In Praise of *Aquanomics*

"Delworth Gardner and Randy Simmons have brought together an important book on *Aquanomics: Water Markets and the Environment*. . . . We cannot walk away from the threats to water quantity and quality that the authors of the chapters in this book lay out clearly—as well as analyzing many of the institutional arrangements that academics and policy makers are contemplating. While it is not fun to read about these severe problems, we must face up to them and this book does so clearly and with substantial depth."

—**Elinor Ostrom**, Nobel Laureate in Economic Sciences; Arthur F. Bentley Professor of Political Science and Co-Director, Workshop in Political Theory and Policy Analysis, Indiana University; Founding Director, Center for the Study of Institutional Diversity, Arizona State University

"When something is not owned, is under government control, or when everyone has a right to it, abuse is guaranteed. Around the world, as in much of the U.S., the failure to adopt strong protective rights has resulted in the degradation of water. Gardner and Simmons's pathbreaking book *Aquanomics* provides clear and crucial understanding of the steps that must be taken to bring discipline to public policies about a misunderstood resource. . . ."

—**Roger E. Meiners**, John and Judy Goolsby Distinguished Professor of Economics and Law, University of Texas at Arlington

"Societies allocate water poorly. The contributors to *Aquanomics* argue convincing that secure property rights to water are necessary, but not sufficient for water to flow from lower to higher valued users; there are numerous transaction costs inhibiting exchange. The authors discuss and illustrate with case studies the economic and political transaction costs of water transfers, and suggest ways to overcome the impediments. This book is essential reading for those wishing to understand water markets and advance more sensible public policies."

—**Lee J. Alston**, Professor of Economics and Environmental Studies and Director of the Institutions Program, Institute of Behavioral Science, University of Colorado

"The strength of the volume is that the authors are united in trying to explain how much of the present waste and misallocation could be prevented by replacing myriad federal and state regulations with markets. While the authors' diagnoses and remedies are not all the same, most of them are based on data and make strong cases. The transactions costs of depending on markets are not forgotten, and there are even a few references to replacing individual trading with trading among competing collectives . . . , *Aquanomics* goes deep and provokes the reader into further reflection and research."

—**Anthony Scott**, Professor Emeritus of Economics, University of Toronto

"*Aquanomics* examines many of the key water issues of the day—the design and use of water markets and pricing for the environment, agriculture and urban use; factors for considering dam decommissioning for eco services and restoration; the role of groundwater management in light of adjacent urban population growth; the paradoxical effects of the Public Trust Doctrine and public irrigation districts; and options for the Sacramento Delta and water trading in California—the state at the epicenter of water tensions. *Aquanomics* is wide ranging and the authors are first-rate scholars. It is a timely volume about our most critical natural resource—water."

—**Gary D. Libecap**, Donald Bren Distinguished Professor of Corporate Environmental Management, University of California

"*Aquanomics* examines the use of markets to address environmental issues. The book provides both a theoretical and historical background, and a wide range of examples that illustrate the usefulness as well as the problems of market approaches to environmental concerns. . . . The book is readable, relevant, and often provocative. Well worth adding to your library and your syllabus."

—**Joel Hamilton**, Professor Emeritus of Agricultural Economics and Statistics, University of Idaho

"This book covers a wide range of current water policy topics, but with a primary emphasis on water markets. *Aquanomics* is authored by a collection of experienced professionals and is always thoughtful, well documented, and informative. It is a good review for those experienced in the water market/policy world and very educational to the uninitiated. It does provide a careful analysis of current water marketing problems in the United States. . . . It will be useful to those in academics, research, and policy development. I look forward to having a copy on my office shelf."

—**Norman K. Whittlesey**, Professor Emeritus of Agricultural Economics, Washington State University

"Water scarcity is already one of the most pressing environmental problems of the 21st century. No resource of water's importance is so mismanaged. The very timely and insightful book *Aquanomics* now explains and details how greater reliance upon water rights and market institutions can help overcome water scarcity and enhance the management of this vital resource. As *Aquanomics* shows, economically and environmentally sound water management is possible, but only if policymakers get the institutions right."

—**Jonathan H. Adler**, Professor of Law and Director, Center for Business Law & Regulation, Case Western Reserve University

"Understanding the institutions that govern water use, including how they create and solve problems, is critical for ensuring there is enough water, of sufficient quality, to meet human needs in the future. The superb work in *Aquanomics* represents an important step toward understanding those institutions, drawing on history, economics, and law to show how water institutions actually work."

—**Andrew P. Morriss**, D. Paul Jones, Jr. & Charlene A. Jones Chairholder in Law and Professor of Business, University of Alabama

"Water is a precious and, in many parts of the world, an increasingly scarce commodity. Yet this precious water often is wasted on low value uses. This tragic incongruity is all the more surprising because we have long ago learned that market-like institutions are an effective way to conserve such scarce resources. By comparison, our institutions for allocating water appear to be broken. With contributions from experts in policy, law, property rights, and economics, *Aquanomics* brings together a diversity of perspectives, all focused on an issue of singular importance: understanding and improving our institutions for allocating water. This book is indispensable for anyone who wants to understand what went wrong and what can still go right with water policy in America."

—**H. Spencer Banzhaf**, Professor of Economics, Georgia State University

AQUANOMICS

The INDEPENDENT INSTITUTE

THE INDEPENDENT INSTITUTE is a non-profit, non-partisan, scholarly research and educational organization that sponsors comprehensive studies in political economy. Our mission is to boldly advance peaceful, prosperous, and free societies, grounded in a commitment to human worth and dignity.

Politicized decision-making in society has confined public debate to a narrow reconsideration of existing policies. Given the prevailing influence of partisan interests, little social innovation has occurred. In order to understand both the nature of and possible solutions to major public issues, the Independent Institute adheres to the highest standards of independent inquiry, regardless of political or social biases and conventions. The resulting studies are widely distributed as books and other publications, and are debated in numerous conference and media programs. Through this uncommon depth and clarity, the Independent Institute is redefining public debate and fostering new and effective directions for government reform.

100 Swan Way, Oakland, California 94621-1428, U.S.A.
Telephone: 510-632-1366 • Facsimile: 510-568-6040 • Email: info@independent.org •
www.independent.org

AQUANOMICS

Water Markets and the Environment

Edited by

B. Delworth Gardner
Randy T. Simmons

Transaction Publishers
New Brunswick (U.S.A.) and London (U.K.)

Library of Congress Catalog Number: 2011020838
ISBN: 978-1-4128-4269-3 (cloth); 978-1-4128-4578-6 (paper)
Printed in the United States of America

Library of Congress Cataloging-in-Publication Data

Aquanomics : water markets and the environment / B. Delworth Gardner and Randy T. Simmons, editors.
     p. cm.
  Includes bibliographical references and index.
  ISBN 978-1-4128-4269-3 (cloth) — ISBN 978-1-4128-4578-6 (pbk.)
  1. Water rights. 2. Water supply 3. Water quality trading. I. Gardner, B. Delworth II. Simmons, Randy T. III. Title: Water markets and the environment.
  HD1691.A68 2012
  333.91—dc23

                                          2011020838

Contents

Acknowledgments

The editors acknowledge vital assistance from the following people in recommending authors for various chapters and in providing useful suggestions for improvement of the manuscript: Alex Tabarrok, David Theroux, Chuck Howe, Herb Fullerton, Terry Glover, Dan Benjamin, Terry Anderson, Ray Huffaker, Norm Whittlesey, and Joel Hamilton.

At the Independent Institute, we are very grateful to David Theroux, President of the Independent Institute, whose vision and support have been crucial to making this book possible. Gail Saari, Anne Paquin, Roy Carlisle, and Martin Buerger have been most adept in handling the copyediting of the manuscript and in performing a variety of administrative functions. The editors are deeply appreciative of the efforts of these people and the entire experience in bringing this book to fruition has been a most positive one.

B. Delworth Gardner and Randy T. Simmons

1

Introduction

B. Delworth Gardner and Randy T. Simmons

When the well is dry, we know the worth of water.

Benjamin Franklin

Water is a ubiquitous but highly contentious substance. It covers over 70 percent of the earth's surface, yet it is constantly being touted as becoming increasingly scarce. Across the globe, water is being discussed and debated, often in bitter and ominous language. Mark Twain was right many decades ago when he quipped, "Whiskey is for drinkin', water is for fightin' over."[1] Many observers see calamity ahead unless water supplies are harnessed and conserved more effectively, and unless water quality can be improved.

Commenting on this worldwide concern about water, *The Economist* reports: "Two global trends have added to the pressure on water. The first is demography. Over the past 50 years, as the world's population rose from 3 billion to 6.5 billion, water use roughly trebled. On current estimates, the population is likely to rise by a further 2 billion by 2025 and by 3 billion by 2050. Diet matters more than any other single factor because agriculture uses about ¾ of the world's water; industry uses less than a fifth and domestic or municipal use accounts for a mere tenth."[2]

Despite the rhetoric of impending doom, is there really a world water crisis? We think the answer to this question is both yes and no. If recent trends in various demands for water are simply extrapolated through time, given the fact there is only a finite water supply, it seems inevitable that serious shortages will occur sooner or later. It is also clear that declining water quality is a pressing problem in many areas of the world, as increasing human activities and, sometimes, natural forces induce high levels of water degradation. What this pessimistic view fails to consider, however, are the ameliorative forces inherent in socio–political–economic systems that can correct and reverse dangerous and ever more costly trends, and indeed are likely to do. One need look no further than improving water quality in many of the economically advanced countries to establish the validity of this point.

1

This book discusses what some of these palliative instruments and policies are and how they may be implemented to effectively postpone, or even eradicate, the onset of water crises. These critical policies critically include establishing secure and transferable private water rights and extending these rights to uses that traditionally have not been allowed, such as instream flows and ecosystem functions. Such policies economize on water quantity and quality as they become scarcer and more valuable. This book contains many examples of how this is being accomplished, particularly in the formation of water markets and market-like exchanges of water rights.

Another focus of the book is to consider remaining impediments to market implementation and how their removal would both improve water quality and effectuate a more efficient allocation among uses. Some extant policies and rules, in fact, even prohibit markets from resolving conflicts over water use. How can this be? Part of the answer is found in the very physical nature of water as a resource as discussed next.

Rethinking Water Policies

Water is most frequently regarded as a "natural resource" somewhat akin to land and air. Yet, for many, water is uniquely different as reflected in the following quotation: "water should not be seen simply as an economic commodity, subject to the usual market laws of supply and demand and to calculations of efficiency, but rather, that it should be viewed as a funda-mental necessity that society chooses (for good reasons) to treat differently from other resources."[3] This view probably has its origins in the indisputable fact that water consumption is necessary for all life to exist. How could such an essential element be left to the vagaries of impersonal markets when life itself is at risk? Therefore, this view holds that everyone ought to have a stake in how water is used. (It is this notion that gives rise to the "anticommons" problem discussed by Bretsen and Hill in chapter 6 and to the promulgation of the "public trust" doctrine discussed by Huffman in chapter 7.) We would argue, in contrast, that viewing water as different from other resources has created much mischief in the form of a vast amount of political tinkering in its governance that has diminished water's productivity and value. All people perceive themselves to be stakeholders in water use and that they, therefore, should have a voice to exert political influence to block any change in water allocations that may strike their fancy.

Going further, water is a fugitive resource in the sense that it tends to move from place to place (especially through the hydrologic cycle in its various forms) and, therefore, is more difficult to manage and govern than is stationary land. Acceptance that "water is special and different" can be clearly observed in the evolution of institutions that govern water's owner-ship, allocation, and use. Still, while granting that water may be different from other resources in some ways does not mean that it is inappropriate to look at water issues under the prism of economic analysis and reasoning in order to account for changing demands and increasing scarcity, which are essentially economic phenomena.

To better understand where we are, why governing rules are so complex, and why changes are so difficult, it is useful to explore briefly the origins of water institutions, particularly those in the American West, the geographic context of much of the discussion of water policies in this book. In the economic and social development of the West, water was generally the most limiting productive factor. Land was plentiful, and labor was relatively mobile and could move to locations with the most favorable employment opportunities. One of the keys to the economic development of the region, therefore, was the harnessing of water supplies and combining them with land and labor in production activities such as mining and agriculture.

Water development began in the mining camps and pioneer settlements that were created long before formal systems of law emerged in the West. These experiences on the frontier, what Frederick Jackson Turner called the region between urbanized civil society and untamed wilderness, were privately organized means of distributing, allocating, and sharing a scarce resource. By "privately organized," we mean they were not sponsored or controlled by a government agency or entity. Water development in the pioneer settlements was often accomplished by a single individual or a few families, but more often by a group of people working together to form a joint stock company in which contributing individuals would receive ownership shares. The stories of these private efforts are often quite astonishing. Much the same thing occurred in the mining camps where initial water diversions were made by an individual or partners, but as the scale of endeavors expanded, larger associations were developed to control and redirect water flows.

Noting that water development happened privately and ahead of government does not mean that there was an absence of governance. Indeed, private systems of governing how rights were established, defined, and enforced evolved along with the private water systems. To borrow a phrase from Anderson and Hill, there were "institutional entrepreneurs"[4] who worked to develop the water management systems that emerged and evolved, and which survive to this day.

Many of the pioneer communities in Utah, Arizona, and New Mexico found remains of Native American irrigation works. Like the aboriginals before them, these European-descended people found that diverting water from the streams was necessary in order to grow crops in the arid West. The settlers first built simple and then more complex irrigations systems. In Providence, Utah, for example, the home of one of the authors of this chapter, the first twelve families arrived in 1859. By the summer of 1861, using pick-and-shovel labor and horse-drawn plows and scrapers, they had dug a four-mile canal and diverted ten second-feet of water from a nearby river to irrigate several hundred acres of cropland. They named their joint-stock company the Providence–Blacksmith Fork Water Company, issued stock to those who helped build it, and sold stock to newcomers. Over the next several years, they extended the first canal and built a second one. The original company continues to operate today and has the right to divert twenty-two second feet from the Blacksmith Fork of the Logan River. Part of the land that was originally farmland is now subdivisions so the water irrigates lawns, gardens, and a city park. Providence City owns shares in the company and, like any other shareholder, pays dues to the company.

The Providence–Blacksmith Fork Water Company is just a small example of the many private water developments that occurred throughout the Western states. Private development was so universal that by 1950, of the 24,869,000 acres of irrigated land in the seventeen Western states, 19,169,000 were irrigated by private irrigation firms.[5]

Water development in Western mining camps is at least as astonishing as in the pioneer agricultural communities. In order to move water to rocker boxes to separate gold from gravel or to hydraulic mining sites where gold was separated by pressurized water, miners built dams, ditches, canals, and flumes. Gold was discovered in California in 1848, and by 1857, water companies had built more than 4,000 miles of canals, ditches, and flumes.[6] In order for all that to happen,

> institutional entrepreneurs hammered out the prior-appropriation system that dominates western water law to this day. Under this system, water rights were granted to a person or a company when they diverted the water from its source; and when not all water claims could be met, the priority of rights was determined by the first-in-time-first-in-right rule. Under this rule, claims were adjudicated on the basis of the date filed. In the years of low water flow, that meant that late claims might not have a right to water, but water owners had a secure right and a reasonable expectation about how much water they could claim under what circumstances.[7]

The same first-in-time-first-in-right rule was applied across the West in both mining and agriculture, allowing the security necessary for people to make investments in water conveyance systems and in mines, farms, and later industries and cities that needed the water in order to survive and prosper. Without secure rights, the investments could and would not have happened. These rights specified a water supply source and established a specific date when the right became effective. Each right also established a point of diversion of the water from its original source, defined the season of permitted use, and named the "beneficial use" to which the water would be put. The first-in-time-first-in-right feature of the water right was of crucial importance, because those who held the most senior rights would have their entire right satisfied before more junior rights received any water at all. The practical consequence of this legal framework was a very high probability that a water supply would be delivered at a time and place that could be accurately anticipated.

In both agriculture and mining, water was diverted from original supply sources such as streams, rivers, and underground aquifers and moved through canals and pipelines to locations of use. (See chapter 13 for elaboration.) In addition, water use could be deferred to more valuable seasons of use by constructing storage reservoirs. Beginning with the passage of the federal Reclamation Act of 1902, massive multipurpose dams and irrigation projects were constructed under federal auspices in every Western state. This development produced a major reorientation in policy and governance. These projects were governed by federal regulations affecting water allocations and pricing, including a huge subsidy to irrigation. In large measure, the changes in water institutions that were invoked were the consequence of this larger government role and included the creation of large water, conservancy, and irrigation public districts. These were empowered by law to tax private real property in order to acquire revenue to manage these complex organizations and to facilitate repaying financial obligations to the federal government. (See chapter 9 for a discussion of some of the consequences of this taxing power.) The important point for us here is that throughout the region's development phase, governing institutions were crafted that were designed to encourage new water development and subsequent diversions of dependable supplies to productive purposes. The codified water law and administration of the various states of the region demonstrate how complex and comprehensive these institutions were and remain.

In our view by far the most significant of these water-governing institutions was prior-appropriation law as described previously. One of the things that worries us most about contemporary trends is the weakening of these private property rights in water.[8] The stability produced by these clear water rights produced an economic environment where investments could be made and planning could occur—obviously necessary conditions for economic progress. But one man's meat may be another's poison. The insecurity of junior rights and the exclusion of those who held no rights but fancied themselves "stakeholders" in water use sowed the seeds of conflict and legal challenges to the existing institutional framework. Much of this book is concerned with these challenges and how best to cope with them.

By their very nature, groundwater aquifers present a vexing problem of inadequate and undefined property rights. If unregulated in the quantity of water that can be pumped, a single pumper captures the full benefits of his activity but shares the cost of lowering water tables with all other users of the aquifer. This is a classic example of the tragedy of the commons. The inevitable result is overutilization and possible depletion of the resource.

States have attempted to deal with this common-property problem in various ways. California, however, is one of the few states that still has no effective regulation of groundwater aquifers. In chapter 12, Brian Steed discusses this issue and its resolution as the County of Los Angeles has acquired effective control of its groundwater resources.

Another complication that continues to harass us is that the world we live in is never static. Changes are manifold and somewhat unpredictable, and in recent years, water has become valued for instream conservation and recreational purposes as well as for the traditional uses that required diversions. Changing institutions to accommodate newly valued water uses, however, is controversial because of opposition from entrenched economic and political interests who fear that granting rights to new uses will diminish the security of water deliveries for their traditional uses. Thus, any changes in the rules could involve large shifts in the creation and distribution of income and wealth. Keeping water instream to protect endangered fish and plants, for example, might well require a reduction in the quantity available for diversions to produce crops. (See chapter 11 for an excellent discussion of this highly visible example from California. See also chapter 4 for a state-by-state review of developing instream flow regulations.) Or, reductions in the federal irrigation subsidy would be expected to increase costs of production in irrigated agriculture and cause reductions in net farm income and in agricultural land values. Conflict is thus inevitable unless institutions can be reshaped to facilitate change without sacrifice by entrenched interests who have created large and expensive lobbying activities designed precisely to protect these interests.

The upshot of this discussion is that institutional arrangements and systems of property rights that were effective in the region's development stages may be inadequate and inefficient now. Those institutions emerged to manage mining, agricultural, industrial, and domestic water uses. Today, demands for instream flows, public access for recreational purposes, and ecosystem preservation compete with those traditional uses, and the conflict between new and established demands are often settled in legislatures and courts in ways that are also inadequate, inefficient, and subject to enormous risk.

But is all hope lost in this morass of competing uses and conflict? We don't think so. Inevitably, as change produces disparities in the value of goods and resources, so long as property rights are fully defined and protected in these commodities and the resources that produce them, markets spontaneously arise to effectuate trades that both parties in the exchange believe will enhance their well-being. One of the authors of this chapter once heard the famous economist, Professor Kenneth Boulding, describe the market as an "old mule" that mankind employs to move resources around to produce gains in wealth that enhance human welfare. Hence, it should not be surprising to observe the spontaneous stirring of markets in water allocation along so many different avenues where value disparities are evident. This book gives major emphasis to these emerging markets and how they are effective in allocating water to higher-valued uses.

Although many of these developments are encouraging, we realize that market formation is often a tortuous and evolving process. Many people, mostly economists, have been advocating policies for over a half-century that would accelerate the implementation of markets for water trading. (See chapter 13 for some of this history.) However, we have been taken aback and surprised at how slow progress has been in this direction. This book also highlights why impediments to market formation exist and what might be done to ameliorate them. Even where many market-induced water transfers are occurring, disparities in value among uses persist, and may even increase as time passes. So much more remains to be done.

A Brief Summary of the Book Chapters

Martin Doyle and Todd BenDor provide a comprehensive review of markets that are developing across the country in ecosystem services in chapter 2, that is, for wetlands, streams, nonpoint source (NPS) water pollutants, and habitat conservation. Special focus is directed to North Carolina where markets for wetlands and stream maintenance were the first to develop and continue to be the most active. Wetland mitigation banking allows private companies to commit to wetland restoration, and these commitments can then be sold as credits to developers who may not have a comparative advantage in this activity and hence do not wish to perform the compensatory mitigation required by law. Where activity in these mitigation investments becomes hindered because the market is thin, an alternative allowed is an in-lieu fee program where funds are collected from developers to undertake investment for the restoration of wetlands.

Doyle and BenDor point out that many ecosystem markets are still in their infancy, and it is difficult to ascertain how quickly they may mature. A major reason for market immaturity is that the government regulatory framework is very unstable and unpredictable. Both existing state and federal policies, if structured incorrectly, can undermine the intent of ecosystem mitigation efforts. Resolving the tensions between the policies developed for specific problems that emerge at the local level and those of broad, federal environmental policy will inevitably remain an ongoing problem inherent to this type of adaptive management. So long as scientific monitoring can play a role in evaluating the programmatic success for maintaining and restoring the integrity of the nation's waters, however, Doyle and BenDor expect that ecosystem service markets can and will play an important role in freshwater ecological restoration.

Chapter 3 by Jeff Peterson and Craig Smith and chapter 8 by Kurt Stephenson and Leonard Shabman focus on marketing activities related to water quality. The Environmental Protection Agency, responsible for water quality under the federal Clean Water Act (CWA), divides water pollution into point sources (PS) and non-point sources (NPS). Most of the former are industrial and municipal, whereas the latter are predominantly agricultural.

Until recently, as Peterson and Smith show, nearly all of the burden of pollution control was placed upon PS, in large part because these sources have observable emissions that can be more easily measured and enforced. Moreover, when a PS is required to meet a new pollutant standard, it is subject to abatement regulations that directly limit pollution. NPS, on the other hand, are regulated on a voluntary basis. A farmer, for example, may voluntarily choose to implement a best-management practice that reduces expected nutrient loading directly, or alternatively, he may reduce production that causes the pollution. For these actions, the farmer may be given "credits" that are commensurate with the amount of pollution reduction. These credits provide an opportunity for a market process to develop if abatement costs vary among polluters—credits may be sold by those who can abate at lower costs to those whose costs are higher. Because per unit of PS abatement tends to be very costly when compared to NPS abatement, the sale of credits from NPS to PS appears to offer sizeable potential gains from trade. Peterson and Smith explore how extensive these pollution-abatement markets are and what the major impediments are to their further utilization. These potential impediments are (1) small abatement cost differences between market participants, (2) "intangible" costs that are not readily observable and measurable but that may affect willingness to trade, (3) varying marketing rules imposed by regulatory authorities, and (4) information costs revealing what pollutant abatement is worth to buyers and sellers. A simulation model is used to quantify the impacts of these impediments on market transactions compared to trading that would occur in a perfect information and frictionless market. The conclusions are that lack of marketplace information as to what abatement is worth to buyers and sellers of credits may severely disrupt market performance, and trading impediments, such as brokerage fees and intangible costs due to unattractive trading rules, will also reduce market activity and performance. These results should prove to be of value to policymakers who are structuring these types of markets.

Chapter 4 by Brandon Scarborough delineates a state-by-state account of recent legislation that permits market water exchanges where instream demanders are beginning to be legitimized as one of the traders. He also presents estimates as to how many instream market transactions have occurred in various states and how much money has been spent to buy instream rights, as well as to show that significant impediments to instream transfers remain and what might be done to eliminate them. Scarborough calls for further legislative reform that would give instream uses the same legal standing as traditional diversion uses have. Integral to this objective is a clear definition and quantification of instream rights along with the enforcement necessary for the development of water markets.

In chapter 5, Ray Hartwell and Bruce Aylward, working in Oregon's Deschutes River Basin, discuss how various types of auctions can be employed to provide for increased stream flows needed to accommodate instream uses and also to provide mitigation credits when pumping reduces groundwater supplies. These auctions appear to be very promising devices since they give owners of water rights and mitigation credits an opportunity to offer their assets for an acceptable price as changing uses are facilitated. Auctions are especially important instruments for generating and revealing information as to what water is worth to people who buy and sell in actual markets. Various types of auctions are evaluated in terms of their suitability, particularly in thin markets where the numbers of buyers and sellers are limited.

The matter of an expanding stakeholder base that can protest and potentially block water transfers has been effectively conceived and analyzed by Stephen Bretsen and Peter J. Hill in chapter 6 on the "anticommons." They point out that the increasing demand for water in industrial and municipal uses and the lower value of water in agriculture creates a puzzle. Most conventional commodity markets respond rapidly to price differentials and market arbitrage reduces those value differentials over time. Bretsen and Hill ask what is different about water markets in the American West, and why have those value differentials grown rather than decreased? Their answer to this puzzle lies largely in the tragedy of the anticommons which occurs when there are multiple rights to veto proposed water transfers regardless of their economic merit. In short, those who hold the rights of exclusion effectively undermine the right to use the resource, especially when exclusion rights and use rights are not bundled together for all rights holders. The effect is to greatly increase transactions costs of making changes in the type and location of water use. And this is not the end of the matter. Even after water transfers have been contracted for, there is still the strong possibility that lawsuits can be brought to invalidate such contracts. The result is that transfers that may be economically efficient do not occur.

Chapter 7 by James Huffman provides an historical and analytical account of the public-trust doctrine and the threat it poses to property rights needed for the efficient functioning of water markets. Huffman argues that the riparian and appropriation legal systems have long provided for reasonably determinate water rights in the United States, and accordingly, these systems have facilitated the transfer of water to more valuable uses. These systems, however, have been seriously impaired by an evolving public-trust doctrine that effectively authorizes the courts to alter vested private rights in the name of inchoate public rights. Huffman points out that the public-trust doctrine originated as a recognition of a public right of access to waters, including those under which the submerged lands are privately owned, for the purposes of navigation and fishing. Why public rights to these particular uses? Because they are instream uses where consumption of the water is mostly nonrival and where property rights are costly to define and protect—representative "public goods" where markets notoriously have been known to fail. But the expansion of these public rights to almost every conceivable interest in water has opened the floodgates of access to the point where few private rights are left. If every self-identified stakeholder can legally protest water transfers, then no market transfers can occur because no holder of a property right can know what he has to trade.

Shabman and Stephenson document in chapter 8 precisely how water-quality trading, as usually proposed and practiced under the Clean Water Act, has only a limited number of real market-like features. Rather, this so-called trading is more an extension of the existing mix of regulatory and voluntary pollutant-reduction programs in water quality management. As distinct from water quality standards, effluent standards apply to limits on the pollutants in wastewater discharge. The effluent standards are included in individual permits issued through the National Pollutant Discharge Elimination System (NPDES), where a permit authorizes a source to discharge a maximum allowable amount of a pollutant in its wastewater. While it is true that trading effluent permits between those whose compliance costs are lower and those whose costs are higher may result in reducing the aggregate cost of meeting an effluent standard, this program falls short of a real market in water quality management. The chapter describes the basic characteristics of market-like program design and stresses the arguments for why market-like approaches should be preferred to the mere trading of effluent permits. Shabman and Stephenson also gives suggestions for ways to add market-like properties to water quality management within the existing statutory and regulatory requirements of the Clean Water Act.

Chapter 9 by Delworth Gardner explores the economic implications of using ad valorem taxes assessed on real property in lieu of direct user charges (prices) to pay for water development and allocation. These taxes are employed mainly at the wholesale level as public districts (generally water conservancy districts) sell water to final urban and agricultural users. In many Western states (Utah is used as a study locale), these districts were created to raise revenues to facilitate financial payments to water developers such as the federal Bureau of Reclamation. Gardner argues that using taxes in lieu of user prices amounts to a subsidy that creates inefficient water use and impedes the optimal amount of water conservation that will be needed in the future to help meet increasing water demand. Using empirically established estimates of price elasticity of demand for water, Gardner shows that higher water prices would induce sufficient water conservation so as to preclude the need for many new water projects that are economically infeasible and environmentally harmful. Changing to a pricing system that permits the elimination of property taxes will require some modifications of existing water contracts with the Bureau, but this does not appear to constitute an insuperable obstacle once the economic and environment benefits are apparent.

Decommissioning of dams is a water issue that is beginning to emerge on the world scene. Worldwide there are more than forty-five thousand large dams (upward of 15 meters tall and having a reservoir capacity exceeding 3 million cubic meters of water), and nearly all the world's rivers are obstructed by large dams.[9] In chapter 10, Pearl Zheng, Ben Hobbs, and Joseph Koonce report that more than 2 million dams have been constructed in the United States, but most of them are small (i.e., storing less than a hundred acre-feet [AF] of water). According to the National Inventory of Dams, however, approximately seventy-nine thousand dams are relatively large (obviously smaller than 15 meters tall in the Benjamin estimate for the world) and pose a "high" or "significant" hazard to life and property in the event of failure.

Observers, especially those of an environmentalist flavor, have been arguing for years that many (most) of these dams have seriously damaged the ecology of natural river systems and now need to be removed. One example of the possibilities and difficulties of removing dams is the September 2009 agreement to remove four dams on the Klamath River, beginning in 2020. The tentative agreement, known as the Klamath Hydroelectric Settlement Agreement, took ten years to achieve and is between twenty-eight different groups including PacificCorp (the electrical utility managing the dams), Oregon, Washington, the federal government, environmental groups, and Indian tribes. The agreement calls for three years of study and then a final decision by the U.S. Department of the Interior, assuming all of the parties sign off on the final agreement.[10]

Zheng, Hobbs, and Koonce provide a valuable analytical instrument for evaluating dam decommissioning that considers cost, ecological effects, and stakeholder preferences as crucial elements. They apply their framework to two case studies—a single dam near Lake Erie and a portfolio of dams in the same area. They draw conclusions about how decision-makers might establish priorities guided by hard empirical results rather than rely on political pressures alone. Dam-removal decisions involve not only numerous trade-offs and complex system interactions, but also varying types and degrees of risks. An important finding of this chapter is that the analysis of a series of dam removals might make more sense than considering them one at a time because for some purposes (such as removing barriers to fish migrations) the dams are interdependent. The benefit-cost analysis becomes skewed if they are investigated one at a time. It goes without saying that this kind of model will be immensely useful if dam decommissioning becomes a worldwide concern as it appears it will.

Three chapters (11 by Goodhue, Sayre, and Simon; 12 by Steed; and 13 by Wahl) have their geographical focus on California, which has been a hotbed of recent controversy and path-breaking legislation. A law enacted in November 2009 "imposes strict conservation rules in urban areas and supports the restoration of the Sacramento–San Joaquin River Delta ecosystem."[11] As part of this legislation, the legislature passed an $11 billion overhaul of California's water system, centering on the Delta. It provides "for the construction of dams, levees and a controversial canal to bypass the Delta and carry water from the Sacramento River to Central and Southern California."[12] The state's voters, however, must decide whether to approve a general obligation bond that would pay for much of the work. Interest groups in various areas of the state are affected differently, and some environmental organizations are vigorous opponents of the new proposals. The vote was scheduled for November 2010 but was postponed until November 2012 because of fears that voters would reject it. California citizens are notoriously independent when it comes to new indebtedness on such a vast scale.

Rachael Goodhue, Susan Sayre, and Leo Simon deliver a penetrating analysis of the very issue discussed in the previous paragraph—what to do about the Delta of the Sacramento–San Joaquin Rivers? This work should be very useful as California voters make their decision about funding. California is the nation's richest agricultural state and depends heavily on the Delta, where water is captured and pumped south via aqueducts to the highly productive Central Valley and to Southern California. The problem is that the levees of the delta that prevent saltwater intrusion and protect the Delta islands that are important as agricultural areas are decaying and very costly to repair. In addition, the Delta ecosystem is the home of endangered species of fish and is used for many other purposes, including recreation and providing supplies of water for homes and industries in the Delta area. Actions proposed to deal with the Delta "problem" include maintaining the status quo, reducing or shutting off water exports to the south, construction of a peripheral canal to bypass the Delta, and building a "dual" system that would export water both through a canal and through the Delta as is presently done.

The goal of the analysis in chapter 11 is to evaluate the political feasibility of the alternative solutions as seen by various stakeholder groups that are affected by the Delta water exports. Five stakeholder groups are identified: (1) the state's taxpayers; (2) urban users who depend on the Delta for some of their water supply; (3) interests within the Delta, including local residents, farmers, and recreational users; (4) agricultural interests in the water-importing zone of the Central Valley; and (5) environmental and conservation interests. The highly rigorous analytical framework incorporates key physical and biological relationships that determine stakeholder groups' welfare under each proposed solution. The conclusion of the analysis is that the dual-conveyance system is the most politically feasible alternative. California will be watched by the whole world as the state grapples with its water future.

In chapter 12, Brian Steed updates the classic studies of water management institutions in the Los Angeles Basin that were first conducted by Vincent Ostrom (1953) and then by recent Nobel Prize winner Elinor Ostrom (1965). Special attention is drawn to local solutions to "common-property" problems. Steed describes how local institutions affecting groundwater governance evolved and how increasing unpredictability about surface water supplies is causing great uncertainty even as the region continues to grow and water demand increases. Enforcement of rights and water contracts has weakened primarily because of changing federal and California state laws, the expanding public-trust doctrine, the competition for new environmental and other instream uses of all surface water sources, and assertions of new stakeholder rights. Because of these uncertainties, evolving California water markets are falling far short of their potential. Still, one of the most important conclusions of the Steed chapter is that as the property rights in groundwater became clear through basin adjudications, extensive water market transfers emerged that have facilitated more efficient use and conservation of this crucial resource.

In the final chapter Richard Wahl provides a description and history of who owns water in California and what types of water rights exist, including the important federal, state, and private water projects, and the rise of market transfers as catalysts for change. Although he concentrates on California, his discussion of these topics applies widely to the whole region. He calls for the replacement of riparian water rights by a permit system that should facilitate market transfers to higher-valued uses. Wahl is uniquely suited to providing the last chapter of this volume because, perhaps more than anyone, he has been at the center of debates over water rights and markets since at least the early 1980s when he was an analyst in the Office of Policy Analysis in the U.S. Department of the Interior. His intuitions that water markets would be environmentally better and more economically efficient than existing federal government policies often led him into conflict with some of his colleagues, especially his bosses. At one point, the loneliness of his position was clearly demonstrated as he was reassigned to an office that was little more than a large closet. His assignment to the closet was only temporary, and he was joined by others in various agencies, universities, and think tanks in exploring the opportunities and limits of water markets. The history is fascinating and, we believe, illuminating about how ideas develop, grow, and are implemented into actual policy.

A Concluding Comment

The coeditors of this book believe that it breaks new ground in two significant ways: (1) it presents a bold new path for reform of water institutions and policies that will be required if this valuable natural resource is to be utilized most effectively in producing social and economic development in the years ahead, and (2) that a broad range of changing and often conflicting demands for water, including increasingly valuable conservation and environmental uses, can be and are being accommodated within a system of private property rights in water and emerging water markets. These indispensable institutions are unsurpassed in providing incentives to increase economic output, and at the same time, for enhancing freedom of human action. But major attention must be given to strengthening and protecting water rights if these goals are to be achieved. Unfortunately, for reasons also discussed in this book, in many circumstances the opposite seems to be occurring, and this is very troubling.

It is also highly important that we as a society get our water prices "right"; that is, prices to final agricultural, industrial, and domestic users must be closer to water supply costs. Attempts by government to fix prices and subsidize some water uses but not others in order to pursue some social or political objective have been disastrously inefficient. Efficient water pricing would induce optimal conservation as well as lead to more efficient development of new water supplies. Prices that become signals to both suppliers and demanders are one of the great tools of free markets—traders are required to face the true opportunity costs of water use. In Peter Boettke's words "The market economy's strength is its dynamic adjustments to constantly changing circumstances. . . . [The] main merit of the price system and the market economy [is] their dynamic adjustment ability as prices, profits, and losses continuously signal, adapt to, and accommodate the ceaseless changes that occur in tastes and technology."[13] Significant differences in the value of water present matchless opportunities for gains from trade. That so many markets are evolving along so many different fronts, as discussed in this book, is persuasive evidence that the economic gains from water trading are huge. Further removal of legal and institutional impediments to water trading, therefore, is likely to produce large societal benefits.

Notes

1. "California's Water Wars: Of Farms, Folks and Fish," *The Economist,* October 24, 2009, 27.
2. "Sin aqua non," *The Economist,* April 11, 2009.
3. Helen M. Ingram, Lawrence A. Scaff, and Leslie Silko, "Replacing Confusion with Equity: Alternatives for Water Policy in the Colorado River Basin," in *New Courses for the Colorado River*, eds. Gary D. Weatherford and F. Lee Brown (Albuquerque, NM: University of New Mexico Press, 1986), 180.
4. Terry L. Anderson and Peter J. Hill, *The Not So Wild, Wild West: Property Rights on the Frontier* (Palo Alto, CA: Stanford University Press, 2004).
5. Alfred R. Golze, *Reclamation in the United States* (New York, NY: McGraw-Hill, 1952), 14.
6. Anderson and Hill, *Not So Wild, Wild West*, 114.
7. Ibid., 113.

8. B. Delworth Gardner, "The Importance of Property Rights in Water," *Water Resources Update*, no. 116 (March 2000): 31–35.

9. Daniel K. Benjamin, "Dams: Do Costs Exceed Benefits," *PERC Reports* (Winter 2007): 22–23.

10. Peter Fimrite, "Deal to Raze 4 Klamath Dams," *San Francisco Chronicle,* September 30, 2009, A1.

11. Wyatt Buchanan and Marisa Lagos, "Legislature Passes Water-System Overhaul," *Chronicle Sacramento Bureau*, November 5, 2009.

12. Ibid.

13. Peter J. Boettke, "What Happened to 'Efficient Markets,'" *The Independent Review* 14, no. 3 (Winter 2010): 368.

2

Markets for Freshwater Ecosystem Services

Martin W. Doyle and Todd BenDor

Introduction

Humans have altered freshwater ecosystems worldwide. With the dramatic increase in irrigation, water storage projects, and land utilization through the twentieth century, the scale of environmental conversion has grown to influence fundamental biophysical processes including fundamental changes to the water cycle, cycling of elements (e.g., carbon, nitrogen, phosphorus), species composition, and climate.[1] These transformations have raised urgent questions about the possibility of conserving and possibly restoring damaged freshwater ecosystems. While environmental conservation and restoration efforts have historically focused on recovering important organisms (flora and fauna), recent scientific and policy endeavors have centered on sustaining the services produced by ecosystems and their components. One way of accomplishing this is through the creation and use of ecosystem service markets.

Ecosystems are often defined as the complex of (1) organisms appearing together in a given area and (2) their associated abiotic environment, which interact through energy fluxes in order to construct biotic structures and material cycles.[2] The study of ecosystems is somewhat distinct from that of the field of ecology in that ecosystem ecologists generally study material or energy fluxes, while other ecologists commonly focus on the behavior or patterns of particular organisms or groups of organisms. Additionally, ecosystem ecologists generally consider ecosystems to be landscape features (physical features in the natural environment) that have the ability to produce various functions. Here, ecosystem functions are the ability of a particular ecosystem (i.e., area) to change the flux or storage of material or energy through time. These functions include photosynthesis, nutrient uptake or retention, metabolism, or any other process characterized by the entirety of the ecosystem

Initial funding for this work was provided by the UNC Institute for the Environment.

feature (physical expression of ecosystem) rather than the process of any particular individual organism or species.

"Ecosystem services" are derived from the beneficial outcomes of ecosystem functions. These services provide the benefits that produce ecological value.[3] For example, streams and wetland naturally function as retainers of nitrogen; in watersheds in which there are nitrogen-driven water quality problems (e.g., hypoxia of estuaries), nitrogen retention would be considered a valuable ecosystem service. The Millennium Ecosystem Assessment groups ecosystem services into four categories: provisioning services (e.g., providing food and water), regulating services (e.g., disease regulation), cultural services (e.g., recreation opportunities), and supporting services (services necessary for the production of other service types).[4] The lists of potential ecosystem services appear to increase with time, and Ruhl, Kraft, and Lant provide a useful review and synthesis.[5]

Markets for these services are as difficult to define as functions and services themselves. Perhaps the most reasonable definition is given by Robertson, who defines ecosystem service markets as those that trade commodities based on ecological assessment criteria, such as wetlands, rather than units of weight or volume, such as the case for the acid rain program.[6] However, the clarity of this definition begins to break down as ecosystem service markets begin to interact with more traditional environmental markets, as in the case when there are both wetland and water quality markets. As we will discuss in this chapter, there are instances in which markets attempt to trade in weight or volume units whose values are estimated using ecological assessment criteria. (We describe this using the example of point source to nonpoint source water quality trading). Given these complicating factors, it is imperative in any discussion of ecosystem markets to understand a range of different resource markets and trading structures. Substantial differences in commodity units and methods of assessment introduce problems that confront researchers and practitioners who study and implement different types of markets.

In this chapter, we focus on freshwater ecosystem markets that currently exist, as opposed to the many that are conceptual or have merely been proposed. Wetlands and streams comprise the oldest ecosystem markets and continue to be the most active at the national scale. In discussing wetlands and streams, we will focus our discussion and examples on markets in North Carolina since they have been active for over a decade and have been the focus of several recent studies as well as recent federal and state regulation revisions. Although the experience of designing and implementing these markets meant successfully navigating certain policy and scientific problems, many others have been exposed and are still in need of further study and remedy. In addition to freshwater ecosystem markets, we also look at habitat conservation banking, an emerging market that presents a new set of opportunities and challenges that will likely interact with these existing markets in the future.

We will describe the policies that created these markets, including those crafted at the federal, state, and local levels. We will also present a series of summary statistics that provide a sense of the scale of these markets. Finally, we use these examples to point toward some of the potential limitations or problems of these markets that merit considerable thought and research attention as comparable markets are developed.

Ecosystem Service Markets: Description and Regulation

The Origin of Wetland Markets

Ecosystem service markets are almost all in some way based on or similar to wetland markets. Wetland regulation in the United States is rooted in the U.S. Federal Water Pollution Control Act of 1972 and the Clean Water Act of 1977, which provides for the protection of "waters of the U.S." under the interstate commerce clause of the U.S. Constitution. Congress designated the U.S. Army Corps of Engineers (Corps) to administer § 404 for waters of the United States with oversight from the U.S. Environmental Protection Agency (EPA). Through judicial interpretation, "waters of the United States" includes navigable waterways, small streams and tributaries, and wetlands.[7] Most development activities that affect waters of the United States fall under § 404 of the Clean Water Act and thus require a permit from the Corps. As part of the 404 program, the permittee must mitigate wetland damage, a process through which they (1) avoid all possible impacts, (2) minimize unavoidable impacts, and (3) provide compensatory mitigation of unavoidable impacts—that is, create, restore, or preserve wetlands such that there is no net loss of cumulative wetland ecosystem function.[8]

In the early years of this regulation (until the mid-1990s), compensatory mitigation was usually performed on-site by the permittee (also often called the "developer" or "impactor"), resulting in the creation or restoration of numerous, small mitigation sites with limited ecological value in comparison to existing, less-disturbed wetlands. During this period, regulations also began promoting off-site compensatory mitigation by permittees. Although this was thought to promote better mitigation, the ecological values of these compensation sites were often extremely low, and the permittee, often a private land developer or a state department of transportation, did not want to be in the business of ecological restoration.

In response to slow § 404 permitting, due to the high volume of compensation sites that had to be approved by the Corps, and high permittee-responsible mitigation costs throughout the early 1990s, entrepreneurs and regulators proposed creating large, consolidated areas of constructed wetlands, known as "mitigation banks," as preimpact or advance compensation.[9] In conjunction with the entrepreneurial mitigation bankers, developers, and EPA staff, Corps districts developed the regulatory guidance necessary to define, create, and maintain markets for mitigation of wetlands by overseeing the banks and the trades that occurred.[10]

Wetland mitigation banking allows private, third-party companies to speculatively restore wetlands, which can then be sold as credits to developers who do not wish to perform their own compensatory mitigation (Figure 2.1). For a mitigation bank to be created and credits from that bank sold, the mitigation banker must have the site approved by a Mitigation Bank Review Team (MBRT; also referred to as the Interagency Review Team (IRT)) which is made up of personnel from the Corps, EPA, and other local or federal natural resource agencies (e.g., U.S. National Marine Fisheries Service, U.S. Fish and Wildlife Service (USFWS), and state departments of environmental conservation).

A key requirement of mitigation banking is that wetlands should be restored in advance of impacts.[11] In less-developed regions of the United States, however, mitigation bankers are unlikely to speculatively invest in banks because it is doubtful that there will be sufficient demand for the created credits over time periods for the mitigation bankers to recoup their investment. In such cases of thin markets, development activities become hindered or slowed by the lack of available mitigation banks in a region since developers cannot

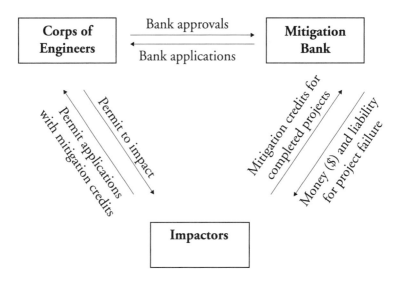

Figure 2.1 Relationships between agencies, impactors (developers), and mitigation bankers in the originally conceived structure of compensatory mitigation banking. Note that once impactors have purchased compensatory mitigation credits, the liability for mitigation site failure is transferred from the impactor to the mitigation bank

easily obtain a 404 permit. Such lack of available advance credits created the impetus for in-lieu fee (ILF) programs. ILF programs are operated by government or nonprofit entities that collect fees from developers (in lieu of actual compensation) and then consolidate these fees over time to build the necessary capital to restore wetlands.[12] Similar to mitigation banks, the obligation and associated liability for providing compensatory mitigation under ILF programs is transferred from the developer to the third-party mitigator. The primary difference between ILF programs and mitigation banks is the time at which mitigation occurs relative to impacts; in banking, restoration is performed prior to impacts, while ILF programs allow mitigation to be performed years after impacts are permitted.[13]

To summarize, compensatory mitigation of wetlands can now take place through three mechanisms: permittee-responsible mitigation, purchase of credits from a mitigation bank, or purchase of credits through an ILF. These and other rules for wetland-related regulation under compensatory mitigation were most recently summarized and formalized by the Corps and EPA in 2008 through the published new regulations governing compensatory mitigation, Compensatory Mitigation for Losses of Aquatic Resources (2008 Compensatory Mitigation Rule).

Emerging Markets for Streams

How, when, and which wetlands merit being considered waters of the United States (and thus subject to federal jurisdiction via the Corps) remains highly contested between land developers and regulatory agencies, and there has been a string of mixed Supreme Court decisions over the past twenty years focused on this topic.[14] The recent *Rapanos/Carabell* cases again raised the question of which waters in the United States should be considered under the regulatory authority of the USACE, and the Corps in part addressed this question through the aforementioned 2008 Compensatory Mitigation Rule. In contrast to wetlands, streams and rivers are more easily justified as "waters of the U.S." that can be regulated by federal power over interstate commerce. Although § 404 of the Clean Water Act is known generally as a "wetlands rule," streams and rivers also fall under its jurisdiction, specifically as a category of "difficult to replace" type of wetland.[15] In the past, either impacts to streams were considered by the Corps to be impractical to compensate, or compensation was performed using wetlands credits. Trading stream impacts for wetland credits is called "out of kind" compensation, since the resources traded are not of the same kind.

More recently, the Corps has begun requiring in-kind compensation for streams, thus increasing the market for stream ecosystems and stream banking separate from wetland banking. Additionally, because streams are a "difficult to replace resource," stream impacts must be compensated by stream restoration. This policy has created a demand for stream restoration credits, and in response, entrepreneurs have created stream mitigation banks similar to those for wetlands. Stream mitigation banking has adapted the wetland mitigation banking model to riverine systems,[16] and while still relatively uncommon, stream markets have surpassed wetlands markets in the number of trades in some states, as in the case of North Carolina (described later).

Water Quality Services

The Clean Water Act provides for trading of credits for nitrogen (N) and phosphorus (P), both of which are leading sources of pollution in the United States, particularly in the Mississippi River Basin and Gulf of Mexico,[17] as well as in many Atlantic river basins, including the Chesapeake Bay, and the Albemarle-Pamlico sound of North Carolina. Under the Clean Water Act, point source (PS) is distinguished from nonpoint source (NPS) pollution: PS pollution is federally regulated under the National Pollution Discharge Elimination System (NPDES),[18] which is focused on discrete pollution emitters (e.g., wastewater treatment facilities), and sets discharge limits and technology standards for PSs. In contrast, NPS pollution is regulated under total maximum daily load (TMDL) requirements, which focus on ambient water quality in watersheds. Nationally, NPS pollution, particularly from agricultural sources, comprises 76 percent of nitrogen and 56 percent of phosphorus reaching waterways.[19] Although the EPA is responsible for NPDES regulation, administration of the NPDES is typically delegated to state agencies. Some states regulating NPDES have allowed water pollution trading districts to form, specifically allowing the emergence of both point source-to-point source (PS–PS) trading and point source-to-nonpoint source (PS–NPS) trading programs.[20]

Under the same theory driving atmospheric emissions trading programs,[21] PS–PS trades should allow PS polluters to come into compliance more efficiently than if each polluter were required to come into compliance individually.[22] Moreover, because NPS polluters can usually make reductions in their pollution for relatively little cost (low marginal nutrient abatement costs) than PS polluters, PS–NPS trades should have even greater potential than PS–PS trades to achieve regulatory compliance at reduced costs. While thirty-seven nutrient trading districts have been created, however, only eight have conducted any trades, and only thirteen trades (one PS–NPS trade) have occurred to date.[23] (Chapters 3 and 8 in this book discuss issues relating to market formation in water quality trading of the kind discussed here.)

Water quality trading does not initially appear to qualify as an ecosystem market since the commodity being traded is a chemical measured in pounds of N or P rather than an ecosystem service measured in ecological assessment metrics.[24] In the case of PS–NPS trading, NPS loads are not measured directly, as they are for PS or in air quality markets. Rather, NPS pollution reductions arise through land use changes, specifically by landowners adopting best management practices (BMPs; e.g., riparian buffers).[25] Just as wetland area or stream length serve as surrogate estimates of wetland or stream ecosystem function, so land use changes through BMPs are used as surrogate estimates of water quality change. Environmental management agencies must develop ecological assessment techniques that provide conversion factors linking land use, soil type, and other variables with their impacts on water quality and nutrient (or other pollutant) loading. As a result, we can consider NPS water quality trading programs to be operating ecosystem service markets under the same definition used to articulate wetland and stream markets.

Habitat Conservation Banking

Habitat conservation banking is a recent development in ecosystem service markets. Conservation banking occurs when habitat for a recognized (listed) threatened or endangered species is impacted and offset with habitat preservation, enhancement, restoration, or creation at a different location. Conservation banking is a similar concept to wetland and stream banking, whereby compensation is performed in one location to offset similar impacts at multiple locations. The advantage of conservation banking is that the conservation bank sites are often large, contiguous, and more strategically sited (to protect habitat) than impact sites.[26] Like wetland banking, these site advantages can produce economies of scale leading to higher quality restoration and ecological benefits not seen in small, fragmented conservation areas.[27]

Conservation banking was first introduced in California by the USFWS to distinguish banks developed specifically for federally listed endangered species from banks designated for wetland mitigation. Unlike stream and wetland mitigation, which now is subject to explicit federal regulation, conservation banking remains regulated by a FWS guidance document.[28] Although this guidance is comparable to early wetland/stream banking guidance documents, the stated goal of conservation banking is to conserve species, which can only be achieved through restoration or enhancement of the habitat needs of that specific species. Thus, while habitat conservation banks operate almost identically to wetland or stream mitigation banks, their evaluation (by a review team similar to the MBRT) is held to species-specific criteria, rather than general criteria used to evaluate wetlands and streams.

Fisheries mitigation banks are perhaps the most relevant conservation bank in the context of water markets, although very few trades have occurred.[29] In two cases in California, over one hundred acres were restored to create the habitat specifically needed for a federally listed endangered species. This area included tidal marsh habitat primarily acquired as habitat for Delta smelt, as well as Sacramento River floodplain habitat for several fish species, including Chinook salmon. In contrast to markets for wetlands, streams, and water quality, fisheries banks exhibit little market activity (trades) or research interest to date, but we expect change as more regions experiment with implementing habitat conservation banks.

Some Regulatory Issues: Monitoring, Service Areas, and In-Lieu Fee Programs

There are several issues with current ecosystem market regulation that require elaboration, particularly given the impacts that regulations can have on promoting successful ecological and economic outcomes. First, regulations governing all of the markets that we have described put very little emphasis on monitoring the ecological service actually being traded. In wetlands mitigation, a range of services is considered to be preserved, enhanced, and restored, including flood attenuation, nutrient retention, and wildlife habitat. The only success criteria (denoting a mitigation project "successful") measured in most Corps districts, however, relate to hydrology (water table elevation), soil type, and vegetation type/survival.[30] While these are ecological components of wetlands, it is unclear whether these components are sufficient proxies to capture the range of ecosystem services that regulations seek to protect under the auspices of the Clean Water Act.

In the case of streams in North Carolina, only physical characteristics of stream channel shape—width, slope, and riparian vegetation—are measured or restored under compensatory mitigation.[31] Although restoring ecological functions (e.g., species recovery, nutrient retention) is the stated purpose of compensatory stream mitigation, specific ecological aspects (e.g., community composition of fish or macroinvertebrates, nutrient retention) are rarely monitored as a requirement for approval of the bank to sell its credits. Evaluating the success of compensatory mitigation programs is difficult because of this disconnect between the purpose of mitigation (functional replacement) and the reality, as it is far from clear what is being achieved when just the physical habitat is being changed.

The second issue pertains to geographic "service areas," which are a key consideration in the economic and ecological success of an overall ecosystem market.[32] When wetlands or streams are destroyed, regulators prefer the mitigation to be as close as possible to the impact, and if possible, within the same watershed. The reasoning for this was articulated in the first federal guidance on wetland mitigation, where regulators argued that wetlands mitigated near impacts were more likely to provide similar ecosystem services.[33] The area that any single mitigation bank can serve is therefore limited to the same watershed (service area) as the impacts for which it provides compensation.

However, the scale of these watershed service areas remains difficult to define explicitly, and the 2008 Compensatory Mitigation Rule has been intentionally vague on this critical issue, essentially leaving it to each district engineer to establish and enforce the scale they consider most appropriate (see § 332.3(c)(4)). If a service area is too large, then many impacts can be concentrated in one geographic area, while all of the mitigation can be geographically distant, leading to impact hot spots and localized net loss.[34] If service areas are too narrowly constrained, then there is potentially insufficient demand in any one area to justify taking on the economic risk of a speculative mitigation bank, that is, a bank residing in a thin market. Also, Corps districts have not been consistent in defining the scale of service areas. Some districts define service areas as U.S. Geological Survey eight-digit watersheds (hydrologic unit classes [HUC]), while others define them as agglomerations of eight-digit watersheds, and still others allow trades across entire states.[35] In many areas, where local regulations augment the Corps authority, these service areas are further constrained by political boundaries such as counties.[36]

Issues involving service area size differ across types of ecosystem service markets: the goal of wetland and stream banking is to sustain the quality of local or receiving water bodies, and thus the geographic service area at the watershed scale makes intuitive and regulatory sense.[37] In contrast, the goal of conservation banks is to preserve viable species populations.[38] Thus, it may be entirely defensible or even preferable to allow the loss of habitat in one region in exchange for mitigation in a distant region, if the distant region is the best source of quality conservation land or genetic conservation resources. Arguably, the inadequate success to date of most ecosystem restoration suggests that there should be a balance between sites that are close but have limited restoration potential, and sites that are further away that have greater restoration potential.[39]

A third issue regards ILF programs.[40] For traditional mitigation trading to occur, offsets (in the case of wetlands and streams, this implies mitigation banks) must be at least partly established before new impacts are permitted. "Advance" mitigation involves speculation on the part of bankers who have limited information on the future of impacts in a region or may have limited confidence in the stability of regulations that govern banking.[41] This uncertainty acts as a barrier to entry for bankers into the mitigation credit market, causing situations in which insufficient credits are available in an area to compensate for new impacts.[42] It is questionable whether ILF programs are ever appropriate, as they undermine both the economic and ecological original intent of mitigation banking. Ecologically, banks are meant to be established prior to impacts, thus reducing the time delay between impacts and an operational ecosystem.[43] When using an ILF, there is an inherent time delay between impacts and establishment of a compensating ecosystem function, thus undermining an important component of ecologically responsible mitigation.[44]

Economically, things are even more problematic: ILF programs accept fees from developers at a rate that is assumed will be adequate to purchase and restore sites in the future. ILF programs could charge fees far in excess of restoration costs, thus holding development projects hostage. As discussed in the North Carolina case in the following section, however, this is often not the case. In fact, ILF programs can (and often do) charge insufficient fees to offset increasing property and restoration costs, which can quickly escalate beyond expectations. Moreover, ILF programs can potentially underprice private mitigation banks operating in the same areas by undercutting the market price for compensation—by collecting fees that are lower than those needed to actually build the project. Because ILF programs are stipulated to be operated by public agencies or nonprofit groups, undercharging for ILF credits acts to subsidize aquatic resource impacts from new public and private development by charging impactors less than the full costs of compensation. That is, ILF programs can place public investments in direct competition with private enterprise.

Characteristics of the North Carolina Stream and Wetlands Market

Policy Structure in North Carolina

In order to illustrate the operation of ecosystem service markets, we will look more closely at a case study of the evolution of markets in North Carolina, particularly focusing on policy structure and extent of market activity. Stream and wetland mitigation banking in North Carolina is regulated by the North Carolina Department of Environment and Natural Resources (NCDENR) and the Wilmington District of the USACE. One of the key characteristics of North Carolina land use and environmental management has been the rapid spatial growth of several urban areas in the state. This rapid suburbanization, combined with the physiography of the state (topographically flat, humid, large wetlands throughout), has led to significant impacts on streams and wetlands. Frequent impacts requiring permits have led to extensive demand for wetlands and stream compensatory mitigation credits.

In North Carolina, the largest impactor of aquatic resources is the North Carolina Department of Transportation (NCDOT). During the mid-1990s, NCDOT began to experience project delays due to insufficient mitigation credits produced by private bankers.[45] In response to this, the state developed the Wetland Restoration Program in 1996, redesignated as the Ecosystem Enhancement Program (EEP) in 2003. The EEP is a state-administered wetlands and stream mitigation program that operates as both an ILF program and a mitigation bank.[46] The EEP was intended to use projected NCDOT construction projects as a platform from which to proactively develop mitigation credits well ahead of time in the needed geographic areas (similar to a mitigation bank). In 1998, the Corps allowed EEP-generated mitigation credits to also be purchased by private developers, effectively opening up the market to a new type of credit consumer for which the EEP was allowed to provide compensation (under an ILF program). Thus, within North Carolina, the market for stream and wetland mitigation credits is (theoretically) made up of trades between private developers and commercial

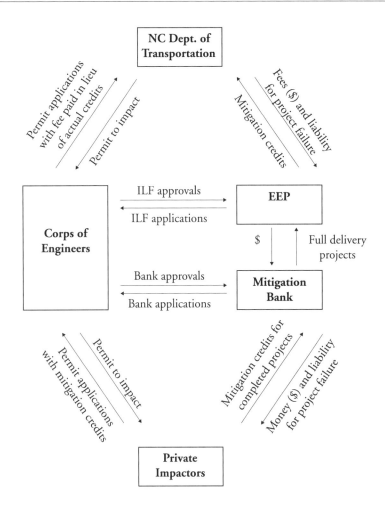

Figure 2.2   Relationships between agencies, impactors, and mitigation bankers in North Carolina in the presence of the Ecosystem Enhancement Program (EEP). Note that private impactors can also pay a fee in lieu of mitigation credits via the EEP, even though that is not shown on the figure

banks, trades between the NCDOT and EEP, and trades between private developers and the EEP (Figure 2.2). Moreover, while the EEP designs and builds some of its own projects (through independent contractors), a major source of wetland and streams credits is attained through reselling credits from "full delivery" sites—sites purchased, designed, and built by private mitigation bank firms. Thus, private mitigation banks can sell credits to private developers, or they can develop sites specifically in response to requests from the EEP.

North Carolina Ecosystem Markets: Economics and Geography

The North Carolina EEP reveals some of the weakness inherent in ILF programs. Templeton and colleagues conducted an economic study of EEP projects for 2006 and 2007 and showed that while the EEP collected fees of $232 per linear foot of stream mitigation, the inflation-adjusted expense for all projects was $242 per linear foot.[47] Moreover, this expense exceeded any inflation-adjusted mitigation fee that EEP charged in previous fiscal years. And Templeton, Dumas, and Session estimate that this is a conservative cost estimate as the projects are likely to still require more costs due to monitoring requirements. Given that the data set analyzed consisted of >191,000 linear feet of stream, the EEP may have undercharged developers by more than $1.9 million. Again, because the EEP is an ILF program, the EEP remained responsible for providing these credits even though they did not collect adequate fees. Presumably, the state provides the necessary funds to fill the gap between costs and fees collected—that is, the state essentially provided >$1.9 million in subsidies for environmental degradation by land developers through the EEP.

In addition to these economic analyses, BenDor and colleagues recently completed an analysis of the North Carolina stream and wetland markets and demonstrated how ecosystem markets affect the locations of ecosystem services throughout the landscape.[48] Between 1998 and 2007, there were 839 transactions (trades) between 607 impact sites and 170 EEP compensation sites, with 431 involving regulated wetlands and 408 involving streams (49 percent). Mitigation sites were spread across the state, while impact sites were concentrated in the rapidly developing urban areas (Figure 2.3). By specifically linking the geospatial coordinates of USACE-licensed impacts with the coordinates of EEP mitigation sites, BenDor and colleagues showed that mitigation transactions traded wetlands an average distance of 54.7 km between impact sites and mitigation (Figure 2.4). Also, impact sites drained, on average, 144 km^2 compared to 43 km^2 at mitigation sites, meaning that mitigation sites were located in streams that were, on average, smaller than streams in impacted sites.

BenDor and colleagues also showed that mitigation performed under the EEP led to virtually no net loss of streams or wetlands at the eight-digit watershed scale, the broadest goal of wetlands and stream regulation. However, there were several ecologically relevant effects: (1) defragmentation, (2) movement upstream in the watersheds, and (3) loss of place-specific functions. The first effect was a spatial defragmentation of streams and wetlands, as numerous small impacts were mitigated by fewer, large sites. While there are economies of scale for compensatory mitigation that drive the desire for large restoration sites,[49] whether there are ecological advantages of single large sites over several small sites are not at all clear.[50]

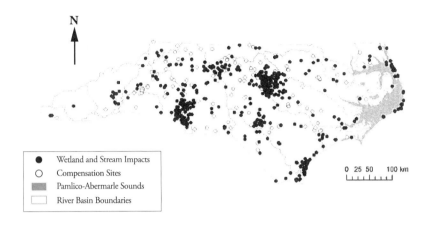

Figure 2.3   Impact and mitigation sites under the auspices of the EEP in North Carolina

Source: Adapted from T. BenDor, J. Sholtes, and M. W. Doyle, "Landscape Characteristics of a Stream and Wetland Mitigation Banking Program," *Ecological Applications* 19, no. 8 (December 2009): 2078–92, doi:10.1890/08-1803.1.

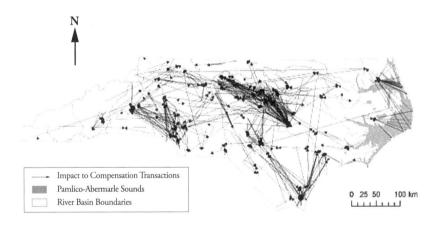

Figure 2.4   Map of EEP compensatory mitigation transactions in North Carolina. Each arrow maps compensatory mitigation transactions, originating at a stream or wetland impact site and terminating at the compensatory mitigation site

Source: Adapted from BenDor, Sholtes, and Doyle, "Landscape Characteristics".

Second, there was a preference to restore streams and wetlands further upstream in the watershed than the impacts for which they were compensating. While this is not surprising, as smaller upstream sites are easier and cheaper to restore than large downstream sites, there will be ecological communities and functions that are both gained and lost through such market-induced pressures for upstream migration of restoration sites.[51] Third, there are place-specific functions that can be lost when impacts are mitigated by restoration sites across the landscape. For instance, when urban wetlands are destroyed and compensated by restoration in remote rural areas, there is less potential benefit for retaining storm water runoff. Thus, there are location-specific benefits that may be particularly problematic to compensate under mitigation banking programs.

North Carolina PS–PS and PS–NPS Market Characteristics

The Division of Water Quality (DWQ) within the DENR is responsible for administering water quality programs and regulations in North Carolina. Also within DENR, the Environmental Management Commission creates water quality regulation within the Neuse River Basin. This 6,192-square-mile basin (Figure 2.5) contains a large portion of the state's population in the headwaters (Raleigh-Durham metropolitan area; a significant source of PS pollution), while agricultural areas dominate the lower watershed (corn,

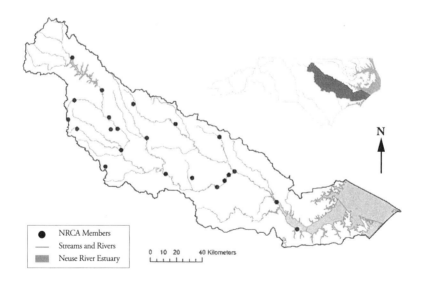

Figure 2.5   Neuse River Compliance Association Map. NRCA members are wastewater treatment plant operators who, as a group, must comply with nitrogen reduction targets

swine; significant sources of NPS pollution). In 1998, the Neuse River Basin adopted rules requiring a reduction in N at the estuary to 70 percent of the 1991–1995 annual average by 2001.[52] Under the rules, PS dischargers who exceed their N discharge allocations are required to purchase offsets from other PS emitters. The rules created an option for wastewater dischargers to meet their N reduction goals collectively by forming an association in which no individual members are fined as long as the group as a whole is in compliance.

Twenty-three wastewater dischargers formed the Neuse River Compliance Association (NRCA), and the association was granted a basinwide NPDES permit. The permit allowed the association an N limit equivalent to the sum of the individual limits. By 2006, the NRCA had reduced total N reaching the estuary by 67 percent, far surpassing their requirements. However, to date there have been no permanent trades among members of the NRCA and only three temporary trades (i.e., year-to-year trades, or leases).

Regulators have also been concerned about the potential creation of N pollution hot spots because the Neuse rules only require N reductions in the river's estuary (see Figure 2.5); there is no regulation of instream water quality. Over time rapidly growing urban areas will need to purchase greater N allotments from the agricultural areas downstream, where population is not increasing as quickly. Upstream N loading from urban areas, combined with a lack of instream water quality regulation, will likely produce a water quality hot spot in the more upstream reaches of the Neuse River. While some of this nitrogen will be retained or removed from the water by natural biogeochemical processes as it is transported downstream, the levels of nitrogen that can be reached within these rivers can be quite large, with potentially toxic or biogeochemically saturating effects.[53]

In addition to the NRCA, which is a PS–PS market, North Carolina also allows PS–NPS trading. It is in this case that nitrogen trading becomes an ecosystem service market as we defined earlier. While the units of trade in the PS–NPS market are in pounds of nitrogen, NPS reductions are based on a land use classification that converts acres to pounds of nitrogen retained per year. Specifically, buffer strips are constructed on riparian lands, and the area of buffer strips is converted into pounds of nitrogen using a conversion factor.[54] These nitrogen credits can be sold to a PS emitter as an offset. In North Carolina, to our knowledge, the first trade between private entities for PS–NPS occurred in 2008. Thus, the state of the market remains unclear. Regardless, it is worth noting that the PS–NPS market mixes the traditional environmental markets, based on pounds or volume, with markets based on complex ecological assessment techniques (ecosystem service markets).

Issues on the Horizon

Science: Do Offsets from Compensatory Mitigation Work?

The critical question underlying all ecosystem service markets is whether or not they work. That is, are restored ecosystems comparable to predevelopment ecosystems? To date, there have been very few studies that have documented actual ecological success of stream restoration projects,[55] and the value and efficacy of wetland restoration continues to be questionable.[56]

Emerging policies are placing greater emphasis on documenting real ecological change rather than relying on indicators or surrogate variables, as has been the standard approach in the past. For instance, in North Carolina, the DWQ in 2008 released its guidance for stream restoration via dam removal, which required substantial documentation of recovery of actual ecological functions (e.g., species, water quality), as opposed to recovery of simple channel geometry, in order to receive approval for the site from the MBRT as a compensation site. Presumably, more rigorous standards for data collection and monitoring will increase the care with which project sites are designed and (more importantly) selected. Regardless of the specific monitoring required, we expect that there will be greater emphasis on regulatory requirements for empirically based evaluation of restoration projects in the future, thereby broadening the information available to guide future programs. Indeed, the 2008 federal Compensatory Mitigation Rule places much greater emphasis on documenting ecological effects of restoration as a part of future compensatory mitigation practices (§ 332.5 and § 332.6).

Policy: Geographic Service Areas and ILF Programs

One of the key considerations for any ecosystem service market is the size of the geographic service area that can be served by a mitigation bank. There has been great inconsistency in the application of service areas to ecosystem markets, be they wetland, stream, or conservation banks. For streams and wetlands, the 2008 Compensatory Mitigation Rule, while establishing a "watershed approach," leaves the scale of the market unspecified, and thus up to the interpretation and discretion of the local district engineer. Determining a bank's service area has critically important implications for the financial viability of individual banks, as well as an ecosystem service market in general.

ILF programs represent another major policy hurdle for the private sector in future ecosystem markets. State regulators, departments of transportation, and many private developers have argued that ILF programs are vitally necessary to prevent development restrictions[57] and for providing compensation in geographic areas that do not generate sufficient impacts (demand) necessary for a private banker to establish a bank. ILF programs suffer from substantial problems, however, potentially leading to insufficient and unsuccessful restoration, as well as the real potential for creating artificially low or high prices.[58]

These factors combine to create a system in which negative resource impacts from land development can be essentially subsidized through the provision of artificially underpriced restoration sites, as shown by the Templeton et al. study for North Carolina.[59] Moreover, many of these ILF restoration sites are completed after impacts, in contrast to their private mitigation bank counterparts, which are required to be (at least partly) completed and certified prior to impacts. Thus, the advantages of ILF programs are, arguably, primarily for developers.

We may now be seeing a distinct shift away from ILF programs, at least in North Carolina. Perhaps the most damning political action against ILF programs came after 2008 state legislature hearings on the EEP. During these hearings, an unusual coalition of environmental groups, private restoration industry, and homebuilders all lobbied against the state's ILF program. The result was unanimous passage of PL 2008-152, "An act to promote compensatory mitigation by private mitigation banks." This bill stipulates that non-NCDOT impactors must use credits from private mitigation banks if those credits are available in the impacted area and that payment to the EEP ILF Program is only acceptable if no mitigation bank credits are available. A critically important aspect of this outcome is that private mitigation banks will no longer have to compete with the EEP in providing wetland or stream credits if the mitigation banks have credits available.

Unfortunately, the North Carolina mitigation bank act does not address the fact that many areas in the state have no private mitigation banks. Increasing the geographic service area of banks (Figure 2.6) is one way to provide compensatory mitigation to these areas without relying on ILF programs. Increasing the service area would provide much greater incentive for private bankers to develop their own sites, which would provide proactive restoration rather than reactive restoration, as is the case in ILF programs. In addition, larger service areas would encourage large restoration projects, as greater certainty in demand would likely lead to greater willingness to invest in larger restoration projects to take advantage of economies of scale.[60] Although we lack empirical evidence, our ecological understanding of other systems and processes (e.g., island biogeography theory)[61] leads us to suspect that large restoration sites are ecologically superior to small ones. Finally, rather than having a discrete banking area, regulators could leverage trading ratios based on the distance away from impacts. Banks that were far away from the impacts, or in a different watershed ("low spatial quality" in Figure 2.6), would be given higher ratios than those that were close. Large mitigation banks would still be desirable to develop since the bankers could be ensured that there would be some demand somewhere in the market for their credits.

In sum, current regulations have sought to avoid the proximity problem by implementing mitigation methods (such as ILF programs) that allow mitigation to occur after impacts. Sacrificing the benefits of advance timing of

Trade-offs in Compensatory Mitigation

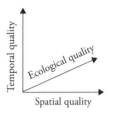

Ideal case: all characteristics of restoration project are high indicating a site close to impacts, restoration completed prior to impacts, with demonstrable ecological benefits.

Near site: typical project to date; located in relatively close proximity; restoration not completed at time of impacts; only minimal indicator data collected to show success of project.

Far-large site: large site with demonstrated ecological benefits beyond surrogate metrics alone; completed prior to impacts including rigorous data for monitoring; located further away from impact site.

Temporal quality: timing of restoration and monitoring relative to impacts; high temporal quality indicates that restoration and monitoring completed in advance of impacts; low temporal quality associated with restoration completed after impacts.

Spatial quality: location of restoration relative to impacts; high spatial quality associated with restoration site in close proximity and landscape position to impacts; low spatial quality associated with distant mitigation site, or out of watershed.

Ecological quality: amount of demonstrable physical, biological, and chemical benefits at restoration site; high ecological quality associated with actual measurements of functional changes (e.g., community composition, nutrient retention, sediment load reductions); low ecological quality associated with no direct monitoring or reliance on surrogate variables.

Figure 2.6   Conceptual model of trade-offs in compensatory mitigation programs between spatial proximity, timing, and quality of restoration

Source: Adapted from BenDor, Sholtes, and Doyle, "Landscape Characteristics".

mitigation is presumably made up by the advantages of geographic proximity. In North Carolina, the stated focus of the EEP has centered on ensuring proximity of mitigation to impact sites, while ecological success criteria receive reduced emphasis, and current guidelines facilitate postimpact mitigation ("low temporal quality" in Figure 2.6) rather than advance mitigation. This approach represents a systemic problem with ILF programs around the United States[62] and has been justified by the argument that spatial proximity between impacts and mitigation sites is of paramount concern—that is, spatial quality is preferred over temporal quality (Figure 2.6). This reflects recommendations that stream and wetland restoration consider "landscape position" and take a "watershed approach" as recommended by the NRC.[63] However, the NRC 2001 review of compensatory mitigation of wetlands throughout the United States also noted that compensatory mitigation should preferably be established prior to permitted impacts. Determining the extent to which spatial proximity, timing, and mitigation project size affect project quality is a critical question that will only be answered through case studies and landscape-scale analysis of mitigation programs (Figure 2.6).

Technical: Limitations to Establishing Property Rights

Property rights are central to environmental trading as they specify who must pay whom to modify actions relating to the environment. These rights also develop in response to changes in economic values, which stem from the development of new technology and the emergence of new markets.[64] Establishing property rights for ecosystem services is particularly difficult because these services are based on ecological assessment criteria rather than direct measurements of weight or volume (even though these assessment criteria are then often used to convert into weight or volume units), and it requires sufficiently precise and accurate measurement of the quantity and quality of the service.

In SO_2 emissions markets, actual SO_2 is measured at the smokestack. That is, the quantity of measurement is mass, and the quality of measurement is precise to the unit being traded (tons of SO_2). In this manner, it is like trading many other commodities for which the unit of trade is precisely known and the quality of the commodity is measured directly (e.g., gasoline, corn, hogs, nickel). In contrast to air quality markets, ecosystem service markets are plagued with uncertainty.

The initial intent of wetland trading regulation was to ensure no net loss of the bundle of wetland ecosystem functions and services in an area. Because of the difficulty in measuring the loss or restoration of functions at individual wetland sites, particularly small sites, measures of wetland spatial extent (area) were deemed to be reasonable surrogates for function. This enshrined the use of size as the primary mechanism for seeking no net loss in wetland mitigation. Subsequent ecosystem service markets, such as streams and endangered species habitat, have adopted similar approaches that establish functional no net loss as a goal, but implement the regulation through size measures (e.g., length for streams, species habitat area). Thus, the currency used to commodify streams, wetlands, and habitat in ecosystem service markets is typically related to size, rather than ecologically derived functional characteristics.

Area can be measured precisely and quickly (some Corps requirements now require compensatory mitigation for impacts over 0.01 acres), but accurately or precisely quantifying measures of ecosystem quality is far more difficult. In a stream or wetland market, critical questions remain unanswered as to what specific functions must be present to determine that the specific site is a "certifiable" ecosystem from which credits can be drawn. In the case of PS–NPS trading, some land area (e.g., riparian buffer) is converted from acres into pounds of nitrogen. A crucial yet unresolved issue is whether the farmer's actions of installing a buffer strip actually produce a measurable reduction in nitrogen loads downstream, or whether the conversion of land itself is sufficient to generate water quality credits. How should water quality improvements be verified? How do changes in ecological quality of traded ecosystems determine the extent to which regulators choose to monitor actions and enforce precise property rights? While monitoring specific ecological functions has received increasing recognition in new regulations (see 2008 Compensatory Mitigation Rule, § 332.5), it remains an ongoing area of study for researchers.[65]

Economic Issues: Unbundling, Un-Stacking, and Double-Dipping

One of the critical issues, or opportunities, in the function of ecosystem markets is the potential for "credit stacking"—selling separate services furnished by the same ecosystem in separate markets. For instance, a hundred acres of a wetland bank might first be sold as wetland mitigation units, and then sold again as water quality credits, endangered species credits, or even carbon credits.

Credit stacking has also been called "unbundling" or "double-dipping," although there are several distinctions between these three concepts. Unbundling is the overarching concept that ecosystem processes and functions can be separated: a wetland can be designated specifically for nitrogen retention, rather than the bundle of ecosystem services that constitute the traditional unit of trade of wetland or stream mitigation credits. Credit stacking specifically involves acquiring credits for a single acre of property that can be independently sold in multiple ecosystem markets. Double-dipping is similar to stacking, except that credits are understood to "double up" natural resource benefits.

The distinction between stacking and double-dipping is unclear. Fox argues that part of the distinction pertains to the additional activities that are necessary to gain the additional credits.[66] For example, if two hundred acres of riparian buffer are established specifically to sell as endangered species habitat credits but are then sold additionally into a market for NPS water quality credits, then Fox argues that the banker would be guilty of double-dipping, because the water quality credits were established separately on the same land with no additional land management activities. To circumvent double-dipping, Fox argues that the natural resource value accounting must be careful and precise; it must clearly separate the riparian buffer needed for water quality provision and that needed for salamander habitat provision, thereby allowing these two areas to be sold separately. The current precision and accuracy of ecosystem service accounting, however, are exceedingly low, thereby causing potential barriers to establishing such closely coexisting ecosystem service markets. If regulators decide that double-dipping is undesirable, then they would need to somehow limit certification of new bank credits (for new markets) to those that are generated by additional land improvements that would not have otherwise been achieved without proactive measures.[67]

There are additional ecological and regulatory arguments against credit stacking. Robertson and Mikota have argued that ecosystem functions do not stack and un-stack like Lego blocks, but rather are interrelated and intertwined.[68] One example is nitrogen trading, where the only pathway to permanent removal of nitrogen from water involves denitrification, the conversion of nitrate (NO_3) into gaseous nitrogen (N_2). The biogeochemical process of denitrification is limited by the availability of carbon, thus inextricably linking carbon to nitrogen markets.[69] Even at the most simple biochemical level, nitrogen and phosphorus are intertwined through basic stoichiometry, making separate water quality markets for these different nutrients scientifically nonsensical. Moving into more complex ecological interactions, such as the species interactions and food webs that are inherent to conservation banks, will undoubtedly be substantially more complex. In the end, unbundling ecosystems is a highly problematic scientific concept.

From a regulatory standpoint, it is clear that it is difficult to "un-stack" ecosystem services derived from ecological restoration projects. There are multiple agencies that regulate ecosystem features and ecosystem service markets: the Corps regulates streams and wetlands via the Clean Water Act, while the USFWS regulates conservation habitat banks through the Endangered Species Act[70] and private organizations oversee carbon trading.[71] Credit un-stacking poses a substantial administrative hurdle for any banker who wishes to engage multiple agencies simultaneously. At the most basic level, unbundling or un-stacking credits makes unclear what actually changes hands when credits are sold.[72]

When a wetland or stream credit is sold for compensatory mitigation, the banker has (1) inevitably sold a permanent easement to that property, ensuring that the physical property will stay in its wetland/stream natural condition, and (2) performed certain management actions that will ensure the viability of the wetland or stream into the future. The transaction, however, has occurred to fulfill the legal requirements of § 404(b) of the Clean Water Act. In the case of un-stacking that same property into water quality credits or endangered species credits, or even carbon credits, the sale of these credits would be to fulfill a completely separate regulatory requirement, such as the Endangered Species Act. Quite simply, the legal status for un-stacking, unbundling, and double-dipping is unclear and will likely only be clarified by a series of court decisions that pit some environmental regulations against others.

Markets: Unintended Consequences

Additional issues emerge in ecosystem service markets from the nonintuitive interactions between ecosystem and market processes. To date, we have insufficient data from which to derive empirical observations about landscape scale ecosystem market behavior, but there are a few modeling studies that provide some additional insight.

In the case of streams, Doyle and Yates linked an economic model of free-entry equilibria with a simple ecological model in order to examine the interactions of stream markets and ecological processes in programs aimed at preventing resource net losses.[73] Their modeling showed that when implementing a no net loss program, a regulator must not only account for the ecological differences between restored and natural ecosystems but also consider the effect of market entry on the number and size of restoration projects. They showed that in a system with little to no restoration scale economies, the number of entrants into an ecosystem service market will be greater than the number that maximizes welfare. The effect of this excess entry on restored ecosystems is to encourage the restoration of smaller sites rather than larger sites, which are generally considered less ecologically desirable than larger sites. Thus, considerations of joint processes are crucial when designing and evaluating such programs. A similar conclusion was reached for a different type of ecosystem market by Armsworth and colleagues, who examined habitat conservation banks within a system that included real estate property market dynamics.[74] They showed that interaction between the local market for land and conservation purchases could actually lead to a decrease in overall biodiversity. Conservation purchases can affect land prices and potentially displace development toward biologically valuable areas or accelerate the pace of development.

While limited in number, emerging studies that link ecological processes and characteristics with economic models suggest that these coupled ecological–economic systems can produce unintended, or at least nonintuitive, consequences. A critical need at this point in time is to more fully explore these types of coupled systems.

Conclusions

Within freshwater ecosystems, ecosystem service markets now span wetlands, streams, NPS water quality, and habitat conservation. Most importantly, the regulatory framework for these markets is very unstable, with major policy changes being the norm rather than the exception.[75] Moreover, under the auspices of compensatory mitigation, the science and economics of ecological restoration taken together is also in its infancy.

There are state and federal policies that can, if structured incorrectly, undermine some of the original intents of compensatory mitigation programs (e.g., ILF programs). There are other policies that can make private provision of compensatory mitigation difficult (e.g., small geographic service areas). Resolving these tensions between the policies developed for specific problems that emerge locally and the initial goals of broad, federal environmental policy will inevitably remain an ongoing problem inherent to this type of adaptive management. So long as scientific monitoring can play a role in evaluating the programmatic success for maintaining and restoring the integrity of the nation's waters, then we expect that ecosystem service markets can play an important role in freshwater ecological restoration.

Notes

1.   P. M. Vitousek et al., "Human Domination of Earth's Ecosystems," *Science* 277 (1997): 494–99.
2.   Millennium Ecosystem Assessment (MEA), *Ecosystems and Human Well-Being: Synthesis* (Washington, DC: Island Press, 2005).
3.   G. C. Daily et al., "Ecosystem Services: Benefits Supplied to Human Societies by Natural Ecosystems," *Issues in Ecology* 2 (Spring 1997). http://www.esa. org/science_resources/issues/FileEnglish/issue2.pdf; D. M. King and L. W. Herbert, "The Fungibility of Wetlands," *National Wetlands Newsletter* 19, no. 5 (1997): 10–13.
4.   MEA, *Ecosystems.*
5.   J. B. Ruhl, S. E. Kraft, and C. L. Lant, *The Law and Policy of Ecosystem Services* (Washington, DC: Island Press, 2007).
6.   M. M. Robertson, "Emerging Markets in Ecosystem Services: Trends in a Decade of Entrepreneurial Wetland Banking," *Frontiers in Ecology and the Environment* 6 (2006): 297–302.
7.   D. M. Downing, C. Winer, and L. D. Wood, "Navigating Through Clean Water Act Jurisdiction: A Legal Review." *Wetlands* 23 (2003): 475–93.
8.   For a historical overview of U.S. wetland mitigation regulations, see P. Hough and M. M. Robertson, "Mitigation Under Section 404 of the Clean Water Act: Where It Comes From, What It Means," *Wetlands Ecology and Management* 17, no. 1(2009): 15–33, doi:10.1007/s11273-008-9093-7.
9.   Robertson, "Emerging Markets."
10.   U.S. Army Corps of Engineers, Federal Guidance for the Establishment, Use and Operation of Mitigation Banks, 60 Fed. Reg. 228: b58605–58614 (1995).
11.   SACE, Federal Guidance.
12.   Environmental Law Institute (ELI), *The Status and Character of In-Lieu Fee Mitigation in the United States* (Washington, DC: ELI, 2006); J. Wilkinson, "In-Lieu Fee Mitigation: Coming into Compliance with the New Compensatory Mitigation Rule," *Wetlands Ecology and Management* 17, no. 1 (2008):53—70.
13.   ELI, *Status and Character.*
14.   See Downing, Winer, and Wood, "Navigating Through Clean Water."
15.   Compensatory Mitigation Rule, 33 C.F.R. § 332.3(e)(3) (2008).
16.   R. Lave, M. M. Robertson, and M. W. Doyle, "Why You Should Pay Attention to Stream Mitigation Banking," *Ecological Restoration* 26 (2008): 287–89.
17.   R. B. Alexander, R. A. Smith, and G. E. Schwaz, "Effect of Stream Channel Size on the Delivery of Nitrogen to the Gulf of Mexico," *Nature* 403 (2000): 758–61.
18.   Clean Water Act § 402, 33 U.S.C. 1342, http://www.epa.gov/npdes/pubs/ cwatxt.txt.

19. Ruhl, Kraft, and Lant, *Law and Policy.*
20. See the review by R. T. Woodward and R. A. Kaiser, "Market Structures for U.S. Water Quality Trading," *Review of Agricultural Economics* 24 (2002): 366–83.
21. J. Boyd et al., "Trading Cases," *Environmental Science and Technology* 37, no. 11 (2003): 216A–223A, doi:10.1021/es032462t.
22. Woodward and Kaiser, "Market Structures."
23. Ruhl, Kraft, and Lant, *Law and Policy.*
24. Robertson, "Emerging Markets."
25. M. M. Robertson, "Discovering Price in All the Wrong Places: Commodity Definition and Price Under Neoliberal Environmental Policy," *Antipode* 39 (2007): 500–26.
26. D. L. Mead, "History and Theory: The Origin and Evolution of Conservation Banking," in *Conservation and Biodiversity Banking*, eds. N. Carroll, J. Fox, and R. Bayon (London: Earthscan, 2008), 9–31.
27. M. W. Schwartz, "Choosing the Appropriate Scale of Reserves for Conservation," *Annual Review of Ecology and Systematics* 20 (1999): 83–108; T. BenDor and N. Brozovic, "Determinants of Spatial and Temporal Patterns in Compensatory Wetland Mitigation Banking," *Environmental Management* 40 (2007): 349–64.
28. U.S. Fish and Wildlife Service (USFWS), *Guidance for the Establishment, Use and Operation of Conservation Banks* (Washington, DC: USFWS, 2003), http://www.fws.gov/endangered/esa-library/pdf/Conservation_Banking_Guidance.pdf.
29. T. Cannon and H. Brown, "Fish Banking," in *Conservation and Biodiversity Banking*, eds. N. Carroll, J. Fox, and R. Bayon (London: Earthscan, 2008), 159–70.
30. National Resources Council (NRC), *Compensating for Wetland Losses Under the Clean Water Act* (Washington, DC: National Academy Press, 2001).
31. USACE, *Stream Mitigation Guidelines for North Carolina* (Wilmington, NC: USACE–Wilmington District, 2003), http://www.saw.usace.army.mil/WETLANDS/Mitigation/Documents/Stream/STREAM%20MITIGA-TION%20GUIDELINE%20TEXT.pdf.
32. R. Bonnie and D. S. Wilcove, "Ecological Considerations," in *Conservation and Biodiversity Banking*, eds. N. Carroll, J. Fox, and R. Bayon (London: Earthscan, 2008), 53–67.
33. Environmental Protection Agency (EPA) and USACE, "Memorandum of Agreement Between the EPA and the Department of Army Concerning the Determination of Mitigation Under the Clean Water Act Section 404(b)(1) Guidelines," February 6, 1990, http://www.wetlands.com/fed/moafe90.htm.
34. T. K. BenDor, N. Brozovic, and V. G. Pallathucheril, "Assessing the Socio-economic Impacts of Wetland Mitigation in the Chicago Region," *Journal of the American Planning Association* 73 (2007): 263–82.
35. Wilkinson, "In-Lieu Fee Mitigation."
36. Robertson, "Emerging Markets."
37. NRC, *Compensating for Wetland Losses.*
38. Mead, "History and Theory."
39. NRC, *Compensating for Wetland Losses.*

40. Wilkinson, "In-Lieu Fee Mitigation."
41. BenDor and Brozovic, "Determinants."
42. Robertson, "Emerging Markets."
43. USACE, Federal Guidance.
44. T. BenDor, "A Dynamic Analysis of the Wetland Mitigation Process and Its Effects on No Net Loss Policy," *Landscape and Urban Planning* 89 (2009): 17–27.
45. Dye Management Group, *Study of the Merger of Ecosystem Enhancement Program and Clean Water Management Trust Fund*, Final Report to the North Carolina General Assembly (Raleigh, NC: Dye Management Group, 2007), http://www.nceep.net/pages/DYE_2007_EEP_CWMTF_Study_Final_Report.pdf.
46. The history and documentation establishing the policies and practices of the EEP are summarized in Dye Management Group, *Study of the Merger.*
47. S. R. Templeton, C. F. Dumas, and W. T. Sessions, *Estimation and Analysis of Expenses of Design-Bid-Build Projects for Stream Mitigation in North Carolina*, Research Report RR08-01 (Department of Applied Economics and Statistics, Clemson University, 2008), http://cherokee.agecon.clemson.edu/curr0801.pdf.
48. T. BenDor, J. Sholtes, and M. W. Doyle, "Landscape Characteristics of a Stream and Wetland Mitigation Banking Program," *Ecological Applications* 19, no. 8 (December 2009): 2078–92, doi:10.1890/08-1803.1.
49. BenDor and Brozovic, "Determinants."
50. Schwartz, "Choosing the Appropriate Scale."
51. R. L. Vannote et al., "The River Continuum Concept," *Canadian Journal of Fisheries and Aquatic Science* 37 (1980): 130–37.
52. Z. A. Hamstead, and T. BenDor, "Nutrient Trading for Enhanced Water Quality: A Case Study of North Carolina's Neuse River Compliance Association," *Environment and Planning C: Government and Policy* 28, no. 1 (2010): 1–17, doi:10.1068/c0887j.
53. J. A. Camargo and A. Alonso, "Ecological and Toxicological Effects of Inorganic Nitrogen Pollution in Aquatic Ecosystems: A Global Assessment," *Environment International* 32 (2006): 831–49.
54. L. L. Osborne and D. A. Kovacic, "Riparian Vegetated Buffer Strips in Water Quality Restoration and Stream Management," *Freshwater Biology* 29 (1993): 243–358.
55. E. S. Bernhardt et al., "Synthesizing U.S. River Restoration Efforts," *Science* 308 (2005): 636–37.
56. NRC, *Compensating for Wetland Losses.*
57. See the preamble to the 2008 Compensatory Mitigation Rule.
58. Templeton, Dumas, and Sessions, *Estimation and Analysis.*
59. Ibid.
60. See Templeton, Dumas, and Sessions, *Estimation and Analysis*, for analysis of economies of scale in stream restoration projects.
61. Schwartz, "Choosing the Appropriate Scale."
62. ELI, *Status and Character.*
63. NRC, *Compensating for Wetland Losses.*
64. H. Demsetz, "Toward a Theory of Property Rights," *American Economic Review* 57 (1967): 347–59.

65. NRC, *Compensating for Wetland Losses.*
66. J. Fox, "Getting Two for One: Opportunities and Challenges in Credit Stacking," in *Conservation and Biodiversity Banking*, eds. N. Carroll, J. Fox, and R. Bayon (London: Earthscan, 2008), 171–80.
67. Fox, "Getting Two."
68. M. M. Robertson and M. Mikota, "Water Quality Trading and Wetland Mitigation Banking: Different Problems, Different Paths?" *National Wetlands Newsletter* 29, no. 2 (2007): 10–15.
69. Alexander, Smith, and Schwaz, "Effect of Stream Channel."
70. Mead, "History and Theory."
71. Fox, "Getting Two."
72. Robertson, "Discovering Price."
73. M. W. Doyle and A. Yates, "Stream Ecosystem Service Markets Under No-Net-Loss Regulation," *Ecological Economics* 69, no. 4 (2010): 820–27, doi:10.1016/j.ecolecon.2009.10.006.
74. P. R. Armsworth et al., "Land Market Feedbacks Can Undermine Biodiversity Conservation," *Proceedings of the National Academy of Sciences* 103 (2006): 5403–08.
75. Robertson, "Emerging Markets."

3

Water Quality Markets: Institutional Design and Performance

Jeffrey M. Peterson and Craig M. Smith

Introduction

More than three decades after becoming law, the Clean Water Act's water quality goals remain an unmet policy challenge. As of 2004, some 44 percent of the assessed stream miles in the United States and nearly two-thirds of the nation's lake acres were categorized as impaired.[1] Particularly in lakes, nutrients were the major cause of the impairment, with nonpoint source (NPS) pollution from agriculture being a leading contributor.

Until recently, a large share of the burden of pollution control of nutrients has been placed upon point sources (PS), in large part because these sources have observable emissions that can be easily measured and enforced. Both industrial and municipal PSs have been regulated, often with requirements to install new treatment technologies, and the discharge limits have become more stringent over time.

In contrast, policies targeted to the major NPSs—agricultural producers—have been voluntary. This voluntary approach is consistent with the long-standing political culture of farm programs in the United States.[2] To improve water quality or to provide other environmental benefits, farmers may apply for various conservation programs offering cost-sharing or other subsidies to install best management practices (BMPs), which reduce environmental

Support for this project was provided by the USEPA's Science to Achieve Results (STAR) program through Agreement No. RD-831J77401-0, by USDA National Needs Graduate Fellowship Competitive Grant No. 2007-38420-17785 from the National Institute of Food and Agriculture, and by USDA Hatch Project KS302. This is contribution number 10-242-B of the Kansas Agricultural Experiment Station. Any opinions, findings, conclusions, or recommendations expressed in this publication are those of the author(s) and do not necessarily reflect the views of the USEPA or the USDA.

damage. However, despite years of effort and the investment of millions of state and federal dollars in these programs, many producers still choose not to participate and/or decide not to implement BMPs on their agricultural fields.[3]

The tightening regulations on PSs, coupled with the limited responses by NPSs, have created a large disparity in costs of water pollution control. Bacon estimated that the cost of obtaining additional nutrient reduction from PSs was up to sixty-five times higher than that from NPSs.[4] Such cost disparities imply that water quality improvements are economically inefficient: the same amount of pollution control could have been achieved at much lower cost if NPSs had increased their abatement activities while PSs had reduced their abatement.

One policy that has been the focus of much recent discussion is water quality trading (WQT). Such a policy would maintain the voluntary participation by farmers, while also creating a mechanism for agriculture to increase its contribution to water quality improvements. In a typical program, the purpose is to limit discharges of a particular nutrient, usually nitrogen or phosphorous,[5] and PSs are allowed to meet their nutrient reduction targets by purchasing water quality credits from agricultural producers in the surrounding watershed. Producers who choose to sell credits are then obligated to implement a BMP that reduces expected nutrient loading by an amount commensurate with the number of credits sold.

As noted previously, substantial evidence exists that NPSs can reduce pollutant loading at a much lower cost than PS polluters in many watersheds, suggesting substantial scope for and gains from point–nonpoint trading.[6] Many states have implemented WQT programs over the past two decades, in part because of the presumed gains from trading, and perhaps in part because of the reported success of trading programs for air emissions such as sulfur dioxide.[7] There are at least thirty-seven WQT programs currently active or under development in over twenty states.[8]

Despite the potential gains, perhaps the most commonly noted feature of existing programs is low trading volume; none of the programs has had extensive trading activity and many have had no trading at all.[9] A widely cited example is the Fox River program in Wisconsin,[10] which had only one trade after its inception in 1981 even though an early study found substantial potential gains from trading among all participating firms.[11]

These outcomes suggest the presence of obstacles to trading that were not anticipated in the design of existing programs. Recognizing and understanding these factors is crucial for the success of trading policies, not only for those targeting water quality but also for the emerging markets for other ecosystem services (e.g., terrestrial sequestration of carbon). The purpose of this chapter is to synthesize the literature on WQT, with particular focus on the studies of possible obstacles to trading and potential means of overcoming them.

The remainder of the chapter is organized as follows. The next section presents a simple conceptual framework of the workings of a point–nonpoint WQT market. The following section relies on this framework to interpret the literature on WQT and its inherent trading obstacles. The subsequent section then quantitatively illustrates the impacts of some of the major obstacles using an agent-based simulation. The final section summarizes and concludes.

Conceptual Framework

Consider a watershed with a large number of both PSs and NPSs generating a water contaminant. An impending regulation will require PSs (e.g., wastewater treatment plants) to install new technology to reduce their emissions of the contaminant. Across all plants in the watershed, emissions must be reduced by a total of $\bar{Q}$ units. Suppose the (annualized) cost of upgrading technology per unit of discharge varies across plants from $\underline{C}$ to $\bar{C}$ and let $C(Q)$ denote the industry-level marginal cost function, where Q is the aggregate quantity of emissions reduction. The industry marginal cost function is depicted in Figure 3.1, under the usual assumption of increasing marginal costs—that is, $C(Q) \geq 0$. If aggregate emissions are reduced by $\bar{Q}$ units, then the industry will bear a total cost equal to area A. Initially, let us assume a very large number of PSs of roughly equal size, so the marginal cost of a particular firm is represented by a single point on the curve.[12]

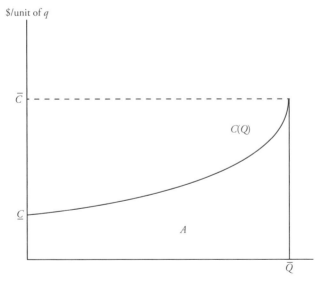

$/unit of q

$\bar{C}$

$C(Q)$

$\underline{C}$

A

$\bar{Q}$

Quantity of emissions reduced by point sources (Q)

Figure 3.1   Point sources' unit cost function

The NPSs (e.g., farms) can reduce discharges of the contaminant by adopting certain land management practices. Unlike PSs, however, they are under no regulatory obligation to do so. Suppose the marginal cost of adopting practices varies within the range $[\underline{c}, \overline{c}]$ and let $c(q)$ represent the aggregate marginal cost function for NPSs, where q is the aggregate amount of emissions reduction achieved through altered land management (Figure 3.2). Here, too, we assume that $c(q)$ is an increasing and smooth function, but we relax this assumption later in the simulations. In the absence of a regulatory requirement, no nonpoint polluter will opt to bear the cost of emissions reduction and no emissions reductions will be obtained from NPSs ($q = 0$). However, if q units of reduction are obtained through incentives created by policies or markets, then the total cost of the land management practices would be area B.

Now suppose a point–nonpoint trading program is introduced, in which PSs are allowed to offset a portion of their emissions reduction by purchasing water quality credits from NPSs. NPSs selling these credits must install management practices to reduce emissions commensurate with the number of credits traded. Such a market would impose the following relationship between emissions reductions from PSs and NPSs:

(1) $Q + q = \overline{Q}.$

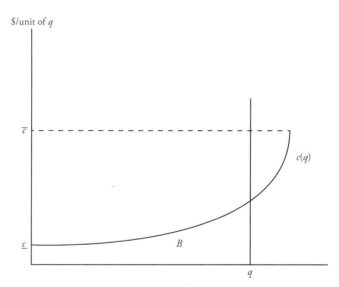

Figure 3.2   **Nonpoint sources' unit cost function**

That is, the emissions reduction target, $\bar{Q}$, must be accomplished through a combination of technology upgrades and land management practices.

WQT Market Research: An Interpretive Review

The trades that actually transpire in a WQT market depend critically on how the market is structured. This section reviews the literature on WQT and related markets, focusing on explanations that have been offered for poor market performance. We first consider the case of an ideal, frictionless market and the conditions under which it would occur. Subsequent sections discuss various departures from these ideal conditions that have been discussed in the literature, each of which offers an explanation for poor market performance observed in actual WQT programs.

Frictionless Market

The case of a frictionless market creates an optimal benchmark of market performance to which other market structures can be compared. The frictionless case assumes that all PS and NPS

1. are rational and obtain utility only from monetary gains;
2. incur zero transactions costs from trading;
3. have complete and perfect information on the market price, which is revealed from a centralized exchange and cannot be influenced by a trader's individual actions.

Under these assumptions, the market equilibrium can be depicted in a textbook demand-and-supply diagram (Figure 3.3). This figure is obtained by projecting the mirror image of Figure 3.1 onto Figure 3.2. In particular, let $P(q)$ denote the inverse demand function for water quality credits purchased by PSs. This function is obtained by solving Equation (1) for Q and substituting it into the PSs' cost function—that is, $P(q) = C(\bar{Q} - q)$. In the frictionless case, the inverse supply function for credits sold by NPSs, $p(q)$, is identical to the NPS cost function ($p(q) = c(q)$). As q increases along the horizontal axis in Figure 3.3, plants are purchasing credits to allow more of the pollution to be controlled by the NPSs (q increases and Q decreases). In the equilibrium of this market, PSs purchase q^* credits from NPSs at a price of P^*. PSs with costs at or above P^* will purchase credits, and those with costs below P^* will upgrade technology. The lower-cost firms who choose to upgrade technology gain nothing from the market, but the higher-cost firms who participate in the market collectively gain area G_1, reflecting their cost savings from buying credits instead of upgrading technology. Area G_2 is the gain to NPSs, or the prices received for the credits sold (P^*) less the cost of generating those credits. The sum of these two areas, $G = G_1 + G_2$, is equal to total benefits from the program, which are often referred to in the literature as total cost savings. Area G is a benchmark

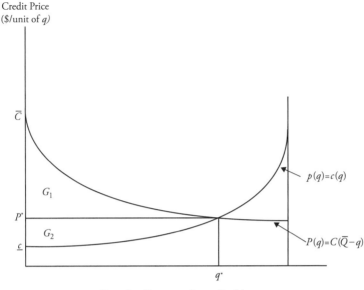

Figure 3.3   Frictionless water quality trading market

representing the maximum possible cost savings; as market imperfections are introduced, only a portion of G is realized in actual trading.

Cost Differences

The first and most obvious explanation for poor market performance is simply little or no potential gains from trading. If area G is empirically small, the incentives for trading will be low and few if any traders will participate. More drastically, if $\underline{c} > \overline{C}$, so that the supply function lies entirely above the demand function, then any trades would generate a loss to one or both parties and no trades would occur.

Several studies have documented a large divergence between control costs of PS and NPS in particular watersheds, implying significant potential gains from trading.[13] On a national basis, the USEPA (United States Environmental Protection Agency) estimated that reducing agricultural background pollution could produce net aggregate savings of $15 billion in capital investments for tertiary water treatment.[14] However, given the importance of site-specific factors on surface water systems, the size of the cost gap is likely to vary across watersheds and could be small or absent in particular cases. Unfortunately, we are aware of no study to date that systematically estimates and compares these costs across locations.

Aside from the geographic factors, the gap in costs depends on the pollutant in question as well as the stringency of the regulatory driver. Rowles evaluated the feasibility of applying WQT in Georgia watersheds with one focus being the development of cost estimates for the treatment of phosphorus by municipal wastewater plants, which were the relevant PSs in the study region. Rowles found there was a substantial increase in treatment costs below 1.0 mg/L total phosphorus.[15] Above that limit, however, PS costs are often competitive with NPS reduction costs, so there may be no incentive to trade until plants are required to reduce discharges to below 1.0 mg/L total phosphorus. In sum, while a small gap in costs may be an explanation for low trading volumes in particular cases—especially situations where the water quality target is not sufficiently stringent—it does not appear to be a universal explanation. More research is needed to determine the relative importance of underlying costs to the other factors discussed later.

Intangible Costs

Assuming that control costs differ across sources, another explanation for limited trading is that traders perceive "intangible" costs that are weighed against any potential gains. That is, the assumption that only monetary trading gains enter traders' utility functions may not hold. A growing literature documents that the behavior of participants in an institution is influenced by institutional processes and rules, independent of the participants' pecuniary outcomes.[16] In many experimental settings, subjects have shown a reluctance to participate in unfamiliar institutions where the expected payoffs of participation are unclear.[17] Such behavior is commonly modeled as ambiguity aversion in the literature—a subject faces risk over the payoff of taking some action and behaves cautiously because the magnitudes of the possible payoffs and/or their probabilities of occurrence are unknown.

In a WQT market, intangible costs may arise from such things as traders' distaste for the institutional rules of trading, or from ambiguous costs due to future public relations problems or WQT opening the door to future regulation. Several authors have proposed specific causes of intangible costs on each side of the market. Regarding NPSs, King noted that farmers, for obvious reasons, do not want government agents examining their on-farm land-management practices.[18] Likewise, if producers had to validate the environmental creditworthiness of their production operation, it may call into question whether they should be regulated any differently than other dischargers. Producers may fear this could lead to future regulation. In addition, farmers may believe that the enrollment process for a WQT market would be burdensome, a factor often cited from farmer surveys to explaining nonparticipation in conservation programs.[19] Regarding PSs, Hoag and Hughes-Popp hypothesize that plant managers are reluctant to participate in WQT markets due to possible public relations problems from "buying the right to pollute."[20]

Figure 3.4 shows how a market reacts to intangible costs. These costs will create a gap between the control cost curves and the market demand and supply functions. If the size of the gap is the same for both PS and NPS, as depicted in the graph, the new equilibrium price, P', will be the same as that in the frictionless case, P^* in Figure 3.3. The quantity of credits traded, however, will decrease from q^* to q'. Similarly, the gains to the point and nonpoint traders will shrink to the triangles bounded by the price line and the new supply and demand curves.

While institutional ambiguity has been documented as an important factor driving behavior in laboratory settings,[21] there is a paucity of empirical evidence about the importance of such factors in WQT market participation. The only study we are aware of that quantifies the impacts of intangible costs in a WQT market was conducted by Peterson et al., in which a series of interviews, questionnaires, and stated choice experiments were undertaken with farmers and wastewater treatment plant managers in Kansas.[22] A comparative analysis of the responses from farmers and wastewater treatment plant managers revealed clear differences in perceptions between the two groups. Plant managers place more importance on liability, risk, and uncertainty, whereas farmers are more averse to government intervention and control. At the same time, both groups put nearly equal weight on insufficient economic incentives as a potential obstacle to participating in WQT.

The choice experiment data collected from farmers were analyzed with an econometric model (specifically, a random parameters logit regression).

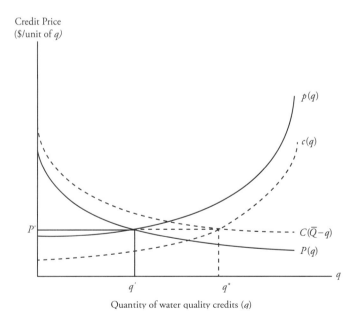

Figure 3.4 Effects of intangible costs on market peformance

The data consist of farmers' stated willingness to participate in a WQT market under varying market rules. Perhaps surprisingly, farmers' choices were not affected by market rules requiring stringent monitoring of their practices. However, producers strongly preferred flexible rules regarding practice installation (e.g., having the option to harvest an installed filter strip for hay or by grazing). Other trading rules, such as the size of the penalty for contract violations and the time required to complete the enrollment process, were found to have widely differing impacts across farmers, with some farmers unresponsive to such features and others highly sensitive to them. Finally, the perceived fear of future regulation was not widespread but would reduce WQT participation by some producers.

The econometric analysis of plant managers' data also revealed the importance of institutional trading rules. Unlike farmers, plant managers were not sensitive to the amount of time needed to enroll in the program, but were somewhat sensitive to the amount of time needed to broker trades after enrollment, and were highly sensitive to the level of perceived risk of contract violations. This uncertainty was presented to managers in the experiments as the probability of having to upgrade technology during the contract period, even though they had purchased water quality credits to offset their emissions.

A set of market simulations based on the econometric results revealed that intangible costs could substantially reduce market gains but may have less of an impact on trading volume. The most preferred and least preferred sets of institutional rules can be inferred from the econometric results. Markets were simulated in both these extreme situations. The simulated market gains were reduced by 52 percent when the rules were switched from the most- to least-preferred combination, while the volume of credits traded remained essentially unchanged.

Transactions Costs

Trades also may be prohibited by high transactions costs, which would include the expenses for searching for trading partners and bargaining over price and other trading terms.[23] Transactions costs are likely to be high in WQT programs that rely on a bilateral negotiation instead of a centralized exchange to generate trades.[24] While the broadest definition of transactions costs would include all of the intangible costs discussed in the last section, for the sake of clarity, we define them to only include the external brokerage charges or other market features that impose a gap between the supply and demand curves when the market clears. (By comparison, intangible costs impose a gap between the traders' underlying marginal cost curves and demand/supply.)

Figure 3.5 illustrates the simplest example of a brokerage fee of \$$t$ per credit traded. The quantity of credits traded is reduced from q^* to q'. The gains to PSs become area C, implying a reduction of $D + H$ relative to the frictionless market. Likewise the gains to NPSs are reduced to area F, implying a reduction of $E + I$. The total losses to the market participants due to transactions costs are $D + E + H + I$. These losses consist of the "direct" losses, due to transaction fees paid to the market administrator (area $D + E$), and the "indirect" losses, due to the deadweight cost of reducing trading volume to q' (area $H + I$).

While a few empirical studies of transactions costs have been conducted for environmental markets,[25] nearly all of this work has focused on markets for airborne emissions rather than WQT. An exception is Netusil and Braden, who simulated a WQT market for soil sediment in Macon County, Illinois, over a range of assumed transactions costs.[26] Transactions costs varied from 5 percent to over 100 percent of the gains from an average trade. The potential traders in the market consisted of seventy-nine land management units owned by fifteen distinct farmers. Transactions costs were only imposed on external trades, which occur between sites on separate farms; internal trades between two sites under common ownership were assumed to incur zero transactions costs. The regulatory driver of the market was a hypothetical limit of three tons of soil erosion per acre per year. Individual sites could exceed this limit if credits were purchased from other sites that fell below it.

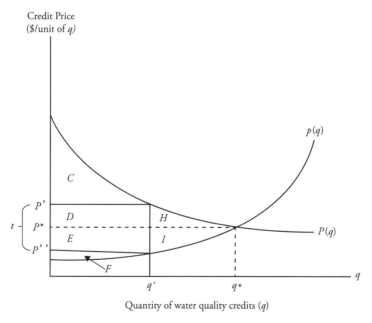

Figure 3.5   Effects of a brokerage fee on market peformance

As transactions costs reached their maximum level, nine trades were executed in comparison to twelve trades when transactions costs were zero. The main impact, however, was in the composition of trades, with 78 percent of trades occurring internally at maximum transactions costs versus 9 percent at zero transactions costs. The gains from trading were reduced by about 34 percent by increasing transactions cost to its maximum level, with about two-thirds of the reduction reflecting the direct transactions expenses (area $D + E$ in Figure 3.5). Overall, the most important impact of transactions costs in this small market was to shift the composition of trades from external toward internal transactions. In markets where there are more independent entities and fewer opportunities for internal trades, the impact on overall market performance is likely to be more drastic.

The Trading Ratio

Another common feature in existing WQT programs is high "trading ratios" between NPS and PS. A typical trading ratio is 2:1, requiring NPSs to install practices that reduce expected loading by two units for each credit sold. The rationale for high trading ratios is that they insure against the greater uncertainty in nonpoint loading reduction.[27] However, this argument misses the point that nonpoint loadings will occur and will be inherently uncertain even if a WQT program does not exist. As credits are sold in a WQT market, practices are being adopted that in most cases reduce the variability of overall nonpoint loading as well as its mean.[28] As such, participation of NPSs in a WQT program actually alleviates some of the environmental risks to society. Shortle and Malik, Letson, and Crutchfield show that, under plausible assumptions about the uncertainty in nonpoint loadings, the economically efficient trading ratio should be no greater than 1:1.[29]

The impact of imposing a trading ratio greater than 1:1 is similar to a percentage tax on credits, reducing the gains from trading as well as trading volume. Figure 3.6 displays the impact of raising the trading ratio from 1:1 to 2:1 trading on an otherwise frictionless market. With the increased trading ratio, the NPSs must reduce pollutant loading by two pounds in order to supply one tradable credit. This essentially doubles the price of all credits sold, resulting in the steeper supply curve, $p(q)$.

The quantity of credits traded reduces to q', and the equilibrium price of credits increases to P'. The gains to PSs with the 2:1 trading ratio is area J, compared to area $J + K + M + R$ in the frictionless market. Thus, raising the trading ratio to 2:1 induces a loss to PSs of area $K + M + R$. The gains to NPSs with a 2:1 trading ratio is area $K + L$, compared to area $L + N + S$ in the efficient market. Thus, the NPSs lose area $N + S - K$. The change in total cost savings from the higher trading ratio is equal to a loss of area $M + N + R + S$.

Previous research on the trading ratio clearly identifies its role in market functioning at a conceptual level. Smith also provides some guidance about

the most economically efficient ratio.[30] However, we are aware of only anec-
dotal empirical evidence about the impact of the trading ratio on observed
trading patterns.

Information Levels

Yet another explanation for poor market performance is limited market
information, which impacts the sequencing of trades. As noted previously, a
frictionless market assumes that trading occurs in a centralized exchange with
full information about prices. In such a setting (a specific such institution would
be a double auction), trades would be executed in order of their market gains:
the first trade would be between the buyer with the highest bid price (the highest price on the $P(q)$ curve) and the seller with the lowest offer price (the lowest
price on $p(q)$), with successive trades yielding progressively narrower gaps between the demand and supply curves until all gains have been exhausted at the
equilibrium point. (Please see chapter 5 for a discussion of actual water auctions that have been occurring in the Deschutes River Basin in Oregon.)

In contrast, trading in existing WQT programs involves bilateral agreements made sequentially with limited information (for instance, an individual
seller likely does not know all potential buyers' bid prices). In the extreme
case, buyers and sellers would be paired together in a random order uncor-
related to the gains from trading. Ermoliev et al. (2000) modeled a sequential

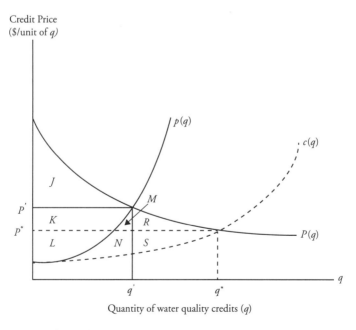

Figure 3.6   Effects of the trading ratio on market performance

market assuming that every participant has the ability to be a buyer and a seller and that there are no transactions costs.[31] In such a setting, traders can back out of earlier trades at no penalty if they find a new trading partner that is more advantageous. Random-ordered, sequential trading will then, ultimately, lead to the efficient outcome (q^* in Figure 3.3). These assumptions, however, are unlikely to hold for WQT programs in practice, where each trade usually involves a binding contract that can only be breached at some financial penalty.

Figure 3.7 shows the effects of different information levels in the market. For this example, the focus will only be on the PSs located at points 1 and 3 along the demand curve (hereafter plant 1 and plant 3) and the NPSs located at points 2 and 4 along the supply curve (hereafter farm 2 and farm 4). For simplicity, let us assume that all four of these entities would trade at most one credit. As in any market, the net gain from a given trade is equal to the difference between the price along the demand curve and the price along the supply curve. In a full-information and frictionless market, the first transaction involving any of these traders would be between plant 1 and farm 4. Plant 3 and farm 2 will not engage in trading because there would be a negative net gain from doing so. So, for the four traders combined, the net gain from trading under full information is $P_1 - P_4$.

A low-information scenario, on the other hand, has the potential to result in different net gains. (Theoretically, it also has the potential to result in the same net gains.) Suppose plant 1 trades with farm 2. The resulting net gain from this transaction is $P_1 - P_2$. Suppose also that plant 3 trades with farm 4 for a net gain of $P_3 - P_4$. The combined net gain from this sequence of trading is $(P_1 - P_2) + (P_3 - P_4) = (P_1 - P_4) - (P_2 - P_3)$. So, assuming that all other traders are paired the same as the full-information scenario, this ill-ordering of trades would reduce the overall market gains by $P_2 - P_3$. This suggests that lower information is likely to increase trading volume while reducing the total gains from trading. However, whether PSs or NPSs gain or lose from less information depends on the order of trading that is realized and cannot be unambiguously predicted.

Previous studies of WQT programs have relied on mathematical programming models to simulate trading, which select trades to minimize the aggregate cost of pollution control, implicitly assuming simultaneous, full-information trading.[32] Atkinson and Tietenberg were the first to simulate a sequential bilateral trading process for air emissions permits.[33] They found that the market equilibrium from this type of trading differs substantially from the programming solution; similar results were later obtained by Burtraw; Klaasen, Forsund and Amann; and Kruitwagen et al.[34]

In addition to studying transactions costs, Netusil and Braden considered sequential bilateral trading under imperfect information in a WQT market.[35] As transactions costs were varied, two types of trading algorithms

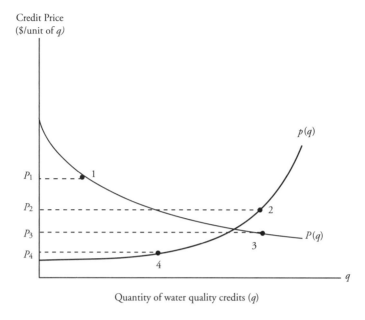

Figure 3.7   Effects of information on market performance

were employed to match buyers and sellers to execute individual trades. In the full-information setting, traders were paired together in the order that maximizes gains. In the limited-information setting, following Atkinson and Tietenberg,[36] traders were paired together randomly. The random ordering of trades reduced the gains from trading even while increasing the number of trades compared to the full-information setting. Their results also revealed strong interaction effects between random ordering of trades and transactions costs. Random ordering reduced the gains from trading by about 3 percent with zero transactions costs but reduced gains by 25 percent when transactions costs were at their maximum.

Summary of WQT Obstacles

To summarize, the WQT literature has identified at least five types of potential obstacles to market functioning. First, the difference in unit costs between PS and NPS may provide an insufficient incentive for trading in some watersheds. Second, there may be a variety of intangible costs induced by market rules that create a gap between unit costs and the prices that buyers are willing to pay and that sellers are willing to accept. Third, transactions costs may inhibit trades with relatively small marginal gains. Fourth, a high trading ratio induces a leftward shift in the supply curve, thus making a certain number of trades infeasible. Fifth, a lack of marketplace information may cause buyers and sellers to be paired together in an economically inefficient manner. Unfortunately, to the extent these obstacles have been studied, they have usually been examined in isolation, so that we have little research evidence about their relative importance.

The first of the obstacles—insufficient cost differences—stands apart from the others in that it cannot be remedied by market design. A first step in designing a WQT market should be an empirical analysis of costs. If the evidence suggests gainful transactions are not present, then any attempt to create a market will be futile. The next three types of obstacles (intangible costs, transactions costs, and the trading ratio) are all similar in that they lead to a market equilibrium with a wedge placed between the unit costs of PSs and NPSs. A Walrasian market (defined as a market that reaches its equilibrium at the intersection of demand and supply curves with an effective market price, as in Figures 3.3–3.6) will increase its performance if each of these impediments is minimized in the market design. The fifth and final obstacle—lack of marketplace information—is also unique because it relies on a non-Walrasian market equilibrium (namely, sequential bilateral trades). As such, it is not clear how the other impediments may interact with the lack of information in a non-Walrasian setting. The simulations reported in the next section attempt to shed some light on this question.

Simulation Model

To examine the ways that various market imperfections may impact the performance of WQT, we constructed and simulated an agent-based model (ABM) of a hypothetical point–nonpoint market. ABMs have been increasingly applied to study the emergent behavior of complex systems driven by microlevel decisions.[37] In economics and other social sciences, agents typically represent autonomous decision-making units such as households, firms, or public entities; in the biological sciences, a structurally equivalent set of models (often called individual-based models) regards agents as individuals in a species population and then simulates population dynamics under a range of ecological settings. ABMs are particularly useful in simulating alternative market institutions where the "market microstructure" plays an important role—that is, cases where agents are heterogeneous and adapt their behavior to institutional rules.

ABMs require specification of two types of computational objects: the agents themselves and the environment in which they operate.[38] In our case, the agents are PS and NPS of a water contaminant (e.g., phosphorous), and the environment is the rules and procedures of a WQT market. We seek to understand how changes in the environment may induce different kinds of trading behavior among the agents, and how the microlevel behavioral changes affect aggregate market performance.

Agents

The PSs are indexed by $i = 1, , .. , I$ and are potential buyers in the WQT market. A new regulation requires each buyer i to either (1) install new technology that reduces its emissions by Q_i units at a cost of C_i per unit, or (2) buy an equivalent amount of water quality credits as offsets. NPSs, indexed by $j = 1, ... , J$, are the potential sellers of credits. Each seller j could generate up to q_j water quality credits at a cost of c_j per unit. Unit costs are assumed to vary across firms but are constant at the firm level. The assumption of constant firm-level unit costs arises from the essentially binary decision about whether to install new technology or to adopt a new practice. These cost properties imply that the aggregate cost curves will have "staircase" structures.

To create our model agents, we generated costs and quantities for each of $I = 10$ PSs and $J = 500$ NPSs using random draws from independent lognormal distributions. The lognormal distribution was chosen to allow for the well-documented skewness in the distribution of costs and environmental impacts across the population of polluters.[39] The parameter values of the lognormal distributions for both buyers and sellers are shown in Table 3.1. The distributional parameters and the population sizes were chosen to be roughly in line with the data used by Smith to model phosphorous trading in the Middle Kansas subbasin.[40]

Because of a variety of market impediments, such as trading ratios, transaction fees, or intangible costs induced by unattractive rules, the effective prices along the demand and supply curves may not coincide with the costs, C_i and c_j. Let $P_i = C_i - \Delta_i$ denote the price that buyer i is willing to pay per credit, where Δ_i is the buyer's implicit monetary cost of market impediments on the demand side of the market. Similarly, let $p_j = c_j + \delta_j$ denote the unit price that seller j is willing to accept, where δ_j is the seller's implicit cost of supply impediments. For simplicity, we abstract from the particular causes of market impediments.

We represent these impediments by shifting the mean of the lognormal distribution of costs from Table 3.1 to obtain a distribution of prices to be offered in the market. In particular, we consider two possible values for the mean cost of the impediments to buyers and sellers, namely $\bar{\Delta} \in \{0,5\}$ and $\bar{\delta} \in \{0,5\}$. Our specification thus considers cases where impediments are either absent or present on each side of the market. When impediments exist on the demand side, the mean of the price along the demand curve is reduced from \$20/credit to \$15/credit. Similarly, impediments on the supply side increase the mean price along the supply curve from \$15/credit to \$20/credit.[41]

The market environment, described next, determines how buyers and sellers are matched together to trade credits. A property of sequential trading is that traders may not fulfill their individual demands, Q_i, or supplies, q_j, in a single transaction. Consider an arbitrary point trading process where the tth trade is about to be made. Accounting for previous transactions,

Table 3.1 Lognormal distribution parameters for buyers and sellers

Item	Mean	Standard deviation
Buyer quantities(Q_i; lbs)	5,000	1,250
Buyer costs (C_i; $/lbs)	20	15
Seller quantities (q_j; lbs)	100	50
Seller costs (c_j; $/lbs)	15	3.74

let $Q_{it} \leq Q_i$ and $q_{jt} \leq q_j$ denote the remaining quantity demanded by buyer i and the remaining quantity supplied by seller j. If the tth trade were to involve buyer i and seller j, their gain per unit traded would be $g_{ij} = P_i - p_j$. Let **G** denote the ($I \times J$) "marginal gains matrix" representing the per-unit gains from trading by all possible trading partners. If buyer i is to trade with seller j, g_{ij} must be positive. If a trade occurs, it is assumed that the two parties will continue trading credits until one of them exhausts their quantity limit; that is, the quantity traded will be

$$(2) \qquad z_t = \min\left\{Q_{it}, q_{jt}\right\}.$$

The total gain from the transaction then will be $z_t g_{ij}$. Depending on the price the two parties agree on, a portion of this gain will be realized by the buyer and the remaining portion by the seller. The prices would depend on the relative negotiating power of the two groups, and we make no attempt here to model the bargaining process nor the resulting prices.

For the agents involved in trade t, the quantities available for trade $t + 1$ are then updated as

$$(3) \qquad Q_{i,t+1} = Q_{it} - z_t \text{ and } q_{j,t+1} = q_{jt} - z_t,$$

respectively. One of these agents will exhaust its available quantity in trade t so that either $Q_{i,t+1}$ or $q_{j,t+1}$ will equal zero. When this occurs, the agent is considered an "inactive" trader. The model records agents as becoming inactive by resetting all entries in row i or column j of **G** to zero. In particular, following trade t, the **G** matrix is updated by setting the following equation:

$$(4) \qquad \begin{aligned} \mathbf{G}_i &= 0 \quad \text{if } Q_{i,t+1} = 0 \\ \mathbf{g}_j &= 0 \quad \text{if } q_{j,t+1} = 0 \end{aligned}$$

where $\mathbf{G}_i$ is the ith row of **G**, and $\mathbf{g}_j$ is the jth column of **G**. As explained in the next section, this change forces the model to exclude this agent from any future transactions. More generally, it identifies inactive traders as those agents who have zero gains from any possible trading partner.[42]

Environment

The environment is the trading mechanism that determines how buyers and sellers are paired together to transact and the order in which these transactions occur. Our trading mechanism is modeled using a variant of the sequential bilateral trading algorithm proposed by Atkinson and Tietenberg.[43]

The trading process occurs by iterating over trades in the sequence they occur. In each trade, indexed by t, the algorithm begins by identifying the trading partners (i, j). Four different ways of doing this are modeled, each of which represents a different level of marketplace information available to agents. These four information regimes are described below.

Once the trading partners are identified, a trade is consummated between the trading partners for z_t units (Equation [2]). This quantity is recorded, along with the marginal gain, g_{ij}, and the total gain, $z_t g_{ij}$. The quantities available and the **G** matrix are then updated following Equations (3) and (4). The model then iterates through additional trades using the same process until no gainful trading partners can be found; trading ceases when the largest element in **G** is nonpositive.

The four information levels modeled are as follows:

1. *Full-information or marginal-gains-ranked trading*: This scenario assumes that every PS and every NPS in the watershed knows precisely all the prices, P_i and p_j, of all agents. In this situation, the most advantageous trades would be executed first. The parties to the tth trade are identified as the (i, j) pair among the active traders with the largest marginal gains—that is, the row and column indexes of the largest value in **G**.

2. *Low-information trading*: The second scenario presumes low information, in which all agents are unaware of other agents' trading prices. Buyers and sellers were paired together randomly. The tth trade is constructed by choosing an i and j at random from the remaining active traders. If $g_{ij} > 0$, then a trade is consummated between the chosen traders; otherwise new (i, j) pairs are randomly chosen until a gainful transaction can be made.

3. *Partial-information trading with buyers' prices known*: The third scenario modeled the case where the buyers' prices, P_i, are known to all traders, but sellers' prices, p_j, are unknown. In this situation, the buyers would drive the market. In each trade t, i is chosen by identifying the agent with the highest price, P_i, among the remaining active buyers, while j is chosen at random from the remaining active sellers. As previously, if $g_{ij} \leq 0$, then a new j is drawn.

4. *Partial-information trading with sellers' prices known*: The fourth scenario modeled the case where the P_is are unknown, but the p_js are

common knowledge. Here, sellers would drive the market. Among the population of active agents, the parties to the tth trade are selected as a randomly drawn buyer and the seller with the lowest p_j. The buyer is replaced with a new random draw of i if $g_{ij} \leq 0$.

Each of the four information scenarios can be combined with the possible mean costs of market impediments (e.g., transactions and/or intangible costs) ($\bar{\Delta} \in \{0,5\}$ and $\bar{\delta} \in \{0,5\}$). Table 3.2 displays the varying assumptions in each of the twelve market environments we simulated. Simulations 1–4 assume idealized market conditions with no impediments to buyers or sellers. These conditions are consistent with the frictionless market depicted in Figure 3.3. However, the level of information varies across these simulations through the scenarios described above. A comparison of simulations 1 and 2 will reveal the effect of full information on market performance. If performance changes significantly between these two cases, simulations 3 and 4 will illuminate the separate effects of marketplace information on P_i or p_j.

Simulations 9–12 are identical to 1–4 except that impediments with an average implicit cost of $5 per credit have been introduced on both sides of the market. The underlying cause of these impediments is not specified. Comparing the outcomes between these sets of simulations allows us to determine the impact of simultaneous demand and supply shifts on market performance. We can also identify the interaction between information levels and a shift in demand/supply.

Simulations 5–8 allow us to separately identify the effect of impediments for buyers and sellers. Simulations 5 and 6 are identical to simulations 1 and 2 except that impediments have been introduced on sellers; simulations 7 and 8 are identical to 1 and 2 except that buyers face impediments. As noted previously, the average implicit costs of the impediments are the same ($5 per credit) for both buyers and sellers. Thus, any simulated difference between the effect of demand and supply impediments will not arise because the two curves have been shifted by differing amounts. Instead, such differences would have to be explained by differences in the shapes of the two curves or from other features of the trading mechanism.

Simulation Results

To evaluate the performance of the WQT market, we compare back to a baseline situation in which buyers would be required to meet the new water quality standard by upgrading technology. Given the cost and quantity parameters in Table 3.1, such a case would require buyers to pay a mean cost of $E[Ci] = \$20$ per pound reduced and would need to reduce a mean quantity of $E[Qi] = 5,000$ pounds. This implies an expected total cost of $E[CiQi] = E[Ci]E[Qi] = \$100,000$ per buyer for an expected aggregate cost of $IE[CiQi] = \$1$ million and an aggregated quantity of $IE[Qi] = 50,000$ pounds. These two values form a baseline to which we can compare our market outcomes.

Table 3.2 The simulation experiments

Simulation	Average cost of impediments		Information level
	Buyers (Δ)	Sellers (δ)	
1	0	0	Full
2	0	0	Zero
3	0	0	P_i known
4	0	0	p_j known
5	0	5	Full
6	0	5	Zero
7	5	0	Full
8	5	0	Zero
9	5	5	Full
10	5	5	Zero
11	5	5	P_i known
12	5	5	p_j known

As trades occur in a WQT market, the same loading reduction is achieved but an increasing share of loading reduction is obtained from sellers of water quality credits. Trading also will reduce the overall cost of achieving the target. We can therefore express cost savings both in dollar terms and as a percentage of the baseline costs. Likewise, we can express the trading volume as the number of credits traded (measured in the pounds of loading reduction borne by sellers) or as a percentage of the loading reduction target. Our main findings are summarized below.

WQT COULD POTENTIALLY REDUCE COSTS, BUT PERFORMANCE DEPENDS ON MARKET RULES.

Table 3.3 summarizes the results of our simulation experiments. The first column serves as a cross-reference to the simulation inputs and assumptions delineated in Table 3.2. The second column reports the number of trades, which is approximately equal to the number of sellers who participate; an individual seller occasionally participates in more than one trade, but this is rare. Our simulations indicate that roughly 50–160 farmers would participate depending on how the market is structured. From the five hundred potential sellers of credits, this would reflect participation rates ranging from about 10 percent to 32 percent, which is similar to the observed participation rates in new conservation programs.[44]

The third and fourth columns report trading volume, both in terms of the number of credits (in pounds of loading reduction borne by sellers) and as a percentage of the baseline loading reduction (50,000 lbs). Simulated trading volume varies widely across simulations, ranging from about 8,600 lbs to over 29,000 lbs, and representing from 17.2 percent to 58.3 percent of the required loading reduction. This reflects market conditions with a potentially large role for WQT in meeting the overall environmental target, but also indicates that volume is sensitive to market rules and design.

The next two columns report the cost savings, as a total in dollars and as a percentage of the baseline total costs ($1 million). Simulated cost savings also vary widely, ranging from about $87,300 to $249,400, or from about 8.7 percent to 25 percent of baseline costs. Again, the potential cost savings are potentially large but also sensitive to market rules.

The last two columns report the final or posttrading costs of achieving the loading reduction target. The next-to-last column is computed simply as the baseline (or pretrading) costs less than the cost savings from trading (e.g., in simulation 1, $1 million—$249,438 = $750,562), while the last column expresses the final cost in average or per-unit terms (in simulation 1, $750,562/50,000 lbs = $15.01/lbs of loading reduction). The last column provides a useful comparison across the simulations in terms of cost effectiveness. With no trading, the cost per unit of loading reduction is the technology upgrade cost of $20/lbs. With trading, this cost ranges from $15.01/lbs to $18.25/lbs.

Table 3.3 Simulation results

Simulation	Number of trades	Volume traded		Cost savings		Final costs	
		Credits (lbs)	Percent (%)	Total ($)	Percent (%)	Total ($)	Average ($/lb)
1	158	26,817	53.6	249,438	24.9	750,562	15.01
2	171	29,141	58.3	208,287	20.8	791,713	15.83
3	169	28,826	57.7	225,354	22.5	774,646	15.49
4	163	27,668	55.3	228,522	22.9	771,478	15.43
5	91	14,292	28.6	127,254	12.7	872,746	17.45
6	95	15,003	30.0	98,940	9.9	901,060	18.02
7	91	14,305	28.6	172,178	17.2	827,822	16.56
8	98	15,530	31.1	138,444	13.8	861,556	17.23
9	57	8,602	17.2	110,071	11.0	889,929	17.80
10	59	8,865	17.7	87,297	8.7	912,703	18.25
11	59	8,915	17.8	100,447	10.0	899,553	17.99
12	58	8,708	17.4	93,803	9.4	906,197	18.12

ACCESSIBLE MARKET INFORMATION IS CRITICAL FOR GOOD PERFORMANCE,
ESPECIALLY IF THE NUMBER OF TRADES IS LIMITED.

The effect of marketplace information on cost savings was unambiguously positive. This can be illustrated by comparing simulation 1 (full information), which resulted in net cost savings of $249,438 (or 25 percent), to simulation 2 (zero information), which resulted in savings of $208,287 (21 percent). This relationship between full and zero information held for all such comparisons modeled (simulations 5 versus 6, 7 versus 8, and 9 versus 10). These results were expected and are similar to the findings of Atkinson and Tietenberg and of Netusil and Braden.[45]

The 4 percent reduction in cost savings from zero information may seem small. However, it should be noted that this measure compares the final value of cost savings after all gainful trades have transpired and does not consider the pace at which gains are accumulated during trading. When the gains by trade are depicted graphically, the effects of information levels on market performance become more pronounced. Figure 3.8 plots the gains by trade with no market impediments (simulations 1–4). Simulation 1 reached its final value ($249,438) after 158 trades, while simulation 2 reached its endpoint ($208,287) after 171 trades. However, simulation 1 accumulates

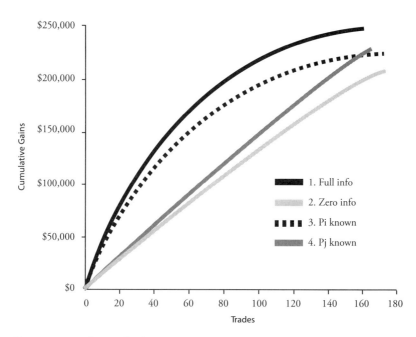

Figure 3.8 **Effects of information levels on cumulative gains by trade, no market impediments**

gains much more quickly in the earliest trades compared to an approximately linear rate of accumulation in simulation 2. Simulation 1 could have ceased after 89 trades (eliminating the last 44 percent of transactions) to obtain the same gains as simulation 2. This same pattern emerged from the other comparisons modeled as well (Figures 3.9 and 3.10). While one benefit of better information is that it leads to more final gains; another, and perhaps more important, advantage is that the gains are realized more quickly with fewer transactions. Alternatively, within a fixed time period where only a certain number of trades are feasible, better marketplace information can increase market performance significantly.

INFORMATION ON BUYERS' ASKING PRICES MAY BE THE MOST BENEFICIAL

The figures also reveal the different effects of marketplace information on buyers' and sellers' prices. The results in Table 3.2 suggest that informing traders of buyers' prices (simulation 3) has nearly the same effect on market performance as informing them on sellers' prices (simulation 4). Simulation 3 has slightly less cost savings than simulation 4 ($225,354 versus $228,522), leading to a slightly higher average cost of loading reduction ($15.49/lb versus $15.43/lb). However, these aggregate measures mask the cumulative patterns shown in Figure 3.8, which reveals that simulation 3 accumulates

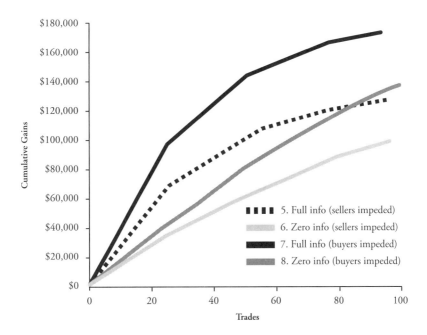

Figure 3.9   Effects of information levels on cumulative gains by trade, with demand or supply impediments

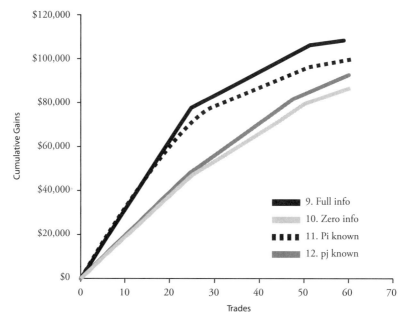

Figure 3.10   Effects of information levels on cumulative gains by trade, with both demand and supply impediments

cost savings much more quickly than simulation 4. Indeed, over about the first eighty trades, simulation 3 behaves very similarly to the full-information case (simulation 1), while simulation 4 closely tracks the zero-information case (simulation 2). A similar pattern is revealed in Figure 3.10 when market impediments are high: over the first 50 percent of trades, simulation 11 (P_i known) is similar to simulation 9 (full information), while simulation 12 (p_j known) is similar to simulation 10 (zero information). These results imply that if only a certain number of trades are feasible—or if the market designers wish to obtain the most benefit out of a limited number of trades—creating an institution that provides accessible information about buyers' prices is preferred to providing information on sellers' prices. However, for overall efficiency, the relative costs of obtaining and disseminating information from the two sides of the market would also need to be considered. These costs are unknown and were not modeled here.

IMPEDIMENTS HURT PERFORMANCE, BUT THEIR EFFECT HINGES ON THE SHAPES OF DEMAND AND SUPPLY.

Comparing simulations 1–4, as a group, to simulations 9–12 reveals that market impediments (the combined effect of transactions costs and any intangible costs from institutional factors) have a significant and negative impact on market performance. With impediments costing an average of $5 introduced on both sides of the market, costs savings are cut by more than half (e.g., from 24.9 percent of baseline costs in simulation 1 to 11 percent in simulation 9) and trading volume is cut by more than two-thirds. These results are straightforward illustrations of the concepts shown in Figures 3.4 and 3.5.

Conceptually less obvious are the separate impacts of demand and supply impediments. Comparing simulations 1 and 2 to simulations 5 and 6 shows the impact of introducing impediments to sellers only. Interestingly, this reduces market performance drastically, with cost savings falling from 24.9 percent of baseline costs in simulation 1 to 12.7 percent in simulation 5. This represents nearly as large a drop as introducing impediments on both sides of the market in simulation 9. On the other hand, simulations 7 and 8 show that impediments faced by only buyers have a milder impact; cost savings fall to 17 percent of baseline costs in simulation 7.

The parallel shifts in demand and supply shown in Figure 3.4 cannot produce such differential impacts. Unlike the curves in Figure 3.4, our lognormal distributions in the simulation impose nonparallel shifts. Figure 3.11 illustrates a case of nonparallel shifts that predicts our simulated results. With no market impediments, the equilibrium of the market is at point 1, yielding cost savings of S_1, equal to area $A + B + C + D$. Introducing impediments only on the sellers shifts the equilibrium to point 2, for a cost savings of $S_2 = A + C$.

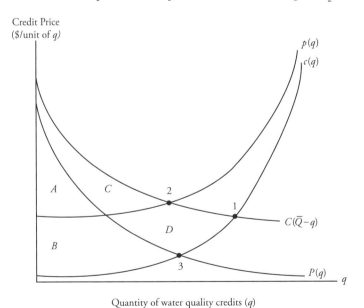

Figure 3.11   Nonparallel shifts in demand and supply

Alternatively, introducing impediments only to buyers would lead to an equilibrium at point 3, where cost savings are $S_3 = A + B$. The loss from impediments on sellers only is then $S_1 - S_2 = B + D$, while the loss from buyer-only impediments is $S_1 - S_3 = C + D$. As area B exceeds C given the nonparallel shifts in the curves, the loss from seller-only impediments is greater.

Such nonparallel shifts would arise from heterogeneity across agents. Figure 3.11 depicts a case where market impediments are viewed as very costly by low-cost firms and less costly by high-cost firms. While the pattern of heterogeneity in any particular market is an empirical question, the simulation results here show that heterogeneity is important to quantify. Market performance may hinge on creating a desirable trading environment for one particular group of buyers or sellers.

Conclusions

A necessary condition for a functioning market for an ecosystem good or service is a legal framework that authorizes market exchanges and creates significant potential gains from trading. The evidence to date strongly suggests, however, that this condition is not sufficient. Rather, the sufficient conditions are a product of purposefully designed institutions that, at a minimum, (1) limit transactions costs, (2) contain transparent rules that minimize ambiguity, and (3) efficiently gather and disseminate price information to participants.

Our simulation experiments illustrate how market performance measures may be sensitive to various institutional factors. Lack of marketplace information may severely disrupt market performance, especially if the time for trading is limited and/or only a limited number of trades are feasible. Meanwhile, other trading impediments, such as brokerage fees, high trading ratios, or intangible costs due to unattractive trading rules, will reduce performance by creating a gap between traders' underlying costs and the prices at which they are willing to trade. Further, impediments to buyers and impediments to sellers may have very different impacts on market performance, depending on the pattern of preference heterogeneity across agents.

Some recent environmental markets have introduced institutional features that attempt to address the challenges named above. For example, some water quality markets have employed a centralized exchange for credits (e.g., http://www.nutrientnet.org), where traders can analyze the economic benefits of trading, post bids, and initiate transactions.[46] Here, the direct link between buyers and sellers is maintained. An alternative approach is to break this link and create an intermediary that acquires and repackages credits for resale. Such an approach has been applied in voluntary carbon offset markets in the United States, where landowners contracted with an aggregator to generate carbon credits, which the aggregator then assembled and sold as a commodity on the Chicago Climate Exchange.[47] A somewhat different intermediary mechanism is a procurement auction, where landowners submit bids to install practices that provide an ecosystem service (or a combination of services).[48] The intermediary would then rank bids, purchase those with the best cost efficiency, and sell the acquired package of services to the final buyer either through a commodity exchange or negotiated contracts.

Much remains to be learned about how to design the most effective market institutions for ecosystem services. In addition to the challenges noted, the most effective design in any particular location is complicated by the biophysical complexities of ecosystem service in question and the various interests of the stakeholders involved. While the potential gains from WQT and other emerging environmental markets may be significant, more research is needed to understand the ways that institutions can be structured to improve market performance as well as to quantify the cost of establishing these structures. Researchers logically could begin by evaluating the performance and establishment costs of some of the recent environmental markets, whose institutional settings differ markedly from earlier approaches.

Notes

1. Environmental Protection Agency (EPA), Office of Water, *National Water Quality Inventory: Report to Congress, 2004 Reporting Cycle*, EPA 341-R-08-001 (January 2009), http://www.epa.gov/305b.

2. R. G. Chambers, "On the Design of Agricultural Policy Mechanisms," *American Journal of Agricultural Economics* 74 (1992): 646–54.

3. C. M. Smith, J. M. Peterson, and J. C. Leatherman, "Attitudes of Great Plains Producers About Best Management Practices, Conservation Programs, and Water Quality," *Journal of Soil and Water Conservation* 62 (September/October 2007): 97A–103A.

4. Elise F. Bacon, *Use of Economic Instruments for Water Pollution Control: Applicability of Point Source/Nonpoint Source Trading for Pollutant Discharge Reductions to Washington State* (Bethesda, MD: Apogee Research, Inc., 1992).

5. Water quality trading programs are complicated by the fact that multiple pollutants are discharged into the same water body and these pollutants are linked together at their source. For example, nitrogen and phosphorous discharges from agricultural runoff tend to be correlated and both are also correlated to other pollutants including sediment and pathogens. In practice, a typical approach has been to design the program around a single nutrient and accept any reduction in correlated pollutants as an ancillary benefit.

6. Paul Faeth, *Fertile Ground: Nutrient Trading's Potential to Cost-Effectively Improve Water Quality* (Washington, DC: World Resources Institute, 2000), http://pdf.wri.org/fertileground_bw.pdf.

7. National Center for Environmental Economics (NCEE), *The United States Experience with Economic Incentives for Protecting the Environment*, EPA-240-R-01-001 (Washington, DC: Environmental Protection Agency, 2001).

8. Faeth, *Fertile Ground*; R. Woodward and R. Kaiser, "Market Structures for U.S. Water Quality Trading," *Review of Agricultural Economics* 24, no. 1 (2002): 366–83; Hanna L. Breetz et al., *Water Quality Trading and Offset Initiatives in the United States: A Comprehensive Survey* (Hanover, NH: Dartmouth College, 2004), http://www.dep.state.fl.us/water/watersheds/docs/ptpac/DartmouthCompTradingSurvey.pdf.

9. D. Hoag and J. Hughes-Popp, "Theory and Practice of Pollution Credit Trading," *Review of Agricultural Economics* 19, no. 1 (1997): 252–62.

10. R. Hahn, "Economic Prescriptions for Environmental Problems: How the Patient Followed the Doctor's Orders," *Journal of Economic Perspectives* 3, no. 1 (1989): 95–114.

11. W. O'Neil, "Transferable Discharge Permit Trading Under Varying Stream Conditions: A Simulation of Multiperiod Permit Market Performance on the Fox River, Wisconsin," *Water Resources Research* 19, no. 1 (1983): 608–12.

12. As an empirical matter, many watersheds will have a limited number of point sources, some of which are very large in terms of discharges. These features create a "lumpy" cost schedule that may influence market outcomes. We assume initially that $C(Q)$ is a smooth function but relax this assumption in the simulations presented later.

13. See, e.g., Faeth, *Fertile Ground*; C. M. Smith, "A Water Quality Trading Simulation for Northeast Kansas" (master's thesis, Department of Agricultural Economics, Kansas State University, 2004); Bacon, *Use of Economic Instruments*.

14. EPA, Office of Water, *1992 Needs Survey Report to Congress*, EPA 832-R-93-002 (September 1993), http://nepis.epa.gov/Exe/ZyPURL.cgi?Dockey=20009NPH.txt.

15. Kristin Rowles, "Why Trade? Searching for the Elusive Cost Savings from Water Quality Trading" (Second National Water Quality Trading Conference, Pittsburgh, PA, May 23–25, 2006).

16. J. Berg, J. Dickhaut, and K. McCabe, "Risk Preference Stability Across Institutions: A Dilemma," *Proceedings of the National Academy of Sciences* 102, no. 11 (2005): 4209–14; R. J. Johnston and J. M. Duke, "Willingness to Pay for Agricultural Land Preservation and Policy Process Attributes: Does the Method Matter?," *American Journal of Agricultural Economics* 89, no. 4 (2007): 1098–115.

17. C. Camerer and M. Weber, "Recent Developments in Modelling Preferences: Uncertainty and Ambiguity," Journal of Risk and Uncertainty 5 (1992): 325–70.

18. D. M. King, "Crunch Time for Water Quality Trading," *Choices* 20, no. 1 (2005): 71–75.

19. Smith, Peterson, and Leatherman, "Attitudes of Great Plains Producers"; W. Hua, C. Zulauf, and B. Sohngen, "To Adopt or Not to Adopt: Conservation Decisions and Participation in Watershed Groups" (presentation, annual meeting of the American Agricultural Economics Association, Denver, CO,

August 1–4, 2004); U.S. Government Accountability Office (GAO), *USDA Conservation Programs: Stakeholder Views on Participation and Coordination to Benefit Threatened and Endangered Species and Their Habitats* (Washington, DC: U.S. Government Accountability Office, 2006), http://www.gao.gov/new.items/d0735.pdf.

20. Hoag and Hughes-Popp, "Pollution Credit Trading."
21. Camerer and Weber, "Recent Developments in Modelling Preferences."
22. J. M. Peterson et al., *Integrating Economic and Biophysical Models to Assess the Impacts of Water Quality Trading,* Final Technical Report to the USEPA-NCER (2009).
23. R. Stavins, "Transaction Costs and Tradable Permits," *Journal of Environmental Economics and Management* 29, no. 1 (1995): 133–48.
24. Woodward and Kaiser, "Market Structures."
25. See, e.g., R. E. Kohn, "Transaction Costs and Optimal Instrument and Intensity of Air Pollution Control," *Policy Science* 24 (1991): 315–32; L. Gangadharan, "Transaction Costs in Pollution Markets: An Empirical Study," *Land Economics* 76, no. 4 (2000): 601–14; E. Woerdman, "Emissions Trading and Transactions Costs: Analyzing the Flaws in the Discussion," *Ecological Economics* 38 (2001): 293–304.
26. N. Netusil and J. Braden, "Transactions Costs and Sequential Bargaining in Transferable Discharge Permit Markets," *Journal of Environmental Management* 61, no. 1 (2001): 253–62.
27. EPA, Office of Water, *Draft Framework for Watershed-Based Trading,* EPA 800-R-96-001 (May 1996), http://nepis.epa.gov/Exe/ZyPURL.cgi?Dockey=20001QL1.txt.
28. J. S. Shortle, "Implications of Comparisons Between the Marginal Costs of Point and Nonpoint Source Pollution Abatement," *Northeastern Journal of Agricultural and Resource Economics* 16, no. 1 (1987): 17–23; R. Horan, "Differences in Social and Public Costs and Public Risk Perceptions and Conflicting Impacts on Point/Nonpoint Trading Ratios," *American Journal of Agricultural Economics* 83, no. 1 (2001): 934–41.
29. Shortle, "Implications"; A. Malik, D. Letson, and S. Crutchfield, "Point/Nonpoint Source Trading of Pollution Abatement: Choosing the Right Trading Ratio," *American Journal of Agricultural Economics* 75, no. 1 (1993): 959–67.
30. Craig Smith, "An Analysis of Alternative Soil, Nutrient, and Water Management Strategies" (Ph.D. diss., Kansas State University, 2011)
31. Y. Ermoliev, M. Michalevich, and A. Nentjes. "Markets for Tradeable Emission and Ambient Permits: A Dynamic Approach," *Environmental and Resource Economics* 15 (2000): 39–56.
32. See, e.g., J. Pan and I. Hodge, "Land Use Permits as an Alternative to Fertilizer and Leaching Taxes for the Control of Nitrate Pollution," *Journal of Agricultural Economics* 45, no. 1 (1994): 102–12; D. Mitchell, "An Examination of Non-Regulatory Methods for Controlling Nonpoint Source Pollution" (PhD dissertation, Oklahoma State University, 2001); J. Eheart et al., "Cost Efficiency of Time-Varying Discharge Permit Programs for Water Quality Management," *Water Resources Research* 23, no. 1 (1987): 245–51; N. Hanley and I. Moffatt, "Efficiency and Distributional Aspects of Market Mechanisms in the Control of Pollution: An Empirical Analysis,"

Scottish Journal of Political Economy 40, no. 1 (1993): 69–87; O'Neil, "Transferable Discharge Permit Trading."

33. S. Atkinson and T. Tietenberg, "Market Failure in Incentive-Based Regulation: The Case of Emissions Trading," *Journal of Environmental Economics and Management* 21, no. 1 (1991): 17–31.

34. D. Burtraw, K. Harrison, and P. Turner, "Improving Efficiency in Bilateral Emissions Trading," *Environmental and Resource Economics* 11, no. 1 (1998): 19–33; G. Klaasen, F. Forsund, and M. Amann, "Emission Trading in Europe with an Exchange Rate," *Environmental and Resource Economics* 4, no. 1 (1994): 305–30; S. Kruitwagen et al., "Trading Sulphur Emissions in Europe: 'Guided Bilateral Trade,'" *Environmental and Resource Economics* 16, no. 1 (2000): 423–41.

35. Netusil and Braden, "Transactions Costs."

36. Atkinson and Tietenberg, "Market Failure."

37. Leigh Tesfatsion, "Agent-Based Computational Economics: A Constructive Approach to Economic Theory," in *Handbook of Computational Economics, Volume 2: Agent-Based Computational Economics,* eds. L. Tesfatsion and K. L. Judd (Amsterdam: North-Holland, 2006), 831–80.

38. D. C. Parker, T. Berger, and S. Manson, eds., *Agent-Based Models of Land-Use and Land-Cover Change* (Bloomington: Indiana University, 2002), http://www.globallandproject.org/Documents/LUCC_No_6.pdf.

39. P.J. Nowak, S. Bowen, and P.E.Cabot, Disproportionality as a Framework for Linking Social and Biophysical Systems. *Society and Natural Resources.* 19 (2006): 153–173, http://lter.limnology.wisc.edu/biblio/disproportionality-framework-linking-social-and-biophysical-systems.

40. Smith, "Water Quality Trading Simulation." To ensure that our final results are not sensitive to a particular set of draws from the lognormal distributions, all our simulations were repeated 10,000 times in Monte Carlo fashion, with a new set of prices and quantities assigned to all agents each time. Using the same model calibrated to data from the Lower Kansas River watershed, Peterson et al. found that 10,000 repetitions was sufficient to ensure that the mean market performance measures computed across the 10,000 repetitions was a stable statistic ("Integrating Economic and Biophysical Models").

41. If impediments to both sides of the market are included, the mean price along demand falls below the mean price along supply. However, the curves still intersect because of the variability among buyers and among sellers; that is, the highest P_i still exceeds the smallest p_j.

42. An additional condition to be an active trader is that enough credits must be available on the other side of the market to satisfy the trader's requirements. In particular, if a buyer i (seller j) cannot find enough gainful trading partners to satisfy his entire demand, Q_i, (entire supply, q_j) then he or she will be designated an inactive trader before trading begins. This "all or nothing" assumption reflects the binary nature of a firm's decision to install a new technology or adopt a new practice.

43. Atkinson and Tietenberg, "Market Failure."

44. Peterson et al., "Integrating Economic and Biophysical Models"; Smith, Peterson, and Leatherman, "Attitudes of Great Plains Producers."

45.   Atkinson and Tietenberg, "Market Failure"; Netusil and Braden, "Transactions Costs."
46.   Woodward and Kaiser, "Market Structures."
47.   J. Williams, S. Mooney, and J. Peterson. "What Is the Carbon Market? Is There a Final Answer?" *Journal of Soil and Water Conservation* 64, no. 1 (2009): 27A–35A.
48.   S. Greenhalgh, J. Guiling, M. Selman, and J. St. John, *Paying for Environmental Performance: Using Reverse Auctions to Allocate Funding for Conservation,* World Resources Institute, Policy Note No. 3 (January 2007), http://pdf.wri.org/pep_reverseauction.pdf; C. M. Smith et al., "Best Management Practice Auctions: Innovative and Market-Based But Are They Cost-Effective?" (annual meeting of WAEA, Kauai, HI, June 24–26, 2009).

4

Buying Water for the Environment

Brandon Scarborough

Introduction

The John Day River and its tributaries in eastern Oregon are home to one of the largest and last-remaining populations of Spring Chinook salmon and summer steelhead as well as the state's only population of westslope cutthroat trout. The basin also has a long history of mining operations as well as very productive agricultural and ranching lands, both vital to local economies. Mining and irrigated agriculture require large diversions of water from rivers and streams, and these industries have water rights that are senior to any instream uses. These water diversions, in conjunction with persistent drought, have reduced stream flows and degraded water quality to the point where the viability of local Chinook and steelhead species is threatened.

Oregon Water Trust (OWT), a private nonprofit organization dedicated to restoring and preserving freshwater ecosystems, approached the conflict between senior diversion rights and potentially threatened fish species from a property rights perspective and proposed leasing and purchasing critical water rights from diverters during critical times of the year. In 2000, for example, OWT entered into the first of five annual agreements with Pat and Hedy Voigt, third-generation ranchers along the Middle Fork of the John Day River, to lease a portion of their water rights. In exchange for compensation, the Voigts reduced their annual water diversions, leaving the water to flow unimpeded downstream for the benefit of fish. The leases proved to be mutually beneficial, satisfying the Trust's demand for increased instream flows while providing additional revenue for the Voigts.[1] In 2006, the Voigts decided to sell a portion of their water rights to OWT, protecting, in perpetuity, up to 10 cubic feet per second (CFS)[2] of water instream for fish. Now, every year from July 21 to September, when flows are most critical for local fisheries, up to an additional 6.5 million gallons a day will flow through the entire seventy-mile reach of Middle Fork.

Demand for instream flows has grown markedly in recent decades in the West, but more than a century of appropriating water for offstream uses has left many streams with insufficient water to meet this demand. In a normally functioning market, new demands are met through voluntary exchanges between holders of existing property rights and the new players in that market—just as was done in the case of the Voigts and OWT. But many states' political institutions governing water use and allocation have not evolved to allow such transfers. Those institutions continue to rely on state-centric provision of instream flows, leaving private marketing opportunities to offstream applications such as agriculture, power generation, municipal, or other industrial uses.

This chapter explores the evolving institutional setting governing instream flows in the West[3] and provides a comprehensive review of the role of markets in restoring stream flows. (See chapter 5 for a discussion of water auctions to protect stream flows in Oregon.) Extensive market data on instream flow transactions are presented, but the institutional battle over market implementation is not over. Substantial barriers remain, and these are discussed state-by-state.

Water Rights

The modern system of water rights in the West, known as prior-appropriation, can be traced to the mining camps of California in the mid-nineteenth century. Shortly after the discovery of gold at Sutter's Mill in 1848, competition became fierce for mining sites and for securing reliable access to water. Lacking an effective governmental authority at the time, the miners established their own extralegal system for allocating and enforcing mining claims.[4] What evolved was a system of property rights to claims based on priority. The first to establish a claim—usually by physically working the land—would gain the rights to that claim.[5]

Like land, water was a critical input in mining operations, from panning along stream banks to washing entire hillsides through wooden sluices.[6] As competition for water grew, miners staked claims farther and farther from natural water sources, which required diverting and conveying water away from streams, sometimes for miles. To secure rights to water, the miners adopted a priority-based system similar to mining claims. The first to establish a diversion secured a right to continued use of a specified amount of water that was protected from injury from subsequent appropriators.

Prior Appropriation Doctrine

The rights-based system for water created in the early mining camps was later adopted by states throughout the West and would formally be known as the prior-appropriation doctrine. (See chapter 13 for discussion of prior appropriation rights in California.) The essence of the doctrine was "first in time, first in right"—the first rights to water were superior to and enforceable against subsequent appropriators. To legally obtain a water right, one had to show intent to use, create a physical diversion, and put the water to beneficial use without harming prior appropriators. In their constitutions, states claimed authority to define beneficial use, which generally included only economic uses, such as agriculture, municipal, mining, or other industrial purposes, including hydropower generation.[7]

Prior-appropriation rights are not property rights in the sense that a right holder takes physical ownership of a volume or flow rate of water; rather, they are an entitlement to use water that is owned by the state. State officials are authorized to grant appropriations for uses the officials deem beneficial and in the public's interest. The rights to use water are generally well-defined and enforceable. They may be transferred wholly or in part to another user, however, with certain limitations as discussed later. Hence, prior-appropriation water rights have been generally secure and can continue indefinitely, assuming the water is used in accordance with state law.[8] Water rights may, however, be lost through nonuse or even wasteful use of water as defined by state officials. This feature of the law is often referred to as "use-it or lose-it." The right to water that is not routinely used or not applied to a beneficial use may be forfeited, in which case the rights are relinquished to the state and may be appropriated by other users.

In short, western water laws evolved to meet the demand of offstream water users. With the exception of maintaining water levels for navigational or hydropower purposes, there was little or no demand to maintain water instream. Today, however, demand to leave water in streams or other water bodies is emerging, and the existing legal framework makes it difficult for people to respond to that demand.[9]

Gradually, and to limited degrees, however, states are expanding some of the provisions of the prior-appropriation doctrine to provide for the protection and improvement of instream flows. All western states now define certain uses of water instream as beneficial,[10] and in most states, water may be appropriated to an instream use or transferred from existing offstream rights to instream uses. There is variation among states, however, particularly in the laws that affect the private sector's ability to provide instream flows and the transferability of water rights to instream uses. Nevertheless, there is a general trend toward less reliance on regulations and restrictions as a means to protect instream flows and a growing interest in market-based strategies. These differences will be described later.

Protecting Stream Flows

There are basically four ways to protect instream flows. The first is to use state restrictions or regulations that limit further declines in flows by essentially closing streams to new appropriations or requiring mitigation of groundwater withdrawals.[11] The second invokes the public trust doctrine or the Endangered Species Act (ESA). In these cases, the right to use water for offstream uses may be denied or diminished to provide adequate flows instream for what is asserted to be the "public benefit" or to meet requirements of the ESA. A third way is to allow appropriation of water for instream uses. Like water rights for offstream uses, private parties or state agencies may apply for rights to leave water in its natural course. A fourth way is to improve and protect stream flows by acquiring existing water rights from offstream users in order to leave water instream that would otherwise have been diverted. This is the method used by OWT described at the beginning of the chapter. Western states have adopted a combination of these strategies to protect instream flows, with mixed results.

Maintaining Status Quo Flows

As the West grew in the late nineteenth and early twentieth centuries, the race to claim water for mining and irrigation severely depleted instream flows. In many cases, the amount of water claimed by rights holders was close to or even exceeded the quantity of water in those streams; that is, the streams were fully appropriated or overappropriated.[12] When a stream is fully appropriated by diverters, there is no water available for environmental or recreational uses.

In response to emerging demand for these nonconsumptive uses, states began to adopt various strategies to protect some of the remaining flows. The earliest efforts relied on legislative restrictions that prohibited additional water diversions. In Oregon, for example, tributaries feeding scenic waterfalls in the Columbia River Gorge were closed to new appropriations in the early 1900s.[13] Similarly, in the 1920s, Idaho's legislature set limitations on new diversions in order to maintain lake levels for the preservation of scenic beauty, health, and recreation.[14]

Later, states adopted more comprehensive policies to protect existing flows from further declines. Most common were the establishment of minimum flows[15] and new instream flow appropriations. In function, the two strategies are very similar. Each legally defines a specified amount or flow of water instream that is not appropriable to other uses in the future. As such, these measures do not impact existing right holders.

Along streams not fully appropriated to other uses, states may designate a minimum flow or level deemed necessary to provide for certain environmental or recreational uses. Any subsequent application to appropriate water from those streams could be expected to be denied if it would reduce the flow below the designated minimum. These minimum flows, like prior-appropriation rights, are generally established by priority and are enforceable against later appropriators but are not protected from more senior users. Given that most streams in the West are heavily or fully appropriated to other uses, minimum flows are often the most junior claimants along a stream. In times of low water supplies due to variation in the hydrologic cycle, this means that these minimum flows cannot be protected.

Most western states have adopted a statutory means of setting minimum flows. For example, in Oregon, a revision to the state's water code in 1955 authorized the Oregon Water Resources Board (predecessor to the Water Resources Commission and Water Resources Department) to set minimum flow levels.[16] By 1987, 547 state-administered minimum flow levels had been established along various stream reaches.[17] In Washington, the Minimum Water Flows and Levels Act of 1967 authorized the Department of Ecology (WDOE), at the request of the Washington Department of Fish and Wildlife, to establish minimum flows for fish, wildlife, water quality, and other instream uses by administrative rule.[18] As of 2008, WDOE had designated minimum flows or stream closures on twenty-five of the state's sixty-two Water Resource Inventory Areas—regions that serve as the geographic basis for the WDOE's basin management and instream resource protection programs.[19] In Montana, minimum flows are maintained through state-administered reservations. The Montana Water Use Act of 1973 authorized the state or any political subdivision of the state to reserve water instream for the protection of recreation, fish and wildlife, or water quality. The Department of Fish, Wildlife, and Parks currently maintains minimum flow reservations on various reaches of eighty-seven streams, in total comprising roughly 2,078 stream miles with some level of minimum flows.[20]

Arizona, Colorado, Idaho, Nevada, Oregon, and Wyoming permit new appropriations for certain instream purposes.[21] Generally, the new rights are defined by priority date, level or flow of water, point or stretch of stream (reach) where flows are protected, and timing of flows. Like diversionary rights and minimum flows, instream rights are protected from injury from more junior appropriators. Commonly, they are established through a process similar to that of diversionary rights.[22] Instream rights have an advantage over minimum flows in that they provide better legal clarity and protection over time.[23]

In Colorado, the state's Water Conservation Board has created nearly 1,500 new instream rights on over 8,600 miles of streams and water levels on 482 lakes.[24] By 2008, Oregon's Water Resources Department had appropriated over nine hundred new instream rights and converted more than five hundred of the state's 547 minimum flows to instream water rights.[25] Far fewer rights have been created in other western states. As two of the driest states in the nation,[26] most of the water in Arizona and Nevada has been appropriated for diversionary uses, leaving few reliable sources for new instream rights.[27] Ninety-three instream rights have been issued in Arizona and eleven in Nevada.[28] Wyoming has approved forty-two of the ninety-seven applications for instream flow rights.[29] In Idaho, the state has established rights on

672 miles of streams and two lakes, roughly 1 percent of the state's total stream miles.[30] The conclusion is that, although there appears to be considerable activity in establishing instream flow rights in most states, the effort is a small fraction of total stream miles.

There are a number of shortcomings to these instream flow protection strategies. First, minimum flows are generally established by administrative ruling,[31] which means they are subject to political motivations rather than economic or ecological criteria. Furthermore, they may be changed under new administrations with different views of the importance of offstream water uses.[32] Second, the late priority date of the right means that there is little assurance that instream flows can be protected, especially during times of drought when flows are most critical to fish and wildlife populations and water demand is highest by offstream right holders. Third, both minimum flows and new appropriations could at best protect existing flows from future diversions, rather than improve or restore dewatered streams. In Montana alone, an estimated 4,000 miles of temporarily or chronically dewatered streams lack sufficient flows to maintain local aquatic species.[33] Establishing minimum flows or new instream rights along dewatered streams would at best perpetuate inadequate flows. So, at the very time that there is growing demand to increase flows on historically dewatered streams in order to restore habitat for fish and wildlife species, reconnect fish migratory routes, and provide adequate flows for recreation or aesthetic uses, there is little chance that these demands can be met in the current legal and administrative framework.

Restoring Flows Through Markets

The inherent limitations of minimum flow designations and new appropriations have made it clear that the only practical way to restore dewatered streams and improve flows is by reducing the amount of water being diverted. The most equitable and efficient way to achieve this is by acquiring offstream water rights from willing sellers and leaving the water in the stream. With markets, demanders of instream flows can enter into voluntary agreements with offstream water users to alter diversions for the benefit of increased flows. Moreover, market transactions and prices provide incentives for improved water use efficiencies and conservation. Water salvaged or conserved from implementing new technologies or measures that reduce waste could, if permissible, be sold or leased to other users, providing additional revenue to the right holder.[34]

Water rights for offstream uses are generally transferable wholly or in part and may be changed in purpose of use, location of use or diversion, or timing of use as long as the change does not injure other water right holders.[35] As a matter of historical record, therefore, transfers among diversionary water users have been common and used to meet changing demands and the need to move water to higher valued uses and places of use. In general, any legal entity may acquire a water right through purchase, lease, donation, or trade provided the water is physically diverted, used in a beneficial manner as defined by the state, and does not harm other water right holders or the public welfare.

Only in recent decades, and to varying degrees among states, however, have these market opportunities been available to demanders of instream flows. The policies of various western states as respect to water markets are summarized in Table 4.1. This list shows that although there is a great deal of inconsistency across states, changes in western water laws have opened the door for a number of state, federal, and private entities to restore dewatered streams, improve flows during drought conditions, and protect, in perpetuity, senior water rights for instream uses through markets. Actual data to determine to what extent market exchanges are occurring will be examined next.

Table 4.1 **Comparison of state instream water laws pertinent to market transfers**

State	State may acquire private water rights to provide instream flows	Private entity is authorized to acquire and hold rights to water for instream uses	Private entity may purchase existing rights and donate to the state to be used instream
Colorado	Yes, CO Water Conservation Board may lease, purchase, or receive as donation	No	Yes
Oregon	Yes, OR Water Resources Department may receive donated water rights	Yes, but instream rights are held in trust by the state	Yes
Montana	Yes, MT Department of Fish Wildlife and Parks may lease water rights (no limit on renewals)	Yes	Yes
Washington	Yes, Department of Ecology through its Trust Water Rights Program may purchase, lease, or receive as donation	Yes, but instream rights are held in trust by the state	Yes

(Continued)

Table 4.1 (*Continued*)

California	Yes, CA Department of Fish & Game and CA Department of Water Resources may lease, purchase, or receive as donation	Yes	Yes
Idaho	Yes, ID Department of Water Resources may lease or purchase water. (Generally through the state's water banking system.)	No	Yes, along the Big and Little Wood Rivers
New Mexico	Yes, Strategic Water Reserve and Interstate Stream Commission may acquire water rights	Unclear	Yes
Arizona	Yes (ADWR via the AZ Water Protection Fund)	Yes from a new appropriation. Generally, may not transfer an existing right to ISF	Yes
Nevada	Yes, NV Division of Wildlife may lease, purchase, or receive as donation	Yes	Yes
Utah	Yes, Division of Wildlife Resources and Division of Parks and Recreation may lease, purchase, or receive as donation	Generally no, however, HB 117 provides for leasing by approved private organizations	Yes
Wyoming	Yes, WY Game and Fish Department may purchase or receive as donation (no leases)	No	Yes

Market Activity

In recent decades, market activity for instream flows has expanded markedly. Between 1987 and 2007,[36] state, federal, and private entities combined acquired more than 10 million acre-feet (AF)[37] of water for instream purposes through short- and long-term leases, donations, and permanent transfers.[38] More than 2,500 transactions[39] were completed with total expenditures exceeding $530 million (adjusted for inflation) (see Figure 4.1).[40]

Market Participants: Who Is Buying Water?

States vary widely in expenditures for instream rights as well as in the roles that federal, state, and private entities play in acquiring water. Market activity has been driven largely by state and federal efforts to restore flows for endangered species and to improve water quality and flows for fish and wildlife habitat. In most states, the legal and institutional setting has limited or even prohibited private entities from acquiring water directly (see Table 4.2). Despite these limitations, private organizations are playing an increasingly important role in restoring stream flows by working cooperatively with state and federal agencies to facilitate transactions and remove barriers to markets.

Between 1987 and 2007, federal agencies entered into 215 leases and 25 permanent transfers. Federal expenditures made up roughly 46 percent of

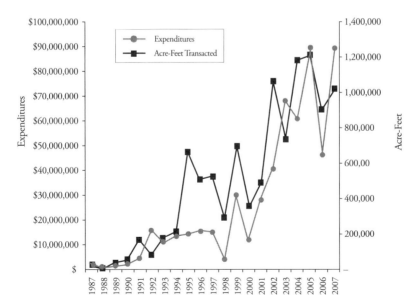

Figure 4.1   Annual instream flow transactions 1987–2007

all market expenditures for water and roughly 56 percent of the total water quantity acquired in markets (see Table 4.2). The U.S. Bureau of Reclamation (USBR)—the single largest federal acquirer—spent more than $240 million on water leases and purchases for nearly 5.5 million AF since 1987. The USBR acquired water from willing sellers in California, Washington, Oregon, Idaho, and New Mexico, primarily to meet instream flow requirements for endangered species. Other federal agencies acquiring water for environmental flows included the U.S. Fish and Wildlife Service and the Bonneville Power Administration.

These data make clear that state agencies too are increasingly using markets to purchase or lease water for instream uses. Since 1987, state expenditures have topped $246 million to restore over 3.3 million AF to streams for environmental and recreational uses (see Table 4.2). State agencies acquired water through 327 leases, 32 purchases, and 199 donation agreements. Temporary and permanent donations continue to increase as landowners retire marginal lands, improve water-use efficiencies, and apparently want to improve flows for fish. In some cases, the donations carry tax benefits for the landowner. State agencies have acquired water for instream purposes in all western states except Wyoming.

Private entities, such as water trusts and conservancies, play an important role in many aspects of stream-flow protection and water marketing, from education and research to water acquisitions. In addition, they work with state policy makers to improve market opportunities and assist in completing trades between governmental agencies and willing sellers. Although private expenditures comprised less than 8 percent of the total since 1987, private entities have participated in more than 1,100 leases, 100 permanent transfers, and received nearly 500 donations—in total, more than double the number of transactions completed by all federal and state agencies combined.

Instream Flow Prices

Table 4.3 summarizes reported market prices between 1987 and 2007 by acquisition method (lease or purchase) and acquiring entity (federal, state, or private). To facilitate time comparisons, all prices have been converted to the price of water per AF per year (AF/yr)[41] and have been adjusted for inflation to reflect constant 2,007 dollars. In order to compare purchases that commit a specified amount of water instream in perpetuity to leases as well as provide flows for a specific term, purchase prices were further adjusted to reflect the annualized cost per AF using a discount rate of 6 percent. To illustrate, consider that a one-year lease of 100 AF at a total cost of $1,000 would have the same cost on a per AF basis ($10) as a water right purchase of 100 AF at the same cost of $1,000 without taking into consideration the term of the contract. Because the buyer is receiving 100 AF each year in perpetuity, the realized cost on a per AF basis would be less than $10. By

Table 4.2   Market activity by transaction type and acquiring entity (1987–2007)

Expenditures	Federal	State	Private	Total
Lease	$ 219,818,383.00	$ 187,965,169.00	$ 6,441,754.00	$ 414,225,305.80
Purchase	$ 29,806,912.50	$ 58,538,202.00	$ 35,858,518.00	$ 124,203,632.50
Total	$ 249,625,295.70	$ 246,503,370.60	$ 42,300,272.00	$ 538,428,938.30
Quantity				
Lease (af)	5,530,594.00	2,338,021.00	441,694.00	8,310,309.00
Purchase (af)	141,596.00	149,673.00	235,978.00	527,247.00
Donation (af)	-	884,961.00	329,489.00	1,214,450.00
Total (af)	5,672,190.00	3,372,655.00	1,007,161.00	10,052,006.00

Table 4.3   Instream flow prices by transaction type and acquiring entity

	Mean	Min	Max	Observations
Federal				
Leases	$ 76.09	$ 1.81	$ 1,017.92	215
Purchases	$ 129.02	$ 5.25	$ 612.96	25
State				
Leases	$ 82.12	$ 0.10	$ 351.36	327
Purchases	$ 175.25	$ 3.09	$ 3,933.68	32
Private				
Leases	$ 12.42	$ 0.29	$ 296.33	1158
Purchases	$ 174.40	$ 2.35	$ 2,785.90	100

discounting the purchase price to reflect the per AF/yr price (annualized lease price), it becomes possible to compare the costs of contracts to deliver water over various time periods. Following the example, the discounted price becomes $0.60 per AF/yr.

Prices for leased water rights ranged from a low of $0.10 to a high of $1,017.92 per AF/yr with an overall mean price of $33.91. State and federal agencies paid significantly higher prices, averaging $82.12 and $76.09, respectively, per AF/yr compared to the mean price of $12.42 paid by private entities (Table 4.3).

The reason for the large disparity in lease prices between private and public acquisitions is not entirely clear but may be explained in part by certain characteristics of the transactions and in part by the objectives of the acquiring organization. First, the transactions costs to transfer or change a water right vary widely depending on the nature of the water right. For example, the transactions costs of trading water within an irrigation district, within a federal or state water project, or through a water bank may be low due to the fact that the water rights (contracts in the case of governmental water projects) are fairly well-defined and transfers may be handled within the organization, not through the state. Often, however, transfers are prohibited outside the "organization," though there are exceptions. For example, state and federal entities may be permitted to lease water from these aggregated sources. In doing so, they generally face lower transactions costs and may be willing to offer a higher price to lease water. By comparison, private entities more often contract directly with individual right holders, which generally involves higher transactions costs, including application fees, clarifying water rights to determine historical and consumptive use amounts, potential legal fees for dispute resolution, and in some cases, tax consequences.[42] Typically these costs are borne by the seller, though private trusts and conservancies will often share in these costs to encourage or speed transactions. Therefore, the reduced costs to the seller may mean that he or she will be willing to accept a lower price received for the actual water rights being transferred than if he or she had to bear the full burden of these costs.

A second reason for the price disparity may stem from the quantity and location of the acquired water. State and federal agencies on average acquire large blocks of water per transaction and from multiple landowners (roughly 7,100 and 26,000 AF per transaction, respectively) compared to private entities (380 AF per transaction). Seeking out individual landowners to negotiate prices would be prohibitively costly; therefore, government agencies often acquire water from aggregated sources using a standing offer or negotiating with a water manager. For example, agencies may contact local irrigation districts, water banks, rental pools (Idaho), or state or federal water projects and offer a set price for water. Anyone interested in selling/or leasing their water may do so at the offered price; however, the price must be high enough to attract sufficient quantities of water, often from multiple landowners to meet the agency's high volume objectives. Private entities, by comparison, generally lack sufficient funding to acquire enough water that would make a noticeable environmental improvement in major streams, thus generally target smaller stream reaches and tributaries where even a small amount of water can make a significant ecological improvement.[43] Moreover, along minor stream reaches and tributaries, there may be fewer competing buyers and lower opportunity costs for the water, thus sellers would be willing to lease water at lower prices.

Purchase prices per AF/yr were markedly higher than lease prices, ranging overall from $2.35 to $3,933.68. State and private entities acquired water rights at a mean price of roughly $175 per AF compared to $129 by federal agencies. Landowners are generally more reluctant to sell rather than lease water rights, thus it is not surprising that sale prices, even when discounted, were much higher than lease prices. Overall, there was much less disparity among acquiring entities in the sale prices compared to lease prices; however, with so few transactions and significant dispersion of prices, making sense of price comparisons becomes more difficult.

Market Barriers

Despite considerable market growth in recent decades, trading water for instream purposes is far from easy. In fact, a number of legal, administrative, economic, and even cultural factors introduce significant transactions costs and obstruct market expansion. States have variously addressed some of these barriers, though there is room for improvement.

Legal Barriers

Historically, the most prominent legal barriers were states' limited definitions of beneficial use and the laws prohibiting either new appropriations for instream flow rights or the transfer of existing water rights to instream uses. Today, however, all western states recognize instream water for certain purposes to be beneficial. The purposes for which states identify instream uses as beneficial, however, are clearly more restrictive in some states than in others, thus limiting the opportunities to protect flows. Washington, for example, has an expansive view of instream uses as beneficial—fish and wildlife maintenance and enhancement, protection of game and birds, and recreation, scenic, aesthetic and all other uses compatible with the enjoyment of the public waters of the state.[44] Wyoming, by contrast, has a more narrow view and limits instream flow rights to the "minimum flow necessary" to "establish or maintain fisheries" (if the water is supplied from stored sources) and to "maintain or improve existing fisheries" if appropriated from unappropriated waters.[45]

The most effective means of improving instream flows is through the acquisition and change of existing offstream water rights to instream uses. Most states, however, legally restrict who may acquire or hold water rights for instream purposes. In particular, most states either prohibit or limit to some degree the role that private entities may play in protecting flows (see Table 4.1). For example, Arizona,[46] California, Montana, Nevada, and New Mexico[47] permit private entities, in addition to public entities, to acquire and hold an instream flow right that was converted from an existing water right. Despite the private sector's legal standing, however, the transfer of water to instream uses is still at the discretion of the state which may deny or amend the application if there is some uncertainty that the water will provide a beneficial use. Washington and Oregon permit private acquisitions but require that once the right is transferred to an instream use, it must be held in trust by the state. In Colorado and along the Big and Little Wood Rivers in Idaho, private parties may donate rights to the state to be converted and held for instream use. In Utah, as part of a recently adopted pilot program (HB 117), private conservancies can lease water from farmers to improve instream flows. In other states, market transactions are generally limited to specific state and federal entities.

A number of arguments in opposition to private appropriation and owner-ship of instream rights generally originate from competing industries.[48] First, agricultural, municipal, and industrial users fear that instream appropriations will reduce potential development by limiting future water supplies. When a governmental or private entity provides instream flows, it is usually with the intention of protecting them in perpetuity—in effect, reducing potential sup-plies of water for other uses. Second, there is concern that transfers of water away from current uses, agriculture in particular, will adversely affect local economies.[49] A large loss of farmland in communities based predominately on agricultural production could affect all sectors of the local economy, from schools and restaurants to equipment suppliers and local repair shops. Third, existing water right holders along streams with instream flow rights in place fear increased scrutiny of their rights and the potential for legal disputes. Because water left instream is easily diverted by other users, enforcement often requires greater oversight to ensure flows are maintained, and this can increase the possibility of disputes and claims against these users.

These arguments are generally unsubstantiated empirically. First, assuming states extend the provisions set forth in the prior-appropriation doctrine to instream users, the risk of injury to existing users is greatly reduced. Under the rule of no injury, transfers may be denied or limited if the change would injure existing senior or junior water users,[50] or in the case of a new appro-priation, no senior water users should be injured.[51] Second, any transfers to instream uses are often isolated and rarely on a scale large enough to affect local communities. Concerns over the effects from transfers are gen-erally less when the transfer is to an environmental or recreational use;[52] however, large scale transfers from agriculture to municipal or industrial uses have been shown to impact local communities.[53] In fact, where the value of water instream exceeds the value of traditional uses, the economic gains from trade may improve local economies by expanding fishing, hunting, and recreational opportunities. Third, the potential for greater scrutiny of existing rights and claims against offstream users is real, but this scrutiny arguably may benefit all legal water users. Only users that are diverting or using water illegally, or in excess of their entitlements, are at risk from water losses. Where water rights are well-defined and enforced, existing users are unlikely to be affected by new instream flows.

Another problem facing the private provision of instream flows is that they are often viewed as a common property resource, in which exclusion of or contracting with all beneficiaries is prohibitively costly. As such, theory suggests that instream flows would be produced below the efficient level if they are only provided by the private sector.[54] Moreover, in the context of markets and acquiring water for instream purposes, pricing of public resources can be difficult.[55] Laws that limit the acquisition of instream flows to state agencies are counter to the fundamentals of property rights inherent in the prior-appropriation doctrine and take allocation decisions out of the hands of water users, including those wishing to enhance environmental amenities. Through legislative changes that codify instream flow rights for private entities, states could increase the pool of buyers and sellers,[56] and, thereby, the opportunities to improve instream flows.

Private-party participation is proving to be an important driver of market expansion, however. Where permitted, acquisitions by private entities continue to increase in frequency, compared to state and federal acquisitions (Figure 4.2). Moreover, state agencies are increasingly looking to private

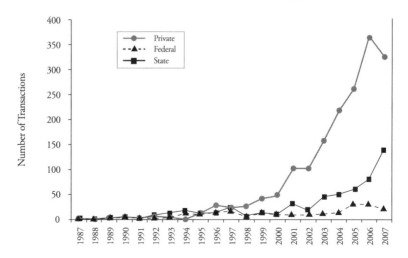

Figure 4.2 Historical transactions by federal, state, and private entities

conservation groups for assistance in facilitating trades for environmental purposes. In states where private acquisitions are permitted, more than 2,400 transactions have occurred since 1987, compared to less than 150 combined in Colorado, Idaho, Utah, and Wyoming, where private acquisitions are highly restricted or prohibited.

Even in states prohibiting private acquisitions, entities such as Trout Unlimited and the Colorado Water Trust have had notable success in restoring stream flows by working closely with state agencies and owners of water rights to facilitate voluntary transactions. In Idaho, Trout Unlimited linked up with irrigators along Rainey Creek, a tributary to the south fork of the Snake River, to obtain the first water donation to the Idaho Water Supply Bank for instream flow protection. In 2007, the Colorado Water Trust acquired consumptive water rights along an important section of Hat Creek that provides resting and refuge habitat for local brook and brown trout populations. The water rights were then donated to the Colorado Water Conservation Board to be converted and held by the state as instream flow rights.

Abolishing restrictions on who may acquire or hold water rights for instream uses would increase the opportunities for trade and expand water markets. Private interests wanting to improve flows could then rely less on political and legal channels and meet their demands directly through voluntary transactions—a more efficient process.[57] Further, demands for environmental or recreational flows could then compete with offstream users in the same market setting, which would improve water allocation and the potential for economic gains.

Poorly Defined Rights

Well-defined, enforced, and transferable rights are critical components of a viable and efficient water market, whether trading for offstream or instream uses. Uncertainty in the entitlement to water or the ability to protect those rights from harm diminishes the incentive to pursue market transfers and reduces the expected gains from trade.

Typically, a surface water right certificate defines the place and nature of use, the amount of water as measured by volume or flow, and the priority date of the right. Throughout the West, however, the actual amount of water in use often differs from what is stated in the water right. "Early appropriations . . . were frequently in excess of actual need because there was no administrative system to police the amounts claimed."[58] Similarly, over time, as irrigators switched crops, implemented new technologies to deliver and apply water, or improved water-use efficiencies, actual water use may have declined, widening the disparity between claims and actual use. Moreover, local hydrological conditions change over time altering the amount of water available to right holders. The same disparity arises in heavily appropriated or over-appropriated basins where more junior water rights may receive little or no water in dry years despite their stated entitlement. Finally, illegal diversions are not uncommon in the West and may go uncontested for decades.

Whenever a transfer is initiated, a dispute is filed, or a state- or basin-specific adjudication is mandated, water rights must be investigated and clarified. Currently, every western state is at some stage of adjudicating water rights, and the process is lengthy, costly, and often contentious. For many states, decades may be required to complete the process. The Montana Water Court, for example, was created in 1979 to facilitate a statewide adjudication and decree of more than 219,000 water rights. The projected completion date is 2020 and is estimated to cost more than $51 million.[59] There can be little doubt, however, that the process of adjudicating rights will help inventory available water resources, uncover illegal diversions, clarify existing rights, and identify abandoned or forfeited rights to water that may be eligible for new appropriation.

Poorly defined rights also influence the willingness of potential sellers to enter into trades. Initiating a transfer application requires state supervision and thus threatens the loss of water if there is a disparity between actual use and the right's claim. A landowner using more water than entitled also risks facing potential state fines. As indicated previously, if historical use is less than the original appropriated amount, there is a risk of forfeiture to the state of the unused water—"use it or lose it." Moreover, the costs of defining rights through adjudication and decree are borne in part by the water right holder regardless of whether the process is initiated by the state in a general adjudication or by a right holder for the purpose of changing use or selling or leasing water. The costs of defining rights, therefore, reduce the gains from trade.

As noted previously, in every western state, junior and senior right holders are protected from injury resulting from a change or a transfer of other water rights. And protection of all legitimate right holders is critical to an efficient market. Where rights are unclear, disputes are common and may tie up transfers for years.[60] Moreover, "the no harm rule makes any trade vulnerable to a variety of constituent claims, some legitimate and some pure holdup."[61] In some cases, disputes may not be limited to only other water right holders. In California, for example, any party, whether a water user or business supported by water users (agricultural product suppliers, local stores, schools, etc.), may protest transfers if they believe they will be adversely affected by the transfer.[62] In other cases, the state or water court may determine if the transfer will adversely impact the public's interest.[63] Irrespective of the reason for the dispute, having multiple parties with veto power against transfers raises transactions costs and can make transfers financially infeasible (see chapter 6). In addition, the risk of disputes and the associated costs themselves restrict market activity by acting as a deterrent to pursuing trades.[64]

Most transfer disputes arise out of trades among offstream users because of fear that the transfer will result in less water available to a downstream user. It is not uncommon, however, for instream flow trades to be similarly challenged, despite the resulting increase of water instream. Other right holders fear the trades may diminish the local agricultural economy or drastically change the stream's hydrology. Changes in the timing of flows and reduction in return flows are real concerns that states are addressing. Most commonly, trades are limited to only the historical consumptive use portion of the water right—the amount that would otherwise have been lost to evapotranspiration[65] or incorporated into crops—thus reducing the probability that less water will be available to other water rights.

Before a transfer can be approved, there must be adequate evidence of no injury to other right holders. But who is responsible for providing this evidence? Providing sufficient documentation and the associated costs fall primarily on the transferor. To encourage water right holders to sell, lease, or donate rights, conservation groups will often initiate the application process and cover all or part of the transactions costs, which may include attorneys' fees, determining historical and consumptive uses, application fees, and negotiations with objectors and relevant state agencies. These costs can be substantial if the water rights are not well-defined.

The benefits from better-defined water rights are clear, but achieving this goal may be costly. In Washington, for example, WDOE, which is the largest acquirer of water for instream uses in the state, contends the transactions costs of pursuing trades of unadjudicated rights can be so high that they exceed the ecological value of increased stream flows.[66]

As the value of water and economic gains from trade, whether for offstream or instream uses, continue to increase,[67] so too does the value of better-defined rights.[68] A growing number of buyers and sellers are now hiring private water consultants to research the status of water rights in order to speed the transfer process. And state agencies are dedicating increased funding to streamline and complete general- and basin-specific adjudications.

Enforcement

Equally important to well-defined and tradable water rights is the protection of those rights by adequate enforcement. Throughout the West, illegal diversions of surface water and pumping from wells further deplete already scarce water resources while directly harming legitimate right holders. Moreover, poorly enforced rights discourage markets and militate against efficient water allocation.

States often lack sufficient technical and financial resources to monitor and police all water users; thus illegal or excess withdrawals can go undetected until a dispute is filed or adjudication is initiated. Even when fines for infractions are imposed, the fines may be so low that they provide little deterrent to infractions. The maximum penalty in Washington, for example, used to be $100 per day, potentially less than the value of the water or the cost of purchasing or leasing water from other users. The fines were increased during the 2003 legislative session to between $100 and $5,000 per day, depending on the severity of the violation; however, few fines (seven between 2003 and 2008) have been imposed because "monetary penalties are difficult, contentious, and require extensive staff time and, in many cases, attorney resources."[69] Similarly, in California, the State Water Resources Control Board lacks sufficient staff resources to enforce instream rights, leaving little assurance that flow targets will be maintained,[70] thus reducing and even eliminating incentives for market trades.

The very nature of instream flows, compared to offstream uses, further complicates enforcement. Once water is diverted for agricultural or municipal uses, other potential users are automatically excluded from its use (with the exception of return flows). By contrast, environmental or recreational flows are defined by a specific flow and reach, but unless closely monitored and enforced are not always excludable from diversion to other users.

The likelihood that rights will be enforced depends in part on who the residual claimant is to water. When the gains from ownership of water rights accrue directly to the user, any threat to the entitlement is more likely to be disputed and resolved. For example, an illegal or excessive diversion that reduces a rafting company's instream flow entitlement is unlikely to go unnoticed or undisputed. Conversely, when water rights are acquired and held by the state for the public, the state is neither the direct beneficiary nor user of the water, and thus any injury to those rights is less likely to be enforced.[71] In other words, the enforcement of state-held rights is dependent upon the ability of the state to police itself on behalf of the public, perhaps an "unlikely prospect."[72] Moreover, traditional water users have a strong political presence, which state regulators are unlikely to disregard.[73]

Greater private involvement in instream flow markets improves the likelihood that stream flows will be enforced. Private parties routinely monitor flows to ensure leased or purchased water remains instream because they have a personal incentive to do so. For instance, the Columbia Basin Water Transactions Program monitors streams on more than 90 percent of their transactions throughout the Pacific Northwest.[74] To reduce monitoring costs, private water trusts and conservancies are employing new technologies that record stream-flow data periodically over time or in real time along streams with instream flow contracts in place, thus ensuring flows are maintained. These efforts not only improve enforcement of instream flow rights but also provide flow data that can be used by fish and wildlife agencies and states to inventory water resources and reduce enforcement costs.

In the end, private organizations are motivated by their constituents' direct benefits gained from improved flows. Thus, putting instream flows in the hands of those that directly benefit from them can help ensure that the intended goals are met, whether restoring the ecological integrity of fish spawning habitat, sufficient flows for recreation, or aesthetics of a free-flowing stream.

Administrative Barriers

The administrative transactions costs in water trades (irrespective of use) can be considerable. Each transfer or change of use is unique, and the timing, complexity, and transactions costs involved depends on the nature of the transfer, third party disputes, the state's application process, and available resources to investigate and process requests and disputes.

The inefficiencies in the existing transfer process are epitomized in the time that is required to complete a transfer. In Washington, for example, instream flow transactions, whether a lease or permanent purchase, can take over a year while few are completed in less than six months. The key problem seems to stem from a lack of adequate resources to process the backlog of applications and settle disputes in a timely manner. In addition, the state lacks an up-to-date and easily accessible database of water rights, complicating the process of researching existing rights and identifying potentially affected third parties. In Montana, if a change-of-use application is not disputed, the process can be completed in less than six months; however, few applications are approved this quickly as disputes are common when rights are not clearly defined. Some of the key problems in Montana, and probably elsewhere, are third-party disputes, irregularities in the application process, changing laws and regulatory procedures, unclear recognition of certain uses of water instream as beneficial, and the methodologies used to determine the consumptive-use portion of water rights.[75]

In contrast, short-term leases and donations in Oregon may be completed in as little as four to eight weeks, with renewals processed even more quickly.[76] Similarly, Colorado permits farmers to temporarily lend water (up to 120 days) to the state Water Conservation Board for use instream, and the transfer requires only approval from the state engineer and eliminates the often lengthy process of going through a state water court. Temporary loans may be approved in as little as a month, while longer-term leases and purchases generally take more than six months to process. In California, short-term transfers (less than a year) may be processed in two to three months, though long-term or permanent change-of-use applications may take years to complete. Hence, the approval process can be administratively cumbersome and costly to the applicant.[77]

To reduce transactions costs and bypass the often lengthy application and approval process, conservation groups may contract directly with landowners and enter into forbearance agreements. In a forbearance agreement, the water right holder is compensated to forbear from exercising their right in whole or in part. Groups such as Montana Water Trust, Trout Unlimited, and OWT have had success in providing needed stream flows for fish and wildlife on relatively short notice while at the same time establishing trust with landowners who may be apprehensive about formal instream flow transactions or dealing with state agencies. There are some important disadvantages; however. Because the water rights do not go through a formal change of use or transfer process with the state, any water left instream is not legally protected from other users. As a consequence, forbearance agreements are not likely to be effective on heavily appropriated or overappropriated streams where improved flows are most needed. Moreover, water that is not diverted may be subject to forfeiture over time. States generally require water be put to a beneficial use (as stated on the claim) at least once every five years to avoid being subject to abandonment or forfeiture. As such, forbearance agreements are only useful in the short term, generally weeks to a few years.

In much of the West, instream flow markets are still in their nascent stages of development. With time and experience, state procedures and requirements are becoming less ambiguous and more efficient. Greater involvement by private entities is helping to streamline the application and transfer processes, while groups like Trout Unlimited continue to propose legislation that better defines and expands the role of private interests in instream flow markets.

Cultural Barriers

Although the various institutional and economic barriers to transfers tend to differ among states, one common characteristic throughout the West is a general apprehension about leasing or selling water back into streams. Traditional thought was that water should be used on the land for productive purposes like farming and ranching[78] and that leaving it in its natural course, undiverted, would be considered wasteful.[79] Landowners looking to trade water for nonagricultural purposes are often met with disfavor from local communities, businesses, and other landowners who fear the economic consequences of losing part of their community's agricultural base.[80] Understandably, after multiple generations of investing in the production of food and fiber under arid conditions, the idea of shifting scarce water resources away from agriculture to protect fish and wildlife populations, sustain recreation activities, and restore aesthetic beauty may seem threatening and may be stoutly resisted. A recent survey of entities throughout the Northwest that have actively acquired water for instream uses revealed that lack of "cultural acceptance" of instream water marketing to be one of the stumbling blocks in expanding these markets. Most respondents believed that the transactions costs attributed to cultural factors were unavoidable; although could be made more manageable by building trust with landowners through adequate personal contact and education.[81]

Another strategy to overcome this cultural inertia might be to pay landowners a premium to encourage sales or leases. WestWater Research, a leading water appraisal firm, estimates that often a 50–100 percent premium over the agricultural value of water may be necessary to entice sellers to move water away from traditional economic uses.[82]

As time passes, improving sentiment toward instream flows and markets will no doubt help to expedite market transfers. Private entities have and will likely continue to play an important role in overcoming existing barriers. By working closely with landowners and communities, trust is being built, and educating landowners about new opportunities to trade water is expanding the pool of interested sellers. Innovative strategies such as cost sharing for improved water use and new technologies, the use of flexible short-term leasing and forbearance agreements that allow landowners to experiment with markets while minimizing perceived risks, and working with state agencies and lawmakers to clarify and streamline the transfer process will help to expand existing markets and create new ones.

Conclusion

One of the most important environmental and economic challenges facing the western states is the efficient allocation of increasingly scarce water resources to new and growing demands, many of which are instream uses. Between 2000 and 2030, the population of the eleven conterminous western states is projected to increase by nearly 50 percent,[83] requiring significant efficiency improvements in water use and reallocation of water away from traditional uses. Concurrent with and in direct conflict of growing urban and industrial demands, there is widespread and increasing interest in preserving and restoring stream flows for a widening list of environmental, economic, and recreational uses.

Regulatory strategies that have limited new water developments coupled with first-in-time first-in-right priority systems that give junior status to new applicants for appropriations (which include most instream demands) have proven to be intrinsically insufficient to accommodate these demands. Markets, however, provide a means of improving stream flows above current levels and for restoring historically dewatered streams. The expansion of water laws that permit free market trades of existing water rights to instream uses will no doubt help to facilitate these uses. During the period from 1987 to 2007, market expenditures for instream flows topped $530 million, restoring over 10 million AF of water to streams for the benefit of fish and wildlife habitat, species conservation, recreation, and even aesthetics. State, federal, and private entities combined completed more than 2,500 transactions with water right holders willing to lease, sell, or donate all or a portion of their water rights.

Despite considerable growth in market activity, opportunities to restore flows through voluntary transactions remain geographically mixed. Many

97

states are reluctant to remove specific legal barriers and invest in institutional changes that would facilitate market transactions by which instream flow demands could compete with demands for offstream uses.

Three important prescriptive changes are needed. The first is basic legislative reform that would extend to private interests the same legal standing for instream flow rights as is currently available for offstream right holders. Private demands for instream flows could then be met through economic means and rely less on political or judicial channels. Second, water rights must be more clearly defined. Unlike legislative reform, this will require substantial investment from both the state and private sectors. Ongoing adjudications in each western state are costly and time-consuming, though they will sharply reduce transactions costs and improve water allocation as they are completed. Where the value of instream flows is high and private acquisitions are permitted, buyers and sellers are increasingly hiring private water consultants, brokers, and appraisers to define rights and assist in water transfers. And third, water rights must be better enforced. Illegal or excessive diversions reduce stream flows, erode legitimate water entitlements, and reduce expected gains from trade. Improving enforcement, however, relies on better-defined rights. Once this is done, the costs of identifying illegal water use are reduced, thus lowering the cost of enforcement and improving stream flows.[84]

The success of instream flow markets in recent decades demonstrates that resources can be devoted to environmental goods without having to rely on state restrictions or regulations that attempt to dictate water use among competing users. Expanding water laws and investing in removing barriers to trade will improve water allocation among various offstream and instream uses, while strengthening incentives for improved water use efficiencies and conservation.

Notes

1. "Stories from the Field," 2006, Columbia Basin Water Transactions Program, accessed November 22, 2008, http://www.cbwtp.org/jsp/cbwtp/stories/stories.jsp?year=2006.

2. "Cubic feet per second" is the rate of water flow passing a given point, amounting to a volume of one cubic foot for each second of time. It is equal to 7.48 gallons per second, 448.8 gallons per minute, or 1.984 AF per day. When discussing instream flows for fish or wildlife, the actual amount (in CFS) does not always convey much information because it is relative to the size of the stream, the amount of water necessary to support the target species or goal, and the current conditions in the stream. For example, in some cases, only a fraction of a CFS may be sufficient to restore migration routes in a small tributary. By comparison that same amount in a large river may provide little or no net benefit.

3. The following eleven western states were included: Arizona, California, Colorado, Idaho, Montana, New Mexico, Nevada, Oregon, Utah, Washington, and Wyoming.

4. The discovery of gold at Sutter's Mill and the subsequent mass migration into the region coincided with the end of the Mexican–American War and was more than two years prior to California's statehood. Much of the land claimed by miners fell under federal jurisdiction; however, there was little or no effective authority governing the allocation or protection of mining claims or water resources. (John Umbeck, "The California Gold Rush: A Study of Emerging Property Rights." *Explorations in Economic History* 14 (1977) 197–226.)

5. Each mining camp devised its own set of rules governing mining claims; for example, limitations on the size of the claim, the number of days each week or year it must be worked, and the number of claims a miner may hold. If these conditions were not met, the claim could be forfeited and staked by another miner. (See Umbeck 1977.)

6. David M. Gillilan, and Thomas C. Brown, *Instream Flow Protection: Seeking a Balance in Western Water Use* (Washington, DC: Island Press, 1997), 16.

7. Hydropower generation requires large volumes of water instream. Despite the instream and generally nonconsumptive nature of water used for hydropower, states consider its use as a diversion, thus satisfying the state's requirements.

8. Water rights may be diminished or eliminated without compensation under certain circumstances. For example, requirements of the Federal Endangered Species Act supersede prior appropriation rights; thus water users may be prohibited from withdrawing water from streams or groundwater in order to protect species habitat. An often-cited case involving the Endangered Species Act occurred in May 2001 when the federal government, reversing a century of practice, cut water deliveries to farmers in the Klamath Basin in Oregon. The water was instead allocated to maintain lake levels and stream flows in order to protect endangered suckerfish and Coho salmon (R. E. Meiners and L. Kosnik, "Restoring Harmony in the Klamath Basin." *PERC Policy Series* 27 (2003) 1–28). Similarly, the public trust doctrine maintains that states must protect waters for the enjoyment and use of the public, which can affect appropriated water rights. Between 1997 and 2007, Slade identifies four cases citing the public trust, in which existing water rights were altered for the protection environmental flows (David C. Slade, *The Public Trust Doctrine in Motion: The Evolution of the Doctrine 1997–2008* (Bowie, MD: PTDIM, 2009). One of the more famous cases occurred prior to that period in 1983. In *National Audubon Society v. Superior Court*, the court found that the city of Los Angeles was diverting too much water from Mono Lake, adversely affecting aquatic and bird life. Despite the city's legal appropriative rights to divert from the lake, the court, in 1989, issued an injunction halting the city's diversions until lake levels recovered (see, e.g., Gary D. Libecap, "The Battle over Mono Lake." *Hoover Digest* 2006, no. 2 (April 30, 2006). http://www.hoover.org/publications/hoover-digest/article/6467. (Chapter 10 explicitly discusses and critiques the public trust doctrine, and chapter 9 discusses the Mono Lake controversy.)

9. James Huffman, "Instream Water Use: Public and Private Alternatives," in *Water Rights: Scarce Resource Allocation, Bureaucracy, and the Environment*, ed. Terry L. Anderson (San Francisco, CA: Pacific Institute for Public Policy Research, 1983), 273.

10. New Mexico laws do not explicitly recognize instream flows as beneficial; however, in 1998, the state's attorney general issued an opinion stating that the state engineer can protect instream flows for "recreational, fish or wildlife, or ecological purposes" (N.M. Attorney General Opinion 98–01 at 1 (27 March 1998)).

11. As our understanding of the connection between groundwater and surface water improved, it has become increasingly common for states to require new groundwater withdrawals to be offset by increases in rights to surface water. For example, a developer may be required to acquire surface water rights equal to (or in excess of) the amount of water that would be withdrawn from a new well.

12. James Earl Sherow, *The Grasslands of the United States: An Environmental History,* ed. Mark R. Stoll (Santa Barbara, CA: ABC-CLIO, 2007), 96. In addition to excessive appropriations, hydrological changes over time reduced the amount of water available for appropriators in many streams, in effect making the most junior water rights useless and others less reliable.

13. Janet C. Neuman, "The Good, the Bad, and the Ugly: The First Ten Years of the Oregon Water Trust," *Nebraska Law Review* 83 (2004): 432–84.

14. Idaho Code Ann. § 67–4301, http://legislature.idaho.gov/idstat/Title67/T67CH43SECT67-4301.htm.

15. States vary in both the terms used to describe minimum flows and the purposes for which they designate them. Montana uses the term "instream reservations"; Washington establishes "base flows," but, like many other states, will often refer to them as "minimum flows" or "minimum stream-flows."

16. Act of March 26, 1955, ch. 707, § 10(g), 1955 Or. Laws 924, 927–28.

17. Following the enactment of the 1987 Instream Water Rights Act, minimum flows designations were replaced with appropriated water rights.

18. Wash. Rev. Code § 90.22, http://apps.leg.wa.gov/RCW/default.aspx?cite=90.22&full=true.

19. "Existing and Future Instream Flow Rules and USGS Gages (Map)," Washington Department of Ecology, January 2008, http://www.ecy.wa.gov/programs/wr/instream-flows/Images/irpp_wrp/wsisf0108-usgs.pdf.

20. Dave Amman, hydrologist, Montana Department of Natural Resources and Conservation, telephone conversation, December 1, 2008.

21. The uses for which water may be appropriated instream vary by state and depend on beneficial use definitions as well as the state's governing agency that handles new appropriations. Common instream uses include water for fish, wildlife, and recreation.

22. The process for applications to appropriate water varies among states but generally includes (1) application filed to the state water regulatory agency, (2) state inspection of the water rights, (3) determination if third parties will be affected by the change, (4) public notice, (5) public comments and protests, (6) hearing (if needed), and (7) final approval or denial.

23. Gillilan and Brown, *Instream Flow Protection*, 144.

24. Colorado Water Conservation Board, Instream Flow and Natural Lake Level Water Rights Database (accessed May 23, 2011), http://cwcb.state.

co.us/technical-resources/instream-flow-water-rights-database/Pages/main.aspx.

25. Oregon Water Resources Department, *Oregon Water Resources Department Summary Presentation—Statewide Roundtables Fall 2008,* accessed December 2, 2008, http://water.oregonstate.edu/roundtables/download/OWRD_Presentation.pdf.

26. Nevada, Utah, and Arizona are the three driest states, receiving on average 8.9, 11.5, and 12.6 inches of annual precipitation, respectively (National Climatic Data Center. "Average Statewide Precipitation for Western U.S. States." Historical Climatography Series 4–2. Accessed April 9, 2009. http://wrcc.dri.edu/htmlfiles/avgstate.ppt.html.

27. Herb Dishlap, "Instream Flow Water Rights: Arizona's Approach," in *Instream Flow Protection in the West,* eds. Lawrence J. MacDonnell, Teresa A. Rice, and Steven J. Shupe (Boulder, CO: Natural Resources Law Center, University of Colorado School of Law, 1989), 173–80.

28. Sasha Charney, *Decades Down the Road: An Analysis of Instream Flow Programs in Colorado and the Western United States (July)* (Denver, CO: Colorado Water Conservation Board, 2005).

29. Thomas C. Annear, and Paul D. Dey, *Water Management Unit Five-Year Plan; 2006 to 2010,* Wyoming Game and Fish Department Fish Division Administrative Report, Project No. AW-SW-EP1–540, 2006, http://gf.state.wy.us/downloads/pdf/Fish/5yearplan2006.pdf.

30. Cindy Robertson, "Idaho's Instream Flow Program—Past, Present and Future," Idaho Department of Fish and Game, 2004, http://www.deq.idaho.gov/water/assist_business/workshops/nps_workshop_04_robertson.pdf.

31. States have variously created or authorized administrative agencies to implement and/or interpret laws governing minimum flows. Depending on how the agency interprets the statute, regulation, or case law, it makes an administrative ruling on whether or not a stream section may be designated for minimum flows.

32. Brian E. Gray, "A Reconsideration of Instream Appropriative Water Rights in California," in *Instream Flow Protection in the West,* eds. Lawrence J. MacDonnell, Teresa A. Rice, and Steven J. Shupe (Boulder, CO: Natural Resources Law Center, University of Colorado School of Law, 1989), 181–235.

33. "Montana Fisheries Information System (MFISH)," Montana Fish Wildlife and Parks, http://fwp.mt.gov/fishing/mFish/.

34. Not all states permit the transfer of salvaged or conserved water.

35. Generally, any transfer of water rights that alters the use in any way requires a formal change of use application to be filed with the appropriate state agency. Once approved, any changes are reflected on the actual water right permit or certificate and filed with the state.

36. Prior to 1987, no western state appeared to be actively pursuing water acquisitions for environmental purposes (Terry L. Anderson and Ronald N. Johnson. "The Problem of Instream Flows." *Economic Inquiry* 24 (October 1986): 535–54.

37. An acre-foot of water is equivalent to 325,851 U.S. gallons (1,233 m^3)—a volume sufficient to cover one acre of land to a depth of one foot.

38. Transactional data were compiled from a number of sources including state and federal agencies, private organizations, and the extant literature. The dataset used is comprehensive and representative of the history of instream flow markets; however, it is unlikely to be complete. In some cases, agencies and organizations did not record transactions, the data were lost, or the data lacked sufficient detail to be included in this research. In other cases, transactions were brokered by entities that chose not to disclose such data, often to protect the identities of the parties involved.

39. Each year of a multiyear lease is considered a separate transaction. For instance, a three-year lease agreement entered into in 2004 would show up as a separate transaction in subsequent years 2005 and 2006 in terms of expenditures as well as water quantity restored instream. Often annual payments are made throughout the lease term, although leases may be paid for in full in the first year. For comparison, recording each multiyear lease as a single transaction would yield 1,997 total transactions.

40. All instream flow acquisition costs and prices have been adjusted to reflect 2007 dollars using the Western Urban Consumer Price Index.

41. For example, a two-year lease of 10 AF per year at a total cost of $200 would have an average cost of $10 per AF per year.

42. For example, in Washington, water rights, "when transferred for valuable consideration" may be subject to a Real Estate Excise Tax (WAC 458–61A-111), payable by the seller.

43. Private entities rely on contributions from donors who expect tangible results. As a consequence, private groups often target specific stream reaches, which requires direct negotiation with landowners and fewer opportunities for standing offer–type transactions.

44. Wash. Rev. Code §§ 90.54.020(1), RCW 90.54.020(3)(a), RCW 90.22.010, http://apps.leg.wa.gov/RCW/.

45. Wyo. Stat. § 41-3-1001, http://legisweb.state.wy.us/statutes/statutes. aspx?file=titles/Title41/T41CH3AR10.htm. It is unclear how designating existing flows ("unappropriated waters") as instream rights can improve fisheries, considering there would be no change to the amount of water instream, only protection from future diversions.

46. Under Arizona law, any individual may change their water right to instream use; however, the process is administratively cumbersome and to date no transfers have occurred. Transactions to enhance instream flows have been limited to the acquisition of federal or state storage water.

47. Current New Mexico statutes and common law do not explicitly preclude or permit transactions for instream flows, and, unless denied by the state engineer or challenged in court, any individual could conceivably lease or purchase existing consumptive water rights and convert them for environmental use while maintaining ownership of the rights.

48. M. L. Livingston and T. A. Miller, "A Framework for Analyzing the Impact of Western Instream Water Rights on Choice Domains: Transferability, Externalities, and Consumptive Use," *Land Economics* 62, no. 3 (1986): 269–77.

49. Jean-Marc Bourgeon, K. Easter, and William Smith, "Water Markets and Third Party Effects," Annual Meeting of the American Agricultural Economics Association (Agricultural and Applied Economics Association), Denver, CO, August 1–4, 2004; Ellen Hanak, *Who Should Be Allowed to Sell Water*

in California? Third-Party Issues and the Water Market (San Francisco, CA: Public Policy Institute of California, 2003), http://www.ppic.org/content/pubs/report/R_703EHR.pdf.

50. The transfer or change in use of a senior water right can result in injury to junior right holders and thus may be disputed. For example, many water users have appropriated water rights that were established on return flows from upstream users, whether more senior or junior. If an upstream right holder alters the timing or quantity of their diversion and thus return flows, it may injure a downstream user's legal water right. Similarly, return flows may be diminished if an upstream user is permitted to transfer more than the historical consumptive use amount—in which case, a more junior user may protest the transfer.

51. Because of the complexity of the hydrological system and inaccuracies in computing consumptive and historic water use, it is unrealistic to assume that all transactions and new appropriations are without some risk of injury to transacting or third parties (see G.P. Green and J. R. Hamilton. "Water Allocation, Transfers and Conservation: Links Between Policy and Hydrology." *Water Resources Development* 16, no. 2 (2000): 197–208.

52. Sabrina Ise and David L. Sunding, "Reallocating Water from Agriculture to the Environment Under a Voluntary Purchase Program," *Review of Agricultural Economics* 20 (1998): 214–26.

53. Between 1905 and 1935, the city of Los Angeles acquired an estimated 95 percent of the agricultural lands and 88 percent of the town lot properties in the Owens Valley of California, effectively eliminating agricultural production in the region. For a detailed discussion of water markets and the Owens Valley case (see Gary D. Libecap, "Rescuing Water Markets: Lessons from Owens Valley." *PERC Policy Series PS-33* (2005) http://www.perc.org/pdf/ps33.pdf and chapter 9).

54. Anderson and Johnson, "The Problem of Instream Flows."

55. Joseph W. Dellapenna, "Markets for Water: Time to Put the Myth to Rest?" *Journal of Contemporary Water Research and Education* 131 (2005): 33–41.

56. Jesse A. Boyd, "Hip Deep: A Survey of State Instream Flow Law from the Rocky Mountains to the Pacific Ocean," *Natural Resources Journal* 43, no. 4 (2003): 1151–216.

57. Jack Sterne, "Instream Rights & Invisible Hands: Prospects for Private Instream Water Rights in the Northwest," *Environmental Law* 21, no. 1 (1997): 203–43.

58. Joseph L. Sax et al., *Legal Control of Water Resources: Cases and Materials*, 3rd ed. (St. Paul, MN: West Publishing, 2000), 236.

59. Krista Lee Evans, "Montana's Water—Where is It? Who can Use It? Who Decides?" Report to the 59th Legislature of the State of Montana Legislative Environmental Quality Council December 2004, http://leg.mt.gov/content/publications/environmental/2004waterreport.pdf. A similar problem exists in other states. In Washington, only a small portion of the more than 165,000 claims submitted has been adjudicated and the state has no time frame for completion (see Washington Department of Ecology, "Water Right General Adjudications." http://www.ecy.wa.gov/programs/wr/rights/adjhome.html). Idaho, after nearly two

decades, recently completed the adjudication of more than 150,000 claims in the Snake River Basin. In 2006, the state began the adjudication process of an estimated 24,500 water rights in the state's northern watersheds. The process is expected to be completed by 2018; however, recent budget cuts and opposition from water right holders are expected to delay completion.

60. Barton H. Thompson Jr., "Institutional Perspectives on Water Policy and Markets," *California Law Review* 81 (1993): 671–764.

61. Gary D. Libecap, "The Problem of Water" (unpublished manuscript, 2005), http://www.aeaweb.org/assa/2006/0108_1300_0702.pdf.

62. Monique Dutkowsky, "Institutions, Third-Parties and Water Markets: An Analysis of the Role of Water Rights, the No-Injury Rule, and Water Code 386 on Water Markets in California Counties," *PERC Workshop Series Paper* (Bozeman, MT: PERC, 2009), http://www.perc.org/files/Dutkowsky%20water%20markets%20third%20parties.pdf.

63. B. Delworth Gardner, "Weakening Water Rights and Efficient Transfers," *Water Resources Development* 19, no. 1 (2003): 7–19.

64. Megan Hennessy, "Colorado River Water Rights: Property Rights in Transition," *University of Chicago Law Review* 71 (2004): 1661–78; C. Carter Ruml, "The Coase Theorem and Western U.S. Appropriative Water Rights," *Natural Resources Law Journal* 45 (2005): 169–200.

65. Evapotranspiration is the sum of water lost through evaporation, primarily from soils, together with the water lost through plant transpiration—the process through which plants transpire water especially through leaves.

66. Hedia Adelsman, senior policy advisor, Washington Department of Ecology, telephone conversation, October 3, 2008.

67. Jedidiah Brewer et al., "Water Markets in the West: Prices, Trading, and Contractual Forms," *Arizona Legal Studies Discussion Paper No. 07–07* (February 2007), http://ssrn.com/abstract=964819.

68. Terry L. Anderson, "Donning Coase-Coloured Glasses: A Property Rights View of Natural Resource Economics," *Australian Journal of Agricultural and Resource Economics* 48, no. 3 (2004): 445–62.

69. Washington Department of Ecology, *2007 Enforcement Report,* Publication No. 08-01-015 (May 2008), 1. http://www.ecy.wa.gov/pubs/0801015.pdf.

70. Greg Wilson, California State Water Resources Control Board, Division of Water Rights, telephone conversation, September 25, 2008.

71. Sax et al., *Legal Control,* 117.

72. Robert D. Pilz, "At the Confluence: Oregon's Instream Water Rights Law in Theory and Practice," *Environmental Law* 36 (2006): 1382–420.

73. Reed D. Benson, "'Adequate Progress,' or Rivers Left Behind? Developments in Colorado and Wyoming Instream Flow Laws Since 2000," *Environmental Law* 36 (2006): 1283–310.

74. Jared Hardner and R. E. Gullison, *Independent External Evaluation of the Columbia Basin Water Transactions Program (2003–2006),* October 7, 2007, http://www.nfwf.org/Content/ContentFolders/NationalFishandWildlifeFoundation/ConservationLibrary/ProgramEvaluations/CBWTP_Eval_Report_10-7_FINAL.pdf.

75. Rankin Holmes, project manager, Montana Water Trust, telephone conversation, September 12, 2008.

76. Short-term transfers or changes in use in Oregon may not be required to undergo a full injury and enlargement investigation, thus streamlining the application and approval process. Longer-term transfers do require a full investigation and are generally completed in six to twelve months, though some may require years.

77. Gregory A. Thomas, "The Future of Water Law Reform in California a Quarter Century After the Governor's Commission," *McGeorge Law Review* 36 (2005): 495–533.

78. Christopher H. Meyer, "Instream Flows: Integrating New Uses and New Players into the Prior Appropriation System," in *Instream Flow Protection in the West,* eds. Lawrence J. MacDonnell and Teresa A. Rice, 2nd ed. (Boulder, CO: Natural Resources Law Center, University of Colorado, 1993, 2-1–2-13); Debby Schoeningh, *Farmers Battle Oregon Water Trust Over In-Stream Water Rights Transfer* (Salem, OR: Capital Press, 2002), 29.

79. Marc Reisner, *Cadillac Desert: The American West and Its Disappearing Water* (New York: Viking, 1986), 12.

80. Natural Resource Law Center, *Restoring the Waters* (Boulder, CO: University of Colorado School of Law, 1997); K. A. Miller, "Managing Supply Variability: The Use of Water Banks in the Western United States," in *Drought: A Global Assessment,* ed. D. A. Wilhite (New York: Routledge, 2000), 70–86.

81. Hardner and Gullison, *Independent External Evaluation.*

82. Steve Parrett, senior project manager, Oregon Water Trust, personal communication, September 14, 2007.

83. "Interim Projections of the Total Population for the United States and States: April 1, 2000, to July 1, 2030," U.S. Census Bureau, Population Division, Interim State Population Projections, 2005, http://www.census.gov/population/projections/SummaryTabA1.pdf.

84. For instance, eliminating illegal diversions in eastern Washington could drastically improve stream flows, at times eliminating the need to acquire water to maintain flows for certain fish species (Hedia Adelsman, senior policy advisor, Washington Department of Ecology, telephone conversation, October 3, 2008).

5

Auctions of Water Rights

Ray Hartwell and Bruce Aylward

Introduction and Background

In many areas, water supplies are insufficient to meet all demands under current allocation schemes. Pressure to balance the emerging needs of development and environmental restoration may require reallocation of water rights away from agriculture and other traditional uses. Market-based mechanisms are widely advocated as a means of accomplishing this on both economic-efficiency and political grounds. These mechanisms are politically appealing because they are voluntary and obviate the need for government takings. In Oregon's Deschutes Basin, significant experience with the use of market approaches to reallocation of water rights provides an opportunity to examine the advantages and disadvantages of different market-based mechanisms.

Posted-offer procurement[1] and negotiated individual transactions have been prominent market-based approaches to acquiring water rights for reallocation, though their success has at times been hindered by scarcity of information on appropriate pricing. Auctions present an alternative approach that is attractive on theoretical grounds because of the potential to minimize costs of water right acquisition in information-poor environments. Despite this, relatively few real-world water right auctions have been implemented, much less studied. This chapter analyzes three water right auctions in two different geographic and policy contexts in Oregon's Deschutes River Basin. This experience in the Deschutes Basin is examined in the context of other efforts to use auction mechanisms in water and natural resource management.

In 2003 and 2004, auctions were used to acquire temporary transfers of water rights to instream use on central Oregon's Crooked River. We examine these auctions in the Ochoco Irrigation District (OID) to showcase a repeated auction process, comparing results with previous efforts to acquire water under a posted-offer scheme. Discussion of a 2004 auction of water development offset credits (or mitigation credits[2]) provides insight into the demand side of the emerging market for water rights in central Oregon. This effort was an ascending-bid "English" auction in which bids were posted online.

Water Markets as a Solution to Water Allocation Challenges

There is an extensive economic literature on the advantages of market-based environmental management approaches as compared to administrative procedures. Economists have long held that the use of "market-based" or "economic-incentive" approaches (principally pollution taxes and systems of tradable permits) to address environmental problems, rather than so-called command-and-control instruments, will yield efficient allocations of these resources.[3] Colby points out that even in the best-case context of effective governments and rule of law, public administration of rights to use natural resources is notoriously inefficient.[4] In contrast, markets create an opportunity cost of resource use and thus encourage efficiency. This is because in the presence of markets for natural resources, the owner's management decisions are always made in light of the opportunity to sell the resource to others (and to receive what others think the resource is worth). Normally, in cases where the owner does not value the resource highly relative to others in the market, he or she will sell it, theoretically allowing it to be put to a more valuable use. Stoneham and colleagues point out that in making resource-use decisions, market prices aid property right holders to understand the value of their property in other uses.[5]

With water rights, the obstacles to trade are often significant. High capital costs associated with canal and other infrastructure development, coupled with electricity costs of pumping water over long distances, combine to limit the geographic scope of trade. As a result, the volume of trade and number of participants in water markets are typically low relative to other commodity markets, even absent political and other administrative restrictions on trade. Water administration is conducted under state law in the western United States and transfers of water rights between states are generally not legal.[6] Additionally, in many states including Oregon, interbasin transfers are not permitted, further limiting the potential trade in water rights. Also, irrigation district interests in maintaining district integrity can make trade between districts hard to effectuate.[7]

Further challenges to establishing functioning water markets include measuring water, defining rights to water, enforcing rights to water, and investing in conveyances. Equity and social concerns, including the sale of rights by cash-poor farmers and imposition of negative environmental costs on society, add another level of complication.[8] Also, statutory protection of third parties from injury associated with water right transfers creates de facto tertiary interests in property rights to water. Administrative transfer procedures aimed at safeguarding common good aspects of water use can also provide the opportunity for challenges to water reallocation, introducing additional elements of cost and risk into transactions. Infrequent transactions add uncertainty to the process. As Colby states, "Transactions, when they first begin to occur in a new area, resemble complex diplomatic negotiations rather than commodity exchanges."[9] These characterizations aptly describe some of the initial market transaction efforts in the Deschutes, where in many cases years passed before the transfers were fully completed.

Despite these impediments to water transfers, growing demand and high costs of developing new water supplies have led to increased interest in real-location of water rights through trade. *A priori*, the low marginal benefit of water use in agriculture compared to that in nonagricultural uses seems to promise extensive gains from trade. And, as expected, water market activity has been on the rise in recent years, though efficient markets characterized by high transaction volumes and liquidity remain rare.

Auctions

In the context of market-based allocation of water resources, auction mechanisms are attractive because they are a cost-effective means to distribute resources in a manner that maximizes economic efficiency. In the case of a single buyer, such as a water administrator or conservation group, competitive auctions allow for the lowest total expenditure cost for a given quantity of water acquired. Crucially, this objective can be met without prior knowledge of the values that others place on the resource.[10] At the same time, minimizing cost is not guaranteed, and an understanding of the different types of auctions is important if an agency or conservation group is to use an auction approach to meet its water management goals.

Types of Auctions

Auction designs vary widely in terms of rules, bidding protocol, the price paid by winners, and the number of items available for sale.[11] In addition, auctions can be used to either sell or buy items. For the sake of simplicity, the following section describes the traditional auction where the auctioneer seeks to sell an item or items.[12] All of the forms described, however, can be used in reverse "procurement" auctions where the auctioneer seeks to purchase some good. These two forms are symmetric, and analysis is applicable across both approaches. An understanding of the aspects of different designs is essential to crafting successful auctions, as the wrong design applied to a situation can have negative unintended results.[13]

An *English,* or ascending-bid, auction uses a bidding process of serial public bids, each higher than the last, until bidding stops, and the item at auction is sold to the highest bidder. In a *sealed-bid auction,* participants submit confidential bids and the highest bidder wins the auction. In a *single-unit auction,* a single item is being sold, while *multiunit auctions* sell multiple like items. If there are multiple winners, then additional considerations enter into the scenario. In a *discriminatory auction,* each winner pays the value of his bid. *Uniform auctions* differ in that bid values are ranked in order to determine bid acceptance, but all accepted bids pay the same amount, typically that of the lowest accepted bid.

Auction Design

While it has been shown that in a controlled environment, diverse auction designs may produce on average the same revenue, this does not imply that choice of auction design is unimportant.[14] Rather, given real-world variation in auction environments, attention to auction design is crucial to meeting an auctioneer's goals. Indeed, Klemperer mentions that while most literature on auctions focuses on results assuming a large numbers of participants and perfect competition, practical auction design is in contrast "mostly good elementary economics."[15] That is, the choice of auction type is less important than the level of participation and competition in determining outcomes.

The central question in auction design is how and to what extent different approaches induce bidders to bid at high values. If bidding is competitive, then water rights will be allocated to the highest value, yielding an economically efficient outcome. A key concept in the analysis of this aspect of auction design is the private value that the bidder places on the item. A bidder will be better off if he is able to acquire the water for any amount up to its value in his private use. Of course, to the extent that a bidder can obtain the water for less than this value, he will be motivated to increase his profit by doing so. To maximize auction prices, an auctioneer will attempt to craft a procedure that will not provide opportunities for successful bidding significantly below one's private resource value. If an auction can avoid being susceptible to such "gaming," then it will generally succeed in the joint aims of (1) maximizing revenue from sales and (2) efficiently allocating resources. Several specific design choices that can have bearing on auction success are discussed next.

Multiple Bidding Rounds

One important aspect of auction design is whether to conduct multiple rounds of bidding. In a traditional auction, a single round of bidding is conducted to determine which bids are accepted. This approach is inexpensive and straightforward, but there can be significant uncertainty as to outcomes, especially if there is little familiarity with past transactions and market prices. Under these conditions, expectations as to likely bid values and auction results may not be consistent for the auctioneer and any participants, and opportunities for gains from trade can be missed. For example, a farmer may overestimate the value of his water right and bid to sell it for more than a conservation buyer is willing to pay. In a single-round auction, no trade would occur, even if the farmer would have been willing to sell for less had he known the value the conservation buyer placed on the water. Multiple rounds of bidding allow participants to learn from the first-round outcome in order to revise their bids, thus increasing the likelihood of a successful transaction in the auction.

Uncertainty regarding potential outcomes can be mitigated by conducting an iterative auction with multiple rounds of bidding and revision of bids permitted between rounds. These "many in one" auctions allow both bidders and the auctioneer to signal their intentions, facilitating rapid learning and (ideally) establishment of a market-clearing price. Bids are provisionally accepted or rejected after each round, and participants can revise bids accordingly in the next round. This provisional disclosure is crucial to bidder learning and auction success.[16] Cummings and colleagues highlight that iterative approaches have advantages including increased predictability of outcomes, which can be crucial in public water purchases where budgets are constrained or price levels are subject to public scrutiny.[17] On the other hand, while multiround formats permit learning from tentative outcomes of previous rounds of bidding, they can also facilitate coordination among participants who may collude to keep prices low.

Budget Constraints and Reserve Prices

Another area of variation in auction design revolves around the constraints or objectives of the auctioneer-buyer or -seller.[18] Specifically, budget constraints and reserve prices can be used to manage risk or signal intentions of the auctioneer. Decisions related to management of these constraints are typically directed to maximize competitive bidding. A budget cap in a multiunit reverse auction designates the total amount to be spent by the auctioneer-buyer on purchases of winning bids. A reserve price is used to ensure a minimum or maximum price for the sale or purchase of a unit in an auction. Limits on the quantity of items the auctioneer will purchase or sell are another form of cap. These constraints serve the primary goal of guarding against unintended auction outcomes.[19]

With both budget caps and reserve prices, a key consideration is whether to disclose either the existence or the amount of the constraint. With caps, disclosure of a liberal budget may suggest that the auctioneer is rich and that bidders need not bid competitively.[20] On the other hand, disclosing the available budget can establish credibility for the auctioneer when entering new water markets. Reserve prices are widely used in both single-unit and multiunit auctions to guard against extreme bids being accepted. Especially in thin markets for goods without well-established values, appropriate reserve prices are essential in avoiding embarrassing failure of an auction. In short, reserve prices should be set at levels that reflect an acceptable outcome to the auctioneer, where the auctioneer at least captures his value of the item being sold. Reserve prices are generally not disclosed, because if there is limited competition, then bidders will bid at the reserve price. However, disclosure of the reserve price can signal the auctioneer-buyer's willingness to pay (in a procurement auction), and thus discourage speculative bidding below that level.

Competition

While informed design and information disclosure decisions can help to discourage strategic or speculative bidding, true competition will render the above concerns moot. As a result, it is crucial that an auction have as many participants as possible. Hailu and Thoyer find that the efficiency of outcomes increases significantly as the number of participants and attendant amount of competition increases from low levels.[21] With this in mind, auctions can be designed in ways that will attract larger numbers of participants. Klemperer points out that participation in auctions is never costless, however, and that individuals will only choose to enter if they believe they have some chance of success.[22] Thus, lowering participation costs can improve outcomes by attracting more bidders, thereby ensuring more competitive bidding.[23]

Competition can be encouraged through information management. Specifically, the auctioneer should take care to not disclose that competition is or may be weak. The expectation of competitive conditions will lead to competitive bidding in a self-fulfilling prophecy. As such, the *perception* of competition is essential. Thus, regardless of the auction design chosen, careful attention to not revealing any information that could betray a lack of competitive conditions is essential.

Auctions of Water Rights

In the application of auction approaches to water rights, several of the theoretical concerns mentioned previously merit additional discussion. In particular, the lack of information about prices in thin markets can be a challenge. Heterogeneity of water rights by location and other parameters demands attention in auction design. Finally, simplicity of auction design and reliability/predictability of the auction outcome can be of large importance.

Informational Asymmetry

Prices for water rights are often not well known, and this poor information environment in water markets makes auction mechanisms particularly attractive because they can catalyze trade without market pricing information. There are several reasons why market prices may be opaque. Even though prices for limited transfers (e.g., between irrigators in the same irrigation district) may be known, the risk and opportunities associated with transfers to new areas or uses may mean that such prices are not relevant. Stoneham and colleagues point out that varied soil quality, microclimates, and other farm-specific traits create information asymmetries even among agricultural users, where the owner of the resource knows more about its value than even sophisticated potential buyers do.[24] Further, conservation buyers may not have accurate information about the value of water used in agriculture, while farmers or ranchers often have little sense of the environmental or development value of their rights. Because the different parties to a potential trade in water rights may have limited or varying information about the value of the resource, negotiating a transaction can be difficult.

In this context, negotiating a trade of water rights is challenging. Potential trades are difficult to identify because parties do not necessarily know with whom there is a high probability of reaping gains from trade. Limited information increases the risk that parties will come to a deal that does not reflect a value that is consistent with public expectations, and will thus be subject to criticism, political rancor, or embarrassment.[25] Auctions, by virtue of the fact that they can solicit bids from all potential trading partners, use competition between potential traders to compensate for the lack of information on prices. A well-designed auction will yield the auctioneer the best price independent of knowledge or negotiating skill.[26]

Heterogeneity of Rights

Water rights can vary greatly in terms of reliability, volume, and delivery cost of the water itself, and this variation can have important implications for auction design. In the American West, variation in priority dates of prior-appropriation rights means that some have constant access to water while others rarely are served. In addition, water rights are variously defined in terms of duty, or volume of water per acre of irrigated land. Further, depending on whether the right is served by a well, direct diversion from a stream, or through an irrigation district, conveyance costs will vary. As explained later, this heterogeneity among rights can be an obstacle to ranking auction bids, and therefore to determining auction winners.[27]

In a multiunit auction, bids are ranked for acceptance based on their attractiveness in terms of price. If there is variation in the rights being auctioned, however, then ranking bids becomes difficult. The most common way to address this problem is to limit the scope of the auction only to rights that are equivalent or that meet some minimum criteria. This can mean limiting eligible rights by location, water source, or some other parameter. This, in turn, will depress the numbers of auction participants, and thus may limit the potential for competition in a small basin. Another approach to this problem is to develop an index to rank bids for different classes of water rights, though this is difficult in actual practice. An implementation of such a mechanism is discussed later in the context of Australian biodiversity and land conservation contracts. The approach to managing varied rights in an auction should be determined on a case-by-case basis depending on the auction objectives.

Other Water Auctions

A few examples of water and natural resource auctions merit specific examination for their approach to managing some of the challenges mentioned. In Georgia, auction mechanisms were used to induce irrigators to suspend irrigation in the Flint River Basin in 2001 and 2002. The Edwards Aquifer Authority in Texas has also used auctions to reduce consumptive use in efforts to protect groundwater flows. Finally, a pilot program in Australia developed a methodology for conducting a multiunit procurement auction of heterogeneous conservation contracts that has applicability in the context of water resources. These efforts are discussed in the following sections.

Georgia Irrigation Reduction Auctions

In response to legislation requiring the use of an "auction-like process" to obtain agreements to suspend irrigation in the event of declared drought in Georgia's Flint River Basin, irrigation reduction auctions were conducted in each of the 2001 and 2002 drought years.[28] Extensive laboratory experiments were used to inform auction design, and in 2001, the state Environmental Protection Division chose a multiround, iterative approach.[29] In this auction, irrigators submitted bids for the per-acre price at which they were willing to suspend irrigation on all of the acres covered by a given permit. Discriminatory pricing was used such that each accepted bid would be paid the amount of the bid to suspend irrigation. While the acquisition budget was public knowledge, the target acreage for irrigation suspension was not disclosed in a deliberate effort to discourage strategic overbidding. Participation was voluntary, but in the event that the auction failed to acquire agreements to suspend sufficient irrigation, the state had the authority to order involuntary suspension of irrigated acres, beginning with the most recently established rights. Clearly, this format implies that the participants faced different incentives depending on when their rights were established, with those holding recently established rights having a strong incentive to participate in order to minimize the risk of having their rights suspended without any compensation. Bidding behavior was not separately explored on this parameter.[30]

The 2001 auction featured multiple rounds of bidding, though the number of potential rounds was not determined in advance. After each round, bidders were informed whether their bid would be accepted if the auction were to end at that time. Bid revisions were permitted in each subsequent round, and rounds were to continue until either the Environmental Protection Division Director ended the auction or no further bid revisions were received.

The multiround approach facilitated price discovery through participant learning in the market. Bids typically declined across rounds as provisionally rejected bidders sought to submit more competitive bids. After five rounds of bidding, a total of 33,006 acres were withdrawn from irrigation at a cost of $135.70 per acre.[31]

In the 2002 auction, a different approach was used, partially to safeguard against bid shading based on learning from the 2001 auction. Specifically, the threshold for accepted bids was radically raised in the final round of the 2001 auction, leading to fears that bidders in 2002 would not bid competitively in anticipation of a high reserve price in the last bidding iteration. Instead, the Environmental Protection Division instituted a sealed bid auction with a publicly known reserve price and a single round of bidding. Petrie and colleagues highlight the advantages that this auction procedure brought in terms of simplicity of administration. They also found that there was sufficient competition that the reserve price did not serve as a benchmark for bids; in fact, the average accepted offer price was lower in 2002 than in 2001.[32] Unsurprisingly, individual bidders tended to reduce their bid level from 2001 to 2002 if their 2001 bids were above the reserve price, while low bidders in 2001 generally raised bids in what was presumably an effort to capture increased rents.

The 2001 and 2002 Flint River Basin irrigation reduction auctions provide a valuable case study in practical auction design. The 2001 auction's multiround framework allowed more control over auction results as administrators could signal the likely success of bids to bidders through the provisional acceptance or denial of bids. In contrast, the 2002 auction's single-round sealed bid approach succeeded in acquiring water rights without a lengthy multiround approach, though price discovery and experience in 2001 surely contributed to this result. In both years, participation numbers led to a competitive outcome despite disclosure of program budgets and the reserve price.

Edwards Aquifer Auctions

Reverse auctions have been used on several occasions to suspend irrigation in the Edwards Aquifer area near San Antonio, Texas. In 1997, the Edwards Aquifer Authority, the administrative body charged with protection and management of the aquifer, used a reverse auction to obtain temporary agreements from right holders to suspend irrigation on 10,000 acres in order to preserve spring flows. While this initial auction was at first opposed by irrigators, in the end, suspending irrigation for payment was more lucrative than farming, and the acreage targets were met.[33]

In 2003, the San Antonio Water System used an online reverse auction to obtain permanent rights to 10,000 acre-feet (AF) of water from pumping rights in the capacity-limited Edwards Aquifer. The auction featured a posted reserve price disclosing the maximum amount that the system was willing to pay per AF of water. Bidders then could submit and revise online bids to sell rights. Nine bids were received, all at the reserve price.[34] Although bids were not lowered through competition, the auction was successful in acquiring water through a voluntary process.

The Edwards experience is interesting for its use of auctions to acquire permanent water rights. Further, it illustrates the potential for bids to cluster at a revealed reserve price when a reserved price system is used. At the same time, given the low number of bidders, the public reserve price may have served to convey a price signal to interested sellers that effectively matched buyers and sellers. Still, compared with a true competitive market, sellers were able to reap some information rents by inflating bids. It also provides an example of a reverse auction used to procure water for municipal use.

The Australian BushTender Trial

The BushTender Trial was a pilot program using auctions to allocate biodiversity contracts in Victoria, Australia. Biodiversity contracts are agreements with landowners to take certain actions to preserve or enhance the conservation value of their land. Actions include fencing of streams, protection of wetland or forests, and suspension of farming or grazing. In the program, a single-round, first-price, sealed-bid auction was used to purchase conservation contracts from landowners.[35] Landowners bid to take certain conservation actions, and the government ranked the bids based on conservation value per unit of cost, accepting the most cost-effective actions. The auction used discriminatory pricing and no reserve price. While this approach is fairly standard, the auction is of interest in the water resources context for its success in allocating heterogeneous goods in a single auction process.

In BushTender, auction administrators essentially developed a score with which to rank a bid on a cost-per-unit basis. This Biodiversity Benefits Index was a function of two subcomponents measuring different aspects of a conservation proposal, the Biodiversity Significance Score and the Habitat Services Score. Using this index, it is straightforward to rank bids and determine which auction offers to accept (though the indexing itself is difficult). The approach is similar to the Environmental Benefits Index (EBI) currently used to rank bids in the USDA's Conservation Reserve Program.[36]

While using the index approach is straightforward, several other considerations emerge. First, administrative costs clearly increase due to the need to assess each proposal in order to assign it a score. Second, there is the separate issue of whether to disclose the score to participants. On the one hand, knowledge of the proposal's score will help mitigate the enormous informational asymmetry that is present in the "market" for something as ephemeral as conservation contracts. On the other hand, if a bidder learns that he has a high score (perhaps due to the presence of unique habitat or populations on his property), he can use this information to raise his bid and extract information rents from the auction in excess of his private resource value. In the end, BushTender chose to navigate this tradeoff by revealing only the Habitat Services Score to landowners, holding the Biodiversity Significance Score in confidence. Stoneham and colleagues also highlight the trade-off between short-term cost effectiveness gains from withholding information from participants and the long-term potential benefits, as knowledge of the conservation value of land spurs investment in habitat, potentially increasing the supply through the substitution effect (investment is shifted to conservation from other uses as the opportunity cost of other uses increases).[37]

Clearly, the BushTender experience could be of value in the auctioning of water rights. The ability to rank water rights that vary in duty, rate, location, and reliability on a single indicator would enable a conservation auction to be conducted on a wider scale. Increased competition could result in lower conservation costs, and increased eligibility might provide access to "unique" water rights that would not otherwise be obtainable through an auction framework. At the same time, implementing a ranking system is a difficult, largely subjective process that is perhaps doomed to be controversial and expensive. Nonetheless, the BushTender trial provides a useful framework for applying auction tools in the natural resources context of heterogeneous commodities.

Ochoco Irrigation District Stream Flow Restoration Reverse Auctions

In 2003 and 2004, the Deschutes River Conservancy (DRC), a nonprofit organization dedicated to using market-based approaches to restore stream flow in the Deschutes River Basin of Oregon, used procurement (or reverse) auctions to acquire annual instream transfers of water ("instream leases") from OID irrigators for environmental restoration in the Crooked River Basin. The experience provides an opportunity to examine an auction approach as it changes over time and to contrast it with the posted-offer approach to lease acquisition used in 2002.

Background/Prior Market Experience

By 2003, the DRC had run an annual program to acquire instream leases from irrigators in several irrigation districts in the Deschutes Basin. Though the program evolved over time, compensation was based on a posted-offer system in which a standing offer was made to all irrigators in a given district to pay a fixed price for the temporary instream transfer of their water rights for the season. The 2001 program paid a fixed price per acre of water rights across all districts, regardless of the volume of water associated with the rights. In 2002, the program was refined to pay a fixed price of $7 per AF of water in rights across all districts. Due to varying duties (AF of water per acre) of water rights, this approach resulted in lease offers from $7 to $39 per acre in different districts in that year. Although this move toward volume-based price discrimination was successful in increasing the amount of water leased for instream uses basinwide in 2002, program participation in the OID was limited. In this district, right holders were offered $28 per acre to forego their right to irrigate and lease their water rights instream.[38] At this price, a single water user participated, leasing a total of 114 acres.

In 2003, the posted-offer program was replaced with a reverse auction for the OID. The posted-offer leasing program was retained in other local irrigation districts. An auction was appealing in the OID district for several reasons: (1) DRC staff recognized that the fixed price methodology was not

117

successful in OID at offer levels extended; (2) lack of knowledge of water values in OID, driven in part by a different composition of water users than in other districts, made revision of a posted-offer approach an exercise in guesswork; and (3) district management accepted the auction as a way to provide additional water management options to irrigators. A reverse auction held the promise of enabling cost-effective water procurement even in the context of DRC's limited knowledge of OID patrons' private water values.

The Columbia Basin Water Transactions Program (CBWTP), in which the DRC participated as a local implementing agency, agreed to fund this novel approach as part of its funding for the DRC's leasing program. The CBWTP is a program promoting transactional approaches to stream flow restoration in the Columbia Basin and is funded by Bonneville Power Administration and managed by the National Fish and Wildlife Foundation out of its Portland office.

Auction Design

After a brief literature review, a single-round, sealed-bid discriminatory auction with a reserve price was selected. This choice reflected several program priorities. First, the single-round auction had the advantage of simplicity, which was a priority given the unfamiliarity of all parties with auction allocation (and indeed market-based allocation) of water rights. Given the importance of avoiding misunderstandings in this first auction, a simple approach was deemed essential. Further, the single-round has lower transactions costs than a multiround approach.

Discriminatory pricing offered the appeal of simplicity and also the potential for lower acquisition costs given a low level of concern about collusion. Concerns about collusion were minor due to the small sums of both water and money involved in the auction. In addition, officials felt that using reserve prices reduced the economic risk of collusive activity by capping the DRC's per acre expenditure. Thus, the DRC chose to implement a reserve price to guard against losses to collusion or unexpectedly high bid values. A budget was set at the level that would just be exhausted if all expected bids below the reserve price would be accepted from lowest to highest.

Bids were enumerated in terms of cost per acre of water rights leased. Because water rights in OID all have the same duty (volume) of water per acre of rights, ranking bids in terms of cost per acre was a valid reflection of the relative amount of water to be transferred to instream use.[39] In essence, bidders had to decide on how many acres of land on which they would be willing to forego irrigation in order to formulate a bid. Importantly, lack of summer precipitation means that foregoing irrigation in the high desert of Central Oregon effectively means foregoing crop production on tracts where water rights are leased. In this respect, the conditions in the OID auction were different from the Georgia irrigation suspension auction, where crop production is possible without irrigation.

Notably, while bidders were free to (and presumably did) bid to lease the water rights appurtenant to their land with the lowest production value (idling their least profitable parcels), they were not able to bid to forego the use of some marginal portion of the water right on lands that would be irrigated. In Oregon, water rights are defined in terms of rate, duty, and acres covered. Unlike in some systems, irrigators are not permitted to spread their volume allotment (duty) over "new" nonpermitted acres. In addition, this prohibition on spreading the water precludes the leasing of a portion of the volume of water from acres that will still be irrigated at a lower volume. For example, a farmer could not choose to underirrigate a pasture and lease the saved volume of water. In sum, the water rights to the acres that have the lowest marginal value can be leased, but the actual marginal water applied to agricultural land cannot be leased.

The 2003 process was different from that of 2002. On January 29, the DRC mailed bid packets to all 147 district patrons who owned at least ten acres with water rights. This limit was imposed because of difficulties in accounting for extremely small water leases. The packets were sent in a district envelope that contained letters from the district and the DRC explaining the auction, a bid form, and a return stamped envelope addressed to the DRC. In the letters, the DRC pledged to accept all bids up to a total of $50,000 as long as the bids were below a reserve price per acre set at the sole discretion of the DRC. The reserve price was not disclosed in the letter. Auction bids had to be received by the DRC by 5 p.m. on February 18, 2003, to be included in the auction. DRC pledged to notify bidders of bid acceptance or rejection by February 28, 2003. Although contact information was provided, no inquiries regarding the auction procedure were received.

As this was the first local auction of water rights and the DRC was serving as buyer and auctioneer, using a transparent and fair process was critically important. To ensure that participants (including participants in subsequent auctions) would trust that the DRC was not manipulating the reserve price after bids were received, the reserve price was set by the DRC and mailed to the OID manager prior to the opening of the bids. The actual opening of bids and the reserve price letter were conducted at 9:00 a.m. on February 19, 2003, at the OID office in Prineville. In attendance were the OID manager, two OID board members, DRC staff, and a DRC board member. The DRC's certified public accountant attended the auction ceremony in order to witness and certify the results.

After the auction, DRC staff notified all auction participants as to whether their bids were successful or not. For accepted bids, the DRC completed the necessary paperwork, collected signatures, filed the lease with the state Water Resources Department,[40] and issued payment checks in the amount of the bids. A stream flow monitoring program was used to ensure that leased water was not diverted from the river during the irrigation season. In 2004, the same process was followed. The letter from the district to patrons reported on the results from the previous year's auction, including the DRC's reserve price and the acres leased.

2003 Results

Establishing the Reserve Price

In 2003, DRC staff established the reserve price at $75 per acre. This figure was supported by multiple analytical approaches based on experience in local water markets. First, the price per AF of stream flow restoration (accounting for reliability of water rights leased) in Tumalo and Squaw Creek irrigation districts from the previous season was applied to expected restoration from the OID leases to calculate a reasonable price for acquisition of restoration water in high-cost districts in the Deschutes Basin. This calculation yielded a price of approximately $30 per AF. Second, academic studies of the potential for leasing water in the North Unit Irrigation District provided some basis for the expectation that water could be leased for $25 per AF in the basin.[41] Third, the DRC evaluated at what price it should be indifferent to between purchasing a district water right (accounting for district fees) and leasing the water in perpetuity. This analysis found that given low risk-free interest rates, $25 per AF was a reasonable amount to pay for a perpetually leased water right in OID relative to outright purchase at existing prices for in-district transfers (note that outright purchase was not necessarily a stream flow restoration option in 2003).

With a range of $25–$30 per AF and an expected average duty of 3 AF per acre, $75 per acre was chosen as a conservative reserve price by the DRC. In the first year of the auction, DRC chose the reserve price primarily to limit exposure to overpaying for water. Given the uncertainty about market prices for leases, learning and experimentation were the main goals—acquiring a specific quantity of water a secondary concern.

Bids Received and Auction Results

The 2003 auction received eight bids from seven different parties to lease 616.7 acres of water rights (one bidder submitted two bids at different prices for different parcels). Bids ranged from $29 to $108.50 per acre, with an average bid of $80. This resulted in the acceptance of three bids and the leasing of 196.9 acres of land. A total of 787 AF of paper water rights were leased at a maximum rate of 2.365 cubic feet per second (CFS). The water was protected from the OID point of diversion downstream through the lower Crooked River to Lake Billy Chinook. The district allotment for the year, based on the available runoff at the beginning of the season, was set at 3 AF per acre yielding a "wet" water lease of 591 AF.[42] The average cost of accepted bids

Table 5.1 2003 Ochoco Irrigation District auction bids

Bidder			Bid 2003 (Reserve Price $75)		
ID	Acres	Total Bid	Per Acre Bid	Accepted	Consumer Surplus
1	40.6	$ 1,189	$ 29.00	✓	$ 1,868
2	6.3	$ 315	$ 50.00	✓	$ 158
3	150.0	$ 9,000	$ 60.00	✓	$ 2,250
4	81.9	$ 6,920	$ 84.50		
4	60.0	$ 6,510	$ 108.50		
5	90.0	$ 7,650	$ 85.00		
6	67.4	$ 6,066	$ 90.00		
7	120.5	$ 11,990	$ 99.50		
			Average		
Total	616.7	$ 49,640	$ 80.49		$ 4,275
Total Accepted Bids	196.9	$ 10,504	$ 53.35		
Percentage of Bids Accepted	32%	21%			

was $53.35 per acre, or approximately $18 per AF of wet water. The complete schedule of bids is presented in Table 5.1.

A simple examination of the bid schedule yields several preliminary insights (see Table 5.1). First, it is clear that the reserve price prevented accepting several relatively expensive bids. Under the assumption that the reserve price was set equal to the conservation value of the water rights, the choice to use a reserve price was validated as the price avoided accepting five high-end bids above $75. Under this same assumption, consumer surplus can be calculated for each bid by multiplying the number of acres sold by the difference between the reserve price and bid. The results suggest the auction yielded a total consumer surplus to the DRC of $4,275, or 41 percent of total lease expenditures in OID.

The wide variance in bids suggests significant heterogeneity in private value of water rights. Wide variance in private resource values is plausible given the mixed land use in OID; in this auction, some participants were commercial farmers, while others did not appear to actively use their water (bidder 1 leased water instream each year from 2002 to 2004, accepting the posted-offer in 2002 and successfully bidding in both 2003 and 2004). In general, the higher bids came from larger landowners who were likely engaged in commercial farming. This is consistent with the experience in the georgia irrigation reduction auction, where participants with rights to irrigate more land bid at higher levels than those with fewer acres. This may reflect higher private resource values due to economies of scale in agricultural production.[43]

On the other hand, lower bids were primarily from small-scale hobby farmers or those who might not have used water rights without the auction. Thus, the auction was successful by both standard measures; assuming that the bid schedule approximated private water values, social efficiency was realized by leasing water from right holders with the lowest marginal use values. At the same time, the DRC was able to acquire water in a cost-effective manner by buying low on the supply curve. Auction results are depicted in Figure 5.1.

The reserve price of $75 was slightly below the average bid value of $80.49. As a result, the auction was not as successful as it might have been in leasing water instream. Several possible explanations present themselves. First, if all bids are taken as accurate representations of the value bidders placed on their water rights, then potential gains from trade are limited because resources are already allocated efficiently. In particular, assuming that the bids above the reserve price were submitted primarily by commercial farmers, then it appears that the potential for market-based allocation of water to environmental use is limited. This would be the case if water were more valuable in agricultural use than in conservation. Crucially, establishing the conservation value of the instream water is a difficult and subjective process.[44] The discussion treats the flat $75 per acre reserve price as a proxy for the conservation value of instream water when in fact it is the DRC's willingness to pay.

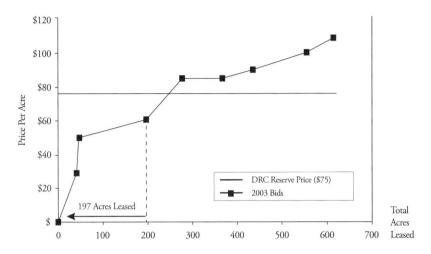

Figure 5.1   2003 Ochoco Irrigation District auction bid schedule, reserve price, and total acres leased

An alternative hypothesis is that bid shading on the part of bidders or the DRC backfired as an effort to gain rents and led to the loss of potential gains from trade. That is, auction participants may have bid higher than their actual valuation of the resource. In so doing, their bids exceeded the reserve price (which may in itself have been shaded downward, below the actual conservation value of the water) and no trade was consummated. As a result, any opportunity for gains from trade was lost. The submission of two bids at different levels by bidder 4 potentially may reveal efforts to shade at least one bid upward in order to take advantage of limited competition and accrue rents. Alternatively, the marginal value of water on the two tracts may differ.

The reality is that strategic overbidding may be a rational response to uncertainty in an iterative situation like an annual water lease. To some extent, both irrigators and the DRC knew that regardless of the mechanism, the DRC would be trying to lease water in OID in the future. Therefore, there was an incentive for the DRC to downplay its willingness to pay and for the irrigators to overstate the value of the water. Ultimately, there is not enough information to conclude whether this motivated bidders.

Although the DRC single-round auction did not allow for bid revision, the implementation of the auction using the same structure in 2004 provides an interesting opportunity to contrast the two years' results. Given that several bidders participated in both years, the repeated auction created opportunities for learning similar to those present between rounds of an iterative auction.

2004 Results

In 2004, the auction in OID was repeated with a few minor modifications. For the second year in a row, the DRC offered to spend up to $50,000 to lease water for stream flow enhancement, accepting bids to sell from lowest to highest subject to a reserve price. Once again, letters were sent to all eligible district patrons explaining the program. The only difference in the 2004 auction from that of 2003 was that the farmers were provided the results of the first year's auction. In this information-scarce environment, the DRC believed that this would decrease the uncertainty for those offering bids.

Establishment of Reserve Price

The DRC examined the 2003 auction results and the program goals for 2004 in choosing the reserve price. Staff noted that in the 2003 auction, an increase of $15 in the reserve price would have doubled the quantity of water obtained. In addition, greater snowpack in 2004 led to expectations that each acre leased would yield more water in 2004 than was available in 2003; hence, the DRC opted to set the reserve price at $91 per acre.

Bids Received and Auction Results

In 2004, nine individuals submitted a total of ten bids to lease 642 acres of water rights at an average cost of $67.20 per acre (Table 5.2). Bids ranged from $29 to $85 per acre, so that all bids fell below the reserve price of $91. Consequently, all bids were accepted, and the DRC leased 642 acres of land with water rights. Due to ongoing revisions of the district water right maps, minor revisions to some bids were made, though the auction results were not significantly impacted. This level of leasing increased stream flow by 6 CFS in the Lower Crooked River for the irrigation season and produced a material increase in flow through the driest section of the river.[45]

The 2004 auction leased more water than the 2003 auction, in which only three of eight bids were accepted. This increase in auction trade was driven by different bid functions and reserve prices between the two years, but ultimately reflected the improved information environment following the 2003 results. While in 2003, the reserve price fell below the average bid, the higher 2004 reserve price at $91 did not disqualify any bids. Further, bids were lower in 2004, probably reflecting learning on the part of repeat bidders. This bidder learning pertained primarily to the likely reserve price—the highest price irrigators can bid while still having their bid accepted. The implication is that bidders are behaving strategically with their new information to maximize rents from auction participation. As a result, their bids are only partially a reflection of the foregone production value of their water used to irrigate and are best considered an upper bound for this (unknown) value.

Figure 5.2 depicts the 2004 OID auction results. The hypothesis that some 2004 bidders scaled their bids in a learning response to the 2003 reserve price

Table 5.2 2004 Ochoco Irrigation District auction bids

Bidder ID	Bid 2004 (Reserve Price $91)					
	Acres	Total Bid	Per Acre Bid	Accepted	Alternative Consumer Surplus (R.P.=$75)	Consumer Surplus
1	40.6	$ 1,177	$ 29.00	✓	$ 1,868	$ 2,517
2	105.4	$ 6,324	$ 60.00	✓	$ 1,581	$ 3,267
3	150.0	$ 9,000	$ 60.00	✓	$ 2,250	$ 4,650
4	35.3	$ 2,085	$ 59.00	✓	$ 565	$ 1,131
4	41.6	$ 3,075	$ 74.00	✓	$ 42	$ 707
5	40.0	$ 3,000	$ 75.00	✓	$ -	$ 640
8	11.0	$ 385	$ 35.00	✓	$ 440	$ 616
9	32.4	$ 2,430	$ 75.00	✓	$ -	$ 518
10	24.9	$ 1,992	$ 80.00	✓	$ -	$ 274
11	161.0	$ 13,685	$ 85.00	✓	$ -	$ 966
			Average			
Total	642.2	$ 43,154	$ 67.20		$ 6,746	$ 15,286
Total Accepted Bids	642.2	$ 43,154	$ 67.20			
Percentage of Bids Accepted	100%		100%			

Note: Bidder ID numbers are consistent between Tables 5.1 and 5.2.

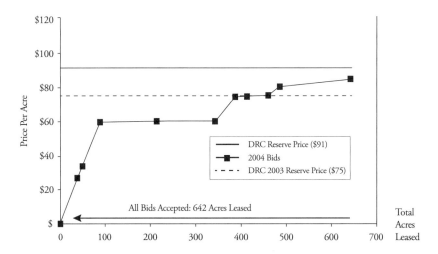

Figure 5.2   2004 Ochoco Irrigation District auction bid schedule, reserve price, and total acres leased

is supported by the clustering of bids at the $75 level. Bidding at $75, these participants presumably sought to maximize rents while still guarding against bid disqualification by slotting bids below the expected value of the reserve price. Of course, the bidding environment did not remain static because the DRC reserve price was raised; as a result, bids above the 2003 reserve price were in the end accepted.

The strategic revision of bids based on the 2003 experience and learning in the emerging water market is further illuminated by examination of behavior by individual bidders.

Table 5.3 facilitates examination of bidder learning by tracing individual bidding behavior from the 2003 through the 2004 auction for the five bidders who participated in both years. Of the three 2003 bidders whose bids were accepted, two elected to leave their bids unchanged in 2004. Bidder 2 submitted a successful bid at $50 in 2003 and revised his bid upward to $60 for 2004. Assuming private water use values remained constant between the years, this revision allowed the bidder to increase rents to his water right lease. It is also noteworthy that the 2004 bid was not increased past the 2003 reserve price (in fact, the 2004 bid was well below the 2003 reserve price of $75); thus, bidder 2's learning arguably reflected a conservative appetite for risk, perhaps resulting from a low private value for water right use. Farmers may face significant weather-related risk to productive use of their land, which may translate into willingness to bid at low levels for a guaranteed income from a parcel.[46]

The fact that two of the three successful bidders from 2003 did not modify their bids in 2004 suggests that these bidders were pleased with their outcomes

Table 5.3 Participant learning between the 2003 and 2004 OID auctions

| Bidder ID | Auction Bids | | | | Strategic Bid Revision 2003 to 2004 | |
	2003 Per Acre Bid	Accepted	2004 Per Acre Bid	Accepted	Present	Description
1	$ 29.00	✓	$ 29.00	✓		
2	$ 50.00	✓	$ 60.00	✓	✓	The measured bid increase likely reflected an effort to increase bidder capture of rents, while at the same time ensuring that the expected reserve price was not exceeded.
3	$ 60.00	✓	$ 60.00	✓		
4	$ 84.50		$ 59.00	✓	✓	The revision lowered the bid to below the 2003 reserve price, while two different bids from this bidder probably reflect hedging risk related to the unknown competition and reserve price.
4	$ 08.50		$ 74.00	✓	✓	The revision lowered the bid to below the 2003 reserve price, while two different bids from this bidder probably reflect hedging risk related to the unknown competition and reserve price.

(*Continued*)

Table 5.3 (*Continued*)

Bidder	Auction Bids				Strategic Bid Revision 2003 to 2004	
ID	2003 Per Acre Bid	Accepted	2004 Per Acre Bid	Accepted	Present	Description
5	$ 85.00		$ 75.00	✓	✓	The revision lowered the bid to match the 2003 reserve price.
6	$ 90.00			✓	n/a	
7	$ 99.50				n/a	
8			$ 35.00		n/a	
9			$ 75.00	✓	n/a	
10			$ 80.00	✓	n/a	
11			$ 85.00	✓	n/a	

Note: Bidder ID numbers are consistent between Tables 5.1, 5.2, and 5.3.

in 2003. At the same time, it does not support any general notion that bidding success makes one less likely to revise a bid in subsequent years, because there is reason to think that these bidders had less information access than some other participants and were less actively engaged in managing their water rights. This conclusion is supported by knowledge of the bidder identities.[47] Further, their initial lower bids suggest low private resource values; in this scenario, it may be that the investment in learning and strategic bid revision was not worth the potential gain.

Of the two bidders (who submitted three bids) who were unsuccessful in 2003 and yet participated in the 2004 auction, both revised their bids in a manner consistent with learning and strategic bidding behavior. In particular, bidders 4 and 5 both submitted 2004 bids that were below the 2003 reserve price of $75.

Bidder 4, who submitted two bids in each year, reduced his bids from $84.50 and $108.50 to $59 and $74, respectively. This bidding behavior reflects not only concern with exceeding the reserve price, but also strategic bidding in competition with other bids. Presumably, the bids falling just below round bidding figures suggest a willingness to forfeit a potential $1 per acre gain in order to increase chances of bid acceptance should the total bidding exceed the $50,000 budget, necessitating the rejection of some bids that were below the reserve price. Finally, bidder 4 submitted two different bids on different parcels of land. This bidding strategy reflects either hedging against the risk of exceeding the reserve price by accepting lower rents on a portion of the leased water rights or varying opportunity costs of foregoing irrigation on the different parcels.

Bidder 5 exhibits similar behavior in reducing a 2003 bid of $85 to a 2004 bid of $75. Assuming that underlying private resource values were approximately constant for this bidder, it seems that learning the 2003 reserve price helped this bidder to calibrate his 2004 bid at a level that maximized expected rents while still guarding against bid rejection through exceeding the reserve price.

The previous discussion provides evidence of learning on the part of bidders between the 2003 and 2004 OID auctions. It is clear that the exchange of information on market norms resulting from the 2003 experience was responsible for a significant component of the increase in success in the 2004 program.

Summary and Enabling Conclusions

The experience in OID provides an interesting case study in the use of auction mechanisms to acquire temporary instream transfers of water rights. Compared with previous posted-offer methods, the auction succeeded in increasing the number of acres leased and ensured low restoration costs. Initial informational asymmetry impeded trade in the first year of the auction; a reserve price served to guard against high-priced offers, encouraged competitive bidding, and signaled a willingness to pay for restoration water. Participant learning informed bidding in the second year of the auction, leading to larger gains from trade and increased stream flow restoration. The improved outcome in 2004 highlights the importance of price discovery through repeated auctions in the information-poor environment of water markets. The experience in OID parallels the success that the Flint River Auction in Georgia enjoyed under its multiround approach. The results suggest that similar learning and improved outcomes can be produced through repetition of single-round auctions over multiple years.

Several tentative conclusions can be drawn from this experience. First, auctions can be used successfully in thin water markets as well as in markets that have numerous bidders. Second, repeating an auction allows for improved outcomes through participant learning. Third, auction design should incorporate reserve prices or other features to guard against unacceptably high costs of obtaining the desired quantity of water. Finally, supply of water available for acquisition exhibits an increasing marginal cost schedule as expected, though the use of a reserve price may flatten the curve over time. It is clear that well-crafted auctions are a valuable tool in market-based stream flow restoration efforts, even on a localized scale.

Deschutes Basin Groundwater Mitigation Auction

The Deschutes Groundwater Mitigation Framework

In response to recognition of a dynamic hydrologic connection between groundwater and surface water in a large portion of the upper Deschutes Basin, the Oregon Water Resources Commission adopted a set of rules whereby new water rights could be established. Under the rules, a moratorium on new groundwater development was lifted and new water right applications could be granted provided applicants obtained offsets to mitigate the impact of well use on existing surface water rights, including those instream.

The rules establish a system of offset units, called "mitigation credits," which must be obtained in sufficient quantity to fulfill an administratively determined "mitigation obligation" proportionate to the impact of the new water development. A mitigation credit is a means of accounting for water that is consumptively used and is measured volumetrically in AF. In addition, mitigation credits are accrued and consumed in specific zones of impact or sub-basins in which groundwater withdrawal has shown a localized effect on aquifer levels.

Mitigation credits can be created through either (1) permanent retirement of an existing groundwater right in the impact zone, (2) instream transfer of a surface water right in or above the impact zone, or (3) a series of annual instream leases in lieu of a permanent transfer. In all three scenarios, the Oregon Water Resources Department awards mitigation credits equivalent to the amount of discontinued use. Mitigation credits are fungible, and the system was designed with the expectation that most new water users would purchase their required mitigation credits rather than purchasing other offsetting water rights for retirement.

By 2004, a large backlog of demand for mitigation credits had developed. This was due to the accumulation of applications for new water rights that were subject to the mitigation rules over several years during the groundwater rulemaking and establishment of initial credits. In fact, even after the rules were adopted, additional time elapsed before the first mitigation credits could be established. As a result, there were relatively few potential sellers and many potential buyers of credits during the initial years of the mitigation credit market.

Auction Methodology

In this context of ample demand and no established market for credits, the first prospective sellers of mitigation credits faced significant uncertainty as to the value of their assets. Consequently, bilateral negotiation entailed significant risk for sellers (and buyers). Without knowing the value that applicants for new water rights put on those rights (and thus on the mitigation credits and other factors required to develop the rights), a seller risked failing to maximize profit or rents by accepting a price that would prove to be too low. On the other hand, if the seller asked for a higher price, he or she might risk losing the opportunity for a market trade and thus forfeit any gains from trade. This risk is all the more severe given that new water development in the basin is often for uses unfamiliar to those who hold the water rights converted to credits, because they may have little sense of the value of water in these uses.

As discussed previously, an auction can be used to maximize seller revenue in such a situation. Further, maximizing value does not require that the seller know in advance of the auction the values that prospective buyers place on the resource. Given this, the DRC proposed the use of an auction to sell mitigation credits on behalf of Deschutes Irrigation, LLC, a client that had acquired permanent mitigation credits. As a niche business aimed at providing full service to prospective groundwater clients, Deschutes Irrigation was motivated by the desire to increase local understanding of the program, to signal that some (even if limited numbers) of mitigation credits were available, and to explore the private resource value held by groundwater applicants.

As part of its effort to develop local water markets, the DRC argued that given the dearth of previous market activity, the auction would prove a valuable source of information on the value of credits (and hence water rights) in this nascent market. The resulting offer of thirty-six mitigation credits by DRC on behalf of Deschutes Irrigation, LLC was the first-ever auction of credits.

Auction Design

To maximize value of the credits for the seller, the DRC proposed a first-price English (ascending-bid) auction. Under this approach, bidders submit open bids to purchase mitigation credits. Bidding information is public, and as auction participants learn of others' bids, they can in turn submit bids at higher levels. This process continues for a specified period of time, so bidders can compete with others for the limited amount of credits. Rather than bringing all auction participants together in one physical space to participate in a live auction run by an auctioneer, the mitigation credit auction was conducted via phone, fax, and the DRC Web site. Bids were submitted by phone or fax. As bids were received, they were posted on the DRC Web site in real time and made publicly available. This online approach has the advantage of being convenient for bidders and allowing time for measured reflection and revision of bids. To participate, bidders were required to register and have an identified mitigation obligation.

In conjunction with this approach, seller Deschutes Irrigation established a reserve price, based on the private value they placed on the credits, and below which bids would not be accepted. The Web site informed participants in real time of the value and scale of all previous bids and whether the reserve price had been met. Bids were accepted from 7:00 a.m. to 7:00 p.m. on the day of the auction. At auction close, the bid at the highest value was accepted, provided it exceeded the reserve price. If this bid was for fewer than the thirty-six mitigation credits for sale, then the second highest bid was evaluated on the same basis and potentially accepted for sale of the remaining credits. This process continued until either all credits were sold or no bids in excess of the reserve price remained to be evaluated. Winning bids paid the amount of their bid; that is, the auction used discriminatory pricing.

Bidding Strategy and Its Implications

In theory, a single-unit English auction will induce participants to continue raising their bids until they reach their private resource values or win the auction. As a result, they are generally considered efficient in that they allocate resources to those who value them most highly. In addition, a sale to the successful bidder maximizes revenue for the seller. This result is notably different than is the case in a multiunit sealed bid auction where competition is obscure due to private bidding. In a single-unit English auction selling a single item, strategic bid shading is not an issue because bidding up to one's private resource value is the dominant strategy. As a result, design is much more straightforward. However, although based on an English design, the mitigation-credit auction differs because bidders were permitted to bid on fewer than the full thirty-six available credits. If all of the bidders could have been expected to bid for the full thirty-six available credits, then this would have been essentially a single-unit auction. However, limiting bids to participants' actual mitigation obligations assured that some bidders would be bidding for fewer than thirty-six credits, creating a multiunit auction where more than one bid could win. It was not strictly necessary, therefore, that a participant submit the highest bid in order to be successful. If the highest (first-winning) bid left enough remaining credits to satisfy the second bidder's bid, then that bidder would profit by *not* bidding his full resource value, because doing so would only increase his cost.

In this case, revising a bid above the current highest bid is only optimal if (1) it is necessary to preserve a chance of winning the auction and (2) the current highest bid is lower than the revising bidder's value for the resource. In a single-unit auction, the first condition is always met, and bidders should revise their bids upward until they reach their private values of the resource. In the multiunit context, this condition is not always met; revision of the bid may not be necessary to preserve the possibility of reaping gains from the auction trade, but it will reduce consumer surplus in the event of a winning bid. In this situation, the optimal strategy is a function of expectations about other bids both in respect to offer price and the quantity of desired credits. Moreover, for the auctioneer, it is not certain that bidders will bid their true values; as a result, the auction may not maximize the value of the sale, and socially efficient allocation is not ensured.

Bidders

Participation in the mitigation credit auction was limited to those with groundwater permit applications and an identified mitigation obligation. Participants were allowed to bid only for the number of credits specified in their mitigation obligation. These requirements limited the auction to those with a bona fide prospective use of the credits. The intent was to avoid speculation or hoarding in the thin market for permanent credits.

As of April 30, 2004, there were forty-seven pending groundwater applications in the Deschutes Ground Water Study Area. In aggregate, these applications were for a rate of 157 CFS and an annual consumptive use of over 41,000 AF of water. Individual applications ranged between 2.67 and 21,000 AF of consumptive use. Twenty-four permit applications were for 36 AF of use or less and therefore had the possibility for satisfying their entire mitigation obligation from the auction.

A list of those groundwater applicants who had received their Initial Review (and, therefore, had an established mitigation credit obligation) from the Oregon Water Resources Department was compiled by the DRC. A letter announcing the auction was sent to a total of forty-three potential participants, explaining the auction. Of these, ten registered to participate in the auction, and seven submitted bids. Apparently the other three for some reason were not serious candidates for the bidding process once they evaluated the potential costs of doing so. Interested parties were required to register with the DRC prior to participating in the auction. To cover administrative costs, winning bids were subject to a $250 administrative fee and the DRC charged the seller a commission equal to 5 percent of the value of the winning bids. Note that this incentive structure aligned broker and seller incentives to maximize the value of the credit sales.

Evaluation of Bidding and Outcomes

The live online auction for mitigation credits was conducted on May 26, 2004. Bids were accepted from 7:00 a.m. to 7:00 p.m. Bidders submitted their bids via either phone or fax to the DRC staff who then immediately updated the publicly accessible bid schedule on the Web site. The confidential reserve price was $2,500 per credit, and bidders were informed whether their bid had satisfied the reserve price. The evolution of the bidding is presented in Table 5.4.

Table 5.4 shows that only the final two bids met the confidential reserve price of $2,500. These bids, submitted by bidders 1 and 2, were for a cumulative 14.4 mitigation credits. The auction resulted in two sales, one of 4.4 credits at $2,600 per credit for a total value of $11,400 and the other of 10 credits at $2,500 per credit for a total value of $25,000.

Bid Analysis

Auction participants can be separated into two groups based on their bidding behavior. One group—comprised of bidders 4, 5, 6, and 7—is characterized by low bidding and no evidence of strategic behavior. Another set of participants includes bidders 1, 2, and 3 and features bids at higher levels that demonstrate some strategic bidding. An analysis of the bidding follows for each of the groups.

GROUP 1—NON-STRATEGIC BIDDERS

The bids submitted by bidders 4, 5, 6, and 7 (found below the horizontal line in Table 5.4) show no clear bidding strategy. They are not revised upward in response to not meeting the reserve price or being surpassed by a subsequent bid. In fact, the bid submitted by bidders 4 and 5 are lower than previously submitted bids which did not meet the reserve price, and thus could have been determined to have no chance of acceptance prior to being placed. Although the intentions of the bidders are unknown, it is plausible that they simply decided in advance to submit a bid at a certain amount and did so without reference to the state of the bids as reflected on the Web site. As they also did not revise their bids, we can conclude that either they had already bid their maximum willingness to pay or they simply were not engaged in the auction. Their bids had little influence on the final auction results.

GROUP 2—STRATEGIC BIDDERS

A second group including bidders 1, 2, and 3 exhibits at least some measure of competitive strategy in the placement of bids. In total, these three

Table 5.4   2004 Mitigation credit auction bids

Time of Submission	Bidder ID	Price per Credit [1]	Number of Credits	Cumulative Credits Bid [2]	Partial Bid Acceptable	Reserve Price Met
18:26	1	$ 2,600	4.4	4.4	✓	✓
17:58	2	$ 2,500	10	14.4	✓	✓
16:59	1	$ 2,200	4.4	14.4	✓	
15:09	2	$ 2,000	10	14.4	✓	
14:56	3	$ 1,800	8.4	22.8	✓	
13:33	1	$ 1,400	4.4	22.8	✓	
12:38	4	$ 500	3.6		✓	
10:55	5	$ 278	36			
9:20	6	$ 1,000	4.2		✓	
8:12	7	$ 500	14.5		✓	

Notes   [1] Bids rounded to the nearest dollar.
[2] The total number of acres bid at the price or above. Not calculated for bids at $1000 or less.

participants submitted six bids at incrementally higher prices until the auction ended. Two of the three bidders revised prior bids in efforts to ensure that they would win the auction. It therefore appears that this group of bidders had consulted the Web site for the status of the auction over the course of the day and informed their bid revisions through this new knowledge. In fact, the last four bids feature two bidders leapfrogging each others' offers until they had both submitted bids above the reserve price. In the end, these two bidders were successful.

Bidders did not fully optimize their bids based on the available information. Specifically, it appears that concerns that bid shading might result from disclosing that the highest bid would not claim all of the available credits were in this case unfounded. Bidder 1, despite the opportunity, failed to exploit this design weakness, and thus failed to maximize information rents. The suboptimality of his strategy is explained next.

Bidder 1's second bid was $2,200 per credit for 4.4 credits. This bid did not meet the reserve price when placed, and therefore some upward revision was required for a chance of the bid being accepted. Bidder 2 subsequently bid $2,500 per credit for 10 credits. This offer met the reserve price, and this fact was disclosed, informing other bidders that the reserve price was at or below $2,500. At this point, a subsequent offer from bidder 1 only needed to meet a single condition in order to be accepted—it must meet the reserve price. It is not necessary that the bid exceeds the $2,500 offered by bidder 2, because if bidder 2 won and purchased 10 credits, there would remain 26 credits to be allocated to lower bids that had also met the reserve price. In this situation, an optimal bidding strategy would involve submission of a series

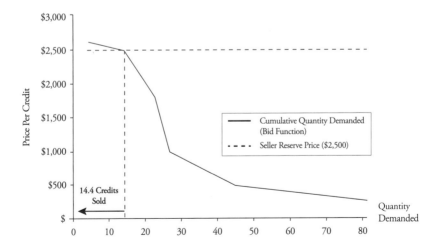

Figure 5.3 Mitigation credit auction bids vs. reserve price

of bids between $2,200 and $2,500 in order to ferret out the reserve price. The lowest bid that met the reserve price would maximize rents for bidder 1. If time or rules did not permit submitting multiple bids as described, then a bid of $2,500 (or $2,501 if equal bids were not allowed) would have given bidder 1 confidence that he had met the reserve price and would therefore be successful in the auction, even in the event that bidder 2 were to submit a subsequent bid (which itself would be suboptimal in the same manner described previously). Bidding a full $100 above the last bid, as was the case with bidder 1's actual bid, increased costs while providing little benefit. One caveat to this statement is that if the bidder feared that a large player might submit a last minute bid that would obtain the entire lot of available credits, a higher bid would have reduced this risk (Figure 5.3).

Conclusions

Analyzing the 2004 mitigation credit auction leads to several conclusions. First, the auction was successful in selling mitigation credits for more than the seller's reserve price at modest transactions cost. The English auction design had some potential weaknesses that created the opportunity for bid shading, however. In future iterations, auctioneers could reduce this risk by selectively disclosing certain information. While efficient bid revision requires that bids per unit be made public, disclosure of the number of credits bid for is unnecessary and potentially counterproductive. This problem could also be mitigated by not disclosing the total number of mitigation credits for sale in the auction.

Finally, in an information-poor environment, the auction effectively enabled learning about the value of mitigation credits. Although there have been few subsequent transactions, it is clear that some willingness to pay over $2,500 per credit does exist. It is equally important, however, that demand was insufficient to allocate all thirty-six credits at this price, suggesting a market-clearing price at a somewhat lower level. For this reason, from the seller's perspective, the auction should be considered a success in capitalizing the value of some credits at a high level. Subsequent development of a cooperative purchase and transfer program between the DRC and local irrigation districts has enabled the provision of a steady supply of permanent credits to the market at a price approaching $1,500 per credit. Even at this lower price, some buyers prefer to "rent" annual credits on an ongoing basis.

Conclusion and Lessons Learned

Through examining the results of multiple auctions of water rights in Oregon's Deschutes Basin, this chapter illustrated both the promise and potential pitfalls of auctions as a tool in water allocation. When contrasted with posted-offer efforts, a reverse auction approach to acquisition of water rights for instream leasing in OID produced superior outcomes. Learning from the initial auction results informed bidding in the second year of the program, allowing for still more gains from trade. An ascending-bid English auction to sell mitigation credits was also a success, though it failed to sell all of the available credits at the seller's desired price level. In general, both of the auction types were well-crafted for the thin market conditions and potential lack of competition of emerging water markets. What few design liabilities existed were not exploited by strategic bidders.

Finally, the key difficulty in actual and potential auctions is the limited ability to create competition among bidders. This problem arises from the naturally thin market conditions for a heterogeneous and extremely localized good such as water. Successful auctions will be those that can find ways to increase competition through higher levels of participation. As markets develop, we can expect that low levels of competition will be the rule rather than the exception; in this context, auctions should incorporate reserve prices, budget caps, and other features designed to make them robust to limited competition.

Auctions have the potential to efficiently allocate resources and maximize value for the auctioneer-seller, even absent any knowledge of participants' private resource values. As market mechanisms are increasingly relied upon to reallocate water resources to emerging environmental and development needs, auctions have a key role to play. Although water has some intrinsic properties that make effective auction design challenging, careful consideration on the part of auctioneers can ensure successful outcomes.

Notes

1. In posted-offer procurement, an entity interested in buying water establishes a price that they are willing to pay for water. Anyone with water to sell then has the option of selling it to this organization at the set price. One challenge is that in the absence of a previous history of water trading, it can be difficult to determine the appropriate price to post.

2. A mitigation credit is a unit of account used to measure the environmental benefit of some restoration action. In many natural resource management schemes, credits can be used to offset or mitigate the impact of natural resource use. The groundwater mitigation program in the Deschutes Basin is explained in the "Deschutes Basin Groundwater Mitigation Auction" of this chapter.

3. R. Stavins, "What Can We Learn from the Grand Policy Experiment? Lessons from SO$_2$ Allowance Trading," *Journal of Economic Perspectives* 12, no. 3 (1998): 69–88.

4. B. Colby, "Cap-and-Trade Policy Challenges: A Tale of Three Markets," *Land Economics* 76, no. 4 (2000): 638–58.

5. G. Stoneham et al., "Auctions for Conservation Contracts: An Empirical Examination of Victoria's BushTender Trial," Melbourne Business School Working Paper Series, Working paper 2002-08, 2002.

6. Colby, "Cap-and-Trade Policy."

7. The concerns of this paragraph are explicitly treated in Chapter 6.

8. A. Dinar, M. Rosegrant, and R. Meinzen-Dick, "Water Allocation Principles and Examples," World Bank and International Food Policy Research Institute, Policy Research, Working paper 1779, 1997.

9. Colby, "Cap-and-Trade Policy," 643.

10. C. Chan, P. Laplagne, and D. Appels, "The Role of Auctions in Allocating Public Resources," Commonwealth of Australia Productivity Commission, Melbourne, Productivity Commission Staff Research Paper, 2003.

11. See Chan, Laplagne, and Appels, "The Role of Auctions," for a comprehensive overview.

12. We describe the auctioneer as the seller of the items at auction—in reality, the auctioneer can be the selling agent for the actual owner of the object at auction.

13. Chan, Laplagne, and Appels, "The Role of Auctions"; P. Klemperer, "What Really Matters in Auction Design," *Journal of Economic Perspectives* 16, no. 1 (2002): 169–89.

14. Chan, Laplagne, and Appels, "The Role of Auctions."

15. Klemperer, "What Really Matters," 170.

16. R. Cummings, C. Holt, and S. Laury, "Using Laboratory Experiments for Policy Making: An Example from the Georgia Irrigation Reduction Auction," *Journal of Policy Analysis and Modeling* 23, no. 2 (2004): 342–63.

17. Cummings, Holt, and Laury, "Using Laboratory Experiments."

18. In most auctions, the auctioneer is the agent of the party buying (such as a conservation group running a reverse auction to purchase water rights) or selling (such as a forest management timber sale) to the bidders. In these cases, this auctioneer-buyer or -seller has goals of buying at a low price or selling at a high price.

19. These unintended outcomes are varied but typically include any potential outcome where the auctioneer would have preferred that no trade take place. Examples include sales at very low prices, sales of more items than are available, purchases at very high prices, or purchases of more units than are needed. Caps help guard against these contingencies.

20. For example, if a conservation group that seeks to purchase water in a specific location discloses that it has a large budget available, water right holders may bid to sell at speculatively high prices.

21. Atakelty Hailu and Sophie Thoyer, "Auction Design for Water Buybacks," (unpublished paper, 2005), http://www.aae.wisc.edu/seminars/papers/2005%20Fall%20papers/AppEcon/Thoyer.09.14.pdf.

22. Klemperer, "What Really Matters."

23. Participation costs could be an explicit fee, but are just as often the administrative costs related to bidding. If an auctioneer requires extensive documentation and legal paperwork prior to allowing a bid, then some participants may choose not to participate, particularly if they feel they have little chance of winning.

24. Stoneham et al., "Auctions for Conservation Contracts."

25. B. Simon, "Federal Acquisition of Water Through Voluntary Transactions for Environmental Purposes," *Contemporary Environmental Policy* 16, no. 4 (1998): 422–32; Cummings, Holt, and Laury, "Using Laboratory Experiments."

26. Chan, Laplagne, and Appels, "The Role of Auctions."
27. While the economic objective of auctions in general terms is to reallocate water to higher value uses and thus to reap gains from trade, conservation buyers may have more specific goals. For example, they may need water at a particular time of year, from a particular source, or at a particular temperature in order to reach conservation objectives. Auction design can address specific circumstances by disqualifying certain rights, for example.
28. R. Petrie, S. Laury, and S. Hill, "Crops, Water Usage, and Auction Experience in the 2002 Irrigation Reduction Auction," Georgia State University, Water Policy Working Paper Series, Working paper #2004-014, 2004.
29. Cummings, Holt, and Laury, "Using Laboratory Experiments."
30. Petrie, Laury, and Hill, "Crops."
31. Ibid.
32. Ibid.
33. Colby, "Cap-and-Trade Policy."
34. G. Eckhardt, "SAWS Takes Online Bids for Edwards Water Rights," *Edwards Aquifer News*, April 2003, http://www.edwardsaquifer.net/news2003.html.
35. Stoneham et al., "Auctions for Conservation Contracts."
36. Chan, Laplagne, and Appels, "The Role of Auctions"; Simon, "Federal Acquisition."
37. Stoneham et al., "Auctions for Conservation Contracts."
38. The Ochoco Irrigation Water rights have a duty of 4 AF per acre, subject to actual water availability.
39. For example, assuming that the water allocation per acre is constant across the district, ranking bids based on price per acre is equivalent to ranking them based on price per acre-foot of water. Because irrigators typically dealt in terms of acres rather than AF, conducting the auction entirely in "acres" was appropriate.
40. Official filing of leases with the State Water Resources Department is important both because it affords legal protection for the instream water and because an instream lease is a recognized beneficial use of water under Oregon law. As a result, leased water rights are protected from forfeiture for nonuse.
41. J..B. Stevens et al., "Benefits, Costs, and Local Impacts of Market-Based Streamflow Enhancements: The Deschutes River, Oregon," *Rivers* 7, no. 2 (2000): 89–108.
42. In Oregon, water rights specify a volume of water that can be diverted from the source for the permitted use. Historically, these "paper" rights have often been for outsize volumes (up to 8 AF per acre) far beyond actual supply or irrigation requirements. Frequently, irrigators do not use the full volume of water specified on their paper rights. If there is a change in water use practice (e.g., from irrigation to instream use), then the new use could demand all of the volume of water on the water right certificate. In cases where this increased water use would harm other irrigators, then the actual "wet" water protected from diversion through the instream lease could be less than the duty found on the paper water right.
43. Petrie, Laury, and Hill, "Crops."

44.   The marginal conservation value per unit of instream water is expected to decrease as stream flow conditions improve toward ecological objectives (which themselves are not fully specified for these areas of the Crooked River). In addition, the value of an annual lease will be a function of hydrological conditions in a given year. Given the limited ability to pay for instream flow restoration, the discussion of true conservation value is largely academic. The DRC's reserve price was the sole conservation demand in the basin and as such is a market price of sorts.

45.   The driest section of the Crooked River is found below the North Unit Irrigation District pumping station just above Smith Rock State Park, some 15 miles downstream of OID. In that section, low flows are typically 10 CFS for much of the summer (before any instream leasing).

46.   Stoneham et al., "Auctions for Conservation Contracts."

47.   These bidders were not commercial farmers engaged in active use of their water rights, nor were they active in the irrigation district. One of these bidders was a trustee for an estate that owned managed water rights along with other holdings. This is in contrast to some other bidders who were members of the irrigation district board.

6

Transactions Costs and Water Markets: The Anticommons Perspective

Stephen N. Bretsen and Peter J. Hill

Introduction

Throughout this volume, the authors have discussed the desirability of using markets to move water to higher-valued uses. They have also described numerous situations where clear gains from trade have resulted from water markets. However, using market mechanisms to allocate water is controversial and costly. In many cases, transactions costs prevent water sales from occurring. This chapter uses the theory of the anticommons to explain why water markets often do not function well.

The marginal value of water in agriculture is much lower than its value for municipal use and for the production of environmental amenities. The increasing demand for water in alternative uses and the lower value of water in agriculture create a puzzle since most commodity markets respond rapidly to price differentials and market arbitrage reduces those differentials over time. What is different about water markets in the American West and why have those differentials grown rather than decreased? The answer lies in the tragedy of the anticommons since the existence of multiple rights of exclusion has impeded water transactions by increasing transactions costs.

First, we describe the tragedy of the anticommons. The next section explains how use rights in water are created under the prior appropriation doctrine. Then, we identify the various rights of exclusion that exist in water transfers generally and in transfers from agricultural irrigation specifically. The combined effect of these multiple rights of exclusion is an anticommons in the water markets in the American West. Finally, we present two case studies that illustrate the difficulty of water transfers due to the tragedy of the anticommons.

The Tragedy of the Anticommons

The tragedy of the anticommons and the tragedy of the commons provide two similar but opposite points of reference for understanding how unbundling property rights can increase transactions costs and lead to economic inefficiencies. In the words of James Buchanan and Yong Yoon, "The basic logic is equivalent in the two cases. The inefficiency arises because separate decision makers, each of whom acts in exercise of assigned rights, impose external diseconomies on others who hold similar rights."[1] The two rights in tension in the twin tragedies are use rights and rights of exclusion (or veto rights).

The tragedy of the commons and the tragedy of the anticommons exist when exclusion rights are separated from use rights.[2] The tragedy of the commons occurs when there are multiple use rights. Those who hold the use rights do not also have the ability to exclude others from access to a resource. In that situation, rents are dissipated by too many entries into the commons. The tragedy of the anticommons occurs when there are multiple rights of exclusion or veto rights. Those who hold the rights of exclusion effectively undermine the right to use the resource, especially when exclusion rights and use rights are not necessarily bundled for all rights holders. The effect is an underuse of the resource. With a linear demand curve, if there are a finite number of users who do not hold exclusion rights, the loss will be identical to that experienced when there is the same number of individuals who have exclusion rights but do not have use rights.[3] Thus, the anticommons becomes "a useful metaphor for understanding how and why potential economic value can disappear into the 'black hole' of resource utilization, a wastage that is quantitatively comparable to the overutilization wastage employed in the conventional commons logic."[4]

Michael Heller introduced the concept of the anticommons based on his observation of retail activity in Moscow after the fall of communism.[5] He was puzzled by the large number of active kiosks on the streets in front of empty stores. His explanation was that four categories of right holders—local government councils, users, balance sheet holders, and regulators—emerged with the transition from socialist property to private property and each had the right of veto over the use of stores. Since a single party who opposed a use could keep the stores from being rented or sold, the transactions costs of coordinating all the veto rights proved to be too great for an entrepreneurial, start-up retailer to overcome. "The tragedy of the storefront anticommons [was] that owners waste the resource when they fail[ed] to agree on a use."[6] Thus underuse of a scarce resource was the problem, rather than the overuse of the resource that occurs under the tragedy of the commons.

The existence of multiple veto rights over water that are not bundled with use rights creates an anticommons in water marketing in the American West. In some cases, no water trades will occur because of the multiplicity of veto rights; in other cases, the tragedy of the anticommons leads to protracted and expensive negotiations with the need for side payments to secure the approval of all concerned. Furthermore, even after water transfers have been contracted for, there is still the strong possibility that lawsuits can be brought to invalidate such transfers. Thus, the tragedy of the anticommons has led to high transactions costs in western water markets. These high transactions costs mean that many transfers that would be economically efficient do not occur.

Use Rights and Exclusion Rights in Water Transfers

Use Rights in Water Under the Prior Appropriation Doctrine

In the western states, ownership of the water resource is vested in the state. However, this ownership interest has not given states or the public rights in water equivalent to use rights. Thus, the Colorado Supreme Court has held that the original 1876 state constitutional provision declaring unappropriated water to be the property of the public "was primarily intended to preserve the historical appropriation system of water rights upon which the irrigation economy in Colorado was founded, rather than to assure public access to waters for purposes other than appropriation."[7] Similarly, in California, although the state water code declares that the state owns all water in trust for the people, the California courts have held that the state is not a property owner in the traditional sense and must follow the state statutory procedures to obtain a water right.[8] However, such declarations provide the legal foundation for the states' regulatory role in the creation and transfer of use rights in water as well as the creation of exclusion rights.

Since the state or the public owns the water, the property right created in water is a usufructuary right. These use rights arise in context of the prior appropriation doctrine, which is the predominant form of water law in the western states. Under this doctrine, water rights are created when a user diverts surface water for a beneficial use. Seniority is granted based on the concept of "first in time, first in right" so that the first appropriator from a surface water source has rights to the water that are senior to subsequent or junior appropriators. Thus, during a drought, junior appropriators are denied access to water to satisfy the water rights of the more senior appropriators based on the order of priority. The property right to water in a prior appropriation system "is not a right to specific water itself, but rather a right to divert a quantity of water, in accordance with one's priority."[9] Although water rights are not permanent, they continue ad infinitum unless they are abandoned or forfeited for failing to divert the water and make beneficial use of it, either due to nonuse or waste. Beginning with Wyoming in 1890, every prior appropriation state except for Colorado, which has a system of special water courts, has replaced common-law adjudications with administrative permitting systems to grant water rights to users, to adjudicate abandonments and forfeitures by users, and to review the transfer of water rights among users.[10]

Exclusion Rights via Mutual Irrigation Companies and Irrigation Districts

One of the major factors in the creation of an anticommons is the way the institutions have evolved to control water in the American West. Since most of the water in question was originally diverted for agricultural irrigation, institutions developed to facilitate that type of diversion. In addition, adequate water supplies for nonagricultural use existed at the time these institutions were created. Thus, the institutional structure facilitated movement of water among agricultural users, but there was little reason to think of constructing institutions to facilitate transactions out of agriculture. As a result, the heavy hand of history has played a large role in water markets today.

The delivery of water to farmers for irrigation has not been a simple matter in the American West due to transactions costs. The high degree of asset specificity in irrigation infrastructure and the number of farmers who receive their water from a single irrigation organization would lead, according to standard transactions costs theory, to vertical integration.[11] However, the economies of scale that existed to provide irrigation infrastructure meant that the optimal size of an irrigation facility was much larger than the optimal size of a farm. In 1920, the number of irrigated acres per irrigated farm was eighty-three, while mutual irrigation companies averaged 1,889 acres, and irrigation districts were, on average, 9,510 acres.[12] Given this enormous mismatch, vertical integration would result in irrigation organizations that would be too small to capture economies of scale or farms that would be too large to operate in a cost-effective manner. This disconnection between the optimal size of the irrigated farm and the irrigation organization meant that alternative organizations had to evolve in the American West to solve the transactions cost problems of organizing irrigation.[13] Two primary forms evolved that are relevant for the effect of the tragedy of the anticommons on water markets—mutual irrigation companies and irrigation districts.[14]

General incorporation statutes were passed in all of the western states in the late nineteenth and early twentieth centuries, and these became the basis for mutual irrigation companies. Most mutual irrigation companies were not-for-profit since their sole function was to provide water at cost and allow farmers to overcome the transactions cost problems of providing irrigation water to their farms. The corporate governance of a mutual irrigation company consisted of shareholders who elected a board of directors that provided management supervision for the organization. As in a closely held corporation, the farmers were typically the shareholders, board members, and officers of the mutual, thus aligning the interests of the water user and the water provider. Shares of stock in the corporation were distributed to the shareholders in accordance with the articles of incorporation and bylaws. Each share of stock usually represented a right to water service and the delivery of a specified quantity of water or to a specified share of the flow of the water source, which varied from time to time between and within seasons of use.[15] In

1920, incorporated mutuals were responsible for over 35 percent of irrigated acres in the seventeen western states. Although the total acreage irrigated by mutuals was approximately the same in 1978, other forms of irrigation organizations had increased enough that they only represented 16 percent of acres irrigated by that date.[16]

Mutual irrigation companies were organized almost exclusively as a farmer-initiated institution and were designed as a means for farmers to cooperate to deliver water to their agricultural lands. Since most of the mutuals were organized by 1920, there was almost no thought that the water would ever be more valuable for uses other than raising crops by the farmers who were members of the mutual. Therefore, it is not surprising that the rules governing the operation of the mutual were designed almost entirely to deal with intraorganization transfers. As a result, several institutional provisions of mutual irrigation companies make it difficult for individual members to transfer any of their water rights outside of the organization.

First, in many cases the individual stockholder does not hold the water rights, but rather they are held by the mutual irrigation company.[17] Since the farmers are the shareholders in the mutual, the issue of whether the company or the farmers hold the water rights might appear to be a moot one. Most of the mutuals, however, also established governance rules for any transfer of rights when they were incorporated. In many cases, these rules require an approval by the majority of voting stock.[18] In theory, there is no reason why the members of a mutual irrigation company should necessarily vote against a transfer of a portion of the water out of their use to a municipal or alternative use so long as account is taken of the return flow from a particular right. Nevertheless, equity issues loom large when a farming community votes on a water transfer, and it can be difficult to secure a majority approval for any transfer of water out of the mutual. Many of these issues focus not on the return flow question, but on the third-party effects, the impact on nonirrigators in a farming community.

Second, perhaps more important than community sentiment and majoritarian voting rules are the even more stringent rules via the articles of incorporation and bylaws that prevent or inhibit transfers of water out of a mutual. In some cases, these rules require the approval of the board of directors to ensure that the transfer will not injure other shareholders or require service beyond the capabilities of the mutual's irrigation system.[19] In other cases, rules create an inseverable appurtenance, in which the shares of stock and hence the water rights are appurtenant or "attached" to the land.[20] With appurtenance, the stock and its associated water right each could not be transferred separate from the other. Appurtenance made sense when water was used almost exclusively for irrigating farmland within a particular agricultural area since it served to limit transfers to outsiders who were not a part of the agricultural community. However, with the increasing

147

differential in the value of water for municipal uses compared to agriculture, the governance rules of mutual irrigation companies and the ways in which rights were formulated and assigned has meant that any transfers out of mutuals have been difficult.

Irrigation and conservancy districts are another institutional innovation that provide irrigation water in the West. These districts differ from mutual companies since they are quasi-public, local government, special use entities rather than closely held, nonprofit corporations. In 1887, California passed the Wright Act, which was the first legislation that allowed farmers to form a taxing district to support the construction and operation of irrigation facilities. Table 6.1 shows the rapid increase in irrigation districts in each of the seventeen western states after the passage of enabling legislation in that state. By 1928, there were 801 irrigation districts, varying in size from a few hundred acres to over 500,000 acres,[21] and by 1930, these districts delivered water to 3,454,272 acres. Today, irrigation districts are responsible for approximately one-fourth of the irrigated acres in the seventeen western states, and their total acreage has increased to 10,769,762.[22]

Irrigation districts have several features that made them uniquely suited to the provision of water for farmers. In the first place, they were farmer initiated, and farmers who wanted to construct irrigation facilities or take over bankrupt irrigation organizations could petition for the formation of an irrigation district. Each state specified particular voting rules for the establishment of the district, and once the district was established, it had the power to tax, issue bonds, and use the power of eminent domain.[23] The power to tax and issue bonds was important for overcoming free-riding problems when irrigation facilities were constructed, and the fact that the approval rate was over 90 percent in irrigation district formation elections in California indicates that many, if not most, farmers saw the district as a useful mechanism for reducing transactions costs.[24] The high number of "yes" votes for the formation of irrigation districts also indicates that farmers were not substantially concerned that the districts would use their taxing power to inappropriately impose costs greater than benefits.

Like the mutual irrigation company, the irrigation district was formed with the single purpose of delivering water to farmers. Hence, it also contained institutional provisions that were not particularly well suited for transfers once water became more valuable outside of the district. In most irrigation districts, the district itself owned the water rights. Placing ownership in the irrigation district was seen as a way of holding the water rights in a form that could easily be transferred for the benefit of the landowners within the district without going through the requirements of the statutory transfer process. In many cases, the water rights, even though held by the district, were appurtenant to specific tracts of land.[25]

Table 6.1 Irrigation districts formed in seventeen western states to December 31, 1928, by years

Year	CA	WA	KS	NV	OR	ID	NE	CO	TX	WY	MT	NM	UT	AZ	OK	SD	ND	Total
1887	(a) 4																	4
1888	7																	7
1889	6																	6
1890	11	(a) 4																15
1891	13	2	(a)															15
1892	3	1		(a)														4
1893	4																	4
1895	1				(a)	(a)	(a) 9											10
1896							3											3
1897							2											2
1898							4											4
1900						1												1
1901						1	1	(a) 1										3
1902						2		1										3
1903								3										3
1904					1	3	1	4										9

(*Continued*)

Table 6.1 Irrigation districts formed in seventeen western states to December 31, 1928, by years (*Continued*)

Year	CA	WA	KS	NV	OR	ID	NE	CO	TX	WY	MT	NM	UT	AZ	OK	SD	ND	Total
1905					2	1	1	2	(a)									6
1906					1	2	2	3										8
1907						1		3		(a)	(a) 2							6
1908						1		5		1								7
1909	2					4	1	19		2	6	(a) 1	(a) 6					41
1910					2	3		18		1	2	1	2					29
1911	2	2			1	1	1	9	1	3	1	1	1					23
1912		5			4	8	4	5				1	1	(a) 2				30
1913	2	2			2	4	2	2	2		3			1				20
1914	1	6		1		2			3		1							14
1915	5	7			1	5	1		1						(a)			20
1916	8	9			7	2			1		2							29
1917	7	14			10	4			3		1	1	3		1	(a)	(a)	44
1918	8	8		1	8	4	3		1		3	1		2			1	40
1919	11	11		1	14	4	2		3		12			2				60
1920	18	16		1	12	12	2		4	1	22		3	2			1	94
1921	14	3			2	3		1	2	2	6		5	2				40

(*Continued*)

Year	CA	WA	KS	NV	OR	ID	NE	CO	TX	WY	MT	NM	UT	AZ	OK	SD	ND	Total
1922	9	7			6	7	1	1	2	1	6		1	9				50
1923	8	6			1	11			2	2	1	1		5		1		38
1924	7	7				2			5	2	1			3				27
1925	9	3			3	6	1	1	5	2	1	1		2				34
1926	3	2		1		2	2		2	1	1			2				16
1927	5	3			1				4	3				2	1			18
1928	2	2			1		1	1	7	1				1				14
Total	168	120		5	79	96	44	79	48	22	71	8	22	35	1	1	2	801

(a)Irrigation district enabling statute passed.

Source: Wells A. Hutchins, *Irrigation Districts, Their Organization, Operation and Financing,* U.S. Department of Agriculture Technical Bulletin No. 254 (Washington, DC: U.S. Government Printing Office, 1931), Table 1.

As a result, any present-day transfer of water by a member of an irrigation district is subject to a complex set of decision rules and a complicated adjudication process to determine whether the farmer even has a clear enough water right to transfer it to a user outside of the district. Even though irrigation districts have public prerogatives, they retain the attributes of a private corporation since the beneficiaries are private landowners and can allocate voting rights and other costs and benefits in different ways.[26] In some districts, voting is on the basis of one vote per water user, while in others, it is apportioned by the amount of water used or the amount of acres irrigated.[27] These different decision rules have a substantial impact on the way that water transfers take place. Where voting rules enable all water users to have an equal vote, securing permission for transfers may be difficult. For example, in the Imperial Irrigation District (IID), the one-person, one-vote voting rule made it time-consuming to gain approval for a transfer of water from the IID to the Metropolitan Water District (MWD).[28] Voting rules that allocate votes based on the number of acres irrigated within the district may allow a numerical minority to veto a transfer of water rights out of the district.

In some states, irrigation districts have actually been given stronger powers than those which existed under their original enabling legislation. For example, in Arizona, an irrigation district can stop the transfer of any water within its particular drainage.[29] This, of course, gives a substantial veto right to an irrigation district over water transfers, even those by individual water rights holders who are not part of an irrigation district and who find it profitable to sell their water right to a nonagricultural user.[30]

The Bureau of Reclamation

Throughout the latter part of the nineteenth century, irrigation projects in the American West were established through substantial private efforts using mutual irrigation companies and associations. Subsequently, the passage of statutes enabled irrigation districts to form, and by 1900, there were 7.5 million acres irrigated in the seventeen western states through localized, bottom-up irrigation institutions.[31] However, there was still substantial pressure for federal involvement, and in 1902, Congress passed reclamation legislation. Funding for the reclamation project was to come from the sale of public land in the sixteen western states with arid land.[32] Land sales revenues declined over time, however, and reclamation projects expanded, so most federal government reclamation was funded out of the general revenues of the government.

Although the original intent of the legislation was to provide irrigation water directly to farmers, this proved impractical because of high transactions costs resulting from the necessity of dealing with a large number of individual farmers, and in 1922, Congress authorized the Secretary of Interior to contract directly with irrigation districts.[33] In 1926, Congress eliminated the possibility of the Bureau of Reclamation delivering water directly to farmers when it required that irrigation districts be the only entity that could enter into a contract with the federal government to receive irrigation water.[34]

By 1929, the Bureau had invested enough money for irrigation projects that the funds invested were 67 percent of the total bonds that had been sold by irrigation districts up to that point.[35] The Bureau has become an important supplier of water throughout the West, with 20 percent of the irrigated acres in the seventeen western states receiving at least some portion of their water from federal reclamation projects.[36] Most of the water from the Bureau projects goes to agriculture. A 1996 study by the Bureau found that 85 percent of reclamation water is used for irrigation.[37]

Because of the heavy involvement of the Bureau in irrigation in the American West, many potential transfers of water from agricultural to nonagricultural use involve the Bureau. Unfortunately, the role of the Bureau in transfers of any water that it has provided to farmers through irrigation districts is unclear. The Bureau does not have administrative guidelines that govern water transfers, and the Supreme Court rulings on various issues involving Bureau water do not provide a consistent understanding of the role of the Bureau in transfers.

There are several reasons for the lack of clarity as to whether the Bureau has to give its approval for transfers of any water from Bureau projects. In the first place, Bureau water is often mixed with water from other sources since many Bureau projects provide supplemental water to existing irrigation organizations. Since these organizations were already delivering water to farmers, the addition of Bureau water confuses ownership issues. "The entire package of rights in reclamation project water can be thought of, as with other property rights, as a 'bundle of sticks.' In most states, the sticks of the project water bundle are divided among at least four entities, the federal government, the state, the district, and the end user."[38] Even more confusing is that the rights of each of these entities are not the same across space and time. This means that a detailed investigation of each case is necessary to determine who has what decision-making power with respect to transfers. This lack of uniformity also means a greater probability of lawsuits since there are precedents, many of them conflicting, in terms of transfers and the right to approve or disapprove of transfers.

Second, Congress has generally deferred to state laws with respect to water rights, especially the state ownership of water and creation of individual usufructuary water rights under the western prior appropriation doctrine. Section 8 of the 1902 Reclamation Act specifically expresses the intention of the federal government to respect state rules governing water use.[39] Nevertheless, the Supreme Court has not interpreted this deference to state law as meaning the Bureau has no control over how its water is used (*Ivanhoe Irrigation Dist. v. McCracken*, 357 U.S. 275 (1958)). Therefore, when it comes to transfers of project water, the Bureau still maintains at least some decision-making authority.

Third, part of the authority of the federal government over water transfers comes not from the actual ownership of water rights by the Bureau, but because of the fact that water is delivered under contract to irrigation organizations. These contract rights, although not the same as a property right to water, limit the rights of water users to engage in transfers.[40]

One of the major contractual restrictions comes from the Reclamation Project Act of 1939, which states that "no contract relating to municipal water supply or miscellaneous purposes or to electric power or power privileges shall be made unless, in the judgment of the Secretary, it will not impair the efficiency of the project for irrigation purposes" (43 U.S.C. 485h(c) (2007)). The ambiguity of the term "impair the efficiency" means there is a great deal of uncertainty as to whether a transfer of project water is legitimate or not. Of course, that creates an opportunity for lobbying by various interests since those who object to the transfers can argue that the efficiency of irrigation has been impaired.

Fourth, other unclear provisions in the enabling legislation for reclamation projects make transfers difficult. Most project-authorizing legislation specifies, at least in a general way, a geographical area that the project is designed to serve.[41] This means that many potential transfers may run into boundary problems since water that is transferred from agricultural to other uses may violate the original boundary provisions.

Fifth, most water transfers are driven by the opportunity for participating individuals or groups to profit from a mutually agreed upon trade. The owner or quasi-owner of the water right expects to be made better off by either leasing or selling that right to another user and that user is willing to make the purchase because of the value of the water in an alternative use. In an examination of the specific provisions of thirty-four contracts, Wahl[42] found fifteen of the thirty-four contracts place some type of restrictions on any income that is generated from water resales by those receiving the water. Six of the thirty-four clearly specify that profits cannot be made until all financial obligations to the Bureau are repaid. Since there is a very large remaining obligation to cover costs incurred in the original construction and ongoing operation of the project in most circumstances, this means there is little reason for present water users to consider a water transfer.[43]

Most of the contracts examined also expressed some sort of limitations on the end use of water, with eleven of them specifying only a single use of that water.[44] Again, these types of restrictions make transfers more difficult, and if they do occur, open up the Bureau to lawsuits for violating the end-use restrictions.

Finally, most of the contracts between the Bureau and water users specify that the Bureau is not liable for water shortages that may arise from any underlying alternative claim that is deemed important enough to trump the rights conveyed in the sale.[45] As a result, if the Bureau reallocates water from irrigation to other uses in order to satisfy particular competing demands, such as the Endangered Species Act or the National Environmental Policy Act, there is no actionable impairment of the water rights of the original users. This, of course, dramatically lessens the security of any property rights to water which farmers may think they hold and also means that farmers have a much less valuable right to transfer to other users. If their water right is not secure or does not represent a fixed amount of water, it is less likely that transfers will occur. Thus, when water deliveries were reduced to 50 percent of the contracted supplies during 1993 in the San Joaquin Valley of California, members of the Westlands Water District claimed the contractual obligations had been abrogated. However, the Ninth Circuit Court of Appeals held that the United States had not breached its contract to Westland's water users since the requirements to meet environmental needs trumped the contractual provisions (*O'Neill v. United States*, 50 F.3d 677 (9th Cir. 1995)). In a period of rising amenity values, it may make sense to transfer water from agricultural to environmental uses. However, doing this through regulatory decree rather than through a formal transfer means that greater uncertainty is introduced into the transfer process. It also means there is a greater likelihood that the multiple claimants upon the water resource will prevent water from going to its highest valued use.

Because of all these issues, apparently for any transfers of Bureau water to be legitimate those transfers would have to be approved by the Secretary of Interior.[46] Thus, the Bureau generally has the right to refuse any district or end-user requests to reassign water deliveries to another party so long as any Bureau water is involved. This discretion, along with the uncertainty introduced by the numerous provisions specifying the use to which water will be put, the boundaries of the project area, the possibility that the efficiency of irrigation has been impaired, and the potential competing claims from environmental uses, means that any transfer that is approved has the potential for being litigated in the court system. Therefore, any water users who are drawing upon Bureau projects face another barrier in their attempts to carry out a transfer of that water.

Exclusion Rights via the Statutory Transfer Process and the Public Interest Standard

The high transactions costs created by the statutory procedures have discouraged transfers both among agricultural users and from agricultural uses to urban and environmental uses due to high transactions costs. Traditionally, these transactions costs arose when holders of water rights (i.e., use rights) exercised statutorily granted veto rights to the amount of water to be transferred. More recently, however, state statutory transfer provisions have been expanded through the concept of the public interest standard to grant exclusion rights to a broader class of potential objectors who do not hold water rights.

The transfer of irrigated farmland and its associated water rights from one farmer to another farmer who will continue the historical use does not normally trigger the requirement for state review and approval.[47] However, a transfer of a surface water right, especially from an agricultural use to other uses, occurs in the context of a change in that water right, either a change in the point of diversion, the time of diversion, the place of use, or the type of use (N.M. Stat. §§ 72-5-3, 72-5-22-24 [2008]). Whenever such a change occurs, the water right holder usually must first receive approval from the state by submitting an application with the administrative agency and following the statutorily mandated procedures. Once an application is filed, notices are published or mailed and opponents can protest the change in the water right. "The major issues that arise in transfer cases are the validity of the original right (e.g., has it been abandoned?), the extent of the right—especially the quantity of water historically used, and whether the transfer will cause injury to other water rights" (N.M. Stat. §§ 72-5-3, 72-5-22-24 (2008)). These issues reflect the nature of water as both a natural resource and a social resource and the interdependencies created among holders of use rights by the prior appropriation doctrine.[48]

The historical use doctrine recognizes that junior appropriators rely on both prior filings and adjudications by senior appropriators as well as the facts on the ground. Allowing junior appropriators to object to the amount of water to be transferred because the senior appropriator proposing the transfer has not historically used all of the water right or has wasted water protects the expectations and use rights of the junior appropriators. "Early appropriations . . . were frequently in excess of actual need because there was no administrative system to police the amounts claimed."[49] "Hence, the fundamental purpose of the change proceeding is to ensure that the true right—that which has ripened by beneficial use over time—is the one that will prevail in its changed form" (*Santa Fe Trail Ranches Prop. Owners Ass'n v. Simpson*, 990 P.2d 46, 55 (Colo. 1999)).

The no-injury rule followed in all western states requires the state to prohibit a change to a water right if the change will injure junior appropriators. The potential for injury arises because irrigation efficiency in the western states stands at about 50 percent and downstream junior appropriators rely on the return flow, which is not part of the transferor's historical use, to satisfy their water rights.[50] As noted by Sax and colleagues,

> If a particular quantity of water is being used over and over, the value of that water is its worth not just to the first user, but to all users.

If the price just exceeds the value of the water to the first user, the transfer may be inefficient. The injury to the junior appropriators who are now without water may exceed the marginal benefit of the water to the city. By protecting junior appropriators, the law "internalizes" that injury and forces the buyer to take it into account.[51]

Given the economic incentives for junior appropriators to protest changes in water rights and given the complex legal, historical, and technical issues that have to be resolved to determine historical use and noninjury, statutory transfer proceedings involve high transactions costs. More recently, the transactions costs of water marketing have been expanded by incorporating a general public interest requirement into the statutory transfer processes. The original concept of the public interest, which is inherent in state statutes and constitutions that declare the state the owner of all water resources, was primarily a way of protecting the property rights of downstream users or junior appropriators. The expanded public interest standard, however, creates new exclusion rights separate from use rights, thus leading to the tragedy of the anticommons in the transfer of rights.

Initially, the expanded concept of the public interest was incorporated into the appropriation statutes of western states. Fourteen of the seventeen western states require state administrative agencies to consider the public interest (or public welfare) when an application is made for a new water right.[52] For example, in an appropriation hearing for a new water right in Idaho, whether or not protested by third parties, the administrative agency "may reject such application and refuse issuance of a permit therefore, or may partially approve and grant a permit for a smaller quantity of water than applied for, or may grant a permit upon conditions" if the proposed use "will conflict with the local public interest," (Idaho Code Ann. § 42-203A(5)(e) (LexisNexis 2008)) where the local public interest is defined as "the interests that the people in the area directly affected by a proposed water use have in the effects of such use on the public water resource" (Idaho Code Ann. § 42-202(B)(3) (LexisNexis 2008)). The Idaho Supreme Court noted that "public interest provisions appear frequently in the statutes of prior appropriation states of the West, but are explicated rarely" (*Shokal v. Dunn*, 109 Idaho 330, 707 P.2d 441, 448 (1985)). Despite this problem, the Idaho Supreme Court determined that the statutory language created an affirmative duty to protect the public interest, including aesthetic and environmental considerations. In arriving at this interpretation, the Idaho Supreme Court quoted with approval an observation by the New Mexico Supreme Court that the "public interest" should be read broadly to "secure the greatest possible benefit from [the public waters] for the public" (*Young & Norton v. Hinderlider*, 15 N.M. 666, 110 P. 1045, 1050 (1910)).

As interpreted by courts, the public interest standard not only creates a broad standard, but also allows multiple third parties to use that standard to veto a transfer of water rights. In a separate case involving an amendment to a permit for additional points of diversion, the Idaho Supreme Court held that parties without use rights could raise objections under the "local public interest" standard (*Hardy v. Higginson*, 123 Idaho 485, 849 P.2d 946 (1993)). Idaho is not unique since most western states permit any interested party to file a protest, although the objections by holders of use rights are given greater attention.[53]

The incorporation of a public interest standard into statutory appropriation provisions for new water rights is significant for water transfers because of the application of appropriation statute standards to the transfer of water rights. The Utah Supreme Court held that an individual without any use rights could protest a change application using the public interest standard contained in the statutory appropriation provisions (*Bonham v. Moran*, 788 P.2d 497 (Utah 1989)). Thus, even though the statutory transfer provision did not contain a public interest standard, the Utah Supreme Court thought it was appropriate for the state engineer to determine whether a change of use would "prove detrimental to the public welfare" (Utah Code Ann. § 73-3-8 (1) (1985)). In particular, the Utah Supreme Court feared that a two-step process of filing for an appropriation for one use and subsequently filing a change application for a different use would allow holders of use rights to eviscerate the intent of the entire statutory scheme of protecting the public interest.

A growing number of western states have codified the public interest standard to apply specifically to water transfers and other changes in water rights.[54] For example, in 1982, California expanded the public interest provision to read "the board may approve any changes associated with a transfer . . . only if it . . . does not unreasonably affect the overall economy of the area from which the water is being transferred" (Cal. Water Code § 386 (2007)).[55] Since 1985 in New Mexico, water rights can be "severed from the land, simultaneously transferred and become appurtenant to other land, or may be transferred for other purposes, without losing priority of right theretofore established, if such changes can be made without detriment to existing water rights and are not contrary to conservation of water with the state and not detrimental to the public welfare of the state, on approval of an application of the owner by the state engineer" (N.M. Stat. § 72-5-23 (2008)).

New Mexico's public interest requirement is closely associated with a lawsuit over an application to transfer water from agricultural irrigation to a commercial, recreational use (*Sleeper v. Ensenada Land & Water Ass'n*, 107 N.M. 494, 760 P.2d 787 (Ct. App. 1988)). Tierra Grande, Inc. and Penasco Ski Corporation dammed a creek to create a recreational lake for a ski resort in violation of state law and were required to breach the dam. The developers then contracted to purchase land and appurtenant surface water rights from two local property owners to create the lake, subject to obtaining the approval of the state engineer to the change application. The Ensenada and

Park View Ditches used water from the same source to water stock in the spring, to fill irrigation reservoirs for use in summer, and to fertilize the soil with its historically high silt content. The Ensenada Land and Water Association protested the transfer alleging that it would impair existing rights and would be contrary to the public interest. As in Utah, the New Mexico statutory appropriation provisions had a public interest requirement while the statutory transfer provisions did not, and, as a result, the state engineer refused to hear evidence that the transfer was contrary to the public interest.

On appeal, the state district court reversed the state engineer's decision on public interest grounds because the ski resort would only create a few menial jobs for local inhabitants and because the proposed development would erode the community's agricultural subsistence economy, which was central to the northern New Mexico culture. The New Mexico Court of Appeals reversed the district court because the statutory transfer provisions did not contain a public interest standard. However, between the decisions of the two courts, the New Mexico legislature amended the statutory transfer provisions to specifically include a public interest requirement.[56]

Incorporating a public interest standard into statutory transfer provisions further increases transfer costs and increases the risk that an anticommons will develop for three reasons. First, the often-undefined term "public interest" or "public welfare" raises a number of questions in the context of water markets. "Is 'public welfare' or the 'public interest' simply the sum of individual's well being" in accordance with utilitarian standards?[57] Is the public interest defined as the interests of all the people in the state in a particular transfer or just the communities or watersheds directly affected? How is the public interest measured in a public policy balancing against private interests, especially when a transfer of water rights from agricultural uses to urban uses represents an economic gain?

Second, is there any feasible way to make the public interest criterion for transfer approval operational? The regulatory authority (the state engineer in most states) charged with determining the public interest has limited resources and expertise for investigating all transfers and then determining what the public interest is.[58]

Third, public interest standards allow third parties who do not hold property rights in water to protest a transfer of water rights. The sheer number of individuals and entities who are able to file a protest along with the broad nature of the public interest standard that forms the basis of the protest only increases the time and costs of a process already fraught with transactions costs. The cumulative effect of the statutory transfer process and the public interest standard is to make the transfer of water rights from traditional agricultural uses to higher value municipal, industrial, and environmental uses even more difficult and unlikely due to a tragedy of the anticommons.

Exclusion Rights via the Public Trust Doctrine

The public interest standard is statutory and thus a creature of the legislature. The public trust doctrine provides an additional, judicially enforced means of creating exclusion rights separate from use rights that can potentially discourage voluntary transfers. The most relevant restrictions are on movement of water rights from lower value agricultural uses to higher value municipal, industrial, and recreational uses, but the public trust doctrine makes more difficult transfers in any direction. (For a detailed discussion of the evolution of the public trust doctrine, see Chapter 7.) As in the public interest standard in the statutory transfer process, the anticommons created by the public trust doctrine arises both because the doctrine expands the number of individuals and entities who can object to a transfer and because the doctrine arms these litigants with additional arguments to employ against the transfer beyond the traditional arguments of historical use and noninjury to downstream junior appropriators.

To this point, this chapter has dealt in principle with the numerous barriers to efficient transfers of water. Now, we will examine the actual functioning of present-day water markets to see how these barriers play out in the real world. In the next two sections, we take up two case studies where water is clearly more valuable in nonagricultural use, but where the transfer process has been prolonged and difficult because of the high transactions costs of the anticommons.

Case Study—The Imperial Irrigation District Transfers

California is a good test case for the efficacy of water markets and for the argument that the tragedy of the anticommons exists in those markets. The state was one of the first to engage in large-scale irrigation projects, and 80 percent of developed water is used in agriculture.[59] Population growth has also been rapid in the state, particularly in the southern, more arid part so water has become much more valuable for municipal use than in farming. The fact that people in cities in Southern California pay one hundred times more for water than farmers in the Palo Verde Valley is one measure of the potential gain from water transfers.[60]

The IID, operating at the Mexican border, uses large amounts of water, and both Los Angeles and San Diego and their surrounding metropolitan areas would like to have a portion of that water. The IID was formed as an irrigation district in 1911 and in 1928 gained more water when the All American Canal, one of the major diversions from the Colorado River, was constructed. The IID, one of the nation's largest irrigation districts, delivers water to 495,000 acres of cropland and 25,000 acres of towns and parks.[61] It also generates power that is sold to forty-five thousand customers.

The water rights held by the IID are complex. The IID is actually third in line in terms of entitlements to Colorado River water, with earlier rights held by the Palo Verde Irrigation District and the Yuma Project Reservation District. However, the IID has generally been able to claim 2.8 million acre-feet (AF) a year, partly because it has first priority on water flowing through the All American Canal. This claim is less secure than it might appear, however, because the Bureau of Reclamation governs Lake Mead, and releases from Lake Mead eventually pass through the All American Canal and eventually are received by the IID. Thus Bureau cooperation is required for the IID to receive its water, a factor that became important in a 2003 agreement discussed later.

The first significant transfer of water out of the IID was initiated in 1985, when the MWD, which includes Los Angeles and San Diego, negotiated a forty-year agreement to receive 100,000 AF a year, with the price set at $100 per AF for the first ten years.[62] However, the IID governing board refused to approve the contract, and it wasn't until 1989 that a final agreement was reached.[63] The water transferred was to come from conservation measures undertaken by the IID. This was problematic though, since the beneficial use doctrine, as interpreted by the California courts, meant that if a farmer used less, he was entitled to less; in other words, he forfeited the right to the water.[64] The IID did secure the right to transfer conserved water in this instance, but the issue of ownership rights of future conserved water was left unresolved.[65]

The 1989 agreement is seen by some as a win-win situation and as a model for future water transfers.[66] But local opposition to the transfer arose soon after the agreement was reached, and it took an additional "five years of negotiations, three agreements, and a side letter from the MWD related to water banking to make the original agreement work."[67] "Although the IID–MWD agreement is hailed as an important example of a water-market transaction, in its details one finds complex arrangements involving substantial risks for both sides and numerous security features . . . Ultimately, no water *rights* transfer ever occurred."[68]

In 1995, the San Diego County Water Authority (SDCWA) began to negotiate with the IID for the transfer of water from agricultural to municipal and industrial uses. This transfer was complicated by the fact that San Diego had no way to transport the water unless the MWD agreed to the use of its canals.[69] Originally, the MWD agreed to deliver the water for $141 per AF,[70] but by the time the final agreement was reached, SDCWA was paying $250 for delivery and another $250 for the purchase of the water.

In 2003, after eight years of negotiation, appeals to the state government for subsidies, and controversy over the circumstances under which the IID actually had the right to transfer water, agreement on delivery of water from IID to SDCWA was reached. However, it was the direct involvement of the federal government through the Secretary of the Interior that finally forced agreement. Secretary Norton threatened to cut California's share of

Colorado River water by 11 percent if the IID didn't agree to move water to San Diego. The threat was based upon the claim of the Interior Department that it could take away IID water because it wasn't putting all of it to "reasonable and beneficial use."[71]

With the real possibility that water would be lost, the IID finally agreed to the water transfer. However, in order to make the deal work, the state provided a subsidy of $235 million. Also, both the public interest and the public trust doctrines created enough uncertainty about the clarity of rights that the SDCWA and the IID each contributed $10 million to a fund to mitigate third-party effects.[72] In 2007, the SDCWA, because of the threat of liability for economic damages under these doctrines, contributed another $29.5 million to the pool for the third-party mitigation fund.[73] Third-party effects are notoriously difficult to define and the concept has no clear principle for determining who should receive compensation and for what amount. Almost anyone in Southern California could claim they were affected in some way by water transfers from IID to SDCWA, either positively or negatively. Furthermore, despite the fact that $20 million was initially allocated to cover the impact of transfers on individuals or firms who were not part of the agreement, a comprehensive study found than the net impact was actually a net gain to third parties of $1.1 million.[74]

The process of transferring water from the IID to municipal uses is a prime example of the tragedy of the anticommons. The tragedy did not prevent the transfer, but only because there was an enormous difference between the value of water in agricultural uses and in urban uses and because the Secretary of the Interior forced it to happen. Even so the process was long, arduous, and costly. Furthermore, the transfer is still subject to lawsuits that may make fulfillment of the terms of the agreement difficult. In September 2006, in response to a suit brought by environmentalists and Mexican agricultural interests, the Ninth Circuit Court of Appeals stopped the lining of the All American Canal. The lining was to prevent seepage and was an important part of the water conservation activities necessary to release water to the SDCWA.[75]

Case Study—Santa Fe, The Middle Rio Grande Conservancy District, and The Estancia Basin

If we don't get this water, I'm certain somebody else will.

Santa Fe Mayor Larry Delgado[76]

If the State Engineer's Office received enough letters against this, they will HAVE to grant us a hearing. This will give us the time we need to be able to go through the proper channels to get this water basin adjudicated so that no more water could be pumped out of this valley in the future.

Shellie Langley, Ewing area resident of the Estancia Basin[77]

New Mexico is a relatively arid state with significant water scarcity issues that are exacerbated by the state's rapid population growth.[78] Most of the growth in New Mexico has been in the urban areas, particularly in the metropolitan areas of Santa Fe and Albuquerque.[79] In 2006, 76.5 percent of the New Mexico's population lived in urban areas.[80] Despite the overwhelming concentration of people in urban areas, water is primarily allocated to agriculture. Ninety-five percent of surface water diversions and 80 percent of groundwater withdrawals in New Mexico are for irrigation.[81] As a result, transferring water from agricultural to urban uses has become a major issue in New Mexico, and the New Mexico Office of State Engineer (NMOSE) has estimated that a 10 percent reduction in agricultural irrigation would allow New Mexico's population to double.

Due to the lack of rainfall and increase in urban growth, obtaining and maintaining an adequate supply of water are important civic objectives for the city and county governments of Santa Fe and Albuquerque.[82] Albuquerque traditionally met its water needs by pumping groundwater from its underlying aquifer but discovered in the 1980s that it was mining the aquifer.[83] Albuquerque has temporarily solved most of its water problems and reduced its reliance on groundwater due to the Bureau of Reclamation's San Juan–Chama Project, which, through a system of diversion structures and tunnels, diverts water from the Colorado River Basin in Colorado to the Rio Grande Basin in New Mexico.[84] When the San Juan–Chama Project was first authorized by Congress in 1962, the Bureau experienced difficulty finding buyers for the water. However, Albuquerque was one of the first buyers in 1963 and contracted for the delivery of 48,200 AF per year (AF/yr), or almost half of the average annual diversion of approximately 100,000 AF.[85] Albuquerque is in the process of building diversion facilities, pipelines, a pumping station, and a water treatment plant that will allow the city to divert 94,000 AF/yr, consume 47,000 AF/yr, and return the remainder of the San Juan–Chama Project water to the Rio Grande through a sewage treatment plant.[86]

The Santa Fe area will not benefit substantially from the San Juan–Chama Project since the city and county contracted for only 5,605 AF in 1976.[87] Further, "Santa Fe allows about half of its San Juan–Chama allocation—about 2,600 AF—to flow down the Rio Grande to offset the effects of the city's ground-water pumping on the river and downstream water users."[88] As a result, local governments in the Santa Fe region are actively searching for other sources of water to meet their current needs and to avoid growth constraints. Given the large percentage of water used in agriculture, both the city and the county have sought to buy or lease water rights from farmers in rural areas across the state, and this has placed both the buyers and the sellers at the crux of the water controversy issues in New Mexico.

The Santa Fe region's demand for water is increasingly reflected in the purchase price for water rights. Since 2005, the city of Santa Fe requires large residential or mixed-use developments to transfer water rights to the city as a precondition to receiving building permits.[89] According to Gary Ehlert, executive officer of the Santa Fe Homebuilders Association, a developer in 2008 paid between $30,000 and $40,000 for an acre-foot of water.[90] In 2007, farmers in the Middle Rio Grande Conservancy District (MRGCD) south of the Santa Fe region were paying $28 per AF for their water, even though the WaterBank, a water rights brokerage firm based in Albuquerque, had sent letters to landowners in the MRGCD offering to buy adjudicated water rights for up to $14,000 per AF.[91] With farmers paying tens of dollars per acre-foot for water for irrigation and developers, cities, and urbanized counties paying tens of thousands of dollars per acre-foot for water for residential and commercial uses, it is clear that there would be huge gains from trade. However, due to the tragedy of the anticommons, water transfers from the MRGCD are neither quick nor certain.

The Middle Rio Grande Conservancy District

The MRGCD is a multipurpose special water district created in 1925 to address problems arising from and related to agricultural irrigation, including flood protection, river control, and land drainage.[92] It extends for 150 miles from the Cochiti Dam in the north to the Bosque del Apache National Wildlife Refuge in the south and encompasses most of the Middle Rio Grande Valley. Within its boundaries are four counties, five cities, including Albuquerque, New Mexico's largest city, and over a quarter of New Mexico's population.[93] Although the MRGCD contains 278,000 acres and 128,787 of those acres are irrigable, only about 70,000 acres are actually irrigated by the 11,000 farmers who receive water from the MRGCD.[94] To deliver this water, the MRGCD manages and maintains four diversion dams and reservoirs, 834 miles of canals and ditches, and 404 miles of riverside drains.[95] The construction of water storage facilities by the MRGCD and the reduction in discharge from agricultural irrigation due to the expansion of the Albuquerque metropolitan area decreased the risk of flooding. The MRGCD's success in reclaiming lands combined with municipal groundwater pumping that has lowered the water table in urban Bernalillo County means that drainage is no longer an important concern.[96] Instead, the MRGCD exists today primarily to support agricultural irrigation. However, as the number of acres devoted to agriculture decreases due to urbanization, the MRGCD has also "portrayed itself as a guardian of riparian habitat, an essential partner in protecting the ecology of the river through its lands and ditch systems, an enhancer of recreational values, and a major source of recharge to the Albuquerque aquifer."[97]

Since 1956, the NMOSE has considered the Rio Grande Basin to be fully appropriated.[98] Permits are no longer issued for new surface water appropriations, and permits for new groundwater diversions are determined on a case-by-case basis in accordance with conjunctive management principles. Growing municipalities seeking water must retire or transfer existing water rights.[99] Given its location near and among cities experiencing rapid growth, such as Albuquerque and Santa Fe, and the differentials in value between agricultural and urban uses of water, the MRGCD should be a likely source of water for these growing municipalities. However, several factors combine to create an anticommons that inhibit the transfer of water from the MRGCD.

The first factor is the mixed and uncertain nature of the ownership of water rights within the MRGCD. When the New Mexico water code was enacted in 1907, existing water rights created by diversion and beneficial use were affirmed and did not require a permit from the NMOSE to confirm their priority date (N.M. Stat. § 72-1-2 (2000)). The MRGCD has taken the position that some of these pre-1907 water rights are appurtenant to 80,785 acres of land within the MRGCD.[100] However, since pre-1907 water rights are vested in the user and predate the creation of the MRGCD, individual landowners who hold such rights within the MRGCD can transfer them without obtaining the approval of the MRGCD. While the MRGCD has agreed that pre-1907 rights are transferable subject only to the statutory transfer process, it has not taken such a position with regards to the small number of individual water rights represented by post-1907 permits issued by the NMOSE before the creation of the MRGCD.[101] As a result, the transferability of these water rights by individual users who have their water delivered by the MRGCD without the approval of the MRGCD is in doubt.

A third set of water rights was created when the MRGCD was organized.[102] The MRGCD claims water rights based on its mission and the language of the Conservancy Act. Since the MRGCD was formed to prevent floods, regulate stream channels and the flow of streams, divert and control watercourses, drain and reclaim inundated lands, and provide for irrigation and develop irrigable agricultural land (N.M. Stat. § 73-14-4(A) (2008)), any new water rights arising from new water supplies developed in connection with these statutory responsibilities belong to the MRGCD and not to individual irrigators.[103] Issues have also arisen about the validity of the MRGCD's water rights because farmers within the MRGCD are irrigating lands that represent less than 60 percent of the MRGCD's claimed water rights. MRGCD takes the position that its water rights are not subject to forfeiture or abandonment.[104] According to the Conservancy Act, "The rights of the [conservancy] district to the waters of the district, or the use thereof, or the land within the district and property owned by it shall not be lost by the district by prescription or by adverse possession, or for nonuse of the waters" (N.M. Stat. § 73-17-21 (2008)). The New Mexico Supreme Court ruled that this provision of the Conservancy Act "precludes abandonment of [a] conservancy district's priority by non-use," noting that the "loss of the priority date is often tantamount to loss of the water right" (*City of Raton v. Vermejo Conservancy Dist.*, 101 N.M. 95, 100, 678 P.2d 1170, 1175 (1984)).

Despite legal precedent and the statutory language of the Conservancy Act, several counterarguments have been raised concerning the validity of the MRGCD's water rights due to nonuse. First, since the New Mexico Supreme Court has only addressed the common-law doctrine of abandonment, its decision does not preclude the MRGCD's loss of water rights due to nonuse under statutory provisions in the water code related to forfeiture or under the public interest standard or the public welfare doctrine.[105] Second, critics have accused the MRGCD of being inefficient in its use of water and, therefore, subject to the laws of water rights due to waste. The total effect of all these issues is to cloud the title of water rights held by the MRGCD and make their transferability less certain since all of these issues would be raised by multiple parties in the statutory transfer process.

In addition to these transferability issues, the MRGCD has a strong commitment to maintaining control over the region's water and in restricting its use to agricultural irrigation. The MRGCD's stated policy is to see as much water as possible remain in agriculture. According to Dennis Domrzalski, spokesperson for the MRGCD, "We want to keep this valley forever green, and the way we do that is to keep agricultural land in production, and the way we do that is to keep water available to those lands."[106] The Middle Rio Grande Water Plan notes that "the 1930 water rights developed by the [MRGCD] have never been available for transfer."[107] The MRGCD's policies are reinforced by the NMOSE's policies of not allowing individual farmers to sell water rights arising from the MRGCD's permits, even though there is no state law prohibiting such transfers.[108]

Also, *acequias*, traditional Hispanic community ditch associations, have a role in the anticommons effect associated with transfers of water rights from the MRGCD. At the time of its formation, seventy-eight existing, independent *acequia* systems were incorporated into the MRGCD, and the MRGCD manages most of the *acequias* in its four-county region.[109] In the United States, the *acequia* culture is unique to northern New Mexico and southern Colorado and reflects a tradition in which water is viewed as a community resource, and decisions about water are made collectively. To support this *acequia* culture, the New Mexico state legislature granted each *acequia* the right to veto any proposed transfers of water rights out of its ditch system (N.M. Stat. § 72-4-24.1 (2008)).

Finally, the Bureau of Reclamation affects the transferability of water from the MRGCD through its claims of ownership to water and water-related infrastructure. The MRGCD contracted with the Bureau in 1963 for 20,900 AF of water per annum from the San Juan–Chama Project. Water from the Bureau carries with it all the uncertainties described earlier in the section "The Bureau of Reclamation" (see page 152)." For example, the Bureau's Web site states that the water contracted by the MRGCD is "supplemental water . . . provided for irrigation," indicating that the water may not be transferable to other uses or may not be transferable if doing so would "impair the efficiency of the project for irrigation purposes."[110] In addition to issues about water, the MRGCD and the Bureau are engaged in an ongoing dispute over who owns much of the MRGCD's infrastructure, especially the El Vado Reservoir, the San Acacia Dam, and the Angastora Dam.[111] During the late 1920s and early 1930s, the MRGCD constructed its four major diversion dams.[112] However, during the 1940s, the MRGCD became financially unstable and was unable to maintain its infrastructure.[113] At the request of the MRGCD, the Bureau and the MRGCD entered into a contract in 1951 in which the Bureau reconstructed and improved the MRGCD's facilities and loaned the MRGCD $15,708,567 on an interest-free basis for fifty years so that it could retire its existing bonds.[114] In return, the Bureau received title to the MRGCD's dams, canals, and ditches.[115] Although the MRGCD paid off the debt in 1999, a federal district court ruled in 2005 that the Bureau continued to own the MRGCD's infrastructure since an act of Congress was required to transfer title back to the MRGCD.[116] As we described in "The Bureau of Reclamation," whenever the Bureau claims ownership rights, water transfers are extremely complicated since there is no clear mechanism by which reclamation water can be legally moved from one party to another.

The overall effect of all these transferability issues is to create an anticommons that makes the MRGCD's water unavailable to cities in the Middle Rio Grande Valley, even if the MRGCD were willing to transfer its water. As a result, the tragedy of the anticommons has forced growing urban areas such as Santa Fe to look to other geographic areas and entities for transfers of water rights, even if those sources are politically or hydrologically questionable.

Santa Fe discovered a double effect of the tragedy of the anticommons when it tried to buy two billion gallons of groundwater rights in the Estancia Basin, which borders the Middle Rio Grande Valley. The first effect was the tragedy of the anticommons in the MRGCD and the Middle Rio Grande Valley which drove Santa Fe to a source such as the Estancia Basin. The second effect occurred when Santa Fe tried to transfer water out of the Estancia Basin and experienced the tragedy of the anticommons in a very direct manner.

The Estancia Basin

The Estancia Basin is located roughly in the center of New Mexico, south of Santa Fe, and southeast of Albuquerque and consists of approximately 2,260 square miles. The western edge of the basin borders on the Middle Rio Grande Basin. As a closed basin, it does not receive any surface water from outside its bowl-shaped boundaries, does not contain any perennial streams, and does not release any surface waters to other watersheds or basins.[117] Most of the Estancia Basin is rural and 97 percent of the water use in the basin is agricultural, although residential housing for Santa Fe and Albuquerque is expanding southward and eastward into the region. Since 1965, the NMOSE has treated the Estancia Basin as a mined basin because groundwater is pumped in excess of the natural recharge.[118]

During 2004, the city of Santa Fe negotiated with Sierra Waterworks LLC for the purchase and transfer of transfer water rights that had been used in the Estancia Basin. Sierra Waterworks had been incorporated in 2003 by a group of Estancia Basin farmers, including the then-incoming board president of the New Mexico Association of Conservation Districts, to construct and maintain reservoirs, canals, and pipelines.[119] The company was headquartered in Moriarty, a town in the Estancia Basin about 50 miles south of Santa Fe, and owned an 8,702-acre farm in the Estancia Basin that had been used for grazing and growing alfalfa and corn silage. Sierra Waterworks pumped 14,500 AF per year from wells located on the farm, which was within the NMOSE's estimates of 2.5 AF of water per irrigated acre.[120]

The proposal that was negotiated between the city and the company was announced by Santa Fe Mayor Larry Delgado on December 23, 2004.[121] Santa Fe would pay $27 million for a 51 percent ownership interest in the Sierra Waterworks' farm and its 7,200 AF per annum of associated water rights.[122] Sierra Waterworks would retain a 49 percent interest, and the farm and water rights would be held by Santa Fe and Sierra Waterworks as joint tenants, giving each party an undivided interest in the whole. Sierra Waterworks would sell its interest in the water rights to Santa Fe based on a reasonable market price per acre-foot, and Santa Fe would lease its interest in the remainder of the farm back to Sierra Waterworks, which would continue ranching operations using a small number of windmill-driven livestock wells.[123] To secure its option to the farm and water rights, Santa Fe would pay Sierra Waterworks $6 million over three years, which would either be applied to the $27 million purchase price if the transaction were finalized or would be forfeited if it weren't.[124] However, the total cost of obtaining the water was estimated at $127 million when an additional $100 million was included to pay for 65 miles of pipeline and rights of ways to transport the water from the Estancia Basin to the city and for a water treatment plant to desalinate the brackish water via a reverse osmosis process. Santa Fe anticipated funding the project infrastructure costs through a combination of long-term bonds and state and federal government assistance.[125] Water delivery was predicted to begin sometime between 2010 and 2012, but the water would be subject to the NMOSE's forty-year planning window for pumping groundwater out of a mined basin.[126]

The supporters of the proposal identified several benefits. First, the transfer of water rights would allow Santa Fe to slow the heavy rate of pumping from its current groundwater wells.[127] Second, the infrastructure created to transport the water to Santa Fe would create the backbone for a regional water system that could deliver water for residential, commercial, and industrial uses and spur economic development in the Estancia Basin.[128] Third, for many farmers, selling their water rights would be more profitable than continuing marginal agricultural activities.[129]

The announcement of the proposed transfer on the day before Christmas Eve in 2004 did not go unnoticed. An emergency meeting called by the Estancia Basin Water Planning Committee, a regional water resources advisory committee consisting of public officials and private citizens, on January 6, 2005, was moved from the county courthouse to the county fairgrounds to accommodate the more than two hundred people who attended. At the meeting, many spoke against the proposal and no one spoke in favor.[130] By mid-January 2005, the Torrance County Commission (representing the largest county by area in the Estancia Basin), as well as the town councils of the larger towns, had passed unanimously resolutions opposing the transfer and had drafted letters to send to the NMOSE.[131] The Estancia Valley Economic Development Association issued a statement indicating that an increase in water exports from the Estancia Basin would be counterproductive to its mission of promoting economic development while preserving the sustainability of the quality of life and unique characteristics of the Estancia Valley. The biggest setback for supporters of the proposal was the creation of the Estancia Basin Resources Association, a grassroots activist organization that opposed transfers from the Estancia Basin.[132] About two hundred people attended the first public meeting of the Estancia Basin Resources Association on January 14, 2005, and the group was instrumental in packing the subsequent Santa Fe City Council meetings with Estancia Basin and Santa Fe residents opposed to the transfer.[133]

The political firestorm proved to be too great for Mayor Delgado and his supporters. Passage of an ordinance by the Santa Fe City Council required two public hearings, and, at the first, only the Sierra Waterworks' president spoke in favor of the proposal.[134] At the second public hearing on January 26, 2005, action on the proposal was postponed indefinitely, and the city staff was directed to cease pursuing any further negotiations with Sierra Waterworks on the proposal.[135]

Since the proposal was defeated before the Santa Fe City Council, Sierra Waterworks never filed an application to transfer water rights with the NMOSE because the company never had a buyer. Although some of the arguments against the proposal, especially by Santa Fe residents, were critical of the economics of the deal and its impact on water rates when combined with the sixty million dollars Santa Fe had already committed to the San Juan–Chama Project, many of the arguments made in the media and before the Santa Fe City Council were dress rehearsals for the arguments the opponents anticipated making at hearings before the NMOSE. These arguments cumulatively created an anticommons in attempts to transfer water from agricultural to urban and other uses.

One of the major issues raised by a transfer of water rights that involves a change in the place and type of use is the legal validity of the water right itself.[136] Since water rights in the Estancia Basin have not been adjudicated and since the Estancia Basin Water Planning Committee estimates "that three or four times the amount of water rights are recognized by the NMOSE than have been beneficially used in the Estancia Basin,"[137] opponents were in a position to raise the issue of whether the Sierra Waterworks' water rights were "paper" rights that had either been abandoned or forfeited or whether they were "wet" rights supported by beneficial use.[138] In addition, questions were raised over whether Sierra Waterworks was pumping more water than needed for its agricultural (i.e., beneficial) use solely to have more water to transfer to Santa Fe.[139]

The New Mexico Water Code and the NMOSE's rules and regulations outline another set of issues available to opponents of a transfer of water rights. In evaluating a proposed water rights transfer, the NMOSE is required to evaluate whether transfers "can be made without detriment to existing water rights and are not contrary to conservation of water within the state and not detrimental to the public welfare of the state" (N.M. Stat. § 72-5-23 (2008); N.M. Code 19.26..2.11.B, Jan. 31, 2005). As a result, opponents of the proposed Sierra Waterworks transfer could question whether the pumping and exportation of groundwater from the Estancia Basin would negatively impact holders of senior water rights and whether it was consistent with water conservation, especially given the NMOSE's guidelines for the sustainability of the groundwater supply in the Estancia Basin as a closed, mined basin.

The public welfare requirement provided opponents of the Sierra Water-work–Santa Fe proposal, who did not have any water rights directly impacted by the transfer, with arguments to use against the transfer, especially since the phrase "public welfare" is not defined and is somewhat elastic. With an interbasin transfer, one issue raised by the public welfare requirement is whose public welfare—the welfare of the residents of the Estancia Basin, the welfare of the residents of Santa Fe, or the overall welfare of the citizens of New Mexico? After the Sierra Waterworks–Santa Fe water rights transfer was defeated, the Estancia Basin Regional Water Plan was updated to clarify that "the exportation of water from the Estancia Basin runs counter to the public welfare of the Estancia Basin" especially given "the inevitable supply versus demand deficiency" created by the mining of a closed basin.[140] However, the updated plan also notes that "the New Mexico State Water Plan (2003) suggests that the NMOSE reserves the right to implement water policies that may not be consistent with the public welfare of specific regions but that are consistent with the public welfare of the State of New Mexico."[141] To overcome these interbasin transfer issues in a public welfare review before the NMOSE, opponents of the proposed Sierra Waterworks–Santa Fe transfer were prepared to make the following arguments, which ultimately present the public welfare as a dichotomy between rural versus urban, agricultural versus residential and commercial, and poor versus rich:[142]

- The residents of the Estancia Basin are part of a long-standing community, and the farmers and ranchers of the Estancia Basin are currently making a contribution to New Mexico through their agricultural activities.
- The Estancia Basin has plans for future economic activity, perhaps industrial, commercial, and residential development linked to the growing communities near Albuquerque along the north western edge that will benefit New Mexico and that require keeping water in the Estancia Basin.
- Santa Fe already has groundwater available in the Espanola Basin and is attempting to mine the Estancia Basin simply to avoid mining its own aquifers. Thus a city with political power is attempting to take water from a region that has less political clout, and Santa Fe becomes to the Estancia Basin what Los Angeles was to the Owens Valley in the early 1900s.
- The Estancia Basin does not have enough water to meet its long-term needs since groundwater is currently being pumped faster than it is being replenished.

Although these arguments were made specifically with respect to the Estancia Basin transfer, they capture quite well many of the objections to water markets and hence are worth discussing in some detail.

The first argument, the long history of a type of economic activity in a particular location, does not mean resources shouldn't be transferred away from that activity if they are more valuable elsewhere. One of the functions of markets is to provide signals about the value of resources and reward individuals who move them from low- to high-valued uses. If one locks all resources into their historic use, economic development cannot take place.

Second, markets take into account future as well as present values. If there is an expectation that the water being sold to Santa Fe will have a higher value if left in the Basin, entrepreneurial foresight will act upon that perception, will bid the water away from those attempting to transfer it, and will profit when the future economic activity occurs.

Third, Santa Fe may have been attempting to buy Estancia Basin water to avoid pumping from its own aquifers. Again, however, market signals enable resource users to determine whether they are better off drawing on their own stock of a particular commodity or whether they should purchase the commodity in the marketplace. A well-functioning water market would allow water users to make appropriate decisions about drawing down their own inventory versus purchasing water in the marketplace.

The last objection to water markets is the only one with possible validity. Since well-defined water rights to groundwater have not been established in New Mexico, it is possible that the water being marketed represented a drawdown of the water stock. The answer to this problem is to better define rights so that it is clear what is being bought and sold when water rights are transferred.[143]

Although the arguments against the transfer were never made before the NMOSE, the Estancia Basin Resources Association did not disappear with the defeat of the proposal before the Santa Fe City Council and stands ready to assert these arguments. Each month, the organization studies reports issued by the NMOSE to determine if anyone in the Estancia Basin is selling water rights that will result in a transfer out of the Basin.[144] In 2006, the Estancia Basin Resources Organization had raised $55,000 toward its goal of developing a $120,000 war chest to fund future legal battles related to transfers from the Basin.[145]

In addition to its goal of creating a legal fund, the Estancia Basin Resources Organization also pursued legislation to protect the groundwater supply of the Estancia Basin. After extensive lobbying by the organization, the New Mexico legislature passed Senate Joint Memorial 17, highlighting the need for transfers of mined groundwater from the Estancia Basin to be "consistent with the public welfare of New Mexico and not contrary to the planning objectives within a regional water plan."[146] The memorial requests that the NMOSE, when evaluating applications to transfer groundwater from the Estancia Basin, require "proof of a need in the importing basin" and "proof that there are no alternative available in-basin sources of water to supply the region seeking to import ground water from the Estancia [B]asin."[147] A memorial is not a statute and is not presented to the governor for signature, hence the "request" made to the NMOSE. Since Senate Joint Memorial 17 was drafted with the assistance of both the Estancia Basin Resources Association and the NMOSE, and the State Engineer spoke in support of the memorial before the New Mexico Senate Rules Committee, the request becomes a part of standard operating procedure for the NMOSE. By providing yet another tool for opponents of transfers from the Estancia Basin, the memorial magnifies the anticommons effect on such transfers.[148]

Conclusion

The tragedy of the anticommons, a situation where several entities without use rights have the right to exclude new uses of a resource, explains an economic anomaly. In the face of increasing demand for water for urban and environmental uses in the western United States, water transfers out of agriculture have been fewer than one would expect based on price differentials, and most of those that have occurred have required extensive and very costly negotiations.[149] The potential for lawsuits that will negate any transfer contracts also exists.

The multiple exclusion rights are the result of the evolutionary path of water institutions and the expansion of certain legal doctrines, such as the public interest and public trust doctrines. Those doctrines were originally quite limited and had the effect of protecting the property rights of people who used navigable waters and who depended on return flows from other irrigators. The efforts to recognize the increased value of nonagricultural water could have been directed to better measuring rights through more precise quantification of the actual nature of the right and the amount of return flow. Instead the path has been one of increased ambiguity as to the legal standing of a water right. Along with this ambiguity came increased claims of legal standing in water transfer disputes by parties that never had it earlier. Both the public interest and public trust doctrines, as presently interpreted, present a wide variety of opportunities for numerous parties to claim injury from a water transfer.

To further complicate matters, the rules governing the operation of mutual companies and irrigation districts were designed to facilitate intraorganization movement of water, but also made transfer outside of the organization difficult. The Bureau of Reclamation was created explicitly to deliver water to agriculture so the rules governing transfer of Bureau water are ambiguous and replete with veto opportunities. Thus, it is accurate to say that in water markets, "'anticommons' is a useful metaphor for understanding how and why economic value can disappear into the 'black hole' of resource utilization."[150]

Notes

This chapter is a shortened and revised version of Stephen N. Bretsen and Peter J. Hill, "Water Markets as a Tragedy of the Anticommons," *William & Mary Environmental Law and Policy Review* 33 (2009): 723–83.

1. James Buchanan and Yong Yoon, "Symmetric Tragedies: Commons and Anticommons," *Journal of Law and Economics* 43 (2000): 2.
2. Ibid, 3–4.
3. Ibid.
4. Buchanan and Yoon, "Symmetric Tragedies," 2. Henry Smith argues that the fugitive nature of water leads to a combination of exclusion and governance rules under both the prior appropriation and riparian doctrines. With increasing and disparate demands for water, information costs may be reduced by using more governance rules under a system that starts primarily with exclusion rules, as is the case with prior appropriation. The combination of exclusion and governance rules creates what Smith calls a semicommons, where "a pattern of valuable uses requires extensive access by multiple parties" ("Governing Water: The Semicommons of Fluid Property Rights," *Arizona Law Review* 51 (2008): 476). While Smith's analysis is helpful, especially in understanding how multiple governance rules evolve, the difficulties in establishing workable water markets is evidence that

the development of those governance rules have created an institutional inefficiency—the tragedy of the anticommons.

5. Michael A. Heller, "The Tragedy of the Anticommons: Property in the Transition from Marx to Markets" *Harvard Law Review* 111 (1998): 621–88. See Heller's book, *Gridlock Economy* (New York: Basic Books, 2008), for additional examples of the anticommons.

6. Heller, "Tragedy of the Anticommons," 621.

7. *People v. Emmert*, 198 Colo. 137, 142, 597 P.2d 1025, 1028 (1979).

8. *California v. Riverside Superior Court*, 78 Cal. App. 4th 1019, 93 Cal. Rptr. 2d 276 (2000).

9. James N. Corbridge Jr. and Teresa A. Rice, *Vranesh's Colorado Water Law*, rev. ed. (Niwot: University Press of Colorado, 1999), 30.

10. Andrew P. Morriss, "Lessons from the Development of Western Water Law for Emerging Water Markets: Common Law vs. Central Planning," *Oregon Law Review* 80 (2001): 861–946.

11. Benjamin Klein, Robert G. Crawford, and Armen A. Alchian, "Vertical Integration, Appropriable Rents, and the Competitive Contracting Process," *Journal of Law and Economics* 21, no. 2 (1978): 297–326.

12. Stephen N. Bretsen, and Peter J. Hill, "Irrigation Institutions in the American West," *UCLA Journal of Environmental Law and Policy* 25 (2006/2007): 290–91.

13. Transactions costs are the costs of specifying, monitoring, enforcing, and trading property rights.

14. Commercial irrigation companies were important in the beginning of the irrigation history of the American West, but because of contracting problems between farmers and the irrigation companies, they were replaced by the mutual irrigation companies and irrigation districts. By 1978, commercial irrigation companies only provided water to 0.5 percent of the irrigated acres in the seventeen western states (see Bretsen and Hill, "Irrigation Institutions," Table 1).

15. Wells A. Hutchins, *Mutual Irrigation Companies*, U.S. Department of Agriculture Technical Bulletin No. 82 (Washington, DC: U.S. Government Printing Office, 1929).

16. Bretsen and Hill, "Irrigation Institutions," Table 1.

17. B. Delworth Gardner, "Institutional Impediments to Efficient Water Allocation," *Review of Policy Research* 5, no. 2 (1985): 353–63.

18. Gardner "Institutional Impediments," 357.

19. Hutchins, *Mutual Irrigation*.

20. Corbridge and Rice, *Vranesh's Colorado Water Law*, 286.

21. Wells A. Hutchins, *Summary of Irrigation-District Statutes of Western States*, U.S. Department of Agriculture Miscellaneous Publication No. 103 (Washington, DC: U.S. Government Printing Office, 1931), Table 3.

22. Bretsen and Hill, "Irrigation Institutions," Table 1.

23. John D. Leshy, "Special Water Districts—The Historical Background," *Proceedings of the Workshop on Special Water Districts* (Boulder: University of Colorado, September 12–13, 1983).

24. Edward P. McDevitt, "The Evolution of Irrigation Institutions in California: The Rise of the Irrigation District" (PhD. dissertation, Department of Economics, University of California, Los Angeles, 1994), Table 3.4.

25. Wells A. Hutchins, H. E. Shelby, and Stanley W. Voelker, *Irrigation-Enterprise Organization*, U.S. Department of Agriculture Circular No. 934 (Washington, DC, 1953).

26. Tim De Young, "Discretion Versus Accountability: The Case of Special Water Districts," *Proceedings of the Workshop on Special Water Districts* (Boulder: University of Colorado, September 12–13, 1983).

27. The constitutionality of restricted and weighted voting systems in irrigation districts was upheld by the U.S. Supreme Court under the rationale that one-person, one-vote requirements do not apply to special purpose districts acting as a business enterprise and benefiting a specific group of landowners (*Ball v. James*, 455 U.S. 355 (1981)).

28. For a more complete discussion of the IID–MWD transfer, see the case study later in this chapter.

29. Robert Glennon et al., "Arizona's Water Future: Where Will the Water Come From?" Unpublished manuscript, 2006.

30. As with the public interest doctrine, this may have originally been designed to protect water rights holders who depended on return flows for a portion of their water. The rule has now been expanded far beyond the consumptive use/return flow issue.

31. Richard W. Wahl, *Markets for Federal Water: Subsidies, Property Rights, and the Bureau of Reclamation* (Washington, DC: Resources for the Future, 1989), Table 1.2.

32. Paul W. Gates, *History of Public Land Law Development* (Washington, DC: Public Land Law Review Commission, 1968).

33. John D. Leshy, "Irrigation Districts in a Changing West—An Overview," *Arizona State Law Journal* (1982): 345–76.

34. Leshy, "Special Water Districts."

35. Bretsen and Hill, "Irrigation Institutions," 318.

36. Reed D. Benson, "Private Rights and Public Authority Over Reclamation Project Water," *Virginia Environmental Law Journal* 16 (1997): 363–427.

37. Ibid., 363–64.

38. Ibid., 367.

39. Ibid.

40. Ibid., 397.

41. Bruce Driver, "The Effect of Reclamation Law on Voluntary Water Transfers," *33 Rocky Mountain Miner Law Institute. 26-1-26-40 (1987).*

42. Wahl, *Markets for Federal Water*. Thirty-four contracts represent a small sample of the over four thousand water contracts under which the Bureau of Reclamation delivers water to users. The contracts examined were "chosen with the assistance of the Bureau's contracting officials to represent a wide variety of geographic areas and contracting circumstances" (see Wahl, *Markets for Federal Water*, 156).

43. The original user often has repayment obligations much smaller than would exist for the new user of the water since farmers do not pay interest charges on Bureau of Reclamation debt and farmers are also subject to "ability to pay" legislation. As a result, the Bureau of Reclamation water delivered to farmers is heavily subsidized (Wahl, *Markets for Federal Water*). If the water is transferred to a nonagricultural use, these subsidies cease and the new user must pay a much higher cost for delivery of the water.

44. Wahl, *Markets for Federal Water*, 167.
45. Benson, "Private Rights," 399.
46. Driver, "The Effect of Reclamation," 26–29; Wahl, *Markets for Federal Water*, 157.
47. Lawrence J. MacDonnell, "Transferring Water Uses in the West," *Oklahoma Law Review* 43 (1990): 119.
48. Gary D. Libecap, *Owens Valley Revisited* (Stanford, CA: Stanford University Press, 2007).
49. Joseph L. Sax et al., *Legal Control of Water Resources: Cases and Materials*, 3rd ed. (St. Paul, MN: West Group, 2000), 236.
50. A. Dan Tarlock, James N. Corbridge Jr., and David H. Getches, *Water Resource Management: A Casebook in Law and Public Policy*, 5th ed. (New York: Foundation Press, 2002).
51. Sax et al., *Legal Control*, 233.
52. See Ariz. Rev. Stat. § 45-153 (LexisNexis 2008); Cal. Water Code § 1255 (Deering 2007); Idaho Code Ann. § 42-203A(5)(e) (LexisNexis 2008); Kan. Stat. Ann. § 82a-711 (LexisNexis 2008); Neb. Rev. Stat. § 46-234 (LexisNexis 2008); Nev. Rev. Stat. Ann. § 533.370(5) (LexisNexis 2008); N.M. Stat. § 72-5-7 (2008); N.D.Cent. Code § 61-04-06(4) (LexisNexis 2008); Or. Rev. Stat. § 537.170(6) (LexisNexis 2007); S.D. Codified Laws § 46-2A-9 (Lexis Nexis 2008); Tex. Water Code Ann. § 11.134(a)(3)(C) (LexisNexis 2007); Utah Code Ann. § 73-3-8(1)(a)(iii) (LexisNexis 2008); Wash. Rev. Code § 90.03.290(1) (LexisNexis 2008); Wyo. Stat. Ann. § 41-4-503 (LexisNexis 2008).
53. Sax et al., *Legal Control*, 229n15.
54. Ibid., 250.
55. Similar restrictions have arisen at the county level, with twenty-two of the fifty-eight counties in the state enacting ordinances that require permits to export groundwater. These restrictions are largely directed at third-party effects, or pecuniary externalities. (See Ellen Hanack, *Who Should Be Allowed to Sell Water in California? Third Party Issues and the Water Market* [San Francisco, CA: Public Policy Institute of California, 2003].)
56. Shannon A. Parden, "The Milagro Beanfield War Revisited in *Ensenada Land and Water Association v. Sleeper*: Public Welfare Defies Transfer of Water Rights," *Natural Resources Journal* 29 (1989): 861–76.
57. B. Delworth Gardner, "Weakening Water Rights and Efficient Transfers," *Water Resources Development* 19, no. 1 (2003): 7–19.
58. Gardner, "Weakening Water Rights."
59. Brent M. Haddad, *Rivers of Gold: Designing Markets to Allocate Water in California* (Washington, DC: Island Press, 2000), 3.
60. Ibid., 66.
61. Ibid., 70.
62. Ibid., 75.
63. Tarlock, Corbridge, and Getches, *Water Resource Management*, 361.
64. Sax et al., *Legal Control*, 147–51.
65. Haddad, *Rivers of Gold*, 79. California has made several attempts to reduce the disincentive for water transfers through statutory revisions (see Brewer et al., "Law and the New Institutional Economics: Water Markets and Legal

Change in California, 1987–2005." Arizona Legal Studies, Discussion Paper No. 07-35, 2007, 5–6). However, there is still considerable uncertainty in this area. See Brian E. Gray, "The Shape of Transfers to Come: A Model Transfer Act for California," *Hastings West-Northwest Journal of Environmental Law and Policy* 4 (1996): 23, and Cal. Water Code § 386 (2007).

66. Tarlock, Corbridge, and Getches, *Water Resource Management*, 362.
67. Haddad, *Rivers of Gold*, 85.
68. Ibid., 92.
69. David Zetland, "Fighting at the Spigot: The Story of a Failing Public Water Cooperative," Experimental Social Science Laboratory (Xlab), Institute of Business and Economic Research, University of California Berkeley, 4, http://escholarship.org/uc/item/9mv6g0vb.
70. Sax et al., *Legal Control*, 646.
71. "Feds Warn Lawsuit May Cost Desert Farmers in Southern California Deeper Water Cuts," *U.S. Water News Online*, February 2003, http://www.uswaternews.com/archives/arcrights/3fedwar2.html.
72. Third-party effects, also known as pecuniary externalities, do not represent an inefficient allocation of resources. Almost all changes in resource allocation in a market economy have some negative effects. Either previous users of a resource have to pay higher prices when a competitor for the resource enters the market, or firms face lower prices for their product with new entrants into an industry. These types of economic change represent an increase in wealth for the economy overall.
73. Michael Gardner, "Water Authority Ups Its Ante to $40 Million," *San Diego Union Tribune*, May 8, 2007, http://www.signonsandiego.com/news/state/20070508-1842-cnswater.html.
74. David Sundig, David Mitchell, and Gordon H. Kubota, *Third-Party Impacts of Land Fallowing Associated With IID-SDCWA Water Transfer: 2003 and 2004*, prepared for San Diego County Water Authority (San Diego, CA, 2004).
75. "Courts Halt Construction on Canal near U.S.–Mexico Border," *U.S. Water News Online*, September 2006, http://uswaternews.com/archives/arcrights/6courhalt9.html.
76. John F. Huddy, "SF May Tap Into Salty Water." *Albuquerque Journal*, December 24, 2004. http://www.abqjournal.com/north/278425north_news12-24-04.htm.
77. Shelley Langley, "Fight to Keep Water in Estancia Basin," *Albuquerque Journal*, January 12, 2005, http://www.abqjournal.com/north/opinion/286959northoped01-12005.htm.
78. From 2000 to 2006, New Mexico's population increased at an annual rate of 7.5 percent compared to the national average of 6.4 percent (U.S. Census Bureau, *State and County QuickFacts: New Mexico*, http://quickfacts.census.gov/qfd/states/35000.html).
79. From 2000 to 2006, the population of the city of Santa Fe increased at an annual rate of 14.5 percent from 62,203 to 72,056 (U.S. Census Bureau, *QuickFacts: Santa Fe*, http://quickfacts.census.gov/qfd/states/35/3570500.html).
80. "The New Mexico Population," University of New Mexico, accessed June 29, 2008, http://www.unm.edu/~nvaldes/326/NMPop06.htm.

81. Susan S. Huston et al., *Estimated Use of Water in the United States in 2000*, U.S. Geological Survey Circular 1268 (U.S. Department of Interior, U.S. Geological Survey, 2004), http://pubs.usgs.gov/circ/2004/circ1268/, Tables 3 and 4.

82. Although the middle Rio Grande region receives less than ten inches of precipitation per year, the region contains "about two-fifths' of the state's population, and is the largest urban water user in the state" primarily due to Albuquerque (see NMOSE, *Middle Rio Grande Regional Water Plan: 2000–2050*, vol. 1 (August 2004), Summary (1) 1).

83. NMOSE, *Middle Rio Grande*, vol. 1, ch. 2, 2-9–2-15. The mining of groundwater may not be an economic constraint depending on the costs involved. In this case, it appeared groundwater supplies would be insufficient to maintain Albuquerque's population growth.

84. NMOSE, *Middle Rio Grande*, ch. 1, 1–2; "San Juan–Chama Project," U.S. Department of the Interior, Bureau of Reclamation, http://www.usbr.gov/projects/Project.jsp?proj_Name=San%20Juan-Chama%20Project&pageType=ProjectPage.

85. Tania Soussan, "San Juan–Chama Transfers Water from 3 Rivers to N.M.," *Albuquerque Journal*, June 1, 2003, http://www.abqjournal.com/drought/43927news06-01-03.htm.

86. "San Juan–Chama Drinking Water Project," Albuquerque Bernalillo County Water Utility Authority, http://www.abcwua.org/content/view/31/24/.

87. Soussan, "San Juan–Chama Transfers."

88. Russell Max Simon, "Area's Water Future Is Flush," *Albuquerque Journal*, September 20, 2006, http://www.abqjournal.com/north/494268north_news09-20-06.htm.

89. Laura Banish, "New Water-Rights Law Upsets Developers," *Albuquerque Journal*, July 28, 2005, http://www.abqjournal.com/north/375460north_news07-28-05.htm.

90. Gary Ehlert, executive officer of the Santa Fe Homebuilders Association, Santa Fe, NM, telephone interview by Peter J. Hill, July 7, 2008.

91. Juan Carlos Rodriguez, "Water Rights Adjudication Put on Hold," *Albuquerque Journal*, March 28, 2007, http://www. abqjournal.com/west/550157west_news03-38-07. The farmers in the MRGCD are being subsidized at $28 per AF (Rodriguez, "It's Rematch For MRGCD in Valencia," *Albuquerque Journal*, June 1, 2007, http://www.abqjournal .com/west/567553_news06-01-07.htm). One can calculate approximate costs of water for the MRGCD from its annual budgets. In 2007, the MRGCD had expenditures of $15.8 million and provided 345,000 AF of water. (Rodriguez, "It's Rematch"; Rodriguez, "Findings in Audit of MRGCD Improve," *Albuquerque Journal*, March 12, 2008, http://www.abqjournal.com/west/292762west_news03-12-08.htm). Thus, water costs are approximately $46 per AF. The figures vary somewhat from year to year depending on the amount of water delivered but are always several orders of magnitude less than the value of water in surrounding cities.

92. Stephen A. Thompson, "Urbanization and the Middle Rio Grande Conservancy District," *Geographical Review* 76, no. 1 (1986): 41.

93. Subhas Shah, *The Middle Rio Grande Conservancy District: Sustaining the Middle Valley for Over 70 Years, Water Growth and Sustainability: Planning for the 21st Century* (Las Cruces, NM: New Mexico State University/New Mexico Water Resources Research Institute, 2000), 2–3.
94. Michael Davis, "Irrigation Season 'Went Really Well,'" *Albuquerque Journal*, December 15, 2005, http://www.adqjournal.com/west/416664west_news12-15-05.htm; Shah, *Middle Rio Grande*, 3.
95. Shah, *Middle Rio Grande*, 3.
96. Lisa D. Brown, "The Middle Rio Grande Conservancy District's Protected Water Rights: Legal, Beneficial, or Against the Public Interest in New Mexico?" *Natural Resources Journal* 40, no. 1 (2000): 4–5; Thompson, "Urbanization."
97. John R. Brown, "'Whisky's fer Drinking' Is It? Resolving a Collective Action Dilemma in New Mexico," *Natural Resources Journal* 43 (Winter 2003): 207.
98. NMOSE, *Water Plan*.
99. NMOSE, *Middle Rio Grande, Administrative Area Guidelines for Review of Water Applications* (September 13, 2000), http://www.ose.state.nm.us/doing-business/mrgbasin/crit9-13.pdf.
100. Shah, *Middle Rio Grande*, 5.
101. Ibid.
102. Two other water rights in the MRGCD are reserved water rights owned by the six Native American pueblos within the MRGCD that are senior to all other rights and individual and MRGCD groundwater rights based on wells drilled before 1956 or permits issued by the NMOSE after 1956 (see Shaw, *Middle Rio Grande*, 3).
103. Charles L. Dumars, David Seeley, and Tanya Scott, "The Middle Rio Grande Conservancy District Water Bank Leasing Program" (presentation at New Mexico Water Markets: A Seminar on Buying, Selling and Leasing Water Rights, Albuquerque, NM, May 14, 2007).
104. Shah, *Middle Rio Grande*, 4; Dumars, Seeley, and Scott, "Water Bank Leasing."
105. Brown, "Whisky's."
106. Rodriguez, "Water Rights Adjudication."
107. Ibid.
108. Tania Soussan, "Village Challenging Water Rights Policy," *Albuquerque Journal*, October 24, 2006, http://www.abqjournal.com/news/state/505466nm10-24-06.htm.
109. Thompson, "Urbanization"; Juan Carlos Rodriguez, "Acequia Users Join on Water Rights," *Albuquerque Journal*, October 28, 2006, http://www.abqjournal.com/west/506903west_news10-28-06.htm.
110. Leshy, "Special Water Districts," 360.
111. Tania Soussan, "Denial of Bid a Blow to Water District," *Albuquerque Journal*, July 27, 2005, http://www. abqjournal.com/news/metro/375253metr007-27-05.htm.
112. Dumars, Seeley, and Scott, "Water Bank."
113. Shah, *Middle Rio Grande*, 2.
114. Ibid.

115. Soussan, "Denial of Bid."
116. Ibid.
117. Estancia Basin Water Planning Committee (EBWPC), *Estancia Basin Regional Water Plan: Year 2008 Update (Final Draft)* (June 2008).
118. EBWPC, *Estancia Basin*, 4-11.
119. Huddy, "SF May Tap."
120. John T. Huddy and Kathy Louise Schuit, "Valley Residents Unite," *Albuquerque Journal*, January 13, 2005, http://www.abqjournal.com/mountain/287215mtnview01-13-05.htm.
121. Huddy, "SF May Tap."
122. Although the Sierra Waterworks pumped 14,500 AF per annum from its farm, the change in water rights from agricultural to urban use would have reduced the amount that could be transferred by approximately half since only about half the water that is used for irrigating crops is consumed and the rest evaporates into the atmosphere or seeps back into the ground. By transferring less than half of its water rights, Sierra Waterworks argued that the transaction would have no hydrological impact on the Estancia Basin.
123. Tania Soussan, "New Mexico Cities Covet Rural Water," *Albuquerque Journal*, January 23, 2005, http://www.abqjournal.com/drought/296333nm01-23-05.htm.
124. Huddy, "SF May Tap."
125. Ibid.
126. EBWPC, *Estancia Basin*.
127. Huddy, "SF May Tap."
128. Kathy Louise Schuit, "Some Say Water Plan to Benefit All," *Albuquerque Journal*, January 6, 2005, http://www.abqjournal.com/mountain/283919mtnview01-06-05.htm.
129. Soussan, "NM Cities Covet."
130. Huddy and Schuit, "Valley Residents." The Estancia Basin Water Resources Planning Committee remained neutral in the controversy and was criticized for its position and lack of preparedness in responding to the Sierra Waterworks–Santa Fe proposed transfer.
131. "Water Transfer Hot Topic," *Albuquerque Journal*, January 13, 2005, http://www.abqjournal.com/mountain/287203mtnview01-13-05.htm. The Santa Fe County Commission was upset about not being included in the development of the proposal, and the chairman, an Estancia Basin farm owner, personally opposed the proposed transfer.
132. Estancia Basin Resources Association, accessed June 9, 2011, http://www.estanciabasin.org/.
133. Kathy Louise Schuit, "Estancia Valley Politicians Lead Charge Against Water Plan," *Albuquerque Journal*, January 18, 2005, http://www.abqjournal.com/drought/291768north_news01-18-05.htm.
134. John T. Huddy and Laura Banish, "Council Hears Water Fears," *Albuquerque Journal*, January 13, 2005, http://www.abqjournal.com/north/287535north_news01-18-05.htm.
135. John T. Huddy, "Santa Fe City Council Kills Estancia Basin Water Plan," *Albuquerque Journal*, January 27, 2005, http://www.abqjournal.com/north/297535north_news01-27-05.htm.

136. See "Exclusion Rights in the Statutory Transfer Process and the Public Interest Standard."
137. EBWPC, *Estancia Basin*, 5-3.
138. Huddy and Schuit, "Valley Residents."
139. Soussan, "NM Cities Covet."
140. EBWPC, *Estancia Basin*, 5-5 and 8-7.
141. EBWPC, *Estancia Basin*, 8-7 and 8-8. See also, NMOSE and Interstate Stream Commission, *New Mexico State Water Plan 2003* (December 23, 2003), 4–12, 44–45, 48–49, http://www.ose.state.nm.us/water-info/NMWater Planning/2003StateWaterPlan.pdf.
142. Schuit, "Estancia Valley Politicians."
143. Vernon Smith, "Water Deeds: A Proposed Solution to the Water Valuation Problem," *Arizona Review* 26 (January 1977): 7–10.
144. Beth Hahn, "Valley Prepares to Protect Water," *Albuquerque Journal*, January 5, 2006, http://www.abqjournal.com/mountain/422358mtnview01-05-06.htm. 145. Hahn, "Valley Prepares."
146. Senate Joint Memorial 17 (2008), 3, http://www.sos.state.nm.us/2008/SJointMemorial17.pdf.
147. Ibid.
148. Laura Nesbitt, "Estancia Basin Memorial OK'd," *Albuquerque Journal*, February 21, 2008, http://www.abqjournal.com/mountain/287282mtn view02-21-08.htm.
149. See Brewer et al., "Law and the New," for a discussion of the increase in transfers over time.
150. Buchanan and Yoon, "Symmetric Tragedies," 2.

7

The Evolving Public Trust Doctrine: An Obstacle to Water Marketing

James L. Huffman

Introduction

Water markets cannot exist without secure and clearly defined property rights in water or in the use of water.[1] Water rights in the United States are defined in various ways, almost entirely by the states. In riparian law jurisdictions, owners of riparian land possess a right of reasonable use of the adjacent waters. In prior appropriation jurisdictions, rights to water are acquired by putting the water to beneficial use. Rights in the use of groundwater are acquired under parallel regimes; one has either the right to reasonable use of the water beneath one's land, or the right to capture any water to which one has legal access. Where conflicts arose historically, water rights were adjudicated by courts, making judicial opinions a source of water rights definition. Some states created recording systems to assist with rights definition. Today, all of these common-law or customary regimes are subject to state permit systems, the records of which give further testimony to existing rights.

But there is more to the water rights definition puzzle. First, there is the state police power to regulate in the public interest. It is long settled, under Supreme Court takings jurisprudence, that police power regulations can impose limits on the exercise of property rights without resulting in an unconstitutional deprivation of those rights. Only if regulations go "too far" do they infringe the Fifth Amendment takings clause (*Pennsylvania Coal v. Mahon*, 260 U.S. 393 (1922)).[2] Second, there are what Justice Scalia labeled background principles of nuisance and the common law (*Lucas v. South Carolina Coastal Council*, 505 U.S. 1003 (1992)).[3] These background principles help to define all property rights. They exist as implied limits on whatever rights the law (or one's deed) might otherwise recognize.

The most important background principle in the context of water is the public trust doctrine. As will be explained in detail later, the doctrine originated as a recognition of a public right of access to navigable waters, including those under which the submerged lands are privately owned, for the purposes of navigation and fishing. This public right is fairly viewed as a background principle because it is held to have existed prior to any private rights in water or riparian and submerged lands. Thus the public rights protected under the public trust doctrine, unless they have been alienated by the state, define a general limit on the scope of private rights.

By its nature, the police power might or might not be exercised, and the public purposes for which it is exercised will change over time depending on circumstances and perceived public needs. Thus, there is a degree of uncertainty about the precise scope and content of all property rights. Those who transact in property markets have no choice but to discount for these uncertainties, knowing (or hoping) that when regulation goes "too far," it will be found by a court to require compensation for taken property interests.

The uncertainties associated with background principles may or may not be similar to those resulting from the prospect of police power regulations. On the one hand, background principles may be understood to be whatever common-law rules existed prior to the acquisition of a property interest. Pursuant to this understanding, one looking to acquire a property interest can, with due diligence, determine with reasonable certainty the parameters and therefore the reasonable value of the property interest. On the other hand, background principles may be understood to be subject to change after a property interest is acquired. In that case, a purchaser of property faces significant uncertainty about the future parameters of the particular property interest and therefore great uncertainty about its value in the market place.

Obviously the latter understanding of background principles will be far less conducive to efficient market transactions than the former. Unfortunately, the trend is in the direction both of expanding police powers and of evolving background principles. Under those conditions, markets will be more difficult to establish and less efficient in their operation.

A Twenty-First Century Tale

On March 7, 1956, Casitas Municipal Water District entered into a contract with the United States providing for the United States to construct the Ventura River Project and for Casitas to repay construction costs over a forty-year period as well as all operation and maintenance costs. The contract also provided that Casitas "shall have the perpetual right to use all water that becomes available through the construction and operation of the Project," subject to the State of California granting to Casitas permits to appropriate the Project water. Those permits were issued by California on May 10, 1956, and the Project was completed and transferred to Casitas for operation in 1959 (*Casitas Municipal Water District v. United States*, 543 F.3d 1276 (Fed. Cir. 2008)).

Thirty-eight years later, the National Marine Fisheries Service (NMFS) listed the West Coast steelhead trout as an endangered species in the Project watershed under the Endangered Species Act of 1973 (ESA). Section 9 of the ESA makes it illegal to "take" any species listed as endangered under the act.[4] On May 2, 2003, the Bureau of Reclamation issued a directive (based on a NMFS biological opinion) advising Casitas that it was required to construct a fish ladder and divert Project water for the fish ladder.[5] This resulted in the permanent loss to Casitas of a fixed amount of water on an annual basis.

Casitas filed a lawsuit in the U.S. Court of Federal Claims asserting that there was a breach of contract on the part of the U.S. government and that their property rights in Project water had been taken without just compensation in violation of the Fifth Amendment to the U.S. Constitution. The Court of Federal Claims granted summary judgment in favor of the United States on both claims (*Casitas Municipal Water District v. United States*, 72 Fed. Cl. 746 (2006); *Casitas Municipal Water District v. United States*, 76 Fed. Cl. 100 (2007)). The U.S. Court of Appeals for the Federal Circuit affirmed the trial court holding on the breach of contract claim but reversed and remanded on the takings claim (543 F.3d at 1279). The government petitioned for rehearing by the three-judge panel that decided the case and also rehearing by the entire Federal Circuit. Both petitions were denied.

Except for a single sentence in Judge Mayer's dissent to the original Federal Circuit ruling on the takings question, there was no hint that the public trust doctrine was at issue in this case. That sentence suggests that the public trust doctrine lies just beneath the surface of virtually every claim that government has taken a property interest in water. "Whether Casitas has a vested property interest in the use of the water is a threshold issue to be determined under California water law," wrote Judge Mayer. "California subjects appropriative water rights licenses to the public trust and reasonable use doctrines, so Casitas likely has no property interest in the water, and therefore no takings claim" (543 F.3d at 1297).[6]

The implications of Judge Mayer's statement are far-reaching. If Casitas has no vested property interest in water it has used for over forty years after paying the full costs of its provision pursuant to a contract with the United States government, it is hard to imagine that any private party has a property interest in the use of water. Despite over a century and a half of legal and popular reference to the appropriative water *rights* doctrine and many centuries of Anglo-American recognition of riparian *rights* to water, Judge Mayer suggests that water users may have no rights at all in their uses because of the public trust and reasonable use doctrines. Such is the power of the public trust doctrine, at least as it has come to be understood by a few American courts. In this chapter, I will explain how those few courts, and the many academics and activists who egg them on, have misunderstood and distorted the common-law public trust doctrine. The implications for water markets are significant.

Because much of the history of the public trust doctrine has reference to riparian and submerged land, rather than water, it is important to understand the critical link between control over riparian and submerged lands on the one hand and control over water on the other. Until the rise of modern concerns for keeping water in streams and lakes for environmental protection reasons, the context of almost every public trust case was a conflict between some activity on the shore or on submerged lands and public use (either navigation or fishing) of the overlying waters. For example, the construction of a pier or a bridge located entirely on private property might obstruct navigation and thereby violate the public trust doctrine. Today, this doctrine that developed largely in the context of such conflicts is said, by many environmental protection advocates and some courts, to limit the exercise of state recognized water rights. For example, it is urged by species protection advocates that, pursuant to the public trust doctrine, private water rights do not include the right to divert water that is necessary to the survival of an endangered species.

Thus while much of the following discussion of the historic public trust doctrine has references to riparian and submerged lands, it has direct relevance to the nature and security of water rights as well.

Roman Foundations

Present-day commentary on the historical foundations of the public trust doctrine often quotes the following from Roman Emperor Justinian's codification of the laws of Rome: "Things common to mankind by the law of nature, are the air, running water, the sea, and, consequently, the shores of the sea; no man therefore is prohibited from approaching any part of the seashore . . . ."[7] From this statement, one could easily conclude that under Roman law, no individual could have exclusive rights in the seashore, or in the air and running water, as mentioned.

That understanding of Roman law dominates modern claims of inalienable public rights in at least the resources mentioned by Justinian. For example, Professors Smith and Sweeney write that "under a remarkable philosophy of natural resource preservation, the Romans implemented a concept of 'common property' and extended public protection of the air, rivers, sea, and seashores, which were unsuited to private ownership and dedicated to the use of the general public."[8] In other words, some things simply cannot be privately owned. The public has a common right of access to these things, and if scarcity should make it necessary to apportion use among members of the public to avoid the tragedy of the commons, some system of public allocation, not private property and markets, must be the solution.

But Justinian did not end his sentence with the assertion that no man could be excluded from the seashore. Rather, immediately after stating that "no man is prohibited from approaching any part of the seashore," he went on to say: "whilst he abstains from damaging farms, monuments, [and buildings], which are not in common as the sea is."[9] Thus, Justinian's codification of Roman law on access to air, running water, the sea, and the seashore stated that no person could be excluded except from existing private enclosures. The unavoidable implication is that these public resources to which all had a right of access could be privatized (as we might say today) to the exclusion of the public. Indeed, the public rights of access noted by Justinian existed "*unless* and *until* a private person or the state required exclusive control of the resource."[10]

While modern advocates for expansive public rights in various resources urge that the Roman concept of *res communes* had reference to resources held in common by the public, the reality is that under Roman law *res communes* (things common to all) had little to distinguish it from *res nullius* (things owned by no one). In either case, these things were free for the taking and for legal conversion to private property, or to the exclusive use of the Emperor.

Thus, the widely asserted claim that the public trust doctrine originated with the Romans is pure mythology. As Patrick Deveney explains:

> Roman law was innocent of the idea of trusts, had no idea at all of a "public" (in the sense we use the term) as the beneficiary of such a trust, allowed no legal remedies whatever against state allotment of land, exploited by private monopolies everything (including the sea and the seashore) that was worth exploiting, and had a general idea of public rights that is quite alien to our own.[11]

The fact that private title in the seashore could be acquired under Roman law did not mean, however, that the public had no rights relative to waters that might be affected by exclusive private use. Obstructions to navigation, docking, and shoreline footpaths and diversion or blocking of natural water flows could be enjoined in some cases or remedied by damages in other cases.[12] In other words, the Roman law with respect to public access to water was very similar to the laws of England that developed several hundred years later.

English Common Law

Two provisions of Magna Carta are said to provide further pedigree for the modern public trust doctrine, although, like Roman law, the connection is far less than claimed. Chapter 16 states that "no riverbanks shall be placed in defense from henceforth except such as were so placed in the time of King Henry . . . by the same places and the same bounds as they were wont to be in his time."[13] As with most of Magna Carta, this provision was not an assertion of public rights against the king, rather it was intended to curtail the king's practice of requiring riparian landowners (the barons who were the other party of interest in the Magna Carta negotiations) to repair, at their expense, roads and bridges necessary to the king's fishing outings on closed ("in defense") waters. Not until the late nineteenth century would Chapter 16 come to be understood as a prohibition on the king's retention or grant of exclusive fisheries, a prohibition that did not guarantee a right of public access to fresh water fisheries, since to this day inland fisheries in Britain are owned by the riparian landowners.

Chapter 23 of Magna Carta, which prohibits fish weirs except on the seashore, was intended to protect the barons' private inland fisheries from the king's placement of weirs to block fish passage for his personal benefit. If Chapter 23 had anything to do with public access to tidal waters, it was its implicit confirmation that exclusive private rights existed in those waters. As Lord Hale observed: "The exception of weares [sic] upon the sea-coast[s] . . . makes it appear that there might be such private interests not only in point of liberty, but in point of propriety on the sea-coast and below the low-water mark."[14]

Thus, Chapter 16 confirmed private rights in inland waters and fisheries, while Chapter 23 did the same with respect to coastal lands and waters, making both provisions of Magna Carta "thin reeds upon which to rest an expansive public trust doctrine."[15] It is not surprising, therefore, that early English law generally provided little foundation for modern visions of the public trust doctrine. The modern doctrine relies heavily on the fact of state title to submerged lands, but the concept of state title was unknown to English law. As in Rome, whose law was introduced to England in the thirteenth century by Bracton, land, whether or not submerged, was either common (meaning free for the taking) or private. In English theory, all common lands were acquired by the king, in his private capacity, at the Norman Conquest. This meant that all private titles derived, though mostly only in theory, from crown grants. While the king did make formal grants, including to submerged and riparian lands, most unclaimed lands were in fact free for the taking. Despite the absence of a formal crown grant, title to such appropriated lands was generally recognized as a legal fiction. In other words, mere possession of most land was presumed to be evidence of a crown grant, though everyone knew there had never been a grant, in fact.

Importantly, for public trust doctrine purposes, the king's claim of title in any lands was in his personal or proprietary, not sovereign, capacity. The only difference between the king and other private property owners was that he owned a lot more than anyone else. In his capacity as sovereign, however, the king held no lands in trust for the public or for any other purpose.[16]

That the king held no lands in trust for the public is important to modern public trust theory because the states' title to submerged land on which the modern doctrine significantly rests is said to derive from the crown's title prior to American independence. But the states succeeded to the king's sovereign powers not his personal property. No title to submerged land could have passed when the states assumed the king's sovereignty. Of course, English law evolved over the post-Magna Carta centuries, but at the time of American independence, the law with respect to title to submerged lands remained little changed from the time of Magna Carta except for the seventeenth-century assertion by John Selden that the *mare clausum* (the closed sea) was crown property.[17] This concept would later be the foundation for national territorial claims in the ocean, but at the time, the English king's claim of title to the sea and its submerged lands was no different than his proprietary claim to uplands. As with the king's uplands, submerged lands could be granted with no legal harm to the public.

What did emerge, but not until the end of the eighteenth century, was a prima facie rule of crown title to submerged coastal lands, including all lands affected by the ebb and flow of the tides. That rule, which is frequently misunderstood to be a precursor to a public trust prohibition on state alienation of submerged lands, required private claimants to prove the existence of an express grant from the crown. Ironically, the rule came into existence not to preserve public access through the sovereign's title, but as a means for the king to take from private claimants lands which they had long occupied but to which they had no express grant of title. Later, it would become a rule designed to assure that the public interest in commercial navigation would only be affected by private claims deriving from express crown grants.

For nineteenth-century Americans, the most relied-upon authority on the law relating to navigable waters and submerged lands was Matthew Hale's 1670 treatise on the law of the sea.[18] Hale described three distinct legal interests in coastal lands: the *jus privatum* held by individuals or the crown; the *jus regium* or royal right, which today we would call the police power; and the *jus publicum,* which are the rights of the public. Of the public rights Hale wrote: "The people have a publick interest . . . of passage and repassage with their goods by water, and must not be obstructed by nuisances or impeached by exactions."[19] Thus, at the time of American independence, the law of England, which was also the law of the American colonies, allowed for private ownership of coastal land subject to a public right of commercial navigation over and past those lands and subject to the power of the king or state to enjoin or remove any obstructions to such navigation. These were important and clearly defined limits on the scope of proprietary interests (whether private or state) in coastal lands.

Early American Adaptations to English Law

English law was "received" as the law of every American state after independence. It was a practical solution to what would otherwise be a massive challenge of creating a legal system from scratch, made all the more sensible since it was already the law of the land during the colonial period. But not everything was the same in America as in England, so modifications were necessary and inevitable. With respect to rights in coastal and inland waters and in submerged lands, the topographical circumstances in North America and the beginnings of the Industrial Revolution required some adaptation of traditional English law.

The importance of water-based transportation to commerce was magnified by industrialization and the associated growth in interstate and international trade. In the United States, particularly with west-ward expansion, inland waterways took on far greater importance than in the British Isles. Certainly England had some inland waterways, but most were affected by the tides, which led to a general association of navigability with tidal waters. Under English law, the significance of waters being navigable was that the *jus publicum* applied, meaning that the public had a right to unobstructed navigation and that, pursuant to the prima facie rule, title to the underlying lands was presumed to be in the crown absent proof of an express grant to a private claimant. But the public right to commercial navigation existed without regard to ownership of the submerged lands.

In the United States, the prima facie rule was understood to establish state title to submerged lands rather than to function as a presumption that the state has title unless private claimants prove otherwise. In an 1805 case, New York's highest judicial officer, Chancellor James Kent, stated that "by the rules and authorities of the common law, every river where the sea does not ebb and flow, was an inland river not navigable, and belonged to the owners of the adjoining soil" (*Palmer v. Mulligan*, 3 Cai. R. 307, 2 A.D. 270 (N.Y. Sup. Ct. 1805)). To the extent Kent was correct in asserting that nontidal waters were not navigable under the common law, it was clearly a rule that would not work in an expanding United States with its thousands of miles of navigable, nontidal waters. Because the public right of commercial navigation is as important on nontidal as on tidal navigable waters, it made no sense to insist that the *jus publicum* applied only where the state held title to submerged lands. But that is what many American courts concluded with the result that most states were found to have title in all submerged lands under navigable waters, whether tidal or not.

The combination of treating the prima facie rule as one of title and link-ing *the jus publicum* to state title led to two significant divergences from the English law. The states held title to vastly more submerged lands than had the crown, and the public rights associated with the *jus publicum* were extended to all waters that are navigable-in-fact, whether or not tidal. But this did not mean that states could not alienate their submerged lands subject to the *jus publicum*, although a century later such a restraint on alienation mistakenly would be claimed to derive from the Roman and English underpinnings of this early American law.

190

Early American Case Law

In 1821, the New Jersey Supreme Court rejected a claim of exclusive private right to oyster beds in the tidal mud flats of the Rariton River (*Arnold v. Mundy*, 6 N.J.L. 1 (1821)). The private claimant proved a chain of title in the oyster beds from the king of England and through the original twenty-four proprietors of East New Jersey. Writing for the court, Justice Kirkpatrick concluded that the king had no authority to grant title to these lands in the first place. Kirkpatrick explained that while everything susceptible of property belongs to the nation and forms its entire wealth, not everything is possessed in the same way. Some things have been granted and are held as private property. Other things are retained and held in a proprietary capacity by the crown (or the state). But a third category of things, including the tidal mud flats of the Rariton River, are the common property of all, held by the crown or state and "protected and regulated for the common use and benefit" (6 N.J.L. at 71).

In reaching this conclusion, Kirkpatrick fully embraced the misunderstandings of English law described previously. Claiming to rely on the law of nature and the true laws of England "to which it were well if we ourselves paid a more sacred regard," Kirkpatrick wrote:

> The navigable rivers in which the tide ebbs and flows, the ports, the bays, the coasts of the sea, including both the water and the land under the water, for the purpose of passing and repassing, navigation, fishing, fowling, sustenance, and all the other uses of the water and its products . . . are common to all the citizens, and that each has a right to use them according to his necessities, subject only to the laws which regulate that use . . . . (6 N.J.L. at 77)

Not only did Kirkpatrick's bold claim of expansive public rights and his conclusion that the king had no authority to grant exclusive rights in submerged tidal lands have no basis in English law, they contradicted the laws and widespread practice of his own state. As recently as 1820, the New Jersey legislature had recognized that individuals owning lands adjacent to waters "wherein oysters do or will grow" can acquire the exclusive right of planting and harvesting oysters (1820 N.J. Laws 162, §9). The reality of exclusive rights in oyster beds was widespread in New Jersey tidal waters and was recognized as necessary to the continued production of economically valuable oysters. While there were many disputes over title to those beds, they were almost always in the context of conflicting private claims rather than claims of common right.

Twenty years later, U.S. Supreme Court Chief Justice Taney relied on Kirkpatrick's common rights argument in *Arnold v. Mundy* to resolve another New Jersey oyster dispute (*Martin v. Waddell*, 41 U.S. 367 (1842)). In holding that the crown had no authority to grant plaintiff a private right in oyster beds, Taney totally ignored the fact that the defendant in *Martin v. Waddell* was claiming private rights pursuant to an 1824 New Jersey statute. A dissenting Justice Thompson posed the obvious question: "If the king held such lands as trustee for the common benefit of all his subjects, and inalienable as private property, I am unable to discover on what ground the state of New Jersey can hold the land discharged of such trust, and can assume to dispose of it to the private and exclusive use of individuals" (41 U.S. at 432). Taney responded to Thompson's query in these terms:

> When the revolution took place, the people of each state became themselves sovereign; and in that character hold the absolute right to all their navigable waters, and the soils under them, for their own common use, subject only to the rights since surrendered by the constitution to the general government. A grant made by their authority must, therefore, manifestly be tried and determined by different principles from those which apply to grants of the British crown . . . (41 U.S. at 410–11).

While Taney did not explain what those different principles are, his decision a decade later in another dispute between private claimants to reclaimed tidal lands in New Jersey confirmed that he saw no restraints on alienation of submerged tidal lands, at least if it was done pursuant to democratically enacted legislation (*Den v. Association of the Jersey Co.*, 56 U.S. 426 (1853)). It is thus puzzling how *Martin*, along with *Arnold*, has survived as cornerstones of modern claims that the public trust doctrine precludes alienation of submerged lands and interests in navigable waters.

This continued modern reliance on *Arnold* and *Martin* is all the more puzzling in light of the fact that *Arnold* was overturned by the New Jersey court only eight years after *Martin* was decided (*Gough v. Bell*, 22 N.J.L. 441 (1850)). In overruling *Arnold*, Chief Justice Green noted that "the view . . . expressed by the Chief Justice in *Arnold v. Mundy*, is incompatible with very numerous acts passed by the legislature of this state" and that many legally established uses of the waters and submerged lands of the state are "destructive to some extent of common rights" (22 N.J.L. at 456). Moreover, argued Green, "whatever doubts may exist in regard to the power of the king to dispose of common rights, there exists none in regard to the power of parliament." After acknowledging that state legislatures, unlike parliament, are limited by their constitutions, Green makes the fundamental point that "the act of the legislature is the act of the people, not that of a mere trustee holding the legal title for the public good" (22 N.J.L. at 457).

Another critical point made by Chief Justice Green in *Gough v. Bell* would later be central to the U.S. Supreme Court's landmark public trust decision in *Illinois Cent. R.R. v. Illinois*, 146 U.S. 387 (1892), though like *Gough*, it would be ignored by those seeking an expansive modern interpretation of the doctrine. Quoting *Arnold*'s holding that "the sovereign power itself cannot . . . make a direct and absolute grant of the waters of the state," (22 N.J.L. at 458–59),[20] Green stated:

> If, by this proposition, it is meant only to assert that a grant of all the waters of the state, to the utter destruction of the rights of navigation and fishery, would be an insufferable grievance, it is undoubtedly true . . .. But if it be intended to deny the power of the legislature, by grant, to limit common rights or to appropriate lands covered by waters to individual enjoyment, to the exclusion of the public common rights of navigation or fishery, the position is too broadly stated (22 N.J.L. at 459).

Illinois Cent. R.R. v. Illinois is the "lodestar" of modern public trust doctrine, or so declared Professor Joe Sax who himself provided the inspiration for the modern revival of the doctrine in a 1970 article.[21] At issue in *Illinois Cent.* was an 1869 grant by the Illinois Legislature of 1,000 acres of submerged lands along Chicago's then existing harbor and lakeshore. The grant was revoked by the legislature four years later. Illinois Central challenged the latter act as a violation of its constitutional rights under the contracts and Fourteenth Amendment due process clauses. The U.S. Supreme Court held that the 1869 grant was not authorized because it violated the state's responsibilities under the public trust doctrine. Thus the 1873 repeal did not result in an impairment of contract or the taking of private property because any alleged contract was invalid and therefore no property rights were transferred by the 1869 act.

That holding has been interpreted by many academic commentators and several courts to mean that the public trust doctrine precludes the alienation of any lands or waters in which the public has a right of access or use. If that was the holding in *Illinois Cent.*, it would clearly be a break with Roman, English, and early American law, although it would be consistent with the rhetoric in *Arnold* and *Martin*. But that was not the holding in *Illinois Cent.* Justice Field, who wrote for the majority, took pains to make clear that submerged and coastal lands affected with the public trust can be alienated.[22] What the court did hold is that the law that applies "to the dominion and sovereignty over and ownership of lands under tide waters in the borders of the sea" also applies to the "lands under the navigable waters of the Great Lakes" *(Illinois Cent.*, 146 U.S. at 437.) As Field had already explained, that law allowed for the alienation of submerged lands. What the applicable law did not allow was the "abdication of the general control of the state over lands under the navigable waters of an entire harbor or bay, or of a sea or lake" (146 U.S. at 452–53). As noted, this restraint on alienation of lands subject to the public trust is precisely that enunciated by the New Jersey court in *Gough.*

The court might have concluded that the public rights of navigation and fishing could be enforced even if the state retained no proprietary interest in the submerged lands of Chicago's harbor. Such public rights had been enforced for centuries in waters over legally alienated submerged lands. But the majority seemed to take the view that the challenges of enforcement and the risks of inappropriate influence justified placing an outer limit on the extent of permitted alienation. As Professors Kearney and Merrill have demonstrated in their in-depth examination of the history of *Illinois Cent.*,[23] the court had good reason to fear that the public's rights might be compromised to political expediency and private rent seeking. At the same time, the court clearly understood that alienation of some submerged lands was essential to the economic future of the state and city.[24]

After *Illinois Cent.*, the U.S. Supreme Court had little to say on the public trust doctrine for several decades. The Supreme Court did take the time in the 1926 case of *Appleby v. City of New York*, 271 U.S. 364 (1926), to confirm that submerged lands can be alienated and to make clear that public trust law is state law. At issue were submerged lands in New York harbor granted to Appleby, the use of which were obstructed by city dredging of adjacent lands. Like Illinois Central Railroad, Appleby claimed that the city's actions resulted in an unconstitutional impairment of his contract rights. Writing for the court, Chief Justice Taft held that under New York law, Appleby had contractual rights that were impaired by the city of New York. With respect to *Illinois Central*, Taft noted the difference between grants of individual parcels to promote commerce and navigation and the grant of a city's entire harbor.

Two other U.S. Supreme Court cases warrant mention in this brief review of the history of the public trust doctrine. In *Summa Corp. v. California State Lands Comm'n*, 466 U.S. 198 (1984), a unanimous court reversed a California Supreme Court ruling that the state of California had conveyed to the city of Los Angeles a public trust easement in a lagoon connected to a privately owned, man-made harbor in the city. The Supreme Court ruled that California could not assert a public trust easement over private property where the predecessors-in-interest had their interests confirmed without any mention of such an easement in federal patent proceedings under an 1851 federal act. The decision has had little notice in modern public trust cases for obvious reasons. It clearly confirmed that public lands can be alienated without being subject to the public trust, as occurred under the 1851 act, and that subsequent construction of a navigable harbor over those lands did not make them subject to the trust. Perhaps the court's decision was made easier by the city of Los Angeles' brazen admission that its claim was rooted in a desire to "dredge the lagoon and make other improvements without having to exercise its power of eminent domain over petitioner's property" (466 U.S. at 202). Such a blatant admission of an attempt to effectively take private property without compensation is not helpful to the usual high-minded arguments of public trust claimants.

The other recent Supreme Court case, which has received more notice from advocates for an expanded public trust doctrine, is similar to *Summa Corp.*, except in its result. In *Phillips Petroleum v. Mississippi*, 484 U.S. 469 (1988), the court upheld a claim by the state of Mississippi to title to submerged lands also claimed by Phillips Petroleum. As in *Summa Corp.*, the state's claim related to the public trust doctrine while the private claimant relied upon recorded titles, property tax payments, and land grants predating U.S. sovereignty.[25] As in *Summa Corp.*, the state's claim had nothing to do with protecting public rights of access and use and everything to do with advancing the financial interests of the state. In the words of a dissenting Justice O'Connor, Mississippi's "belated and opportunistic" (484 U.S. at 492) public trust claim was based on its desire to receive royalties from development of the petroleum reserves beneath the submerged lands.

Freeing the Public Trust Doctrine from Its Shackles

As the foregoing historical account demonstrates, the public trust doctrine of early twentieth-century American law was closely linked to the English common law. The doctrine recognized public rights of access to navigable waters and their associated submerged lands for the purposes of commercial navigation and fishing. At least some English and American cases included bathing as a public trust use. A significant American modification of the English law was the expansion of the definition of navigable waters to include nontidal waters that are in fact navigable for commercial purposes. The other significant modification accepted by most American courts was the application of the prima facie rule as establishing state title to submerged lands, rather than as an evidentiary presumption of title. This change did not affect the scope of the public trust doctrine with respect to either waters affected or public uses protected, but it did provide the basis for the mistaken conclusion, drawn by some late twentieth-century American courts, that the states may not alienate submerged lands without breaching its public trust responsibilities. However, the U.S. Supreme Court made clear, at least through 1984, that submerged lands could be alienated and that the resulting private rights, though subject to the servitude of the public trust, were constitutionally protected like any other property rights.

For emerging environmental interests in the 1960s and 1970s, the public trust doctrine's concept of public rights offered a promising avenue for judicial intervention and, most importantly, for overcoming the obstacle of seemingly vested private rights. Professor Joe Sax, a leading environmental law scholar and environmental rights advocate, launched what became a concerted effort to put the public trust doctrine to work on behalf of environmental interests with his 1970 article calling for "effective judicial intervention."[26] In a second article, in 1980, Sax would acknowledge that for the public trust doctrine to achieve the goals he set for it ten years earlier, it must be liberated from "its historical shackles."[27]

The process of liberation is well along in several states. Indeed, a recent book surveying public trust law developments between 1997 and 2008 is titled *The Public Trust Doctrine in Motion*.[28] The point is that the doctrine has been changing over time to provide protections for claimed public rights broader than those protected by the historic doctrine. A few examples from a handful of states will illustrate recent developments.

The first court to take up Professor Sax's initial invitation to judicial intervention was the Wisconsin Supreme Court in *Just v. Marinette County*, 201 N.W.2d 761 (Wis. 1972). Landowner Just claimed that his property was unconstitutionally taken by the county's denial of a permit to fill wetlands near the shore of a lake. The Wisconsin Court held that the zoning regulation came within the county's police powers and did not, therefore, result in a taking. In addition, the court stated that "[t]he active public trust duty of the state of Wisconsin in respect to navigable waters requires the state not only to promote navigation but also to protect and preserve those waters for fishing, recreation, and scenic beauty" (201 N.W.2d at 768). To the extent the court was relying on the public trust doctrine rather than the police power (actually it was confusing the two), it thus extended the traditional trust doctrine with respect to both protected public uses and geographic scope. Because the Wisconsin legislature had defined navigable waters to include all waters "navigable in fact for any purpose whatsoever,"[29] and the Wisconsin Supreme Court had long upheld a public right in the recreational use of navigable waters,[30] it should have come as no surprise to the Justs that the public trust doctrine has broader reach in Wisconsin than under the historic common law. But prior to *Just*, a riparian landowner would have had no way to anticipate that the doctrine might preclude the filling of wetlands for the purpose of economic development of the land. Indeed, as the court acknowledged, "[S]wamps and wetlands were once considered wasteland, undesirable, and not picturesque" (*Just*, 201 N.W.2d at 768).

Perhaps the most widely recognized modern public trust case is *National Audubon Soc'y v. The Superior Court of Alpine County*, 33 Cal. 3d 419, 658 P.2d 709 (1983), generally referred to as the Mono Lake case. The city of Los Angeles diverted water from tributaries to Mona Lake pursuant to water rights granted by the State of California. As a consequence, the lake level gradually fell with negative consequences for wildlife dependent on the lake. The National Audubon Society challenged the continued withdrawals from the tributary streams as a violation of the public trust responsibilities of the state. When the case finally reached the California Supreme Court, the court noted that the relationship between the prior appropriation water rights and the public trust doctrine was a question of first impression (33 Cal. 3d at 425).

Succinctly put, the question was whether state-recognized water rights are subject to limitations imposed by the public trust doctrine.

The California court identified three issues to be resolved: "the purpose of the trust; the [geographic] scope of the trust, particularly as it applies to the non-navigable tributaries of a navigable lake; and the powers and duties of the state as trustee of the public trust" (33 Cal. 3d at 434). On the first question, the court noted that it had held previously "that the traditional triad of uses—navigation, commerce and fishing—did not limit the public interest in the trust res" (33 Cal. 3d at 434). Quoting language from the earlier opinion, the court said the doctrine must "encompass changing public needs" and be "[un]burdened by an outmoded classification" of public uses. "Growing public recognition" confirmed that "preservation of . . . [tide]lands in their natural state" is "encompassed within the tidelands trust" (33 Cal. 3d at 434).[31] On the second question, the court concluded that the trust "protects navigable waters from harm caused by diversion of non-navigable tributaries" (33 Cal. 3d at 437). Finally, the court concluded that in performing its duties as trustee, the state had no duty to compensate affected property owners because "parties acquiring rights in trust property generally hold those rights subject to the trust, and can assert no vested right to use those rights in a manner harmful to the trust" (33 Cal. 3d at 437).

A year after the Mono Lake case, the Montana Supreme Court ruled in *Montana Coalition for Stream Access v. Curran*, 682 P.2d 163 (Mont. 1984) that the public has a right of access for the purpose of recreation to all waters in the state that can be used for recreation. In reaching this conclusion, the court abandoned the historic definition of protected public uses, and although it did not explicitly abandon the navigability requirement of historic public trust doctrine, its decision had that effect. The court relied on an 1893 Minnesota case in which that state's supreme court said it could see no reason to distinguish "boating and sailing for pleasure" from "mere commercial navigation" undertaken for "mere pecuniary profit" (*Lamprey v. State*, 53 N.W. 1139, 1143 (Minn. 1893)). "Thus," said the Montana court, "the issue becomes one of use, not title" (682 P.2d at 170). The court was correct in dismissing title as a determinant of the geographic scope of the public trust doctrine, but by effectively abandoning navigability as a test of geographic scope and including recreation among the protected public uses, the court made the doctrine applicable to virtually all waters of the state. "The capability of use of the waters for recreational purposes determines their availability for recreational use by the public" (682 P.2 at 170).

The continued broad reach of the *Curran* holding was confirmed by the Montana court in its 2008 holding in *Bitterroot River Protective Ass'n v. Bitterroot Conservation Dist.*, 2008 MT 377, 346 Mont. 547, 198 P.3d 219 (Mont. 2008). In *Curran* and a second 1984 case, the waters at issue were clearly navigable by historic commercial navigability standards (*Montana*

Coalition for Stream Access v. Hildreth, 211 Mont. 29, 684 P.2d 1088 (1984)) so they probably would have been subject to a public right of commercial navigation under the traditional common-law public trust doctrine, absent express alienation of the right by the state. In *Bitterroot*, however, at issue was public access to a clearly nonnavigable slough on indisputably private land. The court held that under the Stream Access Law enacted in response to the *Curran* decision,[32] there was a public right of access and use because the slough "consists of surface water capable of recreation" (*Bitterroot*,198 P.3d at 242).

In the most recent Montana case, the court made clear that the public right of access to the waters of Mitchell Slough did not include "the right to enter upon or cross over private property to reach the State-owned waters hereby held available for recreational purposes."[33] The New Jersey Supreme Court sees no such limitations on the right of public access. In *Raleigh Avenue Beach Ass'n v. Atlantis Beach Club*, 879 A.2d 112 (N.J. 2005), the New Jersey court held that the public trust doctrine requires a private beach club owning the dry sand beach to the high water line to provide horizontal and vertical access to the beach and public use of the dry sands on its property. In reaching its decision the court relied on a series of New Jersey cases dating back to *Borough of Neptune City v. Borough of Avon-By-The-Sea*, 294 A.2d 47 (N.J. 1972). In *Neptune* the court said:

> We have no difficulty in finding that, in this latter half of the twentieth century, the public rights in tidal lands are not limited to the ancient prerogatives of navigation and fishing, but extend as well to recreational uses, including bathing, swimming and other shore activities. The public trust doctrine, like all common law principles, should not be considered fixed or static, but should be molded and extended to meet changing conditions and needs of the public it was created to benefit (294 A.2d at 47).

In 2008, the Utah Supreme Court ruled in *Conatser v. Johnson*, 2008 UT 48, 194 P.3d 897 (Utah 2008), that the public has a right to walk upon and otherwise touch private land beneath state waters. The decision reaffirmed and expanded upon an earlier holding that the public had a right to float over such private submerged land. The earlier decision, *J.J.N.P. Co. v. Utah*, 655 P.2d 1133 (Utah 1982), preceded the Montana Supreme Court's decision in *Curran* and was similar in outcome, though significantly different in legal theory.

The Utah court did not rely on the public trust doctrine. Rather it concluded that because the state of Utah owns all waters in the state pursuant to a 1919 statute, the public has an easement to use those waters for recreational purposes. It is a peculiar theory since if the state owns the waters, there is no reason the public would require an easement to use its own waters. Describing the public right as an easement suggests that the Utah court did not really mean to say that "individuals have no ownership interest as such in natural water" (655 P.2d at 1136). If the public has an easement to use the water, there must be an underlying right in the water possessed by someone other than the public.[34] The Utah court's theory is indistinguishable from the public trust doctrine, which underscores that there is more than one way a court can achieve the end of restricting private water rights by finding a preexisting public right.

The Consequences of a Liberated Public Trust Doctrine

The foregoing examples of Wisconsin, California, Montana, and New Jersey have two things in common: (1) previously unrecognized public rights in relation to water are established in the name of the public trust doctrine; (2) vested private rights in water and land are unavoidably diminished. In each case, a state supreme court purports to act consistent with the long history of American and English public trust law dating from Justinian's codification of Roman law. As the foregoing summary of that history demonstrates, however, the public rights now recognized in these four states have little precedential pedigree. The public right asserted in Utah is an even more egregious intrusion on vested private rights because the statute on which the court relies expressly declared that public ownership of the state's waters was subject to preexisting rights. The *J.J.N.P.* and *Conaster* decisions give no hint that the public easement applies only in relation to private rights first acquired after 1919. Although one cannot doubt that these courts believed they were acting in the public interest, it is equally clear that they modified settled law with significant consequences for private rights in the use of water and riparian and submerged lands.

None of the five courts mentioned was unaware of the impact of its decision on private rights. In *Just*, the Justs claimed that the county's wetlands regulation resulted in an unconstitutional taking of their property. The Wisconsin court responded that a taking occurs only if "the restriction practically or substantially renders the land useless for all reasonable purposes" (201 N.W.2d at 767),[35] and insisted that "this is not a case where an owner is prevented from using his land for natural and indigenous uses" (201 N.W.2d at 768). But the court evidenced some discomfort by insisting that nothing had been taken from the Justs. The court had noted that the statute authorizing the county's regulation allowed that "natural and indigenous" included, among other very limited uses, "harvesting of any wild crop such as marsh hay, ferns, moss, wild rice, berries, tree fruits and tree seeds; . . . hunting, fishing, preservation of scenic, historic and scientific areas and wildlife preserves; . . . [and] hiking trails and bridle paths" (201 N.W.2d at 766 n3). The court was also aware that the Justs already had sold parcels carved from the land they purchased in 1961 (201 N.W.2d at 766). It was obvious to anyone paying attention, including the court, that the Justs' reasonable expectations at the time of purchase were significantly diminished by the zoning regulation. So the court had no choice but to acknowledge that "this case causes us to reexamine the concepts of public benefit in contrast to public harm and *the scope of an owner's right to use of his property*" (201 N.W.2d at 767).

In addressing the scope of the state's duties as trustee in the Mono Lake case, the California court concluded that there is no duty to compensate affected property owners because they "can assert no vested right to use those [water] rights in a manner harmful to the trust" (33 Cal. 3d at 437). This conclusion correctly implies that the state cannot take what a property owner does not possess. Of course, this means that the critical question in a takings case is whether the property owner possesses the right claimed to have been taken. But that query (and the constitutional protection against takings) is meaningless if property rights can be redefined at the discretion of the very state doing the taking.

Although many courts, including the *Just* court, confuse the states' police powers with their responsibilities as trustees under the public trust doctrine, the states' trust duties are a function of the extent of public rights, not of the current political determinations of the public interest. If the public rights that define the states' trust duties are indeterminate, so too will be private rights in the same resources. Any expansion of public rights necessarily results in the contraction of private rights.

The Montana court in *Curran* evaded discussion of this relationship between public and private rights by asserting that public rights are not dependant on the state having title to the submerged lands. While this is true, it does not follow that public rights are not bounded by vested private rights in submerged lands and in the use of water. To the extent the Montana court recognized the relationship between public and private rights, it seemed to take the view that expanding public rights necessarily trump affected private rights. The court's reliance on the Minnesota court's language in *Lamprey* underscores this disparagement of private rights. In rejecting private rights claims in the face of assertions of public rights, the Minnesota court compared "boating and sailing for pleasure" to "*mere* commercial navigation" undertaken for "*mere* commercial profit" (33 Cal. 3d at 437).

The impact of allowing private rights to vary with changing judicial definitions of public rights under the public trust doctrine is made clear by the recent Montana decision upholding a public right of access to the privately owned Mitchell Slough. In response to the *Curran* court's recognition of a public right of access to all waters that can be used for recreation, the Montana legislature enacted the Stream Access Law of 1985 to give more precise definition to the scope of this new public right. Under that law, the public right extends to all "natural water bodies." With an understanding that Mitchell Slough is not a natural water body due to the man-made diversion that delivers a significant share of the Slough's water and the many historic manipulations of the Slough topography, a few landowners invested several million dollars to create a vibrant trout fishery and wildlife habitat in the Slough. After the Montana Supreme Court held that the public had a right of access pursuant to the public trust doctrine, Huey Lewis, a landowner since 1987, reported a consensus among the Mitchell Slough landowners to "quit feeding the fishery. We're going to shut off the headgates like we're supposed to and without maintenance and without cleaning, the slough will slowly go back to the mud ditch it was."[36] The landowners forbidden by the Utah court from excluding the public from their private property on which they have made expensive trout habitat improvements declared themselves similarly deterred from future investment in habitat restoration.[37]

It is not surprising that the Mitchell Slough and Weber River landowners would foreswear future investments in habitat improvement and restoration. Few individuals are prepared to make significant investments if the returns must be shared with anyone who happens along. What is surprising, however, is the ease with which courts have dismissed well-founded, private claims of right in the name of a modern public trust doctrine bearing little resemblance to the historic doctrine on which property owners and their lawyers will have relied. The enforcement of clearly defined property rights is a central attribute of the rule of law. How do the courts explain and justify their expansion of public rights (and corresponding contraction of private rights) in the name of the public trust doctrine?

The answer to that question is particularly evident in the New Jersey court's decision in *Neptune*. "The public trust doctrine, like all common law principles, should not be considered fixed or static, but should be molded and extended to meet changing conditions and needs of the public it was created to benefit." This is a frequent theme in modern public trust decisions, and it is certainly true that the common law has never been frozen in time. But it is also true that property rights lose their vitality as guarantors of reasonable return on wise resource management when they become contingent on judicial perceptions of the public good. The fact that public valuations of particular resources have shifted over time provides no better case for deprivation of property rights than does the fact that neighbors prefer a different use of a resource than does its owner. If the neighbors interfere, it is trespass whether the neighbors or the owner value the resource more highly. The same must be true if the public wishes a different use of the resource than does its owner. A taking in the name of common-law evolution is no less a taking than one in the name of private trespass. The fact that the public trust doctrine is state law that might vary from state to state does not alter the fact that state laws affecting property rights must comply with the U.S. Constitution. The United States Supreme Court made this clear almost a century ago in *Appleby v. City of New York*, 271 U.S. 364 (1926).

Avoiding the Takings Clause?

But a century is a long time and, though *Appleby* did hold that the state could not, in the name of the public trust, limit rights in submerged lands previously alienated by the state, the case did not speak directly to constitutional protection of water rights. Logic suggests that if the state can alienate lands subject to the public trust, it can alienate waters similarly affected. If, as in *Appleby*, the Constitution protects alienated interests in such lands, logic further suggests that property interests in water are also constitutionally protected against state infringement. That was the conclusion of the Court of Appeals in the *Casitas* case discussed at the beginning of this chapter. But there is much in modern public trust law and related water law doctrines casting doubt on that conclusion.

As a background principle of the common law, the public trust doctrine has been claimed to function as a categorical defense available to government in a takings case.[38] The term "categorical defense" is meant to convey that where the state asserts the existence of a public right rooted in the public trust doctrine, there is a presumption that any conflicting private right claim is invalid. The presumption follows from the theoretical proposition that public rights arising from the public trust doctrine predate any claims of private right. So even if one holds paper title to a property right enforceable against other private claimants, it is not enforceable against the state because the conflicting public rights precede and are superior to any private rights. Viewed in the context of a takings case, a government-imposed limitation on the use of private property, undertaken to exercise or enforce a public trust-based public right, cannot result in a taking because the private claimant never possessed the right to engage in the restricted use in the first place.

The principle that one possesses only what one acquired in the first place is sound. One who acquires property subject to an easement or servitude has no legal objection when that easement or servitude is exercised by its owner. The market value of such a property interest should reflect the existence of the easement or servitude, which is why a wise purchaser always performs a title search and other due diligence to affirm precisely what is being acquired. Thus, due diligence in the purchase of riparian land will inform the purchaser as to ownership of the adjacent submerged lands and any related common law or statutory restrictions on the use of those lands. For example, due diligence would have informed Appleby that his title to submerged lands in New York Harbor included the right to construct a wharf, but not the right to thereby obstruct navigation in the harbor. Or, due diligence would have informed a pre-1984 purchaser of property extending from the navigable Bitterroot River across the nonnavigable Mitchell Slough that he could exclude others from floating and wading in Mitchell Slough but not in the Bitterroot River. Neither a New York regulation restricting Appleby's wharf from harbor navigation channels nor a Montana prohibition of obstructions to navigation on the

Bitterroot River would result in unconstitutional takings because there was no right to engage in the prohibited activities in the first place.

In the Montana case, however, the state imposition of a right of public access to Mitchell Slough also is found not to be an infringement of private property because evolving understandings and values allow the courts to recognize public rights where they did not previously exist. But these new public rights are treated as if they always existed, meaning that their enforcement by the state does not result in the taking of private property. This is the wonder and power of the unshackled public trust doctrine. Due diligence by purchasers of properties affected by the public trust will reveal that the public has rights in the nature of a servitude or easement and that the nature and scope of those rights may change. Due diligence by purchasers of properties not yet affected by the public trust will reveal that no limiting public rights exist at the moment, but they might be found to exist in the future.

As with other contingencies mentioned below, if due diligence reveals the threat of an unpredictable and uncompensated public trust taking at an indefinite time in the future, market value of the properties in question will be negatively affected, investment in the improvement of those properties will be deterred, and transfers of the resources to higher-valued uses will be impeded. The result is wealth loss, economic inefficiency, and potential productivity losses. There are other sources, in addition to the evolving public trust doctrine, of potential contingency in the definition of property rights in water and in riparian and submerged lands. As noted at the beginning of this chapter, the police powers of the states make property rights contingent on state regulation to the extent that regulation does not go "too far." The contingencies created by the prospect of police power regulation are not peculiar to property rights in water—they affect all property rights to a greater or lesser degree. But water rights are subject to contingencies arising from particular aspects of water law in addition to the public trust doctrine. Although these water law doctrines are beyond the scope of a chapter on the public trust doctrine, they warrant mention because of their similar impact on water markets. (See chapters 6 and 13 for further discussion of these issues.)

Closely related to the general police power is a public interest standard often applied in the administration of water rights. The granting of permits to appropriate or divert water and to transfer water rights from one use or user to another is often dependant on the proposed action being in the public interest. This means that the water rights administrator has the discretion to grant, condition, or deny a permit based on a public interest determination. Although that public interest determination has some parallel to the beneficial and reasonable use doctrines of appropriation and riparian law, respectively, it does contribute to making water rights indeterminate. The impact on water markets is most apparent where the public interest standard is available to limit water right and water use transfers.

Another source of contingency is the widespread declaration in state law that the state or the people of the state own the water in the state. The significance of such declarations of state ownership is much debated. Those seeking to justify uncompensated limitations on private water use or a public right of access to all waters argue not only that the state owns the water in a proprietary sense but also that the right cannot be alienated. The parallel to public trust-based claims of unalienable, proprietary rights to submerged lands is obvious. The implication for water rights claimants is that their rights are contingent on the state's superior title. This argument for inferior private rights in water is often fortified with the assertion that appropriative and riparian rights are mere usufructs. In combination, these state water law doctrines are taken to mean that the state owns the water and makes revocable grants for private use.

As with modern, shackle-breaking interpretations of the public trust doctrine, the foregoing descriptions of the state ownership and usufructuary rights doctrines are, at best, caricatures of the historic understanding of the law. The assertion of state ownership of water, like the assertion of state ownership of wildlife, "must be understood as no more than a nineteenth-century legal fiction expressing 'the importance to its people that a State have power to preserve and regulate the exploitation of an important resource'" (*Douglas v. Seacoast Prods.*, 431 U.S. 265 (1977)).[39] But even if the state can be said to own the water in the proprietary sense that it owns submerged lands under navigable waters, the insistence that a grant of usufructuary rights is qualitatively different from a grant of possessory rights makes no sense economically. What gives property in land or water market value is the right to use it (including for nonconsumptive purposes) and to exclude others from using it. The negative consequences of making usufructuary rights contingent are every bit as real as of making possessory rights contingent.

Conclusion

Water markets require clearly defined and strictly enforced property rights in the use of water. Although the transient nature of most fresh water supplies poses practical challenges for definition and enforcement of such rights, the riparian and appropriation systems have long provided for reasonably determinate water rights in the United States.

Under the riparian doctrine rights are correlative, meaning that riparian landowners may use water for purposes and in amounts that are reasonable in relation to the uses of other riparians and to the capacity of the water source. The volume or flow of a riparian right thus varies with the available supply and the demands of other riparian landowners. Under the appropriation doctrine, water rights are fixed with respect to quantity (or flow) and priority. This means that each user has an exclusive right to the full amount of his water right unless the supply is insufficient to satisfy the rights of all senior rights holders drawing from the same source. Thus, in both systems, there is an indeterminacy relating to the supply of water at any moment in time. The fact of this unavoidable source of indeterminacy, however, does not argue for further compromising the definition and enforcement of water rights by embracing an evolving public trust doctrine that effectively authorizes the courts to alter vested private rights in the name of inchoate public rights.

The case for public rights has been widely made, most effectively by Professor Carol Rose in her article "The Comedy of the Commons."[40] But accepting that public rights provide benefits and avoid costs that private markets fail to account for, it remains important for achieving the efficiency benefits of markets that private rights be clearly defined and not subject to evolving and inchoate public rights. (Stephen Bretsen and P. J. Hill make this point clearly in chapter 6 on the anticommons character of the public trust and public interest doctrines.)

The historic public trust doctrine was clear with respect to both its geographic scope and protected public uses. The resultant public rights served to define one boundary on private rights held pursuant to the riparian and appropriation systems. To the extent that modern public trust decisions have made public rights less determinate and more likely to change in the future, private water rights have become less determinate. As a result, water markets are made less effective as efficient allocators of a scarce resource.[41]

Notes

1. It is unusual in Anglo-American law to possess a private right to water, if what is meant by that concept is ownership of the physical object. Certainly one can be said to own the water in one's swimming pool or water bottle, but for the most part water is used and then some portion of it returns to a river, lake, ocean, or subterranean geologic formation where it awaits use by others. Indeed, even bottled and pool waters sooner or later resume their journey in the hydrologic cycle. Thus, it is really rights in use of water that are critical to water markets. The legal labeling of such rights as usufructuary has come to suggest, for many commentators and some courts, that they are always conditional subject to superior rights held by the state. If accepted, this understanding of rights of use in water, like the expansive public trust claims discussed in this chapter, makes water markets impossible by making water rights ill-defined and insecure.

2. "The general rule at least is that while property may be regulated to a certain extent, if regulation goes too far it will be recognized as a taking" (260 U.S. at 415).

3. Justice Scalia stated that when uncompensated "regulations . . . prohibit all economically beneficial use of land, . . . limitation[s] so severe . . . must inhere in the title itself, in the restrictions that background principles of the State's law of property and nuisance already place upon land ownership" (505 U.S. at 1029).

4. "Take" is defined as "harass, harm, pursue, hunt, shoot, wound, kill, trap, capture, or collect, or to attempt to engage in any such conduct."

5.   In a lawsuit brought by Casitas, the United States claimed that Casitas was not required to construct the fish ladder and that the amount of water lost was less than claimed. Whatever those facts, it was not disputed that compliance with the ESA had a measurable impact on the volume of water Casitas had available for use in any given year.

6.   The argument suggested by Judge Mayer was made explicitly in briefs presented to the court. See, e.g., Brief of California State Water Resources Control Board as Amici Curiae Supporting Appellee, United States (2007 WL 4984849).

7.   Justinian, *The Institutes of Justinian 2.1.1*, ed. and trans. Thomas Cooper (Philadelphia, 1841).

8.   G. P. Smith II and M. W. Sweeney, "The Public Trust Doctrine and Natural Law: Emanations Within a Penumbra," *Boston College Environmental Affairs Law Review* 33, no. 2 (2006): 307–43.

9.   Justinian, *Institutes*.

10.   P. Deveney, "Title, Jus Publicum, and the Public Trust: An Historical Analysis," *Sea Grant Law Journal* 1, no. 13 (1976): 12.

11.   Ibid., 17.

12.   J. Huffman, "Speaking of Inconvenient Truths—A History of the Public Trust Doctrine," *Duke Environmental Law and Policy Forum* 18, no. 1 (2007): 15.

13.   The quoted language is from the 1225 version of the Magna Carta (http://www.fordham.edu/halsall/source/magnacarta.html). It was derived from chapter 47 of the 1215 version. The reference is to King Henry II, father of King John, the signer of the 1215 charter and grandfather of King Henry III, signer of the 1225 charter. The reference to Henry II is significant as an effective revocation of the crown's intrusions on private rights during the reigns of kings Richard I and John.

14.   M. Hale, "A Treatise De Jure Maris et Brachiorum Ejusdem," reprinted in *A History of the Foreshore and the Law Relating Thereto*, ed. S. A. Moore (1670; Holmes Beach, FL, 1888), 370–89.

15.   Huffman, "Speaking of Inconvenient Truths," 28.

16.   "No line is drawn . . . between those proprietary rights which the king has as king and those which he has in his private capacity. The nation, the state, is not personified; there are no lands which belong to the nation or to the state. The king's lands are the king's lands; the king's treasures are the king's treasures: there is not more to be said" (see, Pollock and Maitland, *History of English Law Before the Time of Edward I,* 2nd ed. Lawbook Exchange Ltd, 1996), 518).

17.   J. Selden, *Mare Clausum: The Right and Dominion of the Sea* (London, 1663), 127–35.

18.   Hale, "Treatise."

19.   Ibid., 404.

20.   Quoting *Arnold v. Mundy*, 6 N.J.L. at 53.

21.   J. L. Sax, "The Public Trust Doctrine in Natural Resource Law: Effective Judicial Intervention," *Michigan Law Review* 68 (1970): 471–89.

22.   See Huffman, "Speaking of Inconvenient Truths."

23.   J. D. Kearney and T. W. Merrill, "The Origins of the American Public Trust Doctrines: What Really Happened in *Illinois Central*," *University of Chicago Law Review* 71 (2004): 799.

24. "The interest of the people in the navigation of the waters and in commerce over them may be improved in many instances by the erection of wharves, docks, and piers therein, for which purpose the state may grant parcels of the submerged lands . . ." (146 U.S. at 452).

25. Mississippi's claim was technically based on the equal footing doctrine pursuant to which states are admitted to the union on an equal footing with the original states. Pursuant to the doctrine states are presumed to have title to submerged lands under navigable waters, consistent with the prima facie rule deriving from English law. The public trust doctrine was critical to Mississippi's claim so long as the court was willing to accept the mistaken conclusion that lands affected with a public trust cannot be alienated.

26. Sax, "Public Trust Doctrine," 471.

27. J. L. Sax, "Liberating the Public Trust Doctrine from Its Historical Shackles," *University of California Davis Law Review* 14, no. 2 (1980): 185.

28. D. C. Slade, *The Public Trust Doctrine in Motion: The Evolution of the Doctrine 1997–2008* (Bowie, MD: PTDIM, 2009).

29. Water Power Act, ch. 652, Laws of 1911 (Wisc.).

30. See *Willow River Club v. Wade*, 100 Wis. 113, 76 N.W. 273 (1898); *Diana Shooting Club v. Husting*, 145 N.W. 816 (Wis. 1914).

31. Quoting *Marks v. Whitney*, 6 Cal. 3d 251, 259–60 (1971).

32. Mont. Code Ann. §23-2-3.

33. Quoting *Curran*, 682 P.2d at 172.

34. It could be argued that the easement is a right of passage over the private submerged lands rather than in the use of state waters, but that is not the way the court describes the easement. "There is a public easement over the water regardless of who owns the water beds beneath the water" (655 P.2d at 1136). Thus, the court describes a public easement over both public and private land.

35. Quoting *Buhler v. Racine County*, 33 Wis. 2d 137, 146 N.W.2d 403 (1966).

36. J. Hull "For the Love of a Ditch," *Montana Quarterly* 5, no. 21 (Spring 2009).

37. R. T. Simmons, "Utah's Stream Access Decision Could Backfire on Anglers," *Salt Lake Tribune*, September 14, 2008.

38. M. C. Blumm and L. Ritchie, "Unlikely Legacy: The Rise of Background Principles as Categorical Takings Defenses," *Harvard Environmental Law Review* 29 (2005): 321.

39. Quoting *Toomer v. Witsell*, 334 U.S. 385, 402 (1948).

40. C. Rose, "The Comedy of the Commons: Custom, Commerce, and Inherently Public Property," *University of Chicago Law Review* 53 (1986): 711.

41. On the effects of uncertainty on water markets, see Barton H. Thompson Jr., "Uncertainty and Markets in Water Resources," *McGeorge Law Review* 36 (2005): 117.

8

Market-like Water Quality Trading: Why It Matters, and How To Make It Happen

Leonard Shabman and Kurt Stephenson

Introduction

Federal and state water quality management agencies are increasingly promoting "water quality trading," claiming that their programs are an application of market-based environmental policy.[1] Considerable variation exists among these operating and proposed trading programs, but as we have argued elsewhere the objectives and the implementation rules rarely have market-like features.[2] The first section of the chapter will show that water quality trading, as usually practiced, is simply an extension of the current Clean Water Act (CWA) command and control regulation; understanding this argument requires an explanation of National Pollutant Discharge Elimination System (NPDES) permits and the permitting process.[3] We will show that it is misleading to call the outcome of these programs "trading" because there is no intent to allow increases in discharges from one source to be offset by equivalent reductions from other sources. Following the explanation of how trading in practice is simply a regulatory extension to conventional NPDES permits, we will describe the basic characteristics of market-like program design. We end with suggestions for ways to add market-like properties to water quality management within the existing statutory and regulatory confines of the CWA.

Current Regulatory and Permitting Strategies for Water Quality Management

Water quality management is oriented around administrative procedures developed to implement the CWA. One focus of the CWA is the attainment of water quality standards, which include state-assigned designated uses (e.g., swimming) for each water body and the measurable criteria used to represent the uses (e.g., clarity of the water). The well-publicized Total Maximum

Daily Load (TMDL) planning process is designed to determine the load (e.g., pounds) of a pollutant (e.g., nitrogen) that can be present in the water per unit time based on the watershed's capacity to assimilate waste and still meet the criterion (water clarity) and attain the designated use.[4] In effect, the maximum allowable load is the result of a social apportioning of the rights to the water between those who benefit from water supply, recreation, aesthetics, or intrinsic values and those who value the waste assimilation service.

Without regard to whether water quality standards are being attained in any location, another provision of the act creates a regulatory mandate to define and enforce effluent standards on certain discharge sources for certain pollutants. As distinct from water quality standards, effluent standards are limits on the pollutants in the flow of wastewater. The limit is specified in a NPDES permit that authorizes a regulated point source (PS) to discharge a maximum allowable amount of a pollutant in its wastewater. NPDES permits for PSs are the only CWA-authorized instrument limiting pollutant discharges.[5]

A PS is where it is technically and financially feasible to trace the pollutant back to an originating location. In contrast, a nonpoint source (NPS) is characterized by any, or all, of the following conditions: a lack of monitoring technology for linking pollutants to their source, costs for tracking pollutants to their source in excess of available resources, or political opposition from sources who could face NPDES permit limits. For one or more of these reasons NPSs are beyond the reach of the CWA, and NPDES permits for PSs are the only CWA-authorized instrument limiting pollutant discharges. This is the case even though in many places NPS loads are the reason water quality standards are not met.[6]

The NPDES permit specifies the allowed concentration of a pollutant in the wastewater flow, and the maximum allowable water flow from the source, where flow and concentration in the flow define an "effluent load limit." Concentration limits are established in a two-tiered process. Initially, the U.S. Environmental Protection Agency (EPA) engages in studies of the available pollutant control technologies, practices, and costs associated with implementing different pollutant control technologies for different industry classes. Based on these studies, the EPA sets technology-based effluent limitations (TBELs) that the agency deems to be the best performing and affordable technology available to control the pollutant. The TBEL is written into the NPDES permit for each individual source.

If the load limit based on the TBEL for all PSs discharging to a water body does not achieve ambient water quality standards, then the second tier of the effluent standard becomes effective. These are water quality-based effluent limits (WQBEL). The allowable concentration of the pollutant must be reduced to that level which can be secured by what the regulator determines to be "limit of treatment technology" (LOT), even then imposing the LOT requirement in NPDES permits still may not secure ambient water quality standards, because of significant loads from unregulated NPSs.

Once the NPDES permit is issued, holders of permits demonstrate compliance with the permit limits when they submit measurements and records of effluent concentration and flow volumes in Discharge Monitoring Reports (DMRs). The regulatory agency conducts random checks of dischargers and inspects control technology to verify the accuracy of the DMRs. From this perspective, effluent limitations are performance standards, identifying only levels of pollutant control performance to be obtained. In principle, a source may choose a less costly alternative technology than the one identified by the EPA to meet its permit limits, as long as the source is confident that the alternative will achieve the same level of effluent performance.

As a practical matter, dischargers usually opt to install and operate the technologies that were used by EPA to set the effluent limits.[7] This behavior is rational because if an alternative proves ineffective, the source would then be required to implement the EPA technology to meet the NPDES limit. On the other hand, if the EPA technology proves ineffective, and the source can show it has properly installed and operated the prescribed technology, that source will still be in compliance with its permit.

Finally, it is worth noting here that the "zero discharge" goal of the act is independent of the CWA's ambient water quality focus. The zero discharge goal has two effects on the NPDES process. First, once an effluent standard is included in an NPDES permit, there can be no future change to the permit that would allow for an increase in loads from that source, even if ambient water quality conditions would suggest such an increase would not violate water quality standards, or if another source could control the same amount of pollutant at lower cost. This provision, called "anti-backsliding," is intended to prevent movement away from the zero discharge goal. Second, regulators are expected to periodically review technologies to revise standards downward over time; called "technology forcing" or "ratcheting down" toward the stated intent of the act to achieve "zero discharge of pollutants."[8] This is an overall directive within the CWA independent of whether the water quality conditions in a water body warrant making further reductions.

Trading Meets the Permitting Process

What is currently referred to as Water Quality Trading has its origins in the regulatory/statutory structure of the CWA, as was briefly described previously. In many places, the pollutant that is causing a violation of water quality standards can be attributed to unregulated NPSs, mostly runoff from agricultural, forest, and some urban and suburban land uses. Reductions of pollutants from these NPSs are secured by using general tax revenues to pay those nonpoint dischargers who agree to adopt pollutant-reducing best management practices (BMPs). In these programs, which are usually administered through the USDA and state cost-share programs, the unregulated dischargers decide whether to accept the payment in return for implementing a government-identified and approved practice that is predicted to reduce pollutant loads.

Most so-called trading programs emerge when ambient standards are not being met and the cause of impairment is NPSs. Since NPSs face no discharge control requirements under the CWA, regulators who administer the CWA look to the only regulatory instrument available—the NPDES permit—and impose ever stricter permit limits on PSs. Most of the current "trading" programs fit the following situation: unregulated NPSs are a significant source of a pollutant, and even with WQBEL limits on regulated sources, water quality standards cannot be achieved. Because water quality standards cannot be met when the NPDES permits are up for their review, or because a facility seeks a permit modification to accommodate growth in flows (from more production from a plant or more population to serve from a public wastewater plant), regulators face unpleasant choices: (1) deny the new PS permit applications unless zero discharge is achieved, effectively prohibiting economic growth of the facility and the local economy; (2) create a new set of permits with technology-based limits for unregulated NPSs, which is a costly, politically contentious process and may require new legal authority; or (3) take no action and let water quality standards be further compromised.

As an alternative to these choices, regulators first require permitted PSs to push toward effluent-control technologies that approach LOT. Even LOT, however, may be insufficient to attain water quality standards. Therefore, additional requirements are placed on the PS because water quality standards are not being met. When PS reduction potential has been exhausted, regulators require that any remaining discharge in excess of revised permit limits must be offset by a permittee elsewhere in the watershed. The off-site reduction is typically secured by encouraging PSs to pay for reductions by agricultural NPSs.

In these programs, acceptable NPS BMPs that are predicted to produce the required offsets to the uncontrolled discharge at the PS are identified by regulators;[9] the regulator encourages the PS to pay for BMP implementation, and the responsibility to assure the implementation of the BMPs is written into the NPDES permit. The requirement to pay for such offsets as a condition of issuing the NPDES permit is what is called trading, although there is no reduction in control responsibility at the PS even when there are increased controls at the NPS. An exchange of legal and financial responsibility for pollutant control is what is normally understood as trading, but that is not how most trading programs work. Offsets are simply an off-site control requirement that is included in the PS's NPDES permit. In fact, securing funding for BMP installation by unregulated sources often appears as a stated goal of trading programs because general tax revenues for these kinds of payment programs are insufficient to induce reductions that will achieve water quality standards. In effect, these are revenue-seeking programs where funds are secured from PSs to be used to subsidize BMPs as described previously.

Some trading programs are designed to work only for PSs, but within the confines of the NPDES process. In those programs, PSs who have short-term difficulty in meeting their individual effluent standard at the end of the compliance year are deemed to be undercomplying with their permit. Meanwhile, other sources may have overcomplied. Overcompliance generates a "credit" in relation to the source's NPDES permit. The programs allow a trade between overcomplying and undercomplying sources, as a means of avoiding an enforcement action for an NPDES violation.

Market-like Water Quality Management

Can most of the current trading program designs based on the NPDES process be considered market-like? When so-called trading programs are focused on securing offsets from unregulated sources, the payments can move only in one direction, from regulated to unregulated sources. Furthermore, the payment is not based on the regulated source increasing its discharge if it secures (presumably at lower cost) offsets. Instead, the PS is encouraged to sponsor offsets only after it has met the most stringent effluent limits deemed attainable by the regulatory authority. Even the simplest understanding of the goal of a market-like program—cost effectiveness—is not advanced by a trading program design that does not include the opportunity for lower cost sources to increase control as higher cost sources increase discharges.

The programs that are focused on short-term NPDES compliance for PSs also are not market-like. In these programs, the credits are based on being above a prescribed effluent limit, and the buyer is only securing the credits as a stopgap until it too can reach its prescribed NPDES limit. The exchange of PS credits defined in this way is not about achieving the ambient water quality standard in the most cost-effective way over time but is rather a mechanism for short-term compliance for an individual source that cannot meet its NPDES permit limit.

Of course, there is much more to the definition of market-like than the objective of cost-effectiveness. In fact, equating "market-like" with cost-effectiveness is a common mistake in the academic literature as well as in policy pronouncements. Consider a water quality program in which a regulator collects current cost and effectiveness data for all nutrient sources in the watershed and uses a computer model to calculate where the most cost-effective nutrient-limiting controls should be implemented. Then the regulator issues permits to each source requiring the implementation of controls identified in the regulator's analysis. For example, the computer model might determine that source A faces relatively high nutrient-limiting control costs compared to source B. So the regulator might allocate controls from source

A to B, as long as the total amount of the nutrient released to the watershed by all sources is limited to the cap. Meanwhile, the total dollars spent on nutrient abatement go down. The regulator also could support research into new methods of cost-effective controls at each source and rerun the computer model. Based on a new analysis, the regulator could reallocate control responsibilities (making "trades" among sources) so that he or she used the most cost-effective control strategy identified by the computer model. Many quantitative studies calculate cost saving in just such a way.[10] We, however, would not recognize such a program as market-like.

Basics of Market-like Systems

A market-like water quality management program must be built on the ambient water quality standards focus of the CWA, as opposed to individual effluent standards and NPDES provisions. Recall that under the act, designated uses for a body of water are established and total pollutant loads that will allow attainment of those uses are identified. The result is a pollutant load limit (cap) defining the maximum amount of pollutant (an amount that is greater than zero) that can be released into a water body. If the cap is treated as an enforceable requirement of the CWA, then a structure for a market in discharge rights, an idea that has been understood for over forty years,[11] could be imagined. The load cap would be divided into a limited number of pollutant discharge rights called allowances. Allowances are time-limited rights to discharge a fixed quantity of a pollutant within a defined geographic area for a period of time.

Allowances are created and defined by government through statute, regulation, or contractual arrangement, and owners of the rights are not allowed to discharge more effluent than their total allowance holdings. Furthermore, the allowances may be bought and sold at the discretion of those dischargers who are required to comply with the cap. Defining an allowance must be accompanied with requirements for the measurement of the total amount of pollutants discharged. Penalties (fines) would be imposed on a source for discharges that exceed allowance holdings.

This allowance-focused system is market-like because it grants dischargers two kinds of decision-making flexibility: waste control flexibility and exchange flexibility. Waste control flexibility means that the discharger (as opposed to the regulator in the NPDES process) determines how pollutants will be controlled at location. A discharger may choose, for example, to alter a production process, install a new piece of pollution control equipment, or even reduce production levels as a means to keep nutrient discharges below or equal to allowance holdings. Dischargers are expected to investigate, experiment, and implement pollution control strategies and technologies that are best adapted to their individual circumstances.

The more widely recognized requirement of a market-like system is exchange flexibility, or the ability to transfer allowances from one party to another—to "trade" the legal and financial responsibility to limit waste discharge. Buyers of allowances could be dischargers who are expanding production. Another buyer might be a source that is experiencing unexpected problems with its control equipment and needs to buy allowances to cover the increase in nutrient loads. Yet another source of potential buyers would be new dischargers who enter a watershed; they must buy allowances (permissions to discharge) just as they must secure land, labor, and equipment in order to operate. Expanding the potential number of buyers and sellers and reducing the costs of exchanging allowances (transactions costs) increase exchange flexibility. Increasing the number of buyers and sellers increases the chances that market participants can negotiate a mutually beneficial trade. Lowering costs of transacting generally means market participants are not required to spend excessive amounts of time and money to locate a trading partner.

Also, this market-like system may allow a discharger to reduce its discharge below what is necessary to meet its allowance limit in one time period, so that it can save allowances, sometimes called "banking" since the allowances generated by such reductions can be used in a later period. By banking the allowances for future use, the party is, in some sense, trading the allowances to itself. Banking thus represents a temporal reallocation of the authorization to discharge for the same responsible party. Exchange flexibility allows a discharger to decide not how, but whether and when, to control a unit of a pollutant.

The responsibility of the regulatory authority in such a system is straightforward: specify the load cap, develop rules for defining and allocating allowances (shares of the cap), and then monitor to assure that each unit of discharge is accompanied by an allowance to make that discharge. In addition, the regulator must enforce penalties against those whose discharge exceeds their allowances. In the following sections, we refer to this system as a Cap and Allowance Market (CAM) and describe the advantages of such a system as compared to the NPDES-focused water quality management program.

CAM Focuses Attention on Water Quality Outcomes

CAM programs are a water quality outcome–focused management strategy. Water quality standards are converted into mass load limits (caps) and then that cap is divided into allowances distributed to individual sources. This approach is fundamentally different from a technology-oriented source-by-source NPDES permitting approach. In the bottom-up NPDES approach, all sources must meet the NPDES prescribed load limits, but the sum of the NPDES permitted loads does not ensure that water quality standards will be achieved. The act's effluent standards approach to regulation anticipated that over time through the continuing "ratcheting down" on the permit limits that the regulated sources would approach zero discharge to the ambient waters. However, not all sources of pollutants are covered by the CWA, and for those that are, the prospect of zero discharge is either technically not feasible or comes at a prohibitively high marginal cost. In addition, zero discharge may not even be warranted to meet the desired water quality standards.

The focus on ambient standards in a CAM approach continuously highlights the importance of working toward a management system that does not push toward load reductions that exceed those required to meet water quality standards but that also seeks to bring all sources under the cap. In such a fully capped system, every discharger would be required to hold allowances before being allowed to discharge. A fully capped program also ensures that actual discharge does not exceed a total maximum load target, increasing the possibility that dischargers' discretion on how to reduce discharges combined with the opportunity for exchanges of allowances will discover and secure least cost combinations of controls over time.

As a practical matter not all sources could be easily required to hold allowances. If only some discharge sources are required to hold allowances, the system is "partially capped." In partially capped systems, the number of issued allowances is some fraction of the total load cap, but a CAM could be developed inside the partial cap, what we will refer to in the following sections as a Group Compliance Permit (GCP).

CAM Reconciles Water Quality Standards and Economic Growth

Dischargers who reduce discharges below allowance holdings can earn revenue from the sale or lease of allowances. Sources which need to expand and increase discharges can avoid becoming buyers of allowances by finding ways to lower discharges per unit of output and thus lower costs. Thus, the opportunity to trade creates both seller and buyer incentives to continuously lower pollutant levels. This continuous innovation will free up allowances for sale, lease, or use at a later time. Innovation means that current dischargers can expand their operations and new dischargers can enter a watershed without increasing total load to the water body.

Unless polluters are given a reason to engage in the difficult and time-consuming process of thinking about wastewater management, many pollution prevention opportunities will simply go unrealized by both dischargers and regulators. With financial incentives offered by exchange flexibility, individual decision-makers who make pollutant generation, treatment, and discharge decisions are alerted to the profitability of pollution prevention opportunities. The combination of financial incentives and decision-making flexibility provides dischargers with both the reason and the means for developing and implementing potential new, low-cost ways to reduce loads.[12]

One of the most fundamental differences between the NPDES process and a CAM approach is the mode and method of innovation. In contrast to a CAM approach, in the NPDES process regulators must assume primary responsibility for ensuring that the cap is achieved through time in the face of growth. The premise is that regulatory agencies are made up of pollution control experts with extensive experience and training in pollution control technologies. Publicly supported research grants are expected to target the most promising pollution control opportunities for development. This position may be reinforced by a belief that dischargers are not as capable of identifying, or as willing to make, pollutant reduction investments.

Meanwhile, the NPDES system substantially diminishes dischargers' willingness and ability to innovate. As has been discussed, under the current system, dischargers are loath to deviate from the practices used to set the effluent standard. A discharger who discovers ways to either lower control costs or improve removal techniques faces the increasing possibility that regulators will significantly reduce his or her permit limit. Indeed, the CWA zero discharge goal and technology-based performance standards compel regulatory authorities to act in just such a manner.

CAM Focuses Attention on Performance

A fundamental characteristic of a CAM is that it focuses attention on verifying the performance of dischargers (outcomes such as pounds of effluent released) and granting dischargers the authority to decide the means by which effluent will be controlled. Thus, monitoring and enforcement is focused on what a source discharges and not what technology it installs and operates. Monitoring approaches range from self-reported sampling procedures of effluent flow and concentrations to continuous monitoring of dischargers. Fines or fees for exceeding the discharge levels are immediate financial penalties that provide strong incentives for compliance.

Therefore, a CAM program will require regulatory agencies to reallocate agency resources and develop new staff expertise. Under conventional water quality management programs, substantial agency resources and attention are devoted to identifying best available control technologies or BMPs. As a result, regulatory staff have assumed the role of an engineer-planner who determines the best waste management strategies for individual dischargers. Under a CAM program, regulatory staff must be less of an engineer working to solve the dischargers' pollution control problems and more of an environmental detective and police officer to protect the public's interest in water quality. Such a change will often require either new agency resources or a reallocation of agency resources to these new tasks. One of the most significant but unrecognized obstacles to the implementation of market-based trading programs is having regulatory agency staff recognize and change agency priorities associated with these new job responsibilities.[13]

CAM Fosters Cooperative Enforcement of Compliance with Allowances

A CAM program can create incentives for dischargers' self-reporting and self-enforcement. Because allowances are limited in number and are a commodity that can be bought and sold, they become assets that have a financial value. As a result, dischargers have financial incentives to protect the value of that asset. If one discharger violates the rules by discharging more than (his or her) allowance holdings, the values of all other allowances are diminished. After all, a rule-breaker reduces the number of potential customers to those selling allowances. Since dischargers stand to lose financially when one discharger breaks the rules, each discharger has incentives to detect and report unlawful behavior. By contrast, noncompliance (discharges in excess of NPDES limits) is a chronic problem in the existing permit system. Incentives for self-regulation among dischargers are nonexistent because the noncompliant behavior of one discharger creates no negative consequences for other dischargers. This self-enforcement incentive is no different than the self-enforcement that ordinary citizens do every day against personal property theft. Few citizens would stand by silently while witnessing a car theft. People help police officers enforce against property theft, not only out of civic duty, but also out financial self-interest—detection of a lawbreaker today may prevent a personal loss of property tomorrow. While markets do not rely exclusively on self-enforcement, broad public support (witnesses, tips, informants, etc.) makes policing against property theft and other forms of crime less costly and more effective.

Market-Like Trading Programs: Working Around The CWA

There is little prospect for near-term reforms of the CWA, so CAM programs must be designed within existing statutory and regulatory constraints. This section describes some of the practical implementation challenges and also suggests opportunities to facilitate implementation of market-like programs for water quality management.

Group Compliance Permits and the Partial Cap

CAM programs can start with a partial cap placed on a group of regulated PS dischargers. As has been explained previously, a combination of factors makes market-like trading of NPDES permits impossible. Fortunately, a practical, and already tested, permitting strategy, the GCP, offers a way to implement the CAM program. The GCP would specify the total aggregate allowable discharge for a group of dischargers in a given watershed. Exchange of control responsibility (trading) could then occur among the sources covered by the GCP. Under such an arrangement, dischargers are free to make choices about control strategies. Failure to participate in the GCP association and to follow association bylaws would activate the source's otherwise dormant individual NPDES permit.

Under a GCP, individual dischargers are not required to use specific control practices, nor are their operational choices constrained by technology-oriented NPDES permit requirements. New and existing sources would not face specific performance or technology requirements as a condition to discharge. Rather, new sources could make a payment to existing sources in an effort to secure membership in the association. The permit also establishes swift and immediate enforcement provisions in the event that aggregate association discharges exceed the association cap.

There are many specific forms that this kind of permit can take. One approach that has been applied for the Neuse River in North Carolina begins with assignment of individual source limits in NPDES as a way to develop a group cap. These NPDES limits are then waived and converted into allowances as long as the source agrees to participate in a discharger association covered by a CGP. The association establishes internal rules for exchanging allowances. Such an organization might be a more effective way to coordinate market participants, particularly when the participants are familiar with each other and are fairly small in number. In essence, the association acts as an umbrella organization to reduce transactions costs between members.

In the program predecessor to the Neuse program, the Tar River (North Carolina) Association, the association members responded to the flexibility of the program by aggressively reducing nitrogen discharges for a fraction of the original cost estimates. With this flexibility, association members were initially able to reduce nutrient loads by making operational changes without expensive capital upgrades. Many of these inexpensive, but effective, operational changes came as a surprise to both the regulators and the members of the association. Relatively simple and inexpensive nitrogen control strategies remained untapped and unknown until the association members had the ability and incentive to discover them. During a period of prolonged economic growth, the association has not exceeded the discharge cap once.[14] Such a compliance record alone is a significant achievement. The establishment of an enforceable cap under a group permit represents a policy with market-like flexibility. (For extended discussion of the Neuse River program see chapter 2.)

Expanding the Partial Cap Through CAM

While uncommon, there are examples of water quality management programs that have placed mandatory mass load limits on NPSs. For example, in the Neuse River Basin, North Carolina has developed a set of regulations that cap all sources including nutrient loads to the river by agricultural landowners and urban areas,[15] in effect creating a kind of GCP for agricultural sources, although the implementation and enforcement aspects are far less stringent than for the PS GCP.

Realistically, there still is limited prospect for mandatory limits on currently unregulated NPSs. Once partial caps are put in place and market-like programs are underway, however, incentives might emerge to incrementally incorporate unregulated NPSs into a GCP. One example would be to reward a municipality's wastewater treatment plant (WWTP) that falls under a partial cap for reaching out to reduce discharges from NPSs. In such an example, a municipality's WWTP might be initially granted some number of allowances under a GCP and then granted additional allowances, if the municipality agrees to connect houses with failing septic systems to the centralized sewer system.[16]

As a condition for issuing the new allowances and added management flexibility, the municipality should be required to measure and report the effectiveness of any NPS controls. Such documentation would include both the means for quantifying nutrient reduction effectiveness (documenting performance) and providing assurances that reductions actually occur and are maintained over time. This requirement would create incentives for discovering and improving measurement and documentation for NPS load reductions.

Nonpoint Source Credit Sales

When cap coverage cannot be expanded, a particularly intriguing feature of the GCP, as implemented in some locations, is the inclusion of fees when the group discharge exceeds the group limit. If the group of regulated sources exceeds its group limit, the group must make a payment to a fund that will secure equivalent load reductions from sources outside the group, usually uncapped NPSs. In both the Neuse and Tar programs, there was a provision for the group to pay for NPSs reductions if the collective discharges exceed the cap. Such payments were another incentive to innovate and find new ways to limit group discharges, so no payments have actually been made.

There are ways to design a program to use these fees, or to use general revenues, to have market-like features. We refer to this kind of design as "nonpoint credit sales." Since allowances are not issued to the unregulated sources, the commodity being created, sold, and bought is a "credit." A credit is created when documented pollutant reductions below some expected baseline are made and then are sold to a GCP program that has exceeded its cap or to governments who are spending general tax revenues to secure NPS reductions.

Credit sales programs differ from the conventional approach to securing NPS control programs that pay for a share of the costs that private landowners incur for BMP installation; BMPs are land-use management practices or structures that can be readily observed (e.g., forested riparian buffers along streams, animal waste storage structures, winter cover crops, etc). Once BMPs are in place, average pollutant removal effectiveness is calculated to estimate the reductions achieved. Rarely is there rigorous monitoring and analysis of the BMPs performance, however. Equally troubling is that the BMP operation and maintenance that is required to secure the predicted performance over time is actually never put into place. Storm water retention ponds, for example, have been required for many years, but there is no reporting requirement on a pond's performance or maintenance. Paying sources that implement agency-identified BMPs is not a market-like program. These payments do not provide sources with either the opportunity or the incentive to develop creative new NPS control strategies or create incentives to improve measurement and monitoring of NPS performance.

One reason for this conventional approach is that documenting load reduction at NPSs is challenging, but a market-like program focuses on performance (load reduction results) and not technology in place. Therefore, a market-like nonpoint credit sales program must overcome the problem of measuring and validating NPS reductions. The measurement and documentation challenge can be met by shifting the responsibility of measurement from government agencies to private entities seeking to create and sell NPS credits, changing the responsibility of the regulatory agency to verification of the reported reductions and away from specifying reduction technologies.[17] Credit providers would have the opportunity to offer different approaches to documentation of load reduction. With the burden of proof on those creating nonpoint credits to document performance, a market-like credit sales program would then allow NPS credit suppliers to experiment with the most effective ways to reduce NPS loading and not be limited to a pre-determined suite of BMPs. Such flexibility might include preventing nutrients from entering waters through the application of conventional BMPs, behavioral changes (e.g., reducing fertilizer application), land conversion (crop to forest cover), or by combinations of these. Given the flexibility to be creative, credit suppliers might also produce NPS credits by removing nutrients after the nutrients have entered the water body. These waste assimilation credits would be created by increasing the biological waste assimilative capacity—for example, through enhanced oyster aquaculture, biomass harvest, or wetland restoration.[18] A market-like credit sales program is based on creating the incentive to explore water quality improvement methods of all types and to be paid only when the efficacy of such methods can be documented.[19]

Whether the payments are made from general revenues or from a GCP that has exceeded its cap, there may be a need to build a new institution that will reduce transactions costs between the buyers and sellers: a credit resale program. The credit resale program would have a designated government agency purchase documented NPS reductions and, if there is a demand from a GCP, resell those credits to capped dischargers who must meet their regulatory obligations through purchasing NPS credits. The fund would be initially capitalized by either private or state funding, but the program would become self-financing as revenues collected from credit sales are deposited back to the fund and then used to purchase additional credits over time. In this approach, the government agency acts as an intermediary between PS (capped) buyers and NPS sellers. An additional likely result from this approach is that private entrepreneurs, looking for opportunities to make a profit, would be likely to invest in identifying credits from urban and agricultural sources and assembling those credits for sale to the credit resale agency. The reasons why government might serve this function and why this might encourage private investors to become credit sellers are complex and are discussed elsewhere in the context of securing wetlands and stream mitigation credits within the North Carolina Ecosystem Enhancement Program.[20] Of key importance is that the credit resale approach be designed to emphasize documentation and assurance of outcomes (not BMPs) and in so doing create the incentives and flexibility for providers of NPS reductions to be innovative, not only in how they provide credits, but also in how they document that the credits created are valid reductions in pollutant loads.

Conclusion

Conventional regulatory and cost share programs implemented under the CWA undermine the conditions necessary for the establishment of more market-like programs.

As a result so-called trading programs based on the NPDES permitting platform cannot incorporate the basic features of a market-like program. A market-like water quality program must contain four design attributes, which are the responsibility of governments. First, it is a responsibility of government to define, set, and enforce a cap on total discharges to ensure that water quality standards are attained. Second, it is a responsibility of government to divide the cap into discharge allowances that clearly specify how much can be discharged, and where and when. It is also a responsibility to make the allowances available to waste dischargers by lottery, auction, or some other distribution method. Third, because the allowances are a commodity that can be bought, sold or leased, among those dischargers under the cap, the government needs to assure that the rules governing the program minimize transactions costs (information and contracting between buyers and sellers). Fourth, rules should assure that holders of allowances have maximum discretion to decide how pollution should be controlled (waste control flexibility) and whether to buy, sell, or lease allowances (exchange flexibility).

If the strong link between water quality management and the individual NPDES process can be broken, water quality trading programs can become more market-like and make a significant contribution to meeting water quality standards. Indeed, there are ways to work around the CWA to employ market-based principles for water quality trading programs. However, while there are examples of such innovation, they are limited in number.

Notes

1. Environmental Protection Agency, 2004; "Water Quality Trading," EPA, last modified October 19, 2010, http://water.epa.gov/type/watersheds/trading.cfm; Maryland Department of Environment, Water Management Administration, *Policy for Nutrient Cap Management and Trading in Maryland's Chesapeake Bay Watershed*, April 17, 2008, http://www.mde.maryland.gov/programs/Water/Documents/www.mde.state.md.us/assets/document/NutrientCap_Trading_Policy.pdf.

2. Kurt Stephenson and Leonard Shabman. 2011 "Rhetoric and Reality of Water Quality Trading and the Potential for Market-like Reform." *Journal of American Water Resources Association.* 47 (February) 1: 15–28.

3. The example used in this chapter is the discharge of the nutrients nitrogen and phosphorus as pollutants because most applications-trading programs are for the control of nitrogen and phosphorus discharges.

4. O. A. Houck, *The Clean Water Act TMDL Program: Law, Policy, and Implementation* 2nd ed. (Washington, DC: Environmental Law Institute, 2002).

5. The NPDES process is required by the CWA, but in most places, it is executed by the states with EPA oversight.

6. While the origins of some NPSs may be untraceable, the source of many such discharges likely could be identified given the expenditure of sufficient time and resources. Indeed, over time the EPA has made administrative decisions that have redefined various NPSs as PSs. In a variety of state and local programs, sources traditionally defined as NPSs have been quantified and measured. In recent years, some urban storm water runoff has been defined as a "point source" and has come under the NPDES process. The same has occurred with agricultural discharges from confined animal feeding operations, and an NPDES program has been established for that source.

7. T. Davies, *Reforming Permitting*, RFF Report (Washington, DC: Resources for the Future, December 2001), http://www.rff.org/rff/Documents/RFF-RPT-reformperm.pdf.

8. Kurt Stephenson, Leonard Shabman, and L. L. Geyer, "Watershed-Based Effluent Allowance Trading: Identifying the Statutory and Regulatory Barriers to Implementation," *Environmental Lawyer* 5, no. 3 (1999): 775–815.

9. The offsets are usually based on practices installed and assumed to provide a pollutant reduction result, as opposed to being a measured reduction in pollutant load.

10. Lynne L. Bennett, Steven G. Thorpe, and A. Joseph Guse, "Cost-Effective Control of Nitrogen Loadings in Long Island Sound," *Water Resources Research* 36, no. 12 (December 2000): 3711–20, doi:10.1029/2000WR900199; M. O. Ribaudo, R. Heimlich, and M. Peters, "Nitrogen Sources and Gulf Hypoxia: Potential for Environmental Credit Trading," *Ecological Economics* 52 (2005): 159–68; James C. Hanson and K. E. McConnell, "Simulated Trading for Maryland's Nitrogen Loadings in the Chesapeake Bay," *Agricultural and Resource Economics Review* 37, no. 2 (October 2008): 211–26.

11. J. H. Dales, *Pollution, Property and Prices: An Essay in Policy-Making and Economics* (Toronto: University of Toronto Press, 1968).

12. Paradoxically, the combination of waste control and exchange flexibility may reduce the number of exchanges that occur. Markets without exchange are a likely initial outcome of a CAM program. Immediately after the implementation of an allowance market, dischargers respond to new incentives and opportunities by aggressively reducing effluent loads below allowance holdings. In many cases, unexpected pollutant reductions are found and pollution control is achieved at a fraction of the anticipated costs. Dischargers would rather find a way to lower nutrient loads and costs rather than paying someone else to do it for them. If all dischargers are all reducing effluent loads below allowance holdings, the need to trade is limited (see note 2, Shabman, Stephenson, and Shobe, "Trading Programs"). Over time, trade may increase as initial improvements are implemented and new nutrient sources enter a watershed and increase allowance demand.

13. Shabman, Stephenson, and Shobe, "Trading Programs."

14. Shabman and Stephenson, "Achieving Nutrient Water Quality Goals."

15. Ibid.

16. Richard Woodward, "Lessons About Effluent Trading from a Single Trade," *Review of Agricultural Economics* 25, no. 1 (2003): 235–45.

17. Stephenson, Norris, and Shabman, "Effluent Allowance Trading."

18. Kurt Stephenson and Leonard Shabman, The Use of Nutrient Assimilation Services in Water Quality Credit Trading Programs, Working paper 2011-01, Department of Agricultural and Applied Economics, Virginia Tech, May 31, 2011, 22 pp.

19. One recent experiment in Pennsylvania made a claim for being market-like because it had landowners compete to sell BMPs as offsets to regulated dischargers (see Greenhalgh et al. 2007, Paying for Environmental Performance: Using Reverse Auctions to Allocate Funding for Conservation. World Resources Institute, Policy Note No. 3 (January 2007) http://pdf.wri.org/pep_reverseauction.pdf.) At a superficial level, competition to sell BMPs might appear to be market-like; however, a key element of any market is that sellers are motivated to, and rewarded for, innovation in how they produce a product. In this auction, there was no financial incentive for innovation as the regulators, not the dischargers, were responsible for identifying control technologies and strategies.

20. Leonard Shabman and Paul Scodari, *Past, Present, and Future of Wetlands Credit Sales*, Discussion Paper 04-48 (Washington, DC: Resources for the Future, 2004), http://www.rff.org/documents/rff-dp-04-48.pdf.

9

The Economic Effects of Using Property Taxes in Lieu of Direct User Fees to Pay for Water

B. Delworth Gardner

Introduction

It is frequently argued that water supplies in the western United States may not be adequate to meet future demand. Transfers out of agriculture, which typically accounts for over 75 percent of water consumption, have accommodated most of the new demand for water in recent decades. But in the face of droughts and continually increasing demand from urban, industrial, and recreational users, is there enough water to sustain agriculture and simultaneously meet the needs of a changing economy? The answer to this question depends partly, if not primarily, on the institutions—federal, state, and local—that price, allocate, and conserve water. Richard Howitt has argued that the costs of institutional change in water tend to be high because the rents from water use and current property right allocations change as institutions change, and concerns for equity (income distribution) are often of dominating political importance.[1] (Chapters 6, 7, 11, and 12 in this book have particularly cogent things to say on the importance of political and legal institutions in efficiently allocating water.)

This chapter explores the economic implications of using ad valorem taxes assessed on real property in lieu of direct user charges (prices) to pay for water development and allocation. Taxes used as a revenue source for government that are unrelated to the quantity of water demanded produce an implicit subsidy to water users, and special focus will be directed in this chapter to the inefficiency in the allocation of water when it is priced below its supply cost.

The geographical focus of the analysis is Utah, the state that ranks second to Nevada as the highest per capita consumer of water and which also has some of the lowest water prices in the western United States.[2] Many of the water institutions and their pricing practices in Utah, however, exist in the other states, so the analysis has broad application to the whole western region of the United States. Public water districts have been created by statute to manage water sales and distribution in many western states,[3] and these districts typically have been given authority to levy property taxes in state and/or in local jurisdictions in order to generate revenues needed to meet repayment obligations to large water developers such as the federal Bureau of Reclamation.

The property tax is a highly dependable source of funds for the districts as it supplements the revenues from direct water sales. Eliminating this revenue source, therefore, could be considered threatening to a district's financial viability and thus will be strongly resisted. Hence, attention and analysis must be directed to whether or not direct water charges as a substitute revenue source for the property tax are politically as well as economically feasible. This chapter, therefore, will also address specific objections by the water districts and their supporters to replacing the property tax with direct user charges. It will also discuss the water-conservation implications of using direct charges in lieu of property taxes to pay for water. In general, it is widely believed that water conservation (reduced water use) can be best effectuated through government-mandated rules, such as requiring water-saving household appliances or limiting lawn irrigation to certain days or to specific times when evaporation losses are thought to be lower. If a certain level of conservation is desirable, however, the effectiveness of these mandated rules must be compared to the conservation efforts that will be made voluntarily by the final users themselves as they respond to higher water prices in lieu of property taxes. The argument advanced here is that voluntary price-induced conservation will usually be more flexible, pervasive, durable, and hence effective than command-and-control governmental regulations. This is not to say that government should have no role to play in conservation—educating water consumers, for example, about economically feasible conservation practices and technologies available may be very useful.

How important are water-related property taxes in Utah as a source of revenue for the water districts? The Utah Rivers Council conducted a study of water suppliers across the eleven contiguous western states, fifty-four of them outside of Utah and eight within.[4] The study found that Utah water districts have statutory authority to levy higher property taxes than districts located in most other states. Moreover, a higher percentage of Utah districts actually used property taxes than was the case in the other states, and these taxes constituted a higher percentage of total district revenues in Utah. Specifically, in the western region outside of Utah, of the twelve districts in the sample that used property taxes, eight received less than 16 percent of their total budget from these taxes. By contrast, in Utah, according to data assembled in the State Auditor's Office,[5] property taxes accounted for between 17 and 20 percent of total revenues in four of the Utah districts, and between 32 and 67 percent in the other four districts. In addition, of the twelve suppliers sampled outside of Utah that collected property taxes, only three used the property-tax revenues for general fund purposes (such as administrative, operation, and maintenance costs), whereas in Utah all of the responding districts (only four of eight districts responded to the River Council's survey) used funds for these general purposes. In sum, Utah districts use the property tax to a greater extent as a revenue source than do comparable districts in other western states. Hence, the data suggest that Utah may be an especially apt location to investigate the economic implications of reducing the property tax in favor of direct water pricing.

The Property Tax and Efficient Allocation of Water Resources

In a market economy prices signal information to consumers and producers. Consider a hypothetical market for water. If water is not rationed by nonprice measures, consumers will consume water until the benefit derived from the last unit of consumption is equal to the price paid. The demand for water taken by a typical consumer is represented by the curve labeled D in Figure 9.1. Following conventional economic theory, the various points along the demand curve represent the marginal valuations by consumers of alternative quantities of water, and because of diminishing marginal utility, these valuations fall as more water is consumed. An aggregate demand curve

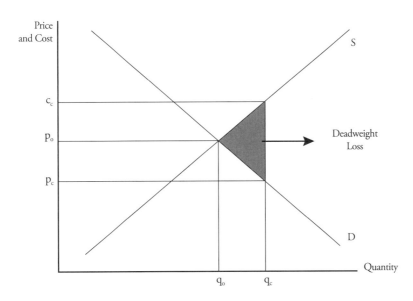

Figure 9.1 Ineffieiency in a water market due to underpricing

for water in a given market can be represented as the horizontal summation of water quantities demanded at various prices across all individual users.

Also, following traditional economic theory, the supply curve (S) represents the marginal opportunity costs of supplying various quantities of water to ultimate users. These costs include construction as well as operating and maintenance costs and are presumed to rise with increasing quantities of water supplied as scarce capital, labor, and management resources are attracted away from increasingly valuable alternative uses.

In such a market, only one water price will equate the marginal costs of supplying water (a point on the supply curve) with the marginal valuations of water by consumers (a point on the demand curve). Let us denote this price as p_o and its corresponding quantity demanded and supplied as q_o. This point is the equilibrium price and quantity that represents an efficient allocation of resources in the water market. Let us see why.

At any quantity lower than q_o, the marginal valuation for consumers of water is higher than the marginal cost of suppliers and, therefore, increasing the quantity of water to q_o would produce a surplus of value over cost. At quantities higher than q_o, the marginal valuation of consumers is lower than the marginal cost of water; thus quantities above q_o are more costly than they are worth. Too many resources have been allocated to supplying water to be efficient. It follows that at quantity q_o, the allocation of resources is efficient since the marginal value of water to consumers is equal to the marginal cost of supplying that water, and the market clears since the quantity demanded is equal to the quantity supplied.

Now, suppose that for one reason or another, the water price is not allowed to rise to the equilibrium price of p_o. Using ad valorem property taxes in lieu of direct water-user prices as a revenue-producing mechanism for a water district would be one such case. The market price, therefore, would cease to function as a mechanism leading to an efficient allocation of resources to water development and use. In effect, taxes on real property owners in the region of water deliveries can be regarded as a "subsidy" to water consumers since the assessed valuation of property for tax purposes is largely independent of the quantity of water use. Hence, the property tax itself is unrelated to the price of water and, therefore, has no direct role in determining how much water will be demanded.[6] Perhaps an indirect effect will be induced if the property tax reduces consumer income and water demand is responsive to real income changes. At most, however, this effect is likely to be small as expenditures for water are typically a small percentage of total income.

In Figure 9.1, assume that the subsidized water price made possible by the property tax is p_c. The associated quantity demanded is q_c, a larger quantity than is the economically efficient quantity of q_o. At p_c, therefore, excess demand exists, and consumers will want more water at this price than at the equilibrium price. The history of water development across the globe is replete with examples of political responses to accommodate this excess demand that exists because of water subsidies. This problem is especially acute in the case of public water suppliers, since the sine qua non of politics is politicians seeking to deliver political favors requested by their constituents.

Note that the marginal cost of water at quantity q_c is c_c, above its value to consumers at p_c. The shaded area in Figure 9.1 represents the difference between what the quantities of water between q_c and q_o are worth to consumers and what it costs to supply that water. This surplus of cost over value is known as "deadweight loss"—a measure of economic inefficiency. This loss suggests that too many resources are being allocated to supplying water to be efficient since society values the "excess" resources devoted to supply water more highly in other uses. Of course, the quantification of the precise amount of deadweight loss is an empirical matter and will depend critically on how far the price is below the equilibrium price and what the elasticities of the demand and supply curves are for water. (These matters will be discussed later in the chapter.) It has been demonstrated elsewhere that water subsidies employed in federal projects have produced inefficient and premature irrigation development in the western United States.[7]

An important political implication of requiring users to pay the total supply cost of water is that then these water consumers will support politically only the construction of projects that are economically feasible—where expected project benefits are at least equal to project costs. On the other hand, if the costs can be shifted to other parties and the water is priced below its cost, then no such assurance would exist that water consumers will support only efficient projects. It follows that if part of the costs of water supply can be shifted from water users to owners of property via the property tax, water users can be expected to enthusiastically support water projects, even if the project costs in aggregate exceed project benefits. Such inefficient projects diminish rather than enhance the wealth and average standard of living of society as a whole. This is the important economic implication of deadweight loss.

Another extremely important consequence of pricing water below its cost for a specific water project is that other potentially lower-cost supply sources may not be given adequate consideration for meeting demand. Water quality reclamation, secondary water systems that provide lower-cost water for non-drinking purposes such as irrigation and industrial uses, more intensive ground water utilization, and water conservation practices, are supply alternatives with potentially lower cost than new water development projects most of which are sponsored by federal and state governments. It should be obvious that wealth is created most effectively by utilizing water supply sources that have the lowest costs.

Evaluating Objections to Eliminating the Property Tax

Many objections to replacing property taxes with increased user fees are raised by those in the water supply business, particularly by the public water districts. Perhaps the most important is the contention that if the price were raised, demand would be insufficient to use all of the available water supply, and hence this valuable resource would be unused or wasted. Another objection is that the public water districts that supply water to final users might not be capable of raising sufficient revenues from user fees to meet their contractual obligations to water wholesalers, especially the federal government. Still another is that raising final user prices to replace property taxes would discourage water conservation by the water districts, since higher prices would reduce the quantity demanded and plenty of water would appear to be available. It has also been argued that giving up property taxes as a revenue source would lower the bond ratings of water district debt and, therefore, cost the districts more to borrow money and thus imperil their fiscal viability. Finally, a frequently heard objection to raising water prices is that this would impose inequitable burdens on poor people. Let us investigate the validity of each of these claims.

Will Higher Prices Result in "Wasted" Water?

Two important questions surface if the price of water rises: (1) the effects on the quantity of water demanded, and (2) the effects on water conservation. Let us analyze these matters in turn.

It has been demonstrated already in the discussion surrounding Figure 9.1 that the quantity of water demanded will be greater at a lower price than would be true if the price were higher. Using a property tax as a price-substitute revenue source implies that the direct water price will be lower than if the price had to bear the entire revenue burden. Now, suppose that a water district has supplies available to meet the quantity demanded at the lower subsidized price. Returning to Figure 9.1, if quantity q_c of water is available for distribution, a final user price that is above p_c would reduce the quantity demanded to a level below the quantity supplied. We might refer to this as excess supply. What would happen to that water at this higher price? In the Utah case discussed, this unused water might well run off into sinks such as the Great Salt Lake or move into storage in reservoirs, lakes, and groundwater aquifers until they are filled to capacity. Hence, it is not clear that this water not demanded would necessarily be "wasted" or even go unused over the long run. In fact, stored water may have high value simply as supply insurance as protection against drought, and some environmental and recreational benefits could accrue from greater quantities of water in storage, even in sinks such as the Great Salt Lake where the salt content makes water unusable for many purposes. The point must be granted, however, that in a year of average or higher precipitation and runoff, lower quantities demanded at higher prices may result in unused water, at least temporarily, or at best may be employed in lower-valued uses.[8]

This situation of unused water supplies is a common occurrence even without the effects of a higher water price. Given the length of time needed to bring new water supplies online and the fact that new water comes in quantity "lumps," water demand and supply are seldom equated in a given year or even over many years. In planning for future population and economic growth, supply agencies generally will have excess water until demand grows to match existing supplies. For example, the Wasatch Front of Utah is a rapidly growing urban area, both in population and economic activity. As pointed out previously, household demand for water is affected by income—as per capita income increases, the demand for water rises. In fact, it is roughly true that even if the price were constant, the demand for water would increase at a rate about proportionate to increases in per capita income and population.[9]

Because surface water supplies are generally stochastic, depending on more-or-less random precipitation and temperature, another pricing issue surfaces. If water storage facilities are not available to stabilize water deliveries through time, an efficient pricing system should incorporate flexible water pricing as available supplies vary. Prices could be raised in years and seasons of short supply and lowered in years and seasons of plentiful supply in order to equate quantity demanded and quantity supplied. Of course, because water prices are generally administratively set, some agency would have to be responsible for gauging supply and demand and setting efficient prices. An objection might be raised that governments have only weak incentives to manage such a system of efficient water prices, even if they have the responsibility and capacity to do so. This problem could be reduced if the pricing schedule as a function of available water supply were promulgated publicly and in advance of any particular supply conditions. The price expectations of water users would then become established as price-setting government would be expected to act in accordance with the rules. Under such a pricing system, arbitrary changes in prices would be more difficult without some formal public-approval process.

Elasticity of Demand and Water Conservation

The critical parameter affecting district revenues from direct water prices, as well as conservation of water by final users, is the price elasticity of demand for water. Price elasticity establishes how much water demanded would be expected to fall as the water price increases. Formally, price elasticity is the percentage change in quantity demanded that accompanies a percentage change in the price. For example, if the price were raised by 10 percent and, as a consequence, the quantity demanded falls by 5 percent, the price elasticity of demand is −0.5; that is, the percentage change in the quantity demanded is half as great as the percentage change in the price. (The negative sign of the elasticity coefficient means that water price and quantity demanded move in opposite directions.)

Given what economists know empirically about price elasticity of demand for water (to be discussed shortly), it is perplexing that water prices are so often ignored in water planning. The most typical plan for increasing supply simply projects changes in population, and water demand is assumed to change proportionately because people have a certain water "requirement." Occasionally income is included as an explanatory variable in projecting the demand for water as it is rightly assumed that high-income people demand more water than do those with lower incomes. Of course, this neglect of price in planning implicitly assumes that demand for water is perfectly price inelastic (an elasticity coefficient of 0), meaning that the quantity demanded is completely unresponsive to changes in the water price. This assumption is surely wrong and usually leads to costly errors (popularly known as the "planner's curse") in anticipating how much water will be demanded when new water is available and some price is established to help defray the costs of providing it.

The author recently (May, 2011) attended a conference where the projected water demand in the years ahead for Las Vegas was discussed by the city's water planner. The price of water was never mentioned as a factor that would help determine the city's future water demand. This is very difficult to understand given the obvious importance of price as will be discussed shortly.

What factors influence the price elasticity of demand for water, and what are the numerical estimates from empirical studies? The responsiveness of quantity demanded to changes in the water price is determined primarily by the number and magnitude of the adjustments that users make. These adjustments are crucially important to what is popularly known as conservation.

Consider domestic (household) use, which will generally include water used outside the home in irrigating lawns, trees, shrubs, and flowers as well as inside the house in bathrooms, kitchens, clothing washrooms, and inside plant watering. Clearly, the type and quantity of adjustments made to the water price change will depend on the time interval over which the adjustments are made. Economists refer to the periods of adjustment as runs (i.e., short run, medium run, and long run). If the time period is very short (e.g., a day or even a week), the adjustment response to a price increase will likely be limited to routine things such as turning off the water tap sooner in the shower or reducing the time the lawn sprinkler is on. These limited adjustments imply that the price elasticity of demand in the shortest of runs will be "low"—perhaps from zero to −0.1. Over the longer run, however, additional quantity adjustments to a price change will be made—plumbing leaks can be repaired, heavy water-using fixtures and appliances in the household can be replaced by those that use less water, and an irrigation technology in the yard can be selected that uses less water. For example, for watering trees, shrubs, and flowers, drip systems (that deliver a very high percentage of water applied to the root zone of the plant) can be used instead of sprinkling technology that generally loses more water to evaporation and percolation below the root zone. Even the plants chosen in and outside the house might be changed to those that require less water, or perhaps landscaping can be designed that has few or no plants at all. It is striking how different landscaping is employed among communities that face sharply different water prices. For example, in Salt Lake City (which has relatively low water prices), urban landscapes contain a plentitude of trees, shrubs, flowers, and lawn grasses that require relatively large amounts of water per unit of land, whereas in Tucson (which has high water prices), yards typically have either very few plants or varieties of plants, such as cacti, that consume little water.[10] In the long run, when all economically feasible adjustments are made to price differences, the price elasticity of demand for water may be high (−1.0, or even higher).

Likewise, over the long run in irrigated agriculture, farmers may make a great number of possible adjustments to changes in water price: different crops, various irrigation technologies and irrigation practices, ditch and canal linings, and recovery of tail water for reuse.[11] Considering all of these adjustment possibilities, especially in the long run, it should come as no surprise that price elasticity of demand for water is much higher (more elastic) than is commonly recognized by water planners and water district managers.

What do empirical studies show the price elasticity of demand for water to be? First, a caveat must be noted. Good reasons exist for believing that the findings of empirical studies might well be biased downward (too low or too inelastic) compared to the "true" long-run elasticity of demand. As suggested previously, the water users at the time they are observed, and at which time the calculations of elasticity are made, may not have completed all of the adjustments they will make eventually. This is easily seen by discussing the two types of estimates of water price elasticity of demand.

Empirical studies are either time-series or cross-sectional, or perhaps a combination of both. In time-series analyses, the water use rates of the same consuming units (say households or farms) are observed at different points in time in which they face different real water prices. In contrast, in cross-sectional studies, different consuming units facing different water prices are observed over the same time period. In both cases, the basic units of observation are users consuming different quantities of water at different prices. Statistical (usually regression) techniques with price as an explanatory variable are then employed to estimate the coefficients of price elasticity of demand. Because the data on prices and quantities are more accessible for the same users at different points in time, time-series studies of elasticity are more common than cross-sectional studies.

A priori, however, a higher price elasticity of demand (more elastic) might be expected in cross-sectional than in time-series analyses. Why? As suggested previously, cross-sectional analysis involves using different spatial units of observation (e.g., firms or households in various communities) at a given moment in time. The variation in prices and associated quantities demanded is normally quite large among various communities with disparate water supply conditions. Hence, as discussed previously, consumers of water probably have had a relatively long period to make quantity adjustments in response to these price differences. In short, the adjustment process will be approximately complete as the observations of water prices and their associated quantities are observed and recorded. On the other hand, in typical time-series analyses, observations will be the same consuming units over some time period such as consecutive years. The real prices of water (the nominal [observed] price corrected for inflation) may change only a small amount from one observation period to the next. This means that the adjustments in observed quantity demanded to even these short-term price changes may be far from complete as the next observation period begins. Hence, less variation in the quantities demanded probably will be observed than if the adjustment period was longer. This logic implies that lower estimates of elasticity of demand (more inelastic) probably will be observed in time-series than in cross-sectional analyses. This is really a variant of the logic that was used previously to suggest that short-run elasticities are lower (less elastic) than long-run elasticities.

This expected finding seems to be confirmed by actual empirical studies. Gardner and Schick made a cross-sectional study of average household water use in forty-four northern Utah communities in the early 1960s.[12] Water prices and average household consumption, along with several other variables such as the average lot size and the average value of the community's houses, were collected from each of these communities. A high degree of variation among these communities in water prices and associated quantities demanded was observed, and the price elasticity of demand was estimated to be –0.77—at the higher end of reported elasticities.

Dr. Gail Blattenberger, Professor of Economics at the University of Utah, has collected price elasticities of demand for urban water use from about fifty studies from the western United States, excluding Utah, and eight additional ones from Utah.[13] Most of these studies were of the time-series variety. As expected, some variation in elasticity estimates exists, but nearly all of them are between 0 and –1.2.[14] Blattenberger's data also suggest that the range of elasticity estimates for Utah are very similar to those for other western states and that –0.5 would be a fairly representative number for both areas.

What are the implications for water conservation of these price-elasticity estimates? Conservation of water may occur at many levels in the water supply chain, but primarily it occurs at the water district (wholesale) level and at the final user level. The water districts sometimes are required by law to implement conservation practices, and the districts often supplement these requirements in order to increase the usable water supply available to their customers.[15]

The districts argue that replacing the property tax with higher direct water prices might reduce their revenues and hence their ability to promote and engage in conservation projects. Also, they maintain that a smaller water quantity would be demanded at the higher direct water price and hence reduce the need for district conservation. These arguments are of doubtful validity for two reasons. First, higher prices as a substitute for property taxes may be set at levels that would be revenue neutral for the districts (discussed later). But, more importantly, the higher prices would result in less water demanded primarily because users themselves would have an incentive to save water, making conservation at the district level less urgent. Of course, elasticity of demand is the critical determinant of how much water market revenues would decline if higher prices were imposed as well as how much final users would conserve on water use.

This relationship between price and conservation warrants further discussion, especially when conservation becomes most urgent in times of drought. As argued previously, if the quantity demanded falls because of a price increase, it is principally because water users are making their own economically optimal adjustments to the higher price. In short, this is price-induced conservation of the most fundamental kind. If conservation is perceived to be in the best interests of consuming units, it is likely to be the most ubiquitous as well as the most effective and permanent. The water districts are limited in their capacity to save water in any case. They may mandate practices such as requiring water-saving showerheads, more water-efficient toilets, smaller urban lot size, or any number of other practices, but the implementation of these practices would likely require a high degree of coercive power that is objectionable to water users if these practices are not really economically feasible for them. On the other hand, if final users face higher prices, they will have an incentive to consider and implement ways to conserve water without being coerced into doing so. This does not mean the water users would like the higher prices. The fact that the districts are concerned about smaller water quantities demanded if the price were raised is proof that they expect voluntary water conservation by the final users. The conclusion must be that the practice of using property taxes in lieu of water tariffs is clearly anticonservation, as has been suggested by Thompson as cited in note 15.

Meeting the Water District's Financial Obligations

Another issue of understandable concern to the water districts of giving up the property tax is potential impairment in meeting their repayment obligations to the developers of water, especially the federal government that distributes water to the districts from large reclamation projects. Facilitating these payments was the principal reason the districts were created in the first place. This revenue-shortage worry, however, is probably overestimated and overstated. Why? Because another important implication of elasticity estimates discussed earlier is that if water demand is price inelastic, then direct water sales at higher prices will generate more market revenues for the districts than lower prices would. Price inelastic demand means that the quantity reduction resulting from a price increase is proportionately less than the price rise, so revenue (price multiplied by quantity) increases. Hence, greater market revenue will be produced by the price rise than may be anticipated by the districts. Of course, whether or not the increased market revenues from price increases will be enough to offset the revenue loss from eliminating or reducing the property tax depends on the magnitude of the price increase, the price elasticity of demand for water, and the proportion of total district revenues that are derived from property taxes.

Some purely illustrative (although quite realistic in the Utah situation) numbers will clarify these relationships. Assume initially that property-tax revenues provide one-quarter of total district revenues and that market sales of water provide the other three-quarters. Suppose that:

> Property-tax revenue = $25 million
> Revenue from water sales = $75 million
> Total revenue = $100 million

Also, assume that the water price is $2 per unit of water (say 10,000 gallons) and that quantity demanded at this price is 37.5 million units.

Now, how high would the water price have to be if revenues from direct market sales were to fully replace the property tax and generate the same total revenue of $100 million? (This may be referred to as a revenue-neutral substitution.) Assume initially that price elasticity of demand for water is −0.3333. This means that if the price were increased 100 percent (doubled) to $4, quantity demanded would fall by 33.33 percent to 25 million units. Total market revenue would be $4 × 25 million or $100 million, and revenues from increasing the price would just offset the lost revenues from eliminating the property tax.

Of course, the more elastic the demand for water (the higher the absolute value of the coefficient), the lower would be the market revenues generated by a given price increase. For example, if the price elasticity of demand was −0.77 (much less inelastic than −0.33, and the number we found in our Utah study of household demand), then the price would have to be much higher to offset the revenues lost from property taxes because the reduction in quantity demanded would be much greater. If the proportion of total revenues provided by the property tax were smaller, then given the elasticity of demand, the smaller would be the necessary rise in the water price to be revenue neutral.

Consider an alternative set of assumed data:

> Property-tax revenues = $10 million
> Revenues from direct water sales = $90 million
> Total revenues = $100 million
> Water price is $2 per unit, and quantity demanded is 45 million units
> Price elasticity of demand is assumed to be −0.5.

What market price would generate revenues of $100 million and thus be revenue neutral? If the price were raised by 33.33 percent to $2.67 per unit, the quantity demanded would fall by 16.67 percent to approximately 37.375 million units. Total market revenues would then be about $100 million.

Comparing the numbers in the two illustrative examples presented, we conclude the following, other things being equal:

1. The lower the dependence on the property tax in raising revenue, the smaller the price increase would have to be to replace the property tax and be revenue neutral.
2. The less inelastic (more elastic) the price elasticity of demand for water, the greater the conservation (quantity) response to a price change would be needed to be revenue neutral.

To summarize, the illustrative numbers suggest that allowing the market price of water to rise to cover the full supply costs and thus eliminate the need for a property tax would not involve Herculean price increases if revenues to the districts remain constant. But could this action be accomplished legally under the contracts held by the water districts? I discuss this question next.

Contractual Obligations to the Bureau of Reclamation

Officials of the public water districts argue that the question of eliminating the property tax is moot since the districts are legally obligated by contract to use property taxes to raise revenues to pay the federal government for water supplied by federal projects. To verify whether or not this is true, several of the repayment contracts between the federal government and the water conservancy districts in Utah were examined, including those for (1) the Uintah Water Conservancy District receiving water from the Vernal Unit of the Central Utah Project; (2) the Emery Water Conservancy District for water supplied by the Emery County Project, a participating project of the Colorado River Storage Project; (3) the Central Utah Water Conservancy District receiving water from the Bonneville Unit of the Central Utah Project; and (4) the Weber Basin Water Conservancy District, which gets water from the Weber Basin Project. The boilerplate stating the terms of these contracts is similar in all four. The relevant parts of the Central Utah Water Conservancy District repayment contract will be examined here as illustrative.

> The District agrees to pay the United States the project repayment obligation of not to exceed $130,673,000 divided into (1) an irrigation repayment obligation of $16,400,000, (2) an ad valorem tax revenue obligation of not less than $38,005,000, and (3) a municipal and industrial obligation of $76,268,000 plus interest, the sum of not less than $47,000,000 shall be collected and paid from ad valorem taxes. . . . The District agrees to levy and collect ad valorem taxes as may be necessary to meet its obligations to the United States. . . . These collections and payments shall be required until the project repayment obligation is paid in full. Revenues from one-half mill levied and collected by the District under Section 73-9-16 of the Utah Code, and, as required, the revenues from one-half mill now authorized by Section 73-9-20, or the revenues from one-half mill levied and collected under said sections based on a projected increase in assessed valuation of property within the District of two and one-half percent per year compounded, commencing in the year of 1965, whichever amount is less, are hereby specifically pledged as security to repay the District's repayment obligation.

A 1985 Supplemental Contract is also relevant to the property-tax issue under discussion here.

> It is mutually agreed that the language in Paragraph 6(d) of the 1965 Repayment Contract regarding the minimum amounts and limitations on the ad valorem tax pledge is hereby superseded and the one-half mill pledge shall be based upon the actual assessed valuation of property within the Central Utah Water Conservancy District; Provided, however, that such pledge will not exceed the then current annual payment. This pledge includes the tax revenues necessary to pay $38,005,000 and $47,000,000 municipal and industrial cost obligation as specified in Article 6 (a) of the 1965 Repayment Contract.

The purpose and effect of the supplemental contract is that since the property values within the district boundaries were increasing at a higher rate than was assumed when the original contract was signed, the supplement provided that the one-half mill levy would apply to the higher valuations.

The contract between the United States and the Weber Basin Water Conservancy District specifies that

> b. Nothing in the contract shall be construed to deny: (4) the United States a prior claim to all or such part of the proceeds of the ad valorem tax of one mill permitted to be levied under the

authority of Section 100-11-16, Utah Code, as amended, as may be necessary in each year to assure the prompt payment of the amount due the United States hereunder in such year, and such prior claim is hereby expressly recognized by the District, but if under any law now or hereafter available the District shall in any year impose an ad valorem tax in excess of one mill on the dollar, the proceeds of such additional tax may be used by the District for mentioned bonds or other securities, free of any claim thereto by the United States.

In effect, this agreement states that property-tax revenues in excess of funds needed for repayment of the federal obligation may be used for the district's other financial purposes.

Actually, in the Weber Basin case, when the project costs turned out to be higher than originally anticipated, the contract was amended so that the district could reimburse the United States for a greater amount. An amended contract in 1961 states that "one-half of the mill levy could be used to generate revenues to repay the United States, and the other one-half shall be available for application on District bonds."

So what does the foregoing say about whether the property tax is an absolute requirement of the districts to raise revenues for their repayment obligations? It is quite explicit in these contracts that a property tax would be used to repay the United States for water deliveries. The financial obligations of the water districts, however, may be greater than the contractual obligations to the federal government, and the districts may borrow to cover these obligations as well and use the property tax as a device to redeem this indebtedness. The use of the property tax as a means of raising district revenues, therefore, cannot be attributed entirely to the contractual obligations to the federal treasury. But the documents are clear that the property tax is a contractual obligation to be used by the districts to raise revenues. But is this obligation irrevocable? This question will be discussed further later in the chapter.

Another issue affecting repayment obligations of the districts arises in the event that federal water is transferred from irrigation to industrial and municipal uses. The repayment charges would then have to be increased to reflect the fact that irrigation use is heavily subsidized in all federal reclamation projects, meaning that irrigators pay a smaller charge per acre-foot (AF) of water than do industrial and municipal users. These repayment changes are covered in official "block notices" given by the U.S. Department of Interior to the relevant water district. For example, a notice dated December 24, 1968, changed the repayment obligation of the Weber Basin Conservancy District when a block of 5,000 AF of irrigation water was transferred to municipal and industrial uses. The block notice specifies how the increased repayment obligation is to be distributed among the repayment categories, and in this particular case, an ad valorem tax was assessed that covered about 12 percent of the additional repayment obligation.

So what can we conclude from the documents reviewed? While these contracts, amended contracts, and block notices clearly indicate that the United States has built an ad valorem property-tax requirement into its contractual repayment agreements with the water districts in Utah, it does appear that changes in the contracts could be made if both parties were to agree. Hence, if direct water prices were to replace revenues derived from property taxes, the federal government must amend its contracts with the districts until repayment has been made in full, at which time the districts would appear to be free to raise revenues in whatever manner they wish.

Is this approval likely to be given by the federal government? Some of the contract amendments cited suggest that both the government and the districts are amenable to contract amendments when they serve the interests of both parties. The federal government, however, may be reluctant to agree to a change in repayment contracts, especially if the financial positions of the districts appear to be weak and there is risk that they may default on their repayment obligations. Given that the districts have been using sinking funds to acquire financial reserves to cover repayment contingencies, however, and the fact that the value of water is increasing through time, the districts appear to be healthy financially. If they could use direct water prices to raise the required revenues if they had the incentive and will to do so, the federal government might agree if requested. But why should the districts do so on their own volition given that the status quo is more than satisfactory from their point of view? It would not appear to serve their interests to give up a secure source of property-tax revenues. If the broader economic-efficiency rationale discussed earlier in this chapter for such action were sufficiently compelling, however, political intervention in the form of new statutes or simple arm twisting might be used to induce them to comply.

Bond Ratings and Debt Management

Another argument of the districts against shifting away from the property tax is that secure revenues from these taxes are indispensable for maintaining the favorable ratings on bonds they issue for water planning and development and other purposes. The ratings determine the rate of interest that must be paid on district debt, a significant component of the district's total costs.

Bond-rating agencies such as Standard and Poors, Moody's Investor Services, and the Fitch Rating Agency use a variety of criteria for rating the debt of states and their public districts among which are whether the debt is insured, the quality of district management services, anticipation of future regulatory or growth restrictions, and the reliability of implementing rate increases or other revenue sources to cover operational or capital costs. The question at issue here is whether collecting property taxes systematically improves bond ratings for those districts that use them?

The Utah Rivers Council survey referred to earlier queried water suppliers about the bond ratings on district debt.[16] For the forty-two agencies sampled outside Utah not using property taxes, eight issued no bonds, while thirty-four districts reported a total of fifty-seven bond issues with ratings. Of these, nine (15.8 percent) received the highest grade, thirty-two (56.1 percent) had a high-grade rating, and sixteen (28.1 percent) reported an upper medium rating. As would be expected, the bonds that were insured generally received the highest ratings. All of the ratings ranging from highest to upper medium, however, are considered to be "quality investment" grade, meaning that the debt is considered to be of low default risk to investors. Since none of these districts used property taxes to obtain revenues to pay off the bonds, it is obvious that a property tax was not a binding requirement for receiving a "quality investment" grade.

For the twelve outside-Utah agencies collecting property taxes, eighteen ratings were reported. Of these, six (33.3 percent) reported having the highest grade, eight (44.4 percent) received a high-grade rating, three (16.7 percent) received an upper medium grade rating, and one (5.6 percent) received a medium grade rating. Comparing these numbers with those in the previous paragraph, those districts using property taxes had 77.7 percent of issues in the top two rating categories, whereas those that did not, had 71.9 percent. At the other end of the rating categories, those that did not use the property tax had a slightly higher percentage in the upper medium and medium ratings, but in both cases, the differences were relatively small.

In Utah, half of the ratings were obtained directly from the water conservancy districts (only half responded to the survey), while the rest were acquired from Moody's Investor Services. The eight districts reported eight bond issues, but one was an unrated state of Utah loan. Of the remaining, seven (28.6 percent) received the highest grade rating, four (57.1 percent) had a high-grade rating, and one (14.3 percent) had an upper medium grade rating.

For those districts outside Utah not using property taxes as a revenue source, 71.9 percent had ratings in the top two categories of highest grade and high grade. Those districts using the property tax had 77.7 percent in these two categories, while in Utah, those using the property tax (all of them) had 85.7 percent in highest grade and high grade. Considering all of these numbers, those districts that collected property taxes had a slightly higher average bond rating (and therefore lower interest costs), but the differences are small. Given the other factors that also affect ratings, this evidence is by no means conclusive that the ability to collect property taxes reduces the interest rate paid on district indebtedness. Moreover, a district always has the option of insuring its bonds to increase its rating whether or not a property tax is levied. Of course, insurance is not without cost, so this may or may not be a financially feasible course to follow, especially since insurance has only a minor effect on the quality of the debt.

For many decades, the state of Utah has acquired highly favorable ratings on its debt for which it is justly proud, and this reputation for financial rectitude might have spilled over to the favorable ratings given to its water districts. (This point may have become increasingly important in recent months as many state and local governments appear to be in serious and worsening financial condition.) What seems to be clear from the data analyzed, however, is that there is no systematic tendency for the rating agencies always to favor those which use property taxes to collect revenues.

Full-Cost Water Pricing and the Poor

A final concern that surfaces whenever proposals are made to increase utility prices (and water deliveries at the retail level are generally considered to be like public utilities that deliver electricity and natural gas) is whether "poor" people can afford to pay these higher prices. So will the replacement of property-tax revenues to the districts by an equal revenue increase provided by direct water charges result in increased burdens on the poorest of the district's customers? The answer is by no means clear. Two considerations seem especially relevant.

First, it is not obvious, *a priori*, that the distribution of direct water charges from metered use would fall disproportionately more on low-income people than does the property tax that would be replaced. People at the lower end of the income distribution also own property (especially homes) that is taxed to raise revenues for the water districts. Unlike the income tax, poor people are not normally exempt from paying property taxes. Hence, property taxes are generally more regressive than income taxes. Moreover, people at the high end of the income-distribution ladder would pay more for direct water charges than their low-income counterparts since they have larger homes and more spacious grounds that use water. They also own more water-using businesses and belong to golf clubs and use other recreational facilities that consume large quantities of water. Therefore, a detailed empirical analysis of the income distribution effects of replacing property taxes with direct water charges is needed to settle this issue.

Second, many cities and other governmental entities have attempted to reduce income inequality by offering utilities at lower rates to low-income customers. These are often referred to as "lifeline" rates. In the case of water, this usually takes the form of a progressive fee schedule for water with a low price charged for the first block (say 10,000 gallons), a higher price for the next block, and so on. One justification commonly given is that people are required to pay a lower price for water they really "need" for drinking and basic household uses and higher fees can be charged for water blocks that are devoted to less valuable uses such as yard irrigation and swimming pools. A casual inspection of the block rates actually used in Utah, however, suggests that the first block of water at the lowest price is typically so large that even middle-income consumers do not exceed that block. This implies that low-income people, compared to those in higher income brackets, are not helped as much by the block system as they could be if the lowest block were not so liberal.

Quite another rationale can be given, however, for a progressive water fee schedule—to induce conservation. As water users pay higher marginal prices for increasing blocks of water, they will undoubtedly be motivated to be more economical in its use.[17]

Unfortunately, no empirical evidence is known to this writer that would shed much light on these income-distribution questions, so any justification for low water prices for the poor is weak. What we do know is that, in general, using price concessions on specific commodities such as electricity or water to effectuate more equality in the distribution of income is inefficient in resource allocation as demonstrated by the discussion of subsidies earlier in the chapter. Much more efficient policy alternatives are available for income equalization, such as direct income support to the poor incorporated in income tax exclusions, food stamps, and welfare programs.

Conclusions

Preserving the property tax as a mechanism for producing revenues for the public water districts has little theoretical or empirical justification. Hence, extra care should be taken to make sure that public water districts that may be created in the future are not burdened with this flawed policy. Failure to price water at market-clearing levels where marginal supply costs are fully covered has produced inefficient water development and allocation that should not be repeated.

As for existing water districts that have extant rules and procedures in place, this analysis suggests that they could survive and even thrive by relying on increasing direct charges on water users that more fully reflect the full supply costs. It may be true that those districts that have relied most on property taxes, and have therefore produced the greatest distortions between consumer valuations and water supply costs, would need to raise prices by a considerable amount in order to replace the lost revenue, but doing so would induce significant increases in water-use efficiency through voluntary conservation, especially in the long run. These conservation effects would be strongly salutary in precluding the necessity of relying on costly development of new water to meet increasing future demands from agricultural, domestic, industrial, and recreational users.

The only important caveat to increasing direct water prices is the "surplus" water problem discussed at length earlier. Water prices should not be raised so much that available supplies would be inefficiently used. This may be a more complex question than appears at first blush, however, since some or most of this water might move into places where it could be stored and used at a later time when demand has increased.

It appears that contracts between the districts and the federal Bureau of Reclamation would need to be renegotiated in order to eliminate the property tax as a revenue source, but it is difficult to see why the federal government would not be interested in increasing water conservation so long as the treasury is fully repaid. The water districts seem to be fully capable of managing their debt and repayment obligations without the property tax, current protestations from them notwithstanding. The argument that they need the tax to retain their financial ratings in order to acquire debt at favorable interest rates seems dubious. In fact, if this argument for the property tax were valid, how is it that water districts without the power to tax have the ability to acquire debt at almost equally favorable rates?

A critical issue is the timing of replacing the property tax with higher user charges. A prudent policy would appear to be to increase the price at approximately the same rate as the rate of increase in demand in order to prevent current supplies from being inefficiently used. After all, the costs of existing supplies are largely sunk costs that have already been expended and are, therefore, irrelevant to efficient water development. Hence, for existing developed water, a gradual shift to direct water charges is probably most feasible if the water market is to clear.[18]

The point relating price to economically efficient allocation of resources deserves further emphasis. Only if the water price is equal to the marginal supply cost will demanders and suppliers receive signals leading to efficient allocations of water. Even if political considerations or contractual agreements prevent the complete elimination of the property tax as a revenue source for the water districts, price can still be used to move toward more economically superior allocations. It must be remembered that what occurs at the margin is what counts most for economic efficiency. Block pricing could be used to meet certain revenue goals and to aid the poor, but economic efficiency and conservation goals would be more nearly achieved if the water price were set at the unsubsidized price (at the marginal supply cost).

For new water development that may be planned to augment future supplies, a requirement should be imposed that the final water users must contract to pay the full incremental costs, and this requirement should apply to irrigators (who traditionally have been subsidized by federal policy) as well as other user types. And there must be no possibility of reneging on the contracts after they have been signed and delivered. This may turn out to be a significant political problem as new supplies are likely to be costly and water users have traditionally been able to influence political benefactors to give them more favorable prices. Only by requiring that the beneficiaries pay the full cost, however, can uneconomic new water projects be prevented. For too long, water projects have been subsidized by separating water prices from supply costs, thus leading to premature and uneconomic development.

The fundamental water problem in Utah (and other western states) is not that existing supplies will prove to be inadequate to meet increasing future demands. This is a fallacy artificially induced by failing to regard water as an economic good like most other goods. The basic problem is that pricing policy has been infected and distorted by political favors in the form of subsidies and concessions to different interest groups. Using property taxes as a revenue substitute for direct water prices is one such example. So many water "problems" could be solved if this commodity were priced at the level required to cover supply costs and equate supply and demand.

Notes

1. Richard E. Howitt, "Drought, Strife, and Institutional Change," *Western Economics Forum* 1, no. 2 (Fall 2002): 11–14.
2. Utah Foundation, *Creating an Oasis: Part Two: Water Consumption, Pricing and Conservation in Utah*, Research Report No. 650, April 2002, http://content.lib.utah.edu/cgi-bin/showfile.exe?CISOROOT=/wwu&CISOPTR=34&filename=35.pdf.
3. Jon R. Miller, "On the Economics of Western Local Water Finance: The Central Utah Experience," *Land Economics* 69, no. 3 (1993): 299–303.
4. Utah Rivers Council, *Mirage in the Desert: Property Tax Subsidies for Water* (2002), http://www.utahrivers.org/wp-content/uploads/2011/03/URC-Property-Tax-Mirage.pdf.
5. Utah State Auditor's Office, *Survey of Local Government Finances Summary Data, various years 1992–2000*. Data for the various water districts by year can be obtained from the website www.sao.ut.gov/lgreports.html.
6. Of course, if the property tax is used as a substitute revenue source for direct water pricing, the resulting lower price can be said to increase the quantity of water demanded. But to the individual property owner who pays the tax, the magnitude of the tax itself is unrelated to the quantity of water demanded by that property owner.
7. B. Delworth Gardner, *Plowing Ground in Washington: The Political Economy of U.S. Agriculture* (San Francisco, CA: Pacific Research Institute for Public Policy, 1995), chap. 12.
8. Unused water could conceivably cause legal difficulties as well. Prior appropriation law requires that water be put to beneficial use; otherwise it can be appropriated by others. In the face of stochastic water supplies due to variations in snowpack, however, all appropriation states have given appropriators some leeway before the forfeiture requirement is exercised. For example, a bill passed in the 2008 legislative session in Utah makes it easier for public entities to own and hold (hoard) water rights for future use. A city can get a nonuse designation and keep the right for a much longer time than was possible under the previous law.
9. This phenomenon of water hoarding by large distributors that must plan for future growth, such as the Salt Lake City Water Department, is already highly controversial as water marketers would like to have this water available for trading to other users who are experiencing tight supplies.
10. Brandon Loomis, "Will Utah Cities Run Dry, or Is Shortage Avoidable?" *Salt Lake Triibune*, June 7, 2008, A1+.

11. B. Delworth Gardner, "Water Pricing and Rent Seeking in California Agriculture," in *Water Rights*, ed. Terry L. Anderson (San Francisco, CA: Pacific Institute for Public Policy Research, 1983), 83–112.

12. B. Delworth Gardner and Seth Schick, *Factors Affecting Household Water Consumption in Northern Utah*, Utah Agricultural Experiment Station Bulletin 449 (Logan, UT: Utah State University, 1964), 1–25.

13. Professor Blattenberger also has collected elasticity estimates from the eastern United States and a few foreign countries, but these appear less comparable to the region discussed here than those from other states in the arid West.

14. An exception is an elasticity estimate for water consumption of –1.57 to –1.63 made by Hewitt and Hanemann (Hewitt, Julie A. and W. Michael Hanemann, "A Discrete/Continuous Choice Approach to Residential Water Demand Under Block Rate Pricing," *Land Economics* 71, no. 2 (May 1995): 173–92), who employed a discrete/continuous choice model rather than standard regression analysis to estimate their price elasticities. Their work shows that the choice of analytic method may also be an important determinant of elasticity estimates.

15. Barton H. Thompson Jr., "Institutional Perspectives on Water Policy and Market," *California Law Review* 81 (May 1993): 671–74.

16. Utah Rivers Council, *Mirage in the Desert*.

17. I am indebted to Randy Simmons, an actual city mayor, for calling this to my attention.

18. The question of an optimal pricing policy as between fixed user charges and a levy on metered quantities used is complex and is discussed in Griffen, Ronald C., "Effective Water Pricing," *Journal of American Water Resources Association* 37, no. 5 (October 2001): 1335–47.

10

The Economics of Dam Decommissioning for Ecosystem Restoration: Making Informed Decisions to Remove Aging U.S. Dams

Pearl Q. Zheng
Benjamin F. Hobbs
Joseph F. Koonce

Introduction

The history of dams is an integral part of the story of civilization. Most dams were first built to provide a variety of vital functions such as flood control, irrigation, water supply, hydropower generation, and flat water recreation. However, nowadays, with increasing numbers of aging and unsafe dams on almost every major U.S. waterway on the one hand, and growing public and government concerns about loss of valuable habitat and farmland and the risk of catastrophic failure on the other hand, society faces two important questions. Why remove certain dams after building them? Which dam(s) should be removed in order to maximize ecological and socioeconomic benefits for a given amount of expenditures?

We address these questions by first reviewing current trends and issues in dam removal in the United Sates. Our review focuses on why it is difficult to make removal decisions. Then, the chapter introduces a quantitative decision analysis (QDA) approach that bridges economic and ecological criteria, in order to facilitate science-informed and consensus-based decisions on dam decommissioning. The decision analysis approach in this chapter features two methods: multicriteria analysis (MA) and optimization. MA supports the quantification of various trade-offs between economics and ecological benefits (nonmarket objectives), and optimization emphasizes the efficient use of scarce economic resources in accomplishing nonmarket objectives, accounting for the complex interactions among multiple dams, habitat creation, and consequent ecosystem responses. This approach views benefits as multidimensional, involving various ecological, economic, and socioeconomic objectives of importance to policymakers, ecosystem managers, dam owners, and local residents, and the purpose of the framework is to help them to better understand the consequences of trade-offs involved in dam removal. In this sense, the framework is a logical extension of the traditional cost-benefit analysis to a situation in which not all criteria can be expressed in dollar terms. Optimization is a computational approach for quickly identifying "efficient" portfolios of candidate dams for removal; by "efficient," we mean that no other portfolio has lower costs and higher ecological benefits. The decision framework has been applied to two case studies with one addressing a proposed removal decision on a single large dam that provides domestic water supply in a major watershed of the Lake Erie Basin. The other case study considers the problem of choosing an optimal portfolio of dam removals in several U.S. watersheds within that basin. The goal of our analysis is not to provide an answer, but rather to provide insights on the general nature of the trade-offs resulting from dam decommissioning expenditures, habitat and ecosystem restoration, and fish community dynamics. This study shows the effect of alternative human value judgments on making the "right" decisions to remove aging U.S. dams.

Dams and Dam Removals in the United States

Background

Dams have changed the American landscape and waterscape. Throughout the country's history, more than 2 million dams were constructed, most of them very small (e.g., storing less than a hundred acre-feet (AF) of water).[1] Failures of such small dams generally led to minor consequences.[2] However, according to the National Inventory of Dams (NID), a database maintained by the U.S. Army Corps of Engineers (USACE) and the Federal Emergency Management Agency (FEMA), approximately seventy-nine thousand dams are relatively large, or pose a "high" or "significant" hazard to life and property in the event of failure.[3] Based on NID records, the most active period of building large or "hazard-potential" dams occurred between 1950 and 1970. This period has been called "the golden age of dam building."[4] As shown in Figure 10.1(a), about one-quarter of these NID-recorded dams in the United States were constructed during the 1960s. Combined, the potential storage behind these dams is close to the nation's total annual runoff;[5] and nearly one-third of them are identified by NID as currently presenting serious threats to downstream public, infrastructure, and natural systems.[6]

Dams have provided important benefits, but have also imposed significant impacts on the environment. They were originally built to provide a variety of

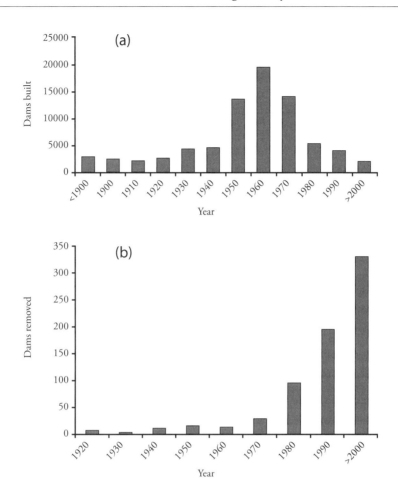

Figure 10.1 (a)—Large and "hazard-potential" dam reconstruction trends and (b)—dam removal trends in the U.S

Source: Figure 10.1a—Number of NID recorded dams constructed over the past 100 years by decade (USACE 2009)). Figure 10.1b—Number of dams removed in different decades (NCHRP 2005; American Rivers 2008).

vital functions (or purposes). The primary ones include recreation (3 percent), flood control (17 percent), fire and farm ponds (15 percent), and irrigation (10 percent).[7] However, dams also impeded fish migration and reproduction; modified natural flow regimes, nutrients, and sediment dynamics of rivers; and thus, substantially disturbed the structure and function of river ecosystems.[8] River ecologists agree that dams are the single greatest cause of the decline of river ecosystems.[9] For example, the Glen Canyon Dam on the

Colorado River has dramatically transformed downstream natural settings and consequently caused severe social and environmental problems.[10] With accumulated knowledge and experience, society has come to understand that in some cases, dams can cause negative impacts that outweigh the benefits they provide.

With the passage of time, the original services provided by dams (e.g., small mill dams) are often no longer required.[11] In addition, dams are not expected to last forever. Due to gradual structural deterioration and sedimentation, the average functional life expectancy of most dams is approximately fifty years.[12] An estimated 30 percent of the NID-recorded dams are now more than half a century old and in need of safety rehabilitation. By 2020, this percentage will reach 85 percent.[13] Very often, these aging dams may not fully pass safety inspections; thus are classified as "unsafe" by the USACE. Nationwide, there are more than 2,400 such unsafe dams nowadays; and many of them have outlived their intended purposes and currently are out-of-service.[14] In 2002, the Association of State Dam Safety Officials estimated that the total cost for rehabilitating the nation's critical dams that pose a direct risk to human life should they fail is over $36 billion; and over the next twelve years, the cost of rehabilitating the most critical ones would exceed $10 billion.[15] Facing such high expected costs, it does not make sense to rehabilitate and maintain all out-of-service, aging, and unsafe dams. But without ongoing and proper maintenance, these dams may pose a serious threat to public safety. In this case, the "no action" alternative, in the end, may be the most costly and dangerous choice because of the potential for failure.[16] Based on an incomplete history of dam failures and near failures in the United States, an estimated more than 4,500 fatalities and a minimum of $3 billion in damages have resulted from dam failure.[17] In many cases, especially where the benefits of the dams are marginal, repair costs exceed removal costs, and so the latter should be considered, especially where ecological benefits would accrue. For instance, the Sandstone Dam, an inactive hydropower dam on the Kettle River in Minnesota, was removed at a cost of $208,000 in 1995, while the estimated repair cost was over $1 million. Its removal opened 30 miles of river for fish migration and whitewater recreation, and fish populations have increased.[18]

Besides economic and social (public safety) benefits, dam removal is now viewed as a viable river and habitat restoration tool.[19] To date, most proposed removals have focused on dams that have significantly impeded migration of anadromous fish (e.g., Coho and Chinook salmon, *Oncorhynchus*).[20] Case studies have shown that restoration of unregulated flow regimes and accessibility of preferred spawning grounds or other fish habitat have increased biotic diversity.[21]

For these reasons, the answer to the first question in our introduction is clear: with increasing numbers of inactive, aging, and unsafe dams, local communities, dam owners, and environmental resource agencies across the country have agreed that dam decommissioning, when appropriate, can serve as an effective river restoration tool that will provide social, economic, and ecological benefits.[22] As a result, dam decommissioning has emerged as a major management issue in the United States.[23]

Trends and Issues in Dam Decommissioning

The available literature related to dam decommissioning reveals several trends and issues. First, existing records indicate that, nationwide, over six hundred sizable dams (mostly small) have been removed[24] (Figure 10.1(b)), mostly since the 1970s. This activity has escalated recently with more than two hundred removals since year 2000. Pohl summarized the primary reasons for dismantling American dams.[25] The leading purposes are to improve or restore species and/or habitat (39 percent), safety (36 percent), economics (18 percent), and failure (5 percent). The recent acceleration of removal reflects increased concern about the problems associated with the aging and substandard dams in the United States and growing agency and public interest in restoring rivers and fish riparian habitat.

Second, dam removal does not always yield an unambiguous ecological and economic improvement.[26] While hundreds of dams have been removed, it does not mean that all dams in question should be torn down. Many dams continue to serve important functions such as flood control, water supply, and hydropower generation. Replacing these services could be too costly or infeasible. In some cases, changing dam operation or design (e.g., adding a fish ladder) will provide enough ecological improvements to the river to justify the continued benefits of dam services.[27] In other cases, dams are retained because they represent a significant aspect of the community's history.[28] While dam removal may benefit many components of local ecosystems, such action may also cause significant environmental damage.[29] In some cases, taking out a dam could release contaminated sediments downstream. For instance, the removal of the Fort Edwards Dam in New York released tons of sediments laden with polychlorinated biphenyls into the Hudson River, which resulted in a cost of $5 million for the clean-up.[30] In other cases, dams serve as barriers to undesirable exotic species (e.g., as barriers to freshwater mussels[31]), and removing such dams may expand their habitat. While it is usually assumed that removing small dams has minimal impacts on geomorphic and ecological processes, debates over removal of larger dams are still ongoing since they can involve large costs and ecological uncertainties.[32] Therefore, dam removal does not always promote a win-win situation in which all interested parties benefit but involves social, economic, and ecological trade-offs that require careful decision analysis.

Third, the science of evaluating geomorphic and ecological effects after dam removal remains at a learning stage.[33] That is, we do not know exactly what will happen after removal. The relatively limited history of dam decommissioning and the insufficient collection of monitoring data are partial reasons. The complexity of river processes, including uncertain and interacting physical, chemical, and biological responses at different temporal and spatial scale, contributes the most to the slow progress in predicting consequences of dam decommissioning.[34] Such slow progress naturally leads to hesitation to remove dams where the consequences are uncertain. Scientific studies determining the rate, magnitude, duration, and spatial extent of the changes in ecological systems following dam removal would improve management decisions.[35]

Fourth, few dam removal research projects have conducted formal cost-benefit or decision analyses. Most studies have considered only a few components of the system (e.g., fish habitat or sediment), rather than an integrated assessment of possible expenditures and system responses.[36] Thus, there is a pressing need for comprehensive studies of these issues so that the trade-offs involved in removal decisions can be fully understood. Table 10.1 compiles a list of benefit and cost categories associated with dam decommissioning. Quantitative research is beginning to emerge that addresses various aspects of dam removal responses/benefits in various environmental settings and for different time scales.[37] However, studies that quantify economic and societal value of dam decommissioning are still scarce.[38]

Fifth, dam removal decisions are considered mostly on a dam-by-dam basis but rarely on a portfolio basis with respect to the cumulative impacts of multiple removals upon fish communities in downstream riparian and lacustrine ecosystems.[39] Instead, riparian habitat recovery (e.g., miles of river reach) is commonly used as a surrogate for ecological benefits.[40] However, due to complex life histories and other ecological interactions and limitations (e.g., lack of available prey), additional habitat at a particular life stage may or may not lead to an increase in the population of target species or an enhancement of ecosystem services.[41] This absence of a focus on the ultimate ecological value provided by dam removal increases uncertainties concerning the benefits of removal and impedes effective decision-making. It also results in vague or incomplete statements of the ultimate goals of ecosystem restoration, and as a result, removal may fail to deliver the desired benefits.[42]

Collectively, these trends and issues indicate that despite the recent increase in the number of completed and proposed dam removals, decisions on dam removal or retention are difficult and sometimes controversial because of the presence of numerous economic and ecological trade-offs and uncertainties, as well as public safety concerns and diverse stakeholders (e.g., dam owners, local communities, dam safety officials, and ecosystem managers). There is still much to be learned about how to make the "right" and the "best" decisions on dam decommissioning.

Table 10.1 Benefits and costs in dam decommissioning

Benefits	Costs
Environmental/Ecological	*Project planning and analysis costs (pre-removal)*
❑ River habitat restoration	❑ Visual/field survey and documentation review
❑ River and lake ecosystem restorations	❑ Environmental/ecological impact evaluation
❑ Threatened and endangered species recovery	❑ Sediment analysis
❑ Biological diversity improvement	❑ Design and engineering
❑ Water quality improvement	❑ Permit acquisition
❑ Restored sediment and energy transport	*Field work costs (expense on site)*
❑ Restored temperature regimes	❑ Dam removal
Economic	❑ Sediment management
	❑ Invasive species control
❑ Operation/maintenance cost reductions	❑ Infrastructure repair and replacement
❑ Repair/upgrade cost reductions	❑ Site restoration
❑ Ownership insurance cost reduction	❑ Historic and archaeological monitoring
❑ Enhanced fishing opportunities	
❑ Enhanced recreational boating opportunities	*Scientific monitoring (postremoval)*
Social	❑ Sediment transports
	❑ Plant recruitment and regeneration
❑ Elimination of dam safety concerns	❑ Water quality
❑ Improved river aesthetics	❑ Riparian wetland response
❑ Improved river access	❑ Aquatic and aquatic-dependent species response
❑ Community revitalization	

Sources: American Rivers, *Paying for Dam Removal—A Guide to Selected Funding Sources* (Washington, DC: American Rivers, 2000); Bowman et al., *Exploring Dam Removal*; Heinz Center, *Dam Removal*; W. L. Graf, ed., *Dam Removal Research: Status and Prospectives* (Washington, DC: H. John Heinz III Center for Science, Economics and the Environment, 2003); W. Price, "Can Analysis Trump Politics in Dam Removal Decisions?," in *Dam Removal: Lessons Learned Workshop* (Portland, OR: American Society of Civil Engineers (ASCE) and Environmental and Water Resources Institute (EWRI), 2004.

Quantitative Decision Analysis (QDA)

Dam removal problems have motivated the development of assessment tools that incorporate scientific, engineering, economic, and social issues.[43] A goal of this chapter is to illustrate how decision analysis can yield useful insights about trade-offs among these issues.

QDA stresses quantification of metrics (criteria) that describe how alternatives perform on various environmental, social, economic, and other objectives; the identification of "efficient" alternatives (for which no other alternative exists that does as well in all objectives and strictly better in some); and description of trade-offs among those efficient alternatives. QDA blends the disciplines of systems analysis and economics, borrowing methods and concepts from (1) statistics, mathematics, and economics; (2) psychology and behavioral science; and (3) operations research and management science.[44] The theory, methods, and practices of QDA are well established. Many books and other publications exist on the topic.[45]

More specifically in applications to ecological assessment and water resources management, QDA can quantify noneconomic objectives, such as habitat restoration and water quality improvement;[46] assess important trade-offs between economic costs and environmental benefits;[47] facilitate consistent and explicit valuation based on the experts' judgment and decision-makers' value or utility preferences;[48] and focus negotiation on stakeholders' ultimate objectives such as ecosystem integrity and human well-being.[49] Compared to many other environmental management problems, however, QDA applications to dam decommissioning have been relatively infrequent and incomplete. Most QDA studies of dam removal have focused on environmental and ecological outcomes but not on assessments of potential economic loss.[50] They seldom explicitly address issues of multiple and conflicting objectives, interactions among multiple dam removal decisions, or ecological linkages between habitat creation and the ultimate ecosystem endpoints of concern to stakeholders.

To gain more insights, the QDA in this chapter takes a systematic and multidisciplinary modeling approach and centers on formal decision analysis methods (MA) and multiobjective optimization (MO). MA emphasizes quantification of trade-offs, user preferences regarding those trade-offs, and transparency in decision-making. (It is an *anti-black box* tool).[51] More importantly, MA can facilitate involvement of diverse stakeholders by helping them to articulate their values and priorities on multiple and typically conflicting objectives. By doing so, it can identify areas of agreement as well as reasons why different parties make different recommendations, which informs negotiation.[52] In contrast, MO focuses on generating a range of choices for decision-makers and describing trade-offs among those alternatives rather than representing value judgments of stakeholders. It is a specific form of optimization whose solutions are members of the efficient set.

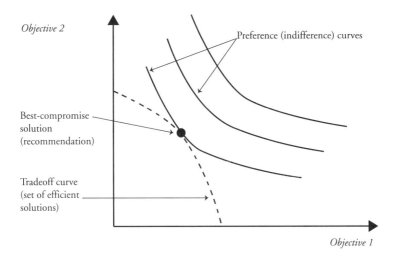

Figure 10.2   Illustration of relationships among tradeoff curve, indifference curves, and best-compromise solution

Once efficient alternatives are identified, trade-offs among objectives can be quantified by calculating the amount of one objective that must be sacrificed to gain improvements in other objectives.[53] As illustrated in Figure 10.2, a decision can then be made by combining a decision-maker's preferences (represented in the figure by a family of indifference curves) and the efficient set to identify the best-compromise solution. In the next section, we provide some mathematical details about MA and MO. For more background, the interested reader can refer to texts on multiple criteria decision-making[54] and multiobjective programming.[55]

Decision Framework and Model Linkages

To implement QDA, a decision framework (Figure 10.3) that integrates regression models, optimization models, and ecological models is developed to answer the second question posed in the Introduction—how to choose which dam(s) to remove or to retain, and what expense to incur in exchange for habitat and ecosystem restoration? This decision framework considers removing dams on U.S. tributaries to Lake Erie to promote habitat restoration. In the case of Lake Erie, we model potential habitat changes for two important fish species: desirable native walleye (*Sander vitreus*) and undesirable invasive sea lamprey (*Petromyzon marinus*). Our QDA approach quantifies important trade-offs, such as management costs versus fish population enhancement, and native species versus exotic species. The framework emphasizes elicitation of values from stakeholders, such as ecosystem managers,

255

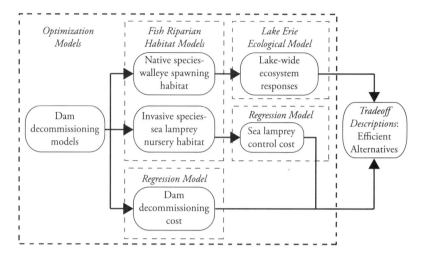

Figure 10.3 Decision framework for dam decommissioning for Lake Erie

and local residents, and establishes critical linkages from dam removal to ecosystem response. Moreover, the framework quantifies dam decommissioning's impacts upon the social, ecological, and economic objectives of importance to managers and stakeholders. These fundamental objectives account for lake-wide and community-based ecological effects of riparian habitat changes following the dam removal decisions.

We use QDA here to aggregate ecological decision criteria (e.g., maximizing native species abundance and total fish community productivity) by an additive value function that weights the individual criteria, yielding a single value that represents the ultimate goal of dam decommissioning and habitat creation: cost-effective improvement in ecosystem health. In our single-dam case study, we also include economic costs of removal in the value index and recommend the alternative (removal or not) that maximizes that index. In contrast, when considering possible collections of dams (portfolios) to remove, we keep the ecological index and expenditures as separate objectives. Cost-effective portfolios are then identified by maximizing this overall ecological index, while accounting for the hydrological and ecological interactions of dam removals at various locations, subject to a maximum allowable budget expenditure.

In the rest of this section, we first provide an overview of the mathematics of the QDA methods used in "Dam Removal QDA Models." We then provide background on the ecological system studied in the case studies (Lake Erie) and summarize the ecological models used in "Ecological Models and Model

Linkages." "Ecological Models and Model Linkages" then presents the economic models (dam removal expense and lamprey control cost).

Figure 10.3 shows the relationships among these models within our
QDA framework. The framework has four basic components: (1) dam removal decision(s) (single or portfolio), (2) management costs (dam removal
and sea lamprey control), (3) habitat changes (walleye spawning and sea
lamprey nursery), and (4) ecosystem responses (criteria representing ecosystem health). The framework takes two critical linkages into account.
One connects dams and the river network, since the ecological benefits of
removing one dam depend on whether others downstream or upstream have
been removed. The other linkage translates tributary habitat changes into
lake-wide ecosystem effects. These linkages are established by four types
of models: removal decision models, fish riparian habitat models, the Lake
Erie Ecological Model (LEEM), and empirical cost models. These will be
discussed sequentially.

Dam Removal QDA Models

For our single dam removal case study, the relative importance of different environmental and economic criteria is reflected in weights (equivalent
to prices) in a multicriteria additive value (MAV) model. MAV is a common
method of MA. In practice, MAVs are widely used to assess a decision-maker's
overall value of an alternative:[56]

$$
V\left(x_1, \cdots, x_I\right) = \sum_{i=1}^{I} \overbrace{W_i}^{\substack{\text{Elicited from} \\ \text{managers or} \\ \text{stakeholders}}} \times \overbrace{V_i}^{\substack{\text{Estimated from} \\ \text{analysis for} \\ \text{each alternative}}} \overbrace{x_i}^{} \;,
\tag{1}
$$

where x_i is the ith quantitative criterion that describes the performance of an
alternative (e.g., remove the Ballville Dam) on a particular objective (e.g., Lake
Erie walleye population); I is the number of criteria; $V(x_1, \ldots, x_I)$ represents
the aggregate value of an alternative; $V_i(\ )$ is a single criterion value function
that scales the performance of each x_i in terms of overall value; and W_i is
the weight accorded x_i representing the rate at which the user is willing to
trade off the criterion. In general, the weights and criterion value functions
are elicited from managers or stakeholders.[57] For example, considering two
criteria of dam removal cost and walleye population, one can ask questions
such as "How much more are you willing to pay for 1,000 more walleye?"
(which can be used to establish the relative weights) and "What are the
least and most desirable levels of the walleye population?" (which would be
associated with the lowest and highest values of that criterion's $V_i(\ )$, which
we define as 0 and 1, respectively). With answers to these questions and

appropriate calculations, criteria weight and value functions can be estimated to reflect the user's preferences.

A recommendation about keeping or removing a particular dam can then be made by noting which alternative has the highest overall value (1). By varying the priority (W_i) placed on the criteria, the effect of alternative perspectives concerning their relative importance can be examined. If changing priorities do not change the decision, then the recommendation is robust, but if priorities matter, then these should be carefully discussed and evaluated by the stakeholders.

In our case study of multiple dam removal decisions, we use a mixed integer linear programming (MILP) model that combines MA and MO. The model identifies cost-effective portfolios of dam removals by maximizing an ecological index in the form of (1) subject to a budget constraint, which we then vary. The MILP method efficiently sorts through a very large number of possible portfolios (in our second case study, as many as 2^{139}) to identify those that are efficient in terms of the ecological index based on (1) and total cost.[58] In summary, like any optimization model, it includes the following three elements: (1) an objective function (the ecological index described by a value function [1]); (2) decision variables (one binary variable per dam representing the decision to keep [0] or remove [1], and variables representing the criteria x_i for all of Lake Erie); and (3) constraints (including functions that relate the x_i to the binary decisions, a constraint limiting expenditures on removals to a budget limit, and logical constraints that force downstream dams to be removed before upstream dams, as the purpose of dam removal is to restore habitat for fish migrating upstream from the lake to spawn).

The solution algorithm searches systematically for the combination of decision variable values that achieve the highest possible value of the objective function, while still meeting all constraints. The constraint relationships between decisions and the ecological criteria are based on understanding of the ecological system (embodied in an ecosystem model), while the effect of decisions on expenditures is based on empirical models estimated using data on dam removal costs and lamprey control expenditures (Figure 10.3). Thus, the MILP model integrates ecological and economic understanding to identify cost-effective dam removal portfolios.

Ecological Models and Model Linkages

In the late 1960s, Lake Erie was called "a dead lake" because of eutrophication from phosphorus inputs from rural and urban sources.[59] After more than five decades of restoration effort, the Lake Erie fish community has shown mixed signs of recovery. Perhaps the most significant milestone has been the resurgence of the Lake Erie walleye population in the 1980s largely due to the implementation of a quota management system and the closure of the commercial fishery in 1970 in the United States.[60] The lake's walleye fishery is widely considered as the best in the world and is heavily exploited.[61] Walleye are also essential for controlling fish community structure via predation.[62] But the rebounding of the Lake Erie walleye population did not continue into the 1990s.[63] Other fish populations (e.g., rainbow smelt [*Osmerus mordax*]) have declined as well in recent years.[64] Among many factors that may have contributed to this recent decline, lack of spawning habitat caused by damming of streams has been hypothesized as playing a critical role.[65]

The focus of the case studies in this chapter is on restoring walleye spawning habitat in the Lake Erie tributaries. Adult walleye swim upstream to spawn every spring.[66] Therefore, walleye populations might benefit from removing dams that block access to suitable spawning habitat upstream. But as a side effect, dam removal may also provide access to favorable spawning and nursery habitat for sea lamprey, an infamous Great Lakes invader, which could negatively impact the Lake Erie fish community.[67]

Sea lamprey prey on a wide range of native game fish in the Great Lakes, such as lake trout (*Salvelinus namaycush*), whitefish (*Coregonus clupeaformis*), and walleye. Sea lampreys attach themselves to host fish, drain blood and body fluids from the hosts, and typically kill the victims.[68] After spreading into Lake Erie in 1921, sea lamprey dispersed rapidly in the other Great Lakes, and their proliferation contributed significantly to the collapse of certain indigenous fish populations during the 1940s and 1950s.[69]

Like adult walleye, adult sea lampreys also leave lakes in spring and migrate up tributary streams to spawn. Without proper controls, dam removal may benefit sea lamprey. However, unlike adult walleye, adult sea lamprey die after laying eggs and larvae sea lamprey live in the muddy streambeds for several years (typically three to seventeen years) before returning to lakes as parasitic adults.[70] Currently, the most effective lamprey control measure is to regularly treat sea lamprey–infested nursery areas in tributaries with lampricides to eliminate larvae populations at their most vulnerable life stage.[71] These measures have been remarkably successful. Sea lamprey is one of the few aquatic invasive species that have been successfully suppressed in the Great Lakes region. Ongoing control efforts have resulted in an estimated 90 percent reduction of sea lamprey populations.[72] We focus, therefore, on the effect on dam removal upon lamprey nursery habitat; furthermore, we assume that any newly accessible nursery habitat will be treated with chemical control and that this control will be 100 percent effective. Consequently, lamprey concerns can be quantified as the additional cost of lampricide application.

Ecological models are used to quantify possible consequences of the removal alternatives and will be discussed briefly in the following subsections. Basically, once a dam removal decision is made, three consequences may follow immediately (Figure 10.3): a potential increase in walleye spawning habitat, a potential increase in sea lamprey larvae nursery habitat, and dam removal cost. Walleye and sea lamprey habitat changes are quantified using data on stream characteristics and habitat suitability models from the literature. Then, in order to link the newly assessable fish habitat to ecosystem responses, we first translate changes in suitable walleye spawning habitat into changes in numbers of walleye young-of-year (YOY)—fish that are less than two years old. Then, changes in YOY are translated into changes in various ecosystem criteria, using a local linear approximation of the LEEM. Meanwhile, using a regression model, changes in sea lamprey nursery habitat are converted into sea lamprey control cost.

Fish Riparian Habitat Models

Fish riparian habitat models based on the habitat suitability index (HSI) concept and geographical information system (GIS) data are used to quantify habitat changes following dam removals for both walleye and sea lamprey. New habitat in both cases is defined as the sum of newly accessible stream reaches of the product of each reach's HSI for the species in question and either the area or length of each reach (for walleye and lamprey, respectively). The HSI for each species depends on the physical characteristics of the reach, including bed particle size (walleye preferring sand, while sea lamprey larvae preferring mud), water depth, and flow velocity during

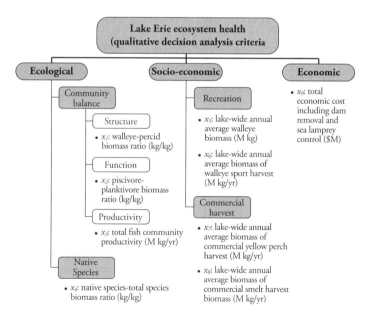

Figure 10.4   Criteria hierarchy for Lake Erie dam decommissioning analysis

Source: Zheng, Hobbs, and Koonce 2009.

spawning season for walleye. The functional form is HSI $= \Pi_k\, y_k \alpha_k$, where y_k are the characteristics, and the exponents α_k sum to 1.[73] The GIS is used to quantify the HSI for each species for each reach, yielding the values of coefficients needed for the MAV and MILP models.

Lake Erie Ecological Model

The LEEM was developed to address the declining populations of major fish species (e.g., walleye), as well as some key factors (e.g., phosphorus loading) affecting the Lake Erie ecosystem.[74] The model includes seventeen species that represent the fish community of Lake Erie. Through predator–prey relationships constrained by energy flow and nutrient availability, LEEM simulates the interactive effects of various stressors, such as phosphorus loadings, toxic substances, the zebra mussel invasion, habitat loss, and fish harvest policy on the Lake Erie ecosystem.[75] We use LEEM here to quantify how dam decommissioning alternatives perform on lake-wide ecological criteria.

The particular ecological criteria we quantify with LEEM are shown in Figure 10.4. They are grouped into three general categories of objectives: ecological, socioeconomic, and economic. Criteria x_1 to x_8 represent ecological and socioeconomic objectives in terms of fish community balance, native species, recreation, and harvest. The economic objective is represented by criterion x_9, the expected cost including dam removal and sea lamprey control. Altogether, these nine criteria can be viewed as quantitative interpretations of the fundamental objectives for restoring the Lake Erie ecosystem.[76]

Habitat–Ecosystem Linkage

Because of insufficient data for understanding complex ecological processes, stream habitat restoration studies seldom attempt to assess ecosystem response. Usually, habitat changes themselves are used as an index of ecological benefits. Additional habitat for a particular life stage for one species, however, may not lead to improvement in the ultimate ecosystem objectives because habitat at that life stage may not be the limiting factor for the organism's population. By explicitly linking removal decisions to ecological criteria, we hope to offer more meaningful insights on the benefits of dam decommissioning.

Our modeling of habitat–ecosystem linkages is based on the life history of walleye and interaction of populations of different fish species in LEEM. In particular, walleye habitat created by dam decommissioning is linked to LEEM. Three steps are involved: (1) estimation of egg production based on walleye spawning habitat changes in each U.S. basin draining into Lake Erie, (2) conversion of egg deposition into surviving walleye YOY that reach lake near-shore nursery habitat, and (3) translation of cumulative changes in walleye YOY recruitment into corresponding lake-wide ecosystem responses based on linearized response functions fitted to LEEM simulation results.

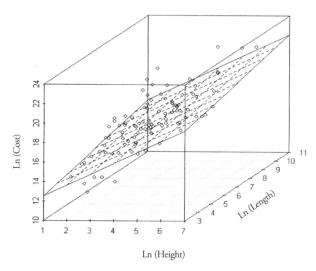

Ln (Height)

Figure 10.5   Scatter plot of dam removal cost versus dam height and length (log-transformed)

Source: Zheng, Hobbs, and Koonce 2009.

Economic Models and Model Linkages

An important objective of dam removals is to minimize an aggregate economic cost. Cost includes both the expected dam removal expense and the cost of controlling sea lamprey in newly accessible habitat. Both cost categories are estimated using regression models.

Dam Removal Cost Model

We have estimated expected dam removal cost as a function of dam size (i.e., height and length), type (i.e., earth or nonearth), and key service function (i.e., water supply, hydropower generation, and flood control) through a multivariate linear statistical analysis based on existing U.S. dam removal records. The results show that the height and length of a dam con-tribute significantly to the removal costs, with (unsurprisingly) larger dams costing more. Figure 10.5 demonstrates this trend, where removal cost data are shown as points and the regression relationship shown as a plane. Scatter around the regression plane indicates that other factors contribute to removal costs as well. First, different dam types require different removal methods. For instance, explosives and heavy equipment (e.g., hydraulic hammers) are often needed to remove concrete dams. Removal of earthen dams, in contrast, seldom requires more than bulldozers, and so would be cheaper.[77] Second, total management cost should include not only dam removal cost but also the value of lost services. The expense of replacing water supply, irrigation, hydropower generation, or even recreational use can be very high.

Information on over six hundred documented dam removals in the United States was collected, of which 117 records included all variables and so could be used to fit the model.[78] After various statistical tests to ensure model quality and robustness, the dam removal cost regression model we have chosen is:

$$\ln(Cost) = 7.35 + \overbrace{0.80(\ln(Height)) + 0.33(\ln(Length))}^{\text{Dam Size}} + \overbrace{1.49(Function)}^{\text{Dam Purpose}} + \overbrace{0.44(Type)}^{\text{Dam Type}} , \quad (2)$$

where *Height* is the structural height (feet) of a dam; *Length* is the length (feet) of a dam; *Function* is a dummy variable representing that a dam currently has an important service function; and *Type* is a dummy variable indicating that a dam type is not earthen (e.g., concrete or stone). Dummy variables are qualitative variables that take on values of zero or one. All coefficients are significant at a 5-percent level or lower. Costs used in the analysis are escalated to year 2006 dollars and include the total removal project costs of engineering consulting, permitting, and removal.

Equation (2) shows that (1) dam height contributes more strongly to removal costs than dam length, (2) removing a dam that currently serves an important purpose (indicated by *Function*) adds additional costs, (3) removing a nonearthen dam (indicated by *Type*) increases total project costs, and (4) additional costs due to lost dam services is larger than the cost difference between removing a nonearthen dam versus an earthen dam. Using Equation (2) and data extracted from a database of existing dams (e.g., NID), we can estimate the decommissioning cost of each structure that is a candidate for removal. This allows us to trade off the cost of different portfolios of dam removals with the ecological benefits estimated by the models of the previous subsection.

Our estimates, however, do have limitations. The statistical fit is not perfect, and important categories of costs, such as dam maintenance costs, sediment management, safety hazards, and recreation benefits, are excluded. Thus, this model should be used as a screen to identify candidate dams that then can be further studied before finalizing any removal decisions.

Exotic Species Control Cost Model

As mentioned earlier, we assume that lampricides will be applied, targeting larval sea lamprey in potentially infested stream reaches following dam removals. Regression analysis based on published data indicates a linear relationship between lampricide usage and treated stream length.[79] With this relationship and unit cost of lampricide application (including purchase and application expenses),[80] we developed a cost model in which lampricide cost is estimated as a function of length of lamprey nursery habitat. An advantage of modeling sea lamprey impact in monetary terms is that this expense can be combined with dam removal costs and then traded off against ecological benefits.

Case Studies of Quantitative Decision Analysis in Dam Removal

Two case studies, a single dam removal case and a multidam removal case, are presented to illustrate the usefulness of QDA for considering ecological-economic trade-offs in dam decommissioning. Both cases consider linkages between dam decommissioning, fish habitat recovery, and ecosystem restoration. They both use multicriteria value functions (1) to assess lake-wide fish community effects as potential benefits of dam removal.

As mentioned, LEEM is used to quantify how dam removal alternatives perform on the eight ecological criteria x_1 to x_8 (Figure 10.4). The weights and single attribute value functions used in (1) were based upon two workshops involving Lake Erie fishery managers and biological researchers.[81] The single criterion value functions $V_i(x_i)$ in Equation (1) are assumed to be linear in the x_i. The economic criterion x_9 is estimated using data from a feasibility study in the single dam removal case,[82] and the regression analysis described in "Economic Models and Model Linkages" is for the dam portfolio case.

Single Dam Decommissioning Case[83]

Background

The Ballville Dam (Figure 10.6) is located on the Sandusky River in northern Ohio and is 18 miles upstream of the Sandusky Bay on Lake Erie.[84] Constructed in 1911, the primary purpose of the Ballville Dam today is to

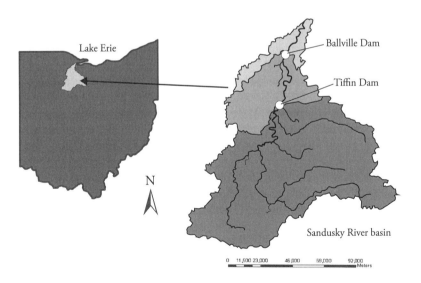

Figure 10.6   Location of Ballville Dam in the Sandusky River basin of Ohio

Source: Corsair et al. 2009.

supply water to the city of Fremont in Sandusky County. Since 1999, there have been ongoing discussions about removing the Ballville Dam.

The most discussed concerns are the dam's diminishing functionality and increasing structural failure risk. Because of aging and other causes, the primary use of the Ballville Reservoir as a public raw water source is threatened by degraded water quality and inadequate supply capacity. The Fremont Water Treatment Plant reported nitrate advisories (a health risk indicator) in recent years, which has caused the city of Fremont to purchase sixty hectares of land for an off-stream water storage facility that would operate as an alternate water source during nitrate alerts.[85] Over time, sediment accumulation has reduced the reservoir's storage capacity by approximately 90 percent, reducing the reliability of water supply.[86] Besides functional deficiencies, the structural deterioration of Ballville Dam may present a hazard to the city of Fremont. The Ohio Department of Natural Resources (ODNR) in 2005 determined that without immediate repairs, the seawall along the north side of the reservoir could not safely pass the probable maximum flood (PMF) standard and the public would be at risk of dam failure.[87] For these reasons, demolition of the Ballville Dam has been proposed to meet Fremont's safety concerns and growing water supply needs (see "Case study Alternatives and Results").

In addition, the ODNR Division of Wildlife and a number of local stakeholders, including fishermen and some environmentalists, endorse removing the Ballville Dam for fish habitat restoration.[88] The Sandusky River offers a wide variety of fishing opportunities and is famous for its spring walleye run. The Ballville Dam is the first river blockage for fish migrating from Lake Erie. Historical fishery data and recent research indicate that there exists a large amount of walleye spawning habitat upstream of the dam[89] (see Figure 10.6).

Large costs and public disagreement, however, make removal of the Ballville Dam controversial. Being a large dam (34-foot high and 423-foot long) that provides important services, the potential cost associated with the removal option would be high (e.g., a reported $7 to $10 million in 2004 dollars).[90] The Ballville Dam is the sole water supply source to the city of Fremont. Removing it means that the city has to find a reliable source elsewhere. A local citizen group (Citizen's Committee to Save the Ballville Dam) opposes the removal, being concerned about the potential loss of various services provided by the reservoir.[91] Moreover, due to complex system interactions, the ecological consequences after the removal would be uncertain. One question is whether increasing walleye habitat would result in increased lake populations of that fish species. A threatening ecological side effect is that dam removal may also provide access to sea lamprey spawning and nursery, which could possibly damage the Lake Erie fish community. In summary, the city of Fremont and other stakeholders face a tough decision: whether to remove the Ballville Dam or not.

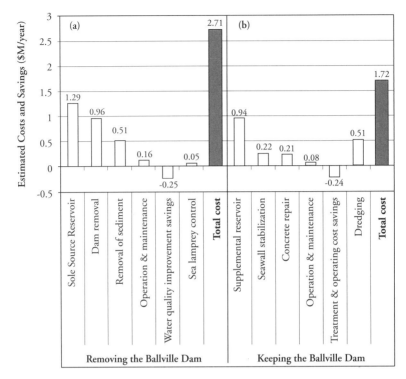

Figure 10.7 Costs and savings for management actions: (a)—removal of the Ballville Dam, and (b)—keeping the Ballville Dam

Case Study Alternatives and Results

The trade-offs among conflicting objectives—the municipal services provided versus the importance of the Sandusky River to walleye populations in Lake Erie—make the proposed Ballville Dam removal problem a good candidate for applying QDA. Two management alternatives exist: to keep or remove the Ballville Dam. To keep the dam in service, seawall stabilization and concrete repair need to be undertaken. Meanwhile, the existing reservoir would have to be dredged to 200 million gallons (MG) and a supplemental reservoir built to a capacity of 300 MG. If instead the dam is removed, a 500 MG sole source reservoir will be built on the land acquired by the city of Fremont. Both proposed alternatives meet the water storage needs of the city of Fremont, anticipated to be 500 MG by 2030.

Each of the alternatives involves several management actions and their corresponding costs and benefits (in terms of savings, e.g., water quality improvement savings for removing the dam and treatment and operation cost saving for keeping the dam). Figures 10.7(a) and 10.7(b) show detailed cost breakdowns of each management action associated with both alternatives, respectively. All costs are escalated to January 2006 dollars and are converted to equivalent uniform annual costs assuming a lifetime of twenty years and a 6 percent interest rate. The total estimated cost to remove the Ballville Dam is approximately $2.7 million/year, while the total estimated cost to keep the Ballville Dam is approximately $1.7 million/year.[92] Thus, removing the dam is more costly than keeping it, largely due to the cost of service replacement (i.e., a new reservoir).

Considering habitat effects, results of the fish habitat model for walleye and sea lamprey show that removing the Ballville Dam will significantly increase not only walleye spawning habitat in the Sandusky Basin (by more than twenty-three-fold), but also potential sea lamprey larvae nursery habitat (more than twentyfold).[93] Such a distinctive trade-off supports the use of QDA. Considering ecological effects, Figure 10.8 presents the overall results of value functions based on Equation (1) for each alternative.[94] These results demonstrate conflicts between walleye fishery improvement and negative impacts on some ecosystem components due to dam removal. In particular, removing the Ballville Dam would improve walleye-related criteria values, namely native fish biomass as a fraction of the total (x_4), walleye population (x_5),

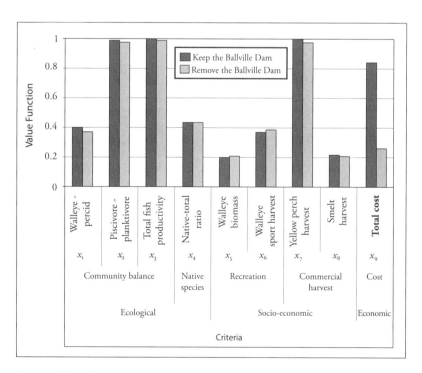

Figure 10.8   Single dam removal case study selected resultes: value functions

and walleye sport harvest (x_6). Because of the increased competition and predation resulting from enhanced walleye recruitment, however, removal negatively affects fish community balance and productivity (x_1, x_2, and x_3). Further, the increase in walleye results in decline in other important commercial fisheries in Lake Erie, such as yellow perch and smelt (x_7 and x_8). The presence of such mixed blessings also supports the use of QDA, as different groups (e.g., commercial versus recreational fishermen) will place different priorities on these ecological criteria.

Incorporating stakeholder values is critical in decision-making, especially for difficult ones such as the proposed Ballville Dam removal. By original criteria weights (based on fishery manager and biologist preferences) elicited from two workshops and using Equation (1), the overall value scores for two alternatives are 0.535 for keeping the Ballville Dam, and 0.529 for removing it. This difference appears small because the functions were assessed for the entire Lake Erie ecosystem, so the ranges are very large relative to the ecological changes that one dam removal could make. This difference can be interpreted by calculating the change in annualized economic cost that would result in the same change in value score of Equation (1); this change is approximately $2 million in annualized cost. This value is approximately double the economic cost difference alone between keeping and removing the dam—indicating that the ecological disbenefits of dam removal (e.g., negative impacts on the yellow perch commercial fishery) are valued approximately as much as the net costs of removal. Thus, under the original weights assigned by decision-makers, keeping the dam is more attractive than removal.

To test the sensitivity of the results to value judgments concerning the importance of walleye, a second weight set was used in which a higher weight was assigned to walleye-related criteria (triple the original values). With additional emphasis on walleye, the overall scores have changed to 0.425 for keeping the Ballville Dam, and 0.427 for removing it. Thus, under the revised weights favoring walleye, removing the Ballville Dam is slightly better than keeping it. This sensitivity analysis shows that value judgments matter, and ecological benefits are ambiguous—different weightings of the components of ecological benefits change the recommendation. This also indicates that stakeholder involvement is important.

In summary, the single dam case study shows that removing the Ballville Dam involves trade-offs between economic costs, walleye-related ecological benefits, and other ecological criteria. Undoubtedly, removing the Ballville Dam will improve walleye population, which, unfortunately as shown in model results, will not lead to an unambiguous enhancement for the whole Lake Erie ecosystem. In the end, the ranking of the alternatives is sensitive to the weights, indicating that the final decision on whether to remove the dam may depend on stakeholders' value judgments.

Note that Figure 10.8 indicates that the ecological performance differences between two alternatives are relatively small. This is because these value functions that evaluate ecological impacts were originally designed to address large changes in lake-wide nutrient and fisheries management problems; thus, lake-wide ecological changes caused by relatively small habitat changes stemming from a single dam removal in just one watershed should be expected to be comparatively small. This observation inspired the next case study: to consider removing multiple dams in various watersheds in order to achieve significant lake-wide ecological improvement.

Multidam Removal Case[95]

Background

According to the Lake Erie Dam Database,[96] there are more than two thousand dams located in the U.S. watersheds of Lake Erie. Many of them are small and were built more than a half-century ago. Some of them are out of service, thus imposing not only adverse impacts on ecosystems but also economic burdens on society. Some of them have deteriorated and face a significant risk of failure, thus giving rise to an imminent public safety hazard. At least twenty-seven dams have already been demolished in the Lake Erie Basin for reasons such as fish and wildlife habitat restoration, cost savings, water quality improvement, and public safety hazard elimination.[97]

Because many dams are seriously being considered for removal in the Lake Erie Basin, there is a reasonable chance that multiple dams will be removed in that basin in the near future. In addition, because removals of multiple dams are likely to have interacting ecological effects due to upstream–downstream relationships, efficient decision-making requires simultaneous consideration of all dam removal possibilities as a portfolio problem. After screening the Lake Erie Dam Database, the case study analyzed here considers possibly removing 139 dams (both large and small size) located in ten watersheds.[98]

Case Study Alternatives and Results

The MILP model described in "Dam Removal QDA Models" is applied to the multidam removal case study. This case study aims to illustrate the use of systems analysis to describe trade-offs among ecological, socioeconomic, and economic objectives (represented by the nine criteria in Figure 10.4) affecting the entire Lake Erie ecosystem. As opposed to two simple alternatives in the Ballville Dam case study, the MILP model considers as many as 2^{139} (approximately 7×10^{41}) alternatives. For each assumed level of the budget for removal, the model chooses the most beneficial portfolio of potential dam removals in terms of the eight ecological criteria. By changing the value of the budget cap, different efficient portfolios (which dams are removed and which are retained) can be generated, and trade-offs cost and ecological

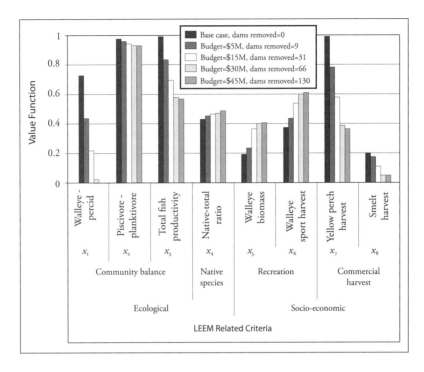

Figure 10.9   Multi-dam case study results; value functions for LEEM criteris for five different portfolios

criteria displayed. For better understanding, the values of the overall ecological objective (in terms of [1], an aggregated multicriteria value function as defined earlier) are rescaled to percentages, where 0 percent represents the base case (no removal), and 100 percent represents the maximum increase (all removals) in ecological value across solutions. Figure 10.9 shows selected results, where trade-offs among LEEM-based ecological criteria are qualitatively consistent with those revealed in the Ballville Dam case study. The magnitude of variations shown in Figure 10.9, however, are much greater than in the Ballville Dam case, since the habitat changes from multiple dam removals in ten watersheds are much larger.

The display of trade-offs among efficient portfolio solutions can inform negotiations among managers and stakeholders. Considering trade-offs between cost and other criteria, the results in Figure 10.9 show that in general, when the budget cap (and thus expenditures on removal and lamprey control) increases, the number of dams chosen for removal increases. With more removals, both habitat creation and ecological benefits are amplified. However, the magnitude of the increases in dam removals and various objectives are not proportional to increases in expenditures. For instance, under a budget of $5 million, nine removals are optimal, creating approximately 11 km² of suitable walleye habitat and yielding 35 percent of the maximum ecological benefit. However, when spending increases sixfold to $30 million, there would not be a sixfold increase in the number of removals and their consequences. Instead, the removal number grows by more than sevenfold (from nine to sixty-six removals), but both walleye habitat creation and ecological enhancement increase by less than threefold. Spending an additional $15 million (for a total of $45 million) contributes little incremental ecological benefit. Such nonlinearities illustrate the complexities inherent in multidam removal decisions.

A detailed look at the efficient portfolios shows that dam size, current service, location, and associated habitat potential are key factors in selecting which dams to remove. When the allowable budget is low, most selected removals are relatively small dams that provide few if any services. In addition, they are chosen also because they are close to the river mouth, blocking significant walleye habitat, while posing a minimal threat of sea lamprey invasion because there is little habitat upstream for that exotic species. Figure 10.10 is a map showing one of the model solutions with nine removals under a $5 million budget. Solid white points are selected dams for removal, while solid black points are candidate dams that are left intact. Wide lines represent river reaches that would become accessible had the chosen dam been removed. Note that most removals are in the Sandusky River Basin where

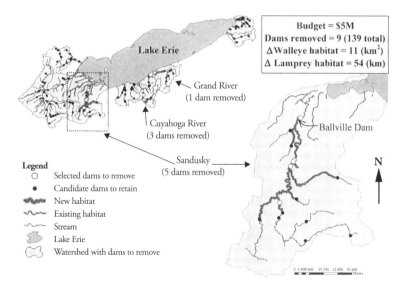

Figure 10.10 Multi-dam removal case study results example: locations of 139 candidate dams and nine removals under a $5M Budget (Sandusky River basin with five dams removed is enlarged)

the Ballville Dam is located. Through Equation (2), the estimated removal cost for "removing" the Ballville Dam is about $1.3 million dollars (the third highest estimate among the 139 dams), which is significantly lower than the first case study's estimated removal cost that includes building a new reservoir and removing the sediment (more than $10 million in present worth terms, based on Figure 10.7(a)). Clearly, Equation (2) underestimated the actual removal cost for the Ballville Dam; this illustrates our conclusion in "Economic Models and Model Linkages" that due to its inaccuracies, the cost regression model should be used only to screen potential dam removals for further study. With this lower cost estimate, the Ballville Dam is removed under a $5 million budget. Together, removing these nine dams out of 139 candidate dams would provide 34 percent of the potential increase in basin-wide habitat for walleye spawning, but only 11 percent of the potential increase for sea lamprey. When the budget is increased, it turns out that the number of removals does not increase monotonically with the economic costs—sometimes the number decreases. This is because removing a single large dam can be equivalent to or be more effective than taking out several small ones. An increased budget allows substitution of one or a few large dam removals for several small dam removals.

Discussion and Conclusion

With increasing numbers of aging and substandard dams in the United States, decision-makers face difficult decisions on dam decommissioning. Often there is no obvious solution, since these decisions deal with multiple and sometimes conflicting social, economic, and environmental goals and involve diverse stakeholders, impending hazards, and various uncertainties. Particularly, decisions on whether to remove some large dams are controversial because of strongly conflicting objectives (e.g., the Ballville Dam). On the other hand, decisions to remove small and abandoned dams are more straightforward. Nevertheless, with the large number of candidate dams for removal and limited budgets, selecting which ones to remove can still be challenging.

Dam decommissioning decisions can benefit from using QDA. QDA provides insights by quantifying the achievement of both economic and noneconomic objectives, identifying cost-effective alternatives, describing important trade-offs, and translating managers' and stakeholders' priorities into recommendations. In this chapter, QDA is implemented through a decision framework that analyzes the benefits and costs of dam decommissioning problems as a habitat restoration strategy in the Lake Erie Basin.

To achieve the goal of cost-effective environmental improvement, it is important to have good estimates of removal costs and environmental benefits. One focus of our work has been to estimate a cost function that can be used in dam removal screening studies. Our regression model estimates removal cost based upon dam parameters (size, type, and purpose) that are relatively easy to obtain. Another focus has been to couple habitat and ecological models so that ultimate ecological goals (such as populations of valued fish species) can be considered rather than habitat proxies. By doing so, dam removal decisions are made based on the evaluations of the criteria that address lake-wide ecological effects, instead of the sometimes misleading criterion of much more "good" habitat that would be recreated.

Because of complex life histories and interactions among different species, habitat improvements alone cannot be counted upon to improve ecological health. In our case study, had habitat restoration alone been used as the ecological criterion, trade-offs among conflicting ecological criteria would not have been described (for instance, walleye[99] versus commercial fish species) and the ultimate decision would be less informed and could be different.

Perhaps the most important focus of our decision framework has been on explicit consideration of stakeholder preferences. As illustrated in the two case studies, by varying the stakeholders' relative priority among the objectives or by changing the budget, trade-offs can be revealed and the sensitivity of decisions to these priorities can be assessed. The case studies demonstrate that QDA can make a complex decision process more transparent.

In sum, a quantitative decision framework can bridge the gaps between dam management and ecosystem restoration, allowing for better understanding of the relationship of habitat improvement expenditures and environmental improvement. It is important to realize, however, that there are many uncertainties in the economic and ecological parameters of the various models used in our decision framework. This means that this framework should only be used in a screening mode, and further site-specific study would be needed to finalize dam removal plans.

Finally, dam removal decisions involve not only numerous trade-offs and complex system interactions, but also varying types and degrees of uncertainties and risks. Future work should quantify and analyze uncertainties in the economic, hydrological, and ecological processes affected by dam removal decisions, including safety risks.

Acknowledgment

This work was supported by the National Center for Earth-surface Dynamics (agreement number EAR-0120914), a Public Safety Canada Research Fellowship in honor of Stuart Nesbitt White, and Abt Associates Inc.

Notes

1. William L. Graf, "Landscapes, Commodities, and Ecosystem: The Relationship Between Policy and Science for American Rivers," in *Sustaining Our Water Resources* (Washington, DC: National Academy Press, 1993), 11–42; Heinz Center, *Dam Removal: Science and Decision Making* (Washington, DC: Heinz Center for Science, Economics, and the Environment, 2002).

2. Association of State Dam Safety Officials (ASDSO), *Dam Safety 101—Dam Safety: A National Concern* (Lexington, KY: ASDSO, 2011), http://www.damsafety.org/news/?p=d42cd061-cae2-4039-8fc6-313975f97c36.

3. U.S. Army Corps of Engineers (USACE), Engineer Research and Development Center, National Inventory of Dams (accessed in June 13, 2005), http://geo.usace.army.mil/pgis/f?p=397:1:2125472315633851. The NID records dams that are six feet high or more and impound at least 50 AF of water, are twenty-five feet high and impound at least 15 AF, or present high or significant downstream hazards to the public (see note 1, Heinz Center, *Dam Removal*). A high hazard potential classification refers to cases in which dam failures will probably cause loss of human life, and significant hazard potential classification refers to potential failures that would not probably cause loss of human life but can cause economic loss, environment damage, or disruption of lifeline facilities (see USACE, "National Inventory of Dams").

4. Martin W. Doyle et al., "Dam Removal in the United States: Emerging Needs for Science and Policy," *Eos, Transactions, American Geophysical Union* 84, no. 4 (1993): 29–33, doi:10.1029/2003EO040001.

5. Heinz Center, *Dam Removal*.

6. ASDSO, *Dam Safety 101*; USACE, "National Inventory of Dams."

7. USACE, "National Inventory of Dams."

8. Elizabeth Maclin and Matt Sicchio, eds., *Dam Removal Success Stories: Restoring Rivers Through Selective Removal of Dams That Don't Make Sense* (Washington, DC: American Rivers, Friends of the Earth, and Trout Unlimited, 1999); Martin W. Doyle, Jon M. Harbor, and Emily H. Stanley, "Toward Policies and Decision-Making for Dam Removal," *Environmental Management* 31, no. 4 (2003): 453–65.

9. World Commission on Dams, *Dams and Development—A New Framework for Decision-Making* (London: Earthscan Publications, 2000).

10. Graf, "Landscapes, Commodities, and Ecosystem."

11. Karen L. Bushaw-Newton et al., "An Integrative Approach Towards Understanding Ecological Responses to Dam Removal: The Manatawny Creek Study," *Journal of the American Water Resources Association* 38, no. 6 (2002): 1581–99.

12. Margaret Bowman et al., *Exploring Dam Removal: A Decision-Making Guide* (Washington, DC: American Rivers and Trout Unlimited, 2002); Heinz Center, *Dam Removal*.

13. Heinz Center, *Dam Removal*.

14. ASDSO, *Dam Safety 101*.

15. ASDSO, *The Cost of Rehabilitating Our Nation's Dams: A Methodology, Estimate, and Proposed Funding Mechanisms* (Lexington, KY: ASDSO, 2003).

16. Heinz Center, *Dam Removal*.

17. ASDSO, *An Incomplete History of Dam Failures and Near Failures in the U.S.* (Lexington, KY: ASDSO, 2007).

18. Maclin and Sicchio, *Dam Removal Success Stories*.

19. Angela T. Bednarek, "Undamming Rivers: A Review of the Ecological Impacts of Dam Removal," *Environmental Management* 27, no. 6 (2001): 803–14; Bushaw-Newton et al., "Integrative Approach"; Doyle, Harbor, and Stanley, "Toward Policies."

20.   John R. Shuman, "Environmental Considerations for Assessing Dam Removal Alternatives for River Restoration," *Regulated Rivers—Research and Management* 11, nos. 3–4 (1995): 249–61; Emily H. Stanley and Martin W. Doyle, "Trading Off: The Ecological Removal Effects of Dam," *Frontiers in Ecology and the Environment* 1, no. 1 (2003): 15–22.

21.   J.V. Ward, and J. A. Stanford, "Ecological Connectivity in Alluvial River Ecosystems and Its Disruption by Flow Regulation," *Regulated Rivers—Research and Management* 11, no. 1 (1995): 105–19; N. Leroy Poff et al., "The Natural Flow Regime: A Paradigm for Conservation and Restoration of River Ecosystems," *Bioscience* 47, no. 11 (1997): 769–84; Liba Pejchar and Keith Warner, "A River Might Run Through It Again: Criteria for Consideration of Dam Removal and Interim Lessons from California," *Environmental Management* 28, no. 5 (2001): 561–75.

22.   N. Leroy Poff and David D. Hart, "How Dams Vary and Why It Matters for the Emerging Science of Dam Removal," *Bioscience* 52, no. 8 (2002): 659–68.

23.   Doyle, Harbor, and Stanley, "Toward Policies."

24.   National Cooperative Highway Research Program (NCHRP), *A Summary of Existing Research on Low-head Dam Removal Projects* (Lexington, MA: NCHRP, Transportation Research Board, prepared by ICF Consulting, 2005); American Rivers, *Dams Slated for Removal in 2008 and Dams Removed from 1999–2005* (Washington, DC: American Rivers, 2008).

25.   Molly M. Pohl, "Bringing Down Our Dams: Trends in American Dam Removal Rationales," *Journal of the American Water Resources Association* 38, no. 6 (2002): 1511–19.

26.   Stanley and Doyle, "Trading Off."

27.   Bednarek, "Undamming Rivers."

28.   Heinz Center, *Dam Removal.*

29.   Doyle et al., "Dam Removal."

30.   Shuman, "Environmental Considerations."

31.   G. Thomas Watters, "Small Dams as Barriers to Freshwater Mussels (*Bivalvia, Unionoida*) and Their Hosts," *Biological Conservation* 75, no. 1 (1996): 79–85.

32.   Bednarek, "Undamming Rivers"; Doyle, Harbor, and Stanley, "Toward Policies."

33.   David D. Hart et al., "Dam Removal: Challenges and Opportunities for Ecological Research and River Restoration," *Bioscience* 52, no. 8 (2002): 669–81; Jim Pizzuto, "Effects of Dam Removal on River Form and Process," *Bioscience* 52, no. 8 (2002): 683–91.

34.   Poff and Hart, "How Dams Vary"; Charles Gowan, Kurt Stephenson, and Leonard Shabman, "The Role of Ecosystem Valuation in Environmental Decision Making: Hydropower Relicensing and Dam Removal on the Elwha River," *Ecological Economics* 56, no. 4 (2006): 508–23.

35.   Poff and Hart, "How Dams Vary"; Heinz Center, *Dam Removal.*

36.   Doyle, Harbor, and Stanley, "Toward Policies"; Pearl Q. Zheng, Benjamin F. Hobbs, and Joseph F. Koonce, "Optimizing Multiple Dam Removals Under Multiple Objectives: Linking Tributary Habitat and the Lake Erie Ecosystem," *Water Resources Research* 45, no. 12 (2009): W12417, doi:10.1029/2008WR007589.

37. See, e.g., Pejchar and Warner, "River Might Run"; Bushaw-Newton et al., "Integrative Approach"; James E. Evans et al., "Assessment Using GIS and Sediment Routing of the Proposed Removal of Ballville Dam, Sandusky River, Ohio," *Journal of the American Water Resources Association* 38, no. 6 (2002): 1549–65; Hart et al., "Dam Removal"; Pizzuto, "Effects of Dam Removal"; Fang Cheng et al., "Modelling the Effects of Dam Removal on Migratory Walleye (*Sander vitreus*) Early Life-History Stages," *River Research and Applications* 22, no. 8 (2006): 837–51.

38. See, e.g., Gowan, Stephenson, and Shabman, "Role of Ecosystem Valuation"; Lynne Y. Lewis, Curtis Bohlen, and Sarah Wilson, "Dams, Dam Removal, and River Restoration: A Hedonic Property Value Analysis," *Contemporary Economic Policy* 26, no. 2 (2008): 175–86.

39. Ed Whitelaw and Ed MacMullan, "A Framework for Estimating the Costs and Benefits of Dam Removal," *BioScience* 52, no. 8 (2002): 724–30.

40. Hope J. Corsair et al., "Multicriteria Decision Analysis of Stream Restoration: Potential and Examples," *Group Decision and Negotiation* 18, no. 4 (2009): 387–417.

41. Ibid.

42. Bednarek, "Undamming Rivers"; Doyle, Harbor, and Stanley, "Toward Policies."

43. Hart et al., "Dam Removal"; Heinz Center, *Dam Removal*; Graf, "Landscapes, Commodities, and Ecosystems"; Stanley and Doyle, "Trading Off."

44. David E. Bell, Howard Raiffa, and Amos Tversky, *Decision Making: Descriptive, Normative and Prescriptive Interaction* (Cambridge, MA: Cambridge University Press, 1988); Jared L. Cohon, *Multiobjective Programming and Planning* (1978; repr., Mineola, NY: Dover Publications, 2003).

45. See, e.g., M. Granger Morgan, Max Henrion, and Mitchell Small, *Uncertainty—A Guide to Dealing with Uncertainty in Qualitative Risk and Policy Analysis* (New York: Cambridge University Press, 1990); Ralph L. Keeney, *Value-Focused Thinking: A Path to Creative Decisionmaking* (Cambridge, MA: Harvard University Press, 1992); R. J. Kopp and V. K. Smith, *Valuing Natural Assets: The Economics of Natural Resource Damage Assessment* (Washington, DC: Resources for the Future, 1993); Charles S. ReVelle, Elbert E. Whitlatch, and Jeff R. Wright, *Civil and Environmental Systems Engineering*, 2nd ed. (Upper Saddle River, NJ: Pearson Prentice Hall, 2004).

46. See, e.g., Richard M. Anderson et al., "Using Decision Analysis to Choose Phosphorus Targets for Lake Erie," *Environmental Management* 27, no. 2 (2001): 235–52.

47. See, e.g., B. Grove and L. K. Oosthuizen, "Establishing a Benchmark for Comparing Relative Cost-Effectiveness of an Alternative Policy Instrument for Controlling Non-Point Source Pollution," *Water SA* 33, no. 5 (2007): 609–14.

48. See, e.g., Jong B. Kim, Benjamin F. Hobbs, and Joseph F. Koonce, "Multicriteria Bayesian Analysis of Lower Trophic Level Uncertainties and Value of Research in Lake Erie," *Human and Ecological Risk Assessment* 9, no. 4 (2003): 1023–57.

49. See, e.g., Corsair et al., "Multicriteria Decision Analysis"; Zheng, Hobbs, and Koonce, "Optimizing Multiple Dam Removals."

50. See, e.g., Calvin N. Peters and David R. Marmorek, "Application of Decision Analysis to Evaluate Recovery Actions for Threatened Snake River Spring and Summer Chinook Salmon (*Oncorhynchus tshawytscha*)," *Canadian Journal of Fisheries and Aquatic Sciences* 58, no. 12 (2001): 2431–46; Stanley and Doyle, "Trading Off"; Michael J. Kuby et al., "A Multiobjective Optimization Model for Dam Removal: An Example Trading Off Salmon Passage with Hydropower and Water Storage in the Willamette Basin," *Advances in Water Resources* 28, no. 8 (2005): 845–55.

51. Ralph L. Keeney and Howard Raiffa, *Decisions with Multiple Objectives: Preferences and Value Tradeoffs* (New York: Wiley & Sons, 1976).

52. Valerie Belton and Theodor J. Stewart, *Multiple Criteria Decision Analysis: An Integrated Approach* (Norwell, MA: Kluwer Academic Publishers, 2002).

53. Cohon, *Multiobjective Programming*.

54. Keeney and Raiffa, *Decisions with Multiple Objectives*; Belton and Stewart, *Multiple Criteria Decision Analysis*.

55. Ralph E. Steuer, *Multiple Criteria Optimization: Theory, Computation, and Application* (New York: Wiley & Sons, 1986); Cohon, *Multiobjective Programming*.

56. Richard M. Anderson and Benjamin F. Hobbs, "Using a Bayesian Approach to Quantify Scale Compatibility Bias," *Management Science* 48, no. 12 (2002): 1555–68.

57. Keeney, *Value-Focused Thinking*.

58. The full MILP model formulation can be found in Zheng, Hobbs, and Koonce, "Optimizing Multiple Dam Removals."

59. Joseph H. Leach, "Lake Erie: Passage Revisited," in *State of Lake Erie: Past, Present and Future*, eds. M. Munawar, T. Edsall and I. F. Munawar (Leiden, The Netherlands: Backhuys Publishers, 1999), 5–22.

60. Richard W. Hatch et al., "Dynamics of the Recovery of the Western Lake Erie Walleye (*Stizostedion-vitreum*)," *Canadian Journal of Fisheries and Aquatic Sciences* 44, no. S2 (1987): S15–S22.

61. Lake Erie Lakewide Management Plan (Lake Erie LaMP), Environment Canada and the U.S. Environmental Protection Agency (EPA), *The Lake Erie Lakewide Management Plan 2000* (2000), http://epa.gov/greatlakes/lakeerie/lamp2000/index.html.

62. Roger L. Knight, "Successful Interagency Rehabilitation of Lake Erie Walleye," *Fisheries* 22, no. 7 (1997): 16–17.

63. Joseph F. Koonce, W. Dieter N. Busch, and Thomas Czapla, "Restoration of Lake Erie: Contribution of Water Quality and Natural Resource Management," *Canadian Journal of Fisheries and Aquatic Sciences* 53, no. S1 (1996): S105–S112.

64. P. A. Ryan et al., "Great Lakes Fishery Commission (GLFC)," *Fish-Community Goals and Objectives for Lake Erie*, Spec. Publ. 03-02 (March 2003), http://www.glfc.org/pubs/SpecialPubs/Sp03_2.pdf.

65. Koonce, Busch, and Czapla, "Restoration of Lake Erie"; Daniel B. Hayes, "Issues Affecting Fish Habitat in the Great Lake Basin," in *Great Lakes Fisheries Policy and Management: A Binational Perspective*, eds. William W. Taylor and C. Paola Ferreri (East Lansing, MI: Michigan State University Press, 1999), 209–37; Lake Erie LaMP, *Management Plan 2000*; Ryan et al., *Fish-Community Goals*.

66. Stanley J. Bolsenga and Charles E. Herdendorf, eds., *Lake Erie and Lake St. Clair Handbook*, Great Lake Books, eds. P. P. Mason and C. K. Hyde (Detroit, MI: Wayne State University Press, 1993).

67. Zheng, Hobbs, and Koonce, "Optimizing Multiple Dam Removals."

68. Great Lake Fishery Commission (GLFC), *Sea Lamprey: A Great Lakes Invader* (Ann Arbor, MI: GLFC, 2000).

69. W. Paul Sullivan et al., "The Sea Lamprey in Lake Erie: A Case History," *Journal of Great Lakes Research* 29, no. S1 (2003): S615–S636.

70. Bolsenga and Herdendorf, *Lake Erie*; Sullivan et al., "Sea Lamprey."

71. Sullivan et al., "Sea Lamprey."

72. GLFC, *Sea Lamprey*.

73. Pearl Q. Zheng, "Multiobjective Decision Analysis and Risk Analysis of Multi-dam Removal: Optimizing Dam Failure Risk, Removal Cost, and Ecosystem Benefit" (PhD dissertation, Johns Hopkins University, 2009).

74. Joseph F. Koonce, Ana B. Locci, and Roger L. Knight, "Contributions of Fishery Management to Changes in Walleye and Yellow Perch Populations of Lake Erie," in *Great Lakes Fisheries Policy and Management: A Binational Perspective*, eds. William W. Taylor and C. Paola Ferreri (East Lansing, MI: Michigan State University Press, 1999), 397–416.

75. Koonce, Locci, and Knight, "Contributions of Fishery Management"; Ana B. Locci and Joseph F. Koonce, "A Theoretical Analysis of Food Web Constraints on Walleye Dynamics in Lake Erie," in *State of Lake Erie: Past, Present and Future*, eds. M. Munawar, T. Edsall, and I. F. Munawar (Leiden, The Netherlands: Backhuys Publishers, 1999), 497–510.

76. Corsair et al., "Multicriteria Decision Analysis"; Zheng, Hobbs, and Koonce, "Optimizing Multiple Dam Renewals."

77. Maclin and Sicchio, *Dam Removal Success Stories.*

78. Maclin and Sicchio, *Dam Removal Success Stories*; NCHRP, *Summary of Existing Research*; American Rivers, *Dams Slated for Removal.*

79. Sullivan et al., "Sea Lamprey."

80. Joseph F. Koonce, Randy L. Eshenroder, and Gavis C. Christie, "An Economic Injury Level Approach for Establishing the Intensity of Sea Lamprey Control in the Great Lakes," *North American Journal of Fisheries Management* 13, no. 1 (1993): 1–14.

81. Workshops were held in Cleveland in Ohio in early 2000 as parts of two previous research projects (see Kim, Hobbs, and Koonce, "Multicriteria Bayesian Analysis"; and Anderson and Hobbs, "Using a Bayesian Approach") that address other decision problems related to Lake Erie ecosystem management.

82. Finkbeiner, Pettis, and Strout (FPS), *Raw Water Supply Study, Prepared for City of Fremont, Ohio* (Toledo, OH: FPS, 1999).

83. Details available in Corsair et al., "Multicriteria Decision Analysis."

84. Michael L. Jones et al., "Does the Value of Newly Accessible Spawning Habitat for Walleye (*Stizostedion vitreum*) Depend on Its Location Relative to Nursery Habitats?" *Canadian Journal of Fisheries and Aquatic Sciences* 60, no. 12 (2003): 1527–38.

85. S. Gainer, "Sediment Samples Will Aid Decision on City Reservoir," *The News Messenger* (Fremont, OH), October 19, 2001.

86. Evans et al., "Assessment Using GIS."

87. Ohio Department of Natural Resources (ODNR), *Dam Safety Inspection Report—Ballville Dam* (Columbus, OH: ODNR, Division of Water, 2003); Arcadis, *Investigation Program Report for the Ballville Dam, Prepared for the City of Fremont, Ohio* (Toledo, OH: Arcadis, 2005).

88. M. Tressler, "Fremont's Dam Blocks State's Vision of River," *Toledo Blade*, January 3, 2000, 9–10.

89. See, e.g., M. B. Trautman, "The Fishes of the Sandusky River System, Ohio," in *International Joint Commission on the Great Lake, Tiffin, Ohio* (1975), 33–241; Jones et al., "Value of Newly Accessible Spawning."

90. Finkbeiner, Pettis, and Strout, *Raw Water Supply Study*; Sarah A. Kruse, "Creating an Interdisciplinary Framework for Economic Valuation: A CVM Application of Dam Removal" (PhD dissertation, Agricultural, Environmental, and Development Economics Graduate Program, Ohio State University, 2005).

91. "Dam Backers Say City Has Enough Water," *Toledo Blade*, January 21, 2000, 13.

92. Corsair et al., "Multicriteria Decision Analysis."

93. Ibid.

94. For details on the definition and interpretation of these indices, see Corsair et al., "Multicriteria Decision Analysis."

95. Details available in Zheng, Hobbs, and Koonce, "Optimizing Multiple Dam Removals."

96. C. Geddes, Institute for Fisheries Research, University of Michigan, Personal communication, 2006.

97. This is based on data provided by R. Archer, Division of Water, Ohio Department of Natural Resources, 2006.

98. Figure 10.10 shows the locations of the candidate dams (solid white and black points).

99. Commercial fishing in Lake Erie was banned by the U.S. Government in 1972. It was reopened in 1976. Recreational walleye fishing in the Lake Erie region has never been closed.

11

The Sacramento–San Joaquin Delta and the Political Economy of California Water Allocation

Rachael E. Goodhue, Susan Stratton Sayre, and Leo K. Simon

Introduction

Large-scale water problems of the nature discussed in this book are inherently difficult to solve. Water distribution and use decisions must be made within a complex system with economic, political, engineering, legal, and ecological dimensions. Any policy choice will impact all of these dimensions. Two critical tasks in the resolution of such debates are to characterize these multidimensional impacts for each potential solution and to identify instruments capable of implementing particular choices. Because of the system's complexity, however, it is virtually inevitable that stakeholders' interests will conflict under any chosen policy path. These conflicts would be relatively manageable in a world in which (1) property rights were fully defined, (2) benchmarks were available and generally accepted as bases for interpersonal welfare comparisons, and (3) interpersonal compensation was feasible. In such a world, the logical approach would be to choose the policy that maximized aggregate welfare, thus ensuring economically efficient outcomes. The winners could then compensate the losers to guarantee that all stakeholders ended up better off, thus ensuring that all equity effects are incorporated into the outcome.

In water allocation problems, typically, none of the conditions listed previously will be satisfied, which makes it very difficult to identify a single, social welfare-maximizing solution. There is almost always ambiguity about what property rights exist and who holds them. For instance, environmental and agricultural stakeholders often value objectives like "ecosystem health" or the "agricultural way of life." It is difficult to assign a precise property right to these diffuse objectives. Moreover, many of the scarce resources at issue in water debates—especially those relating to the environment and "ways of life"—are nonmarket goods. Because they are not traded, there is no market price that can provide a basis for welfare comparisons.[1] Finally, to the extent that a property right can be defined, it is often unclear who holds that right. For example, the Endangered Species Act (ESA) could perhaps be interpreted as endowing each endangered species with a property right to survival. Obviously, however, one cannot compensate a species for its extinction.

Without some degree of consensus about how to weigh competing interests, expert assessments of the policy route that most equitably balances these interests are bound to be challenged by stakeholders, whose subjective views about the appropriateness of any given inter-stakeholder trade-off will surely be wildly divergent. In such contexts, political factors will play a particularly important role in shaping the ultimate policy outcome. In order to understand the political process from which a solution may emerge, it will be helpful to analyze the relative impacts of alternative policies on each stakeholder group. A policy option that is ranked reasonably high by all stakeholders may provide a natural starting point from which to construct a politically viable way forward, even if it is not economically efficient.

In this chapter, we conduct an analysis along these lines of the political debate over the future of California's Sacramento–San Joaquin Delta (the Delta). The Delta serves a critical role in the state's water distribution system. Water that flows through the Delta provides drinking water to two-thirds of the state's residents and irrigation water for nearly 2.5 million acres of some of the most productive agricultural land in the world. The Delta also occupies a unique and important ecological niche. It is part of the largest estuary on the west coast of North America and is home to fifty-five species of fish and 750 species of plants and wildlife.[2]

It is widely acknowledged that currently the Delta is in crisis. While many of the concerns expressed regarding the Delta are familiar to long-time observers of California water policy, we do not attempt here to provide a history of the evolution of California water policy. Today, there is a remarkable degree of consensus that the Delta's condition is ever-worsening and that now is a critical time for action. The Delta's ecosystem is changing, and as a result, it is failing to provide some of the ecological functions it has performed in the recent past. Due at least in part to this failure, several species are on the verge of extinction. Moreover, its infrastructure is highly vulnerable to floods and earthquakes. Since 2007, at least five major reports have been released detailing alternative management strategies and providing policy recommendations. In 2006, Governor Schwarzenegger signed an executive order creating several entities tasked with studying the Delta's problems and recommending a solution. The entire initiative is known as Delta Vision.

The Vision process seeks to meet two objectives that it terms "coequal" goals: "environmental quality of the Delta" and "the economic and social well-being of the people of the state."[3] Two key entities are the Blue Ribbon Task Force and the Delta Vision Committee. The Blue Ribbon Task Force is an independent group of experts from a variety of backgrounds charged with examining a broad variety of possible solutions and recommending a strategic direction. The Delta Vision Committee consists of five members of the governor's cabinet whose responsibility is to review the Task Force's work and make final recommendations. The Task Force released a report outlining its objectives, *Delta Vision: Our Vision for the California Delta,* in late 2007 (*Delta Vision*; finalized in 2008) and its final report, *Delta Vision Strategic Plan,* at the end of October 2008 (*Strategic Plan*), and the Delta Vision Committee released its recommendations for implementation about two months later (*Implementation Report*).[4]

In addition to the work initiated by the governor, several independent organizations have issued substantial reports on policy options for the Delta. Through the Public Policy Institute of California (PPIC), a multidisciplinary group of researchers has released two reports on the Delta. (The 2008 report will be referred to as the PPIC Report throughout this chapter.)[5] Immediately following the publication of the PPIC Report, the Pacific Institute and the Environmental Defense Fund (EDF) each issued their own analyses.[6] Each of these reports evaluates a variety of policy options for the Delta's future. Most of them provide specific policy recommendations.

Finally, in response to the Delta's failing ecosystem, a number of state, federal, local, and private agencies have joined forces to create what will be known as the "Bay Delta Conservation Plan" (BDCP).[7] This group has released several documents.[8] In the words of one of these documents, "The purpose of the Bay Delta Conservation Plan (BDCP) is to help recover endangered and sensitive species and their habitats in the Delta in a way that also will provide for sufficient and reliable water supplies."[9]

In this chapter, we use these analyses as a starting point to investigate the political dimensions of the debate over policy alternatives. Our goal is to evaluate their political consequences in a comprehensive framework capable of identifying politically feasible solutions to the Delta crisis. The framework incorporates key physical and biological relationships that determine stakeholder groups' welfare under each possible solution. An analysis focused on identifying economically efficient outcomes would attempt to monetize these welfare measures to permit the construction of a social welfare function. In contrast, our focus is on identifying politically feasible solutions. Since economic efficiency does not guarantee political feasibility, we assess the feasibility of an alternative directly from its impact on the welfare of each stakeholder group. Because we do not evaluate the economic efficiency of the alternatives, we are not required to take the controversial step of monetizing different objectives. Instead, we offer a discussion of what alternatives are likely to be politically feasible given the identified impacts on the stakeholder groups.

In the remaining sections of this chapter, we begin by providing a description of the Delta's role in the state's water system, a description of the current pressures facing the Delta, and a discussion about the political debate over the region's future. We then construct a stylized model of the major policy decisions and their impacts on several key stakeholders. Next, we use that model to discuss the political feasibility of the policy alternatives currently under consideration. And finally, we offer concluding comments, including a discussion of further uses of the model developed within this chapter.

The Sacramento–San Joaquin Delta

Water has been a critical issue in California since the first days of its development. One of the state's most striking geographical features is the immense Central Valley in its middle. This 42,000-square-mile region is drained by two large river systems: the Sacramento River in the northern half and the San Joaquin River in the southern half. These rivers meet east of the Coastal Range in the Delta.[10] (See Figure 11.1 for a stylized map of the Delta region.) Under natural conditions, water from both the Sacramento and San Joaquin Rivers flows through the Delta to Suisun Bay, and on to San Francisco Bay and then the Pacific Ocean. In an average year, absent water diversions, the Sacramento and San Joaquin River systems would transport approximately 30 million acre-feet (AF) of water to the Pacific Ocean.

An important consequence of the state's climate is that water supply is highly variable, both within a given year and across years. In an average year, after accounting for rainfall used directly by crops and other vegetation before entering the water supply, evaporation and flows to the ocean and other salt sinks, precipitation and imports from neighboring states, most importantly from the Colorado River, provide approximately 80 million AF of water available to meet California's specific water demands. In a dry year that number could shrink to approximately 65 million AF, while in an unusually wet year, it could be as high as 95 million AF.[11] Typically, the state receives most of its precipitation during the winter and little to none over the hot, dry summers. Much of the winter precipitation falls as snow in the Sierras.

Since the Delta drains nearly half of the state's annual precipitation, this variability has important consequences for the Delta's natural ecosystem. Historically, under natural flow regimes, conditions in the Delta varied substantially with variations in water flows. In the spring, as the snowpack melted, huge quantities of fresh water flowing down the Sacramento and San Joaquin Rivers flooded the Delta with cold, fresh water. As flows in the rivers

Figure 11.1 Delta region

(*Sources:* California Spatial Information Library, *Hydrologic Features,* State of California, 2008. http://projects.atlas.ca.gov/projects/casil/; California Department of Fish and Game, *Delta Vision: Interactive Map,* http://imaps.dfg.ca.gov/viewers/delta_vision/app.asp.)

lessened over the summer and into the fall with the snowpack gone, salt water from San Francisco Bay would move further into the Delta creating brackish conditions in parts of the western and northern Delta. In dry years, brackish conditions would prevail for longer periods and penetrate further into the Delta, while in wet years, the reverse would be true.

Development has dramatically altered this system. Prior to large-scale settlement, the Delta was a marshy region with shifting channels and varying water salinity. In the 1860s, farmers began settling parts of the Delta, dredging channels through the marsh to facilitate shipping and using the sediments to build levees and convert marshland into farms. These activities changed the

Delta from a region of shifting channels and landmasses to a progressively more static system of islands and channels. By 1930, approximately 1,100 square miles of land had been reclaimed in the Delta.[12]

While settlement drastically changed the nature of the Delta itself, the state's water infrastructure has changed flow conditions. The heavy spring floods typical of California were a problem for early settlers for two reasons: the floods themselves could damage houses and farms, and the water contained in those spring floods would have been extremely valuable in the dry summer and fall months that followed had it been available. The solution was to dam the rivers, permitting flood control and a means to capture and store the snowmelt for later use. Today, large quantities of water are diverted upstream of the Delta. Even after accounting for return flows, more than 25 percent of the water that would naturally flow to the Delta never reaches it.[13] Diversions on the San Joaquin River are so large that a substantial section of the riverbed is actually dry in all but the wettest periods. Water that reaches the Delta through this river today is the result of drainage canals that flow into the riverbed, carrying water polluted with agricultural runoff.[14]

During the twentieth century, the Delta system was altered further by two large water projects. In 1937, Congress authorized the Central Valley Project (CVP), which constructed facilities for water storage upstream from the Delta in both the Sacramento and San Joaquin River systems and water transportation facilities in the Delta. Water from the Sacramento River system, our focus here, is released from storage and flows through the Delta. It is then diverted from the southern end of the Delta and sent south to water users in the Central Valley. In 1960, California voters approved construction of the State Water Project (SWP), which performs a similar function and also supplies water to urban Southern California. Together these projects divert approximately 5.5 million AF of water each year.[15]

Water conveyed through the Delta provides critical supply for many of the state's water users. Nearly two-thirds of the state's residents are at least partially dependent on the Delta for drinking water. These include residents of urban Southern California and parts of the Bay Area. Farmers, especially in the southern and western Central Valley, are dependent on the Delta for irrigation water. In addition to users who rely on the Delta for water conveyance, farms and communities within the Delta region divert water directly from the Delta for their uses. Since 1990, less than half of the Delta's natural outflows have reached the ocean.

While this system has fueled substantial economic growth in many regions, it has drastically changed the character of the Delta. Today's Delta is a series of static, levee-lined channels that flow between reclaimed islands, home to farms and communities. Carefully timed water releases from projects upstream on the Sacramento River keep salinity within the

Delta at a relatively constant level that is low enough to be useful for drinking water and agricultural purposes. As documents released through the BDCP process point out, "In an effort to engineer the Delta for water conveyance and agriculture, we have created a fairly static environment—while the water still flows, and the tides still fluctuate, the land and the water have become disconnected, and the complexity of the ecosystem has diminished considerably."[16]

The Delta in Crisis

Stakeholders in the region agree that the Delta is in crisis, due to a large and complex set of interrelated problems. They disagree, however, on the relative contribution of various causes and the potential performance of various solutions. In simple terms, there are two major concerns: the health of the Delta ecosystem and the risk of levee failure. As the *Strategic Plan* notes:

> The Delta ecosystem, by almost any measure, is in serious decline and threatened by catastrophic failure from earthquake, floods, sea level rise, global warming, land subsidence, and urban development. These ecosystem threats equally endanger the current Delta water export system.

These problems guarantee that today's Delta has a limited lifespan. The PPIC Report notes that "the Delta of the future will be very different from the Delta of today and the Delta of the past, regardless of what management and policy actions are taken and what happens to California's environment and economy." This statement should not be interpreted as suggesting that current policy choices are irrelevant. The choice of management and policy actions today will determine the nature of the Delta of the future.

The substantial alteration of the Delta's natural ecosystem described in the previous section has had severe consequences. One ecologically and politically important effect has been the severe decline in the populations of several fish species in recent years. Some populations have declined to the extent that the species have been listed under the ESA. Fish declines in the Delta are likely the result of many factors, but water export operations are widely believed to play a major role.

Exporting water through the Delta in the current fashion causes three major problems for fish: water flow reversals, deaths at the pumping facilities, and altered hydrodynamics within the Delta.[17] The pumping plants in the southern Delta that deliver export water to the CVP and SWP are extremely powerful. When operating, they reverse the direction of water flow in much of the Delta. While San Joaquin River water would naturally flow northward through the Delta, the pumps pull water from the Sacramento River south. These flow reversals confuse native fish species and draw them toward the pumps. Once near the pumps, the fish face extreme dangers from the pumps themselves. Large numbers of fish (particularly Delta smelt) are killed at the pumping plants each year, despite the presence of a fish recovery operation designed to mitigate this impact.

Within the Delta, altered hydrodynamics have caused considerable changes. As noted previously, the Delta today is a much more static system than it was historically. Many biologists believe this has been detrimental to native fish species, through two mechanisms. First, the reduced variability has altered the ecosystem to which native species evolved and adapted. In particular, fish species that adapted to live in an environment of varying salinity are at a disadvantage in one with constant salinity. Second, the altered Delta ecosystem has provided a home to several invasive species and has favored certain predatory ones. These species have exacerbated the pressures on several species of native fish.[18]

The government has already undertaken ESA-mandated efforts in order to address fish population declines. In 2007, federal court Judge Oliver Wanger ruled that the effects of current water operations in the Delta on the Delta smelt violated the ESA. In response, exports from the Delta were reduced by nearly a third in 2008, reducing the water available for urban and agricultural uses.[19] Enforcement of the ESA for the fall-run Sacramento River salmon has also required government action. The National Marine Fisheries Service closed all commercial salmon fishing off the California and Oregon coasts in 2008 due to a particularly low count of fall-run Sacramento River salmon.

In addition to its failing ecosystem, the Delta in its current form is threatened by a large risk of island flooding with potentially disastrous consequences. When farmers built levees around marshy land in the Delta and reclaimed the land, they initiated an ongoing change in the system. Over the intervening years, the land making up these diked islands has subsided, primarily, due to the decomposition of organic carbon in the peat soils characterizing the Delta.[20] Sea levels have also increased, causing water levels in San Francisco Bay to rise approximately eight inches over the last century,[21] leading to an increase in water levels in the Delta. Today, many Delta islands are as much as twenty feet below sea level and continue to subside at long-run rates estimated at one to three inches per year.[22] Moreover, the levees surrounding many islands are considered insufficient for flood protection, either because they are too low given current water levels, because they have not been adequately maintained, or both.

As the islands continue to subside, and as sea levels continue to increase, as many observers predict, the likelihood of levee failure will increase. The consequences of a levee failure are expensive and severe. As soon as a levee is breached, water rushes in to fill the "bowl" and equalize water levels. This causes immediate destruction of homes and farms. In 2004, a levee breach along the Middle River within the Delta flooded an island known as the Jones Tract. Within a day, twenty homes and fifty other structures were under approximately twelve feet of water.[23] Repairs cost approximately $90 million and were largely funded by the state.[24]

Although the Jones Tract failure involved only one island, observers are increasingly concerned about the possibility of multiple, simultaneous levee failures. Two likely scenarios for such an event are a massive flood on the Sacramento River system or an earthquake on one of the faults that runs through the region. Geologists warn that such an earthquake *will* occur, the only question is *when*.

The result of a massive levee failure event is likely to be the destruction of the Delta system in its current form. Water from the Delta would rush in to fill multiple islands simultaneously, and Delta water levels would drop precipitously. As a result, salty water from San Francisco Bay would be drawn into the Delta, creating brackish conditions. Exporting water through the Delta for either residential or agricultural uses would cease to be an option until levees were repaired and sufficient fresh water from the rivers feeding the Delta reached the area. The negative consequences of such a large and sudden disruption of the state's water supply cannot be overstated. A sudden change to the Delta's salinity regime would also have adverse consequences for the region's ecosystem. Although many biologists believe that greater variation in salinity would benefit native Delta fish species, it is unlikely that a sudden and drastic change in salinity would benefit any fish, native or otherwise.

According to all major policy reports regarding the Delta in recent years, climate change is expected to exacerbate the Delta's problems over the coming years. Three major negative impacts on the Delta are anticipated. The first two are the consequences of increased climatic variability: more frequent droughts and larger floods. More frequent droughts will further stress an already stressed water supply. Minimum water needs for fish will likely mean little to no water available for other uses in a growing number of critically dry years. On the other hand, increased frequency of heavy floods raises the risk of a large flood event triggering simultaneous levee failures. The third impact of climate change may be even more problematic for the Delta (over the long run). Sea levels are expected to rise over time. Estimates of the degree of sea level rise vary widely, but all major analyses of the Delta include some projected sea level rise. The PPIC Report considered sea level increases of between 0.5 and 1.5 feet by 2050. This sea level rise exacerbates the problem of levees that are insufficient to protect islands from floods. The PPIC Report argues that the probability of a massive levee failure event by 2050 could be as high as 95 percent.

The Debate over the Delta's Future

Due to the Delta's role as the hub of the state's water system, decisions about its future affect a broad set of stakeholders. Any policy decisions will create winners and losers. Unsurprisingly, discussions over the region's future have triggered an active political and scientific debate. As discussed in the introduction, this debate has resulted in the publication of several major reports providing recommendations for the Delta's future.

We proceed by providing a general description of the policy options available to the state and a discussion of the strengths and weaknesses of each option. In the process, we discuss the recommendations made by each report along with the justifications for those recommendations. We divide our examination into two sections. The first discusses possible strategies for water exports. The second discusses other policy options.

Water Export Strategies

The PPIC Report argues that the fundamental choice facing the state is the selection of a strategy for Delta water exports. It identifies four basic options: continue through-Delta exports ("through Delta"), stop exporting water ("no exports"), build a canal to convey all water exports around the Delta ("peripheral canal"), or build a canal and export water both through the canal and through the Delta ("dual-conveyance"). In this subsection, we describe each of these alternatives and review the major arguments for and against each option.

The first option is to continue exporting water through the Delta using the current system. To be viable, this option would require upgrading and improving Delta infrastructure to minimize the risk of system collapse due to levee failure. A key element of any successful through-Delta strategy would be a substantial reduction in export volumes in order to comply with the ESA. The PPIC Report estimates that reductions of 25–40 percent from historical levels prior to the Wanger decision are likely. Pursuing this strategy means accepting a growing risk of numerous simultaneous levee failures. It also requires export users to continue to spend significant resources treating Delta water to meet quality standards. If rising sea levels cause the Delta to become more saline, treatment costs would increase. Over time, the desirability of the through-Delta option will likely deteriorate. The PPIC Report argues that this option is likely to be dominated by other choices on both cost and environmental performance criteria.

This conclusion is far from universal, however. In particular, many groups representing in-Delta interests believe that a modified through-Delta strategy could be successful. For instance, the South Delta Water Agency (SDWA), which delivers water to farmers in the southern Delta, argued in their public comments on drafts of the *Strategic Plan* that "the potential for a greatly improved through-Delta system without a canal was . . . ignored."[25]

The second option—the "no export" strategy—represents the extreme alternative of reducing Delta exports: stopping them altogether. This approach would likely result in the best environmental outcomes as all issues related to fish deaths at the pumps and altered flow regimes would be eliminated.

However, if this approach were adopted, water users who rely on Delta exports would be forced to reduce their use and/or seek alternative supplies. Conservation efforts and reductions in irrigated acreage would meet some of the shortfall, as shown by growers' responses to the dramatic reductions in SWP deliveries for 2009. Likely alternative water supplies include desalination, reclaimed wastewater, and, perhaps, increased reliance on groundwater. This shift in supplies would impose a monetary burden on all export users.

The third option is the "peripheral canal" alternative. This alternative would convey water around the Delta instead of through it by constructing a canal. The canal would start on the Sacramento River upstream of the Delta and transport water around the Delta to the existing pumps in the southern Delta. The idea of building such a canal is not new. In 1982, a bond initiative for the construction of a peripheral canal supported by then-Governor Jerry Brown was defeated due to overwhelming opposition from Northern California. The canal proposed at the time would have provided for a dramatic increase in water exports. Following the initiative's defeat, building a canal was considered a nonviable option, politically, for many years. Due to ESA-mandated water delivery restrictions in the past few years, however, the possibility of canal construction has been reintroduced. Here we do not compare in detail differences between the peripheral canal options discussed today and the 1982 peripheral canal proposal. In today's context, the goal is not to increase water deliveries to Southern California, but to separate as much as possible the needs of the state's water supply system from those of the Delta's ecosystem. Optimal timing of water releases and flow patterns with the Delta for ecosystem management differs from the optimal timing of water releases and flow patterns for agricultural and urban uses in Southern California. While a canal would mitigate the timing and flow problems, it cannot increase the total available water supply. As such, the proposals call for a much smaller canal than that proposed thirty years ago.

Today, a revised canal plan is a very real part of the debate, although it is subject to much controversy. In fact, even the name is controversial. Proponents of a canal plan generally avoid the term "peripheral canal," likely due to its negative associations with the failed 1982 bond initiative. Instead, many documents refer to an "isolated conveyance." For instance, neither the *Delta Vision* nor the *Strategic Plan* contains the word "peripheral," although both recommend exploring the construction of an isolated conveyance. In this chapter, we adopt more popular usage and refer to a "peripheral canal" rather than an isolated conveyance.

Proponents of a peripheral canal argue that it provides several potential benefits. First, it insulates the state's water supply from the risk of Delta levee collapse. In the event that a major levee collapse increased salinity levels in the Delta to the point that water in the Delta was unusable, the existence of an entirely isolated facility would permit the transport of fresh water from Sacramento south. Similarly, the canal would reduce the costs to export users of treating exported water, since its passage through the Delta currently contributes much of the salinity and other pollutants, which must be treated.

While the canal provides clear benefits for export users, its environmental effects and hence the environmental benefits it might provide are highly uncertain. Stakeholders disagree regarding their potential existence and importance. Proponents of the canal argue that it would have three major ecosystem benefits. First, by routing exports around instead of through the Delta, the canal would eliminate problems with reverse flows as water is sucked south toward the pumps. Although the existing pumps would still be used, water would not be drawn across the Delta toward them. Second, exporting water through the canal would mitigate entrainment problems at the pumps, especially for the smelt whose habitat is downstream of the proposed new intakes.[26] Finally, conveying water around the Delta would allow water managers greater flexibility in managing salinity. Today, fresh water is released from storage to manage salinity in the interior Delta so that water quality standards are met. If water exports were instead conveyed around the Delta, the salinity within the Delta could be allowed to fluctuate. Some biologists believe this fluctuation will favor the native Delta species that evolved in response to the natural salinity fluctuations in the system.

Stakeholders disagree about the effect increased salinity variability will have on fish populations. While agreeing that altered salinity standards and regimes could be beneficial, the draft BDCP urges caution. It states:

> Predictions of the response of various fish and other aquatic organisms to changes in the salinity regime, is uncertain . . . . Large-scale changes in the salinity regime within the estuary have the potential to result in large-scale biological benefits (increased species diversity and resilience) or to large-scale degradation (jeopardy of extinction).[27]

Other groups disagree that a peripheral canal would provide any ecosystem benefits. Restore the Delta, a coalition of Delta residents and environmentalists, argues that building a peripheral canal is a poor solution because it would worsen water quality in the Delta. The diversion of freshwater into the canal would reduce the amount of freshwater flowing through the Delta, thus worsening water quality. Restore the Delta argues that this would "lead to the death of the Sacramento–San Joaquin Delta's ecosystem."[28]

The canal would also have negative impacts on Delta residents and farmers. The fluctuating salinity that some biologists believe will help native fish species is a serious problem for Delta farmers and residents who rely on Delta waters for irrigation and drinking water. If all water exports were conveyed through a peripheral canal, carefully timed releases to maintain low salinity would no longer be necessary for water exports. Water quality in the Delta would likely become too saline for either irrigation or drinking water most of the year. The SDWA asserts that the peripheral canal "will destroy the southern Delta and so we must justify that death. This is why the Plan makes no reference to protecting southern Delta agriculture; it seeks to remove southern Delta agriculture."[29] One particularly important consideration for the southern Delta is that if through-Delta exports are eliminated, high-quality fresh water from the Sacramento River will no longer be drawn southward, diluting the low-quality water from the San Joaquin River. While the SDWA focuses on the effects on its clientele, other in-Delta users will face negative impacts due to changes in water quality and flows.

The final option—the "dual-conveyance" alternative—is to pursue a mixed strategy under which a canal around the Delta would be constructed, but some through-Delta exports would also continue. This approach involves improving the fortifications along a channel in the middle of the Delta in addition to building a canal. Exports would be routed through both the in-Delta channel and the canal. In the remainder of this chapter, we reserve the term "peripheral canal" for proposals that involve routing all exports through a canal and use the term "canal" to refer to a generic canal whether part of a single- or dual-conveyance system.

The PPIC Report argues that "there seems little reason to prefer a dual facility over a peripheral canal." Its authors believe that the environmental performance of a dual-conveyance system is unlikely to be better than that of a peripheral canal. Moreover, the dual-conveyance alternative would involve both building a canal and pursuing substantial upgrades to the existing levee system. As a result, it is likely to be more expensive. As stated in the report, "a dual conveyance alternative with significant investments to support through-Delta pumping is unlikely to be worth the additional costs, given the water quality and environmental risks of through-Delta pumping."[30]

In contrast, the Delta Vision Committee has recommended the dual-conveyance option over the peripheral canal. In the *Strategic Plan*, they point out "the need to maintain flows through the Delta for water supply and eco-system health" and note that "a dual conveyance system offers extra insurance against such disasters by creating an additional path for water conveyance."[31] They note that substantial additional analysis will be required to determine the feasibility and desirability of a dual-conveyance option. Such analysis should consider both single- and dual-conveyance options.

> Most stakeholders who are skeptical of the construction of a canal make little distinction between the stand-alone peripheral canal and the dual-conveyance options. Most environmental groups involved in the debate have stopped short of outright rejection of a peripheral canal, but remain concerned about the degree to which

the desirability of such a canal is considered a foregone conclusion. For instance, the Bay Institute and the Natural Resources Defense Council (NRDC) argued in their comments on the second draft of the *Strategic Plan* that a major change in Delta conveyance could have dramatic unintended consequences on *Delta Vision*'s co-equal goals.[32] The process of developing specific proposals for facilities and operations, and the analysis of potential impacts, benefits and costs, has just begun. *Delta Vision* can best support this process by urging the careful development and analysis of alternatives, rather than by encouraging a rush to judgment.

Groups representing in-Delta interests have been more vocal in their opposition to the peripheral canal and dual-conveyance alternatives. In particular, they object to the *Strategic Plan*'s identification of the dual-conveyance as the preferred alternative. In their comments on the fifth (and penultimate) draft of the *Strategic Plan*, the SDWA stated:

> There can be no "preliminary" choice of an isolated or dual facility *until* all of the analyses have been done. Perhaps the PC [peripheral canal] costs $25 billion and creates warm stagnant zones on the Sacrament [*sic*] system which adversely affects the fisheries while creating no new water supply? Clearly it is premature to make any comments on what is best for fisheries or the State. The Plan suggests DWR and other [*sic*] investigate a dual facility. The Plan should recognize this reality and not assume DWR is capable of some sort of fair analysis of the issues.[33]

Restore the Delta expressed concern that whether part of a joint system or not, the presence of a peripheral canal would drastically reduce state incentives to maintain and repair the levees that protect Delta communities today. Specifically, they argued that if a peripheral canal is built, "in the event of a natural disaster, the Delta would be written off in the same way that New Orleans was abandoned after Hurricane Katrina."[34] Moreover, extensive newspaper reports in the *Sacramento Bee* and *San Francisco Chronicle* on plans to build a canal were met with a chorus of overwhelmingly negative comments denouncing the Southern California "water grab." In an online forum, a *Sacramento Bee* reader with the username "tgianco" wrote:

> I remember these debates from when I was a kid. We really need to start up Northern CA as the 51 state again. The people of SoCal chose to live in a desert . . . that's their problem, not ours' or anyone else's.[35]

Despite this opposition to a canal, the governor's office plans to proceed with canal construction, likely as part of a dual-conveyance system as recommended in the *Strategic Plan*. The *Implementation Report* sets a target date of 2011 to begin construction of the facility. In fact, Mike Chrisman (chair of the

Delta Vision Committee and head of the state's Natural Resources Agency) claimed that the state has the legal authority to build the canal without approval from the legislature or the voters. However, most observers agree that the plan is likely to end up in the courts, especially if the administration fails to seek approval.[36]

Other Decisions

While the choice of a long-term strategy for Delta (water) exports is particularly critical, discussions over the Delta's future are not solely focused on exports. In this section, we discuss three additional decisions facing the state that will have a profound influence on the long-term health of the Delta and the state's water system.

The first decision concerns Delta governance. It is widely believed that the existing institutions responsible for managing the Delta have contributed to the current crisis. The *Strategic Plan* endorses this opinion, pointing out that under the current system "everyone is involved; no one is in charge." Some groups charge that the entities responsible for protecting fish and the ecosystem in general have failed in that duty. For instance, the SDWA notes that

> The agencies of the State charged with protecting endangered species and operating and regulating the State Water Project *never tried to comply with CESA; never.* During the time DWR knew that it did not have sufficient supply to fulfill its contracts, and while it increased exports to fill those contracts, it didn't comply with CESA, or more correctly never attempted to comply with the law.[37]

The Wanger decision described previously that triggered massive reductions in water exports reached a similar conclusion. This decision called a biological opinion that allowed (but did not require) increased export volumes through the Delta "arbitrary and capricious."[38]

In response, many stakeholders believe that new governance institutions are necessary. The *Implementation Report* released by the Delta Vision Committee lists as one of its fundamental actions developing "an improved governance system that has reliable funding, clear authority to determine priorities and strong performance measures to ensure accountability to the new governing doctrine of the Delta: operation for the coequal goals."[39] It further states that "completion of this fundamental action is absolutely essential to the sustained operation and maintenance of all of these recommendations."[40]

Environmental groups are insistent that the institutions for governing the Delta must be changed. They believe that the existing governance structure has allowed too much managerial flexibility, which has been exercised in ways that are detrimental to the environment. Therefore, they are pushing for new institutions that restrict this flexibility. For instance, EDF argues that

A bedrock element of environmental reliability is therefore a provision for automatic, non-discretionary changes in water project operations and other diversions in the event that the program elements above—such as water or money—do not materialize or the performance measures are not achieved by established deadlines.[41]

As with other elements of the Delta debate, there is disagreement about how best to reform the governance structure. Current proposals call for the creation of a new governing body called the California Delta Ecosystem and Water Council (CDEW). While many believe that new leadership and rules are necessary, not all stakeholders support the idea of new governing bodies. In particular, in its comments on the fifth draft of the *Strategic Plan*, SDWA states

> SDWA strongly opposes the creation of a new super Delta agency or governing board. It is not possible to do away with the various federal and state regulatory authorities or to combine them with interests that have goals contradictory to their duties. . . . If we learned anything from the CalFed debacle, it should be that putting the regulators in with the regulated, and encouraging them to reach consensus is the worst possible approach.[42]

A coalition of water export users known as the "Business Water Caucus" endorses the idea of governance change but expresses concern that changing too much will delay the implementation of other recommendations.[43] In particular, they note

> We continue to support the overall structure of the governance proposal but reiterate the need to limit the California Delta and Ecosystem Council to an oversight role, using the strategic plan to delegate specific and direct responsibility to implementing agencies, eliminating the cost and delay from yet another three-year planning process as envisioned by the CDEW plan.[44]

The Delta Vision Committee appears to agree with the need to act quickly. Although they acknowledge that governance is important, their plan suggests moving forward with canal construction while governance rules are developed. In response to this, The Nature Conservancy (TNC) announced that it supported the construction of a canal *conditional* on the development of new governance institutions more capable of safeguarding the Delta ecosystem. TNC's water program director for California, Anthony Sacarino, argued "We need to explore something that's new and has more independence, and we need to do that as soon as possible . . . The trick really isn't in the engineering; it's in the governance."[45] Thus, some environmental interests and some exporter interests favor institutional reform. This suggests that both groups feel that their interests have not been as well served by current institutions as they might be by alternative ones. However, it does not by any means suggest that the two groups would support the *same* set of alternative institutions.

A second critical element of the debate concerns water infrastructure. Many water users believe that additional investments in water infrastructure beyond the construction of a peripheral canal or a fortified through-Delta system are essential. Much of the public debate centers on the construction of new storage facilities either upstream on the Sacramento River system or south of the Delta. Upstream storage would offer managers greater ability to optimize the timing of water flows into the Delta. Storage south of the Delta would enable large volumes to be exported through or around the Delta at times when it would have the smallest impact on the ecosystem, but still be available for water users at their preferred times.

Many water user groups, along with the governor and many members of the Assembly, believe that storage investments are necessary and must be part of a comprehensive solution to the state's water problems. Although environmental groups do not universally reject the notion of new storage, they urge caution and reject the notion that all possible surface storage plans should be pursued. In particular, the Bay Institute and NRDC argued that

> The draft recommends proceeding with surface storage options without any real criteria for prioritizing potential projects, any examination of the cost-effectiveness and financing of these projects, and a meaningful discussion of innovative storage alternatives . . . . The discussion of surface storage would be significantly strengthened by the addition of an action requiring a careful analysis of the cost-effectiveness of specific projects, the optimal sizing and location of potential projects and the relative cost of alternative approaches.[46]

While storage investments have captured most of the political attention, additional investments in conveyance facilities outside the Delta proper are also under consideration. The PPIC Report argues that additional investments in expanding existing or constructing new conveyance facilities permitting more flexible movement of water between water user groups will be more cost effective than new storage.[47]

A third important element under discussion is expenditures on ecosystem restoration. One of the *Strategic Plan*'s seven goals for the Delta is to "restore the Delta ecosystem as the heart of a healthy estuary." The BDCP rests heavily on the notion of ecosystem restoration, and a draft plan containing several specific restoration opportunities is available.[48] The idea of ecosystem restoration within the Delta has widespread support. However, in-Delta interests are concerned about many of the specific measures proposed in this plan. For instance, the Sacramento County Farm Bureau noted in its comments on the first draft of the *Strategic Plan*, which endorses the adoption of the BDCP, that it

> vigorously opposes ecosystem performance measures, which set targets for conversion of 300,000 acres of productive agricultural land to tidal marsh, active floodplain, seasonal wetlands, and channel habitat. This is unacceptable and will do major damage to Delta agriculture.[49]

Altogether, policymakers and stakeholders addressing the Delta's future must make several difficult and interconnected decisions about the best direction to take. In the next section, we develop a stylized model of the choices and their consequences for several key stakeholder groups.

The Model

In this section, we develop a numerical model of the policy choices facing the state and the effects of each of these choices on the well-being of several key stakeholders. Our goal is to create a comprehensive framework for evaluating stakeholder payoffs from various policy choices. To do so, we identify a set of vectors from which the state (policymakers) must choose. Each of the four policy options described previously corresponds to a specific vector belonging to this set.

The model we develop has three basic components: policy choices, outcomes, and utilities. Figure 11.2 is a schematic of how these components relate. The first box denotes a set of policy choices, represented by a vector x. Following the PPIC Report, we focus on the state's choice of how much water to export. As shown in the diagram, policy choices induce a set of outcomes that are of interest to particular stakeholders, including financial, ecological, and employment impacts. In our model, the vector of outcomes resulting from the policy vector x is denoted by the vector $y = f(x)$. The final element of the model is a set of utility functions that define the well-being of several major stakeholder groups. These are given by the vector-valued function, $u(y)$. In this analysis, we focus on five broadly specified stakeholder groups: urban users of exported water, the agricultural regions of the San Joaquin Valley that rely on exported water, environmentalists, state taxpayers, and in-Delta interests.

The remainder of this section elaborates on the details of each element in Figure 11.2 and concludes with a discussion of several caveats regarding the model.

Policy Choices

As described, our model focuses on the state's decision about how much water to export and the manner in which it will be exported. We define two continuous variables that represent the state's policy choices:

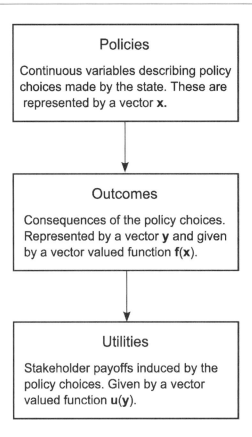

Figure 11.2 Model schematic

- *ThruExports*—the quantity of water exported through the Delta
- *PCExports*—the quantity of water exported around the Delta through a canal.

Each of the choices discussed in "Water Export Strategies" can be represented using these two variables. Table 11.1 summarizes how each alternative is modeled in our framework. The values are chosen to be representative of the alternatives discussed in the PPIC Report. The PPIC Report does not include a precise plan for how to allocate exports between the canal and through-Delta pumping for the dual-conveyance alternative; we divide the exports evenly between the two.[50]

Outcomes

As shown in Figure 11.2, policy choices map to outcomes that are of interest to particular stakeholder groups. In this section, we describe each of the outcomes in our model and explain how they are calculated as functions of policy choices. The functions presented in this section draw heavily on the analysis presented in the PPIC Report.

Many of the outcomes that affect stakeholders involved in the Delta debate are financial. In particular, different export regimes impose different types of costs that are borne by different stakeholder groups. Our model contains three groups that bear some financial burden for different alternatives: agricultural users and urban users that rely on Delta exports for some of their water and the state's taxpayers. The five specific costs included in our model are costs due to reduced water exports, water treatment costs, levee maintenance costs, costs associated with a major collapse of the levee system, and repair costs following a major collapse. In the following several paragraphs, we describe in detail each of these costs and their allocation across users.

The first major set of costs relates to the consequences of reduced exports. These costs are driven by reductions in total water exports rather than changes in export conveyance. We therefore compute two water use outcomes:

$$TargetExport = ThruExport + PCExport$$

and

$$ReductionShr = \frac{HistoricalExports - TargetExports}{HistoricalExports},$$

where *HistoricalExports* is a measure of the pre-Wanger level of exports from the Delta (approximately 6 million AF per year). *TargetExports* measures the planned amount of total exports. As discussed in "Event Uncertainty," this level may or may not be achieved in practice. *ReductionShr* measures the portion of exports that are no longer allowed; a value of 1 indicates a complete cessation of exports, and a value of 0 indicates restoration of pre-Wanger levels.[51]

We rely on the analysis in the PPIC Report to calculate the cost of export reductions. The report's authors used a model of the state's water demands

Table 11.1   Values specified for modeling PPIC policy choices

PPIC policy option	ThruExports (million AF)	PCExports (million AF)
Continue through-Delta exports	6	0
No exports	0	0
Peripheral canal	0	6
Dual-conveyance	3	3

Note: These values refer to targeted export volumes and are prior to ecosystem driven export reductions.

and infrastructure to estimate the scarcity costs imposed by reductions in exports from the Delta. They computed the total scarcity cost associated with a discrete set of export levels. To convert these discrete points into a continuous function relating total scarcity cost to export reductions, they used the following functional form:

$$C(CutShare) = CostNX * CutShare^{\phi},$$

where $CostNX$ is the cost of ending all exports, and ϕ is a parameter determining the curvature of the relationship between scarcity costs and export reductions.

There are several continuous cost variables in our model. We calibrate each of these variables to discrete cost estimates obtained from the PPIC Report. We adopt its method of extrapolating from discrete numbers to continuous functions, defining

$$Cost_i(NewValue) = BaseCost_i \frac{NewValue^{Exp_i}}{BaseValue_i},$$

where $NewValue$ is the value whose cost we want to compute, $BaseCost_i$ represents a baseline cost (drawn from the PPIC Report) for a value $BaseValue_i$, and Exp_i determines the curvature of the relationship. This functional form will be either convex or concave, depending on whether Exp_i is larger or smaller than 1.

The PPIC Report's conclusions are driven by aggregate costs of scarcity. We use information provided in the report's Appendix G to allocate these costs between the two stakeholder groups in our models that are responsible for them: agricultural users south of the Delta and urban users in both Southern California and the Bay Area.[52] We therefore construct two separate functions: $Cost_{agExport}(CutShare)$ and $Cost_{urExport}(CutShare)$ with the form given above. Note that in these functions, the value being changed is the cut share, not the value of exports. The base value is a 100 percent cut or the cessation of all exports. Thus, these functions have the form

$$Cost_i(CutShare) = CostNoExports_i CutShare^{Exp_i}.$$

In these constructed functions, the exponent $Exp_{agExport}$ is much lower than $Exp_{urExport}$. Both exponents indicate that the cost of cuts increases at an increasing rate. The rate of increase is faster for urban users, because urban users can absorb small cuts more easily. Therefore, the relative difference in cost between a small cut and a large cut is greater for urban users than for agricultural ones.

For each of the remaining cost types, given the lack of any information suggesting otherwise, we assume the share of total cost paid by each stakeholder is independent of the aggregate cost. We define a vector φ_i giving the share of that cost borne by each stakeholder. We use the notation φ_{ij} to denote the share of cost i borne by stakeholder j. The total cost paid by stakeholder j is thus

$$C_j = \sum_{ij} \varphi_{ij} Cost_j$$

.

The first such cost is treatment of water exported through the Delta. We scale the baseline level of treatment costs from the PPIC Report to a specific level of through-Delta exports using the function $Cost_{treatCost}(ThruExport)$. For our base case simulations, we set the value of $Exp_{TreatCost}$ to 1, thus assuming away any economies or diseconomies of scale in treatment costs. We allocate half of the computed cost to agricultural users and half to urban users. Although agricultural users use more water than urban users, their treatment standard is lower.

If water is exported through the Delta, additional resources will need to be spent on maintaining the Delta infrastructure, particularly the levees. The primary purpose of these expenditures is levee maintenance to keep the Delta water fresh enough for export. Therefore, this cost depends on the degree to which water is exported through the Delta. As with other costs, we scale using the function $Cost_{MaintainCost}(ThruExport)$. Since a high portion of the costs must be paid for even small levels of exports, we set the value of $Exp_{MaintainCost}$ to be very low (0.1 for our base case simulations).

Another cost component is the cost of constructing a canal if one is built. Current plans call for the vast majority of these expenses to be paid by the water users dependent on Delta exports. We allocate 45 percent of the costs to each of the water user groups (agricultural users south of the Delta and urban users receiving water exports) and allocate the remaining 10 percent to taxpayers. Because current plans call for building a canal capable of conveying far more than current export levels in order to enable large export volumes during wet periods, we assume that the cost of canal construction is independent of the target level of canal exports.

While most interest groups focus primarily on the direct financial impacts of any policy choice, they are concerned about other considerations as well. The PPIC Report predicts that large reductions in exports would lead to water transfers from San Joaquin Valley agriculture to urban water uses. Although the water right holders themselves would be compensated for these transfers, San Joaquin Valley agricultural interests are concerned about the impact on regional employment as well. Using the PPIC's modeling results, we compute an outcome variable related to agricultural employment:

$$AgEmploy\ (TotalExports) = BaseJobs - JobLossNX * CutShare$$

where *BaseJobs* is the current level of agricultural jobs in the San Joaquin Valley, and *JobLossNX* is the level of job loss predicted if all exports were stopped.

The long-term success or failure of any policy proposal is intimately connected to its environmental performance. While there are many elements of ecosystem performance, we follow the PPIC Report in focusing on the survival probabilities of two bellwether fish species: fall-run Sacramento River salmon and Delta smelt, and utilize the Report's definitions of what survival means. Formally, there are two outcomes related to ecosystem performance: ρ_{salmon}, the probability that salmon populations will recover enough to support a commercial fishery, and ρ_{smelt}, the probability that Delta smelt populations will recover allowing the species to avoid extinction. As discussed previously, fish are likely to be affected by exports either through or around the Delta and by the aggregate quantity of water flowing into the Delta. We thus introduce a new outcome variable, *DeltaInflow* measuring the quantity of water flowing into the Delta from the Sacramento River. Its value is given by:

$$DeltaInflow = SacFlow - PCExports$$

where *SacFlow* is the flow of water in the Sacramento River after upstream diversions.

We model both probabilities as functions of the two export variables and the inflow level in the following fashion:

$$\rho_k(ThruExport, PCExport) = \alpha_k + \beta_k DeltaInflow^2 + \gamma_k ThruExport^2 + \delta_k PCExport^2$$

for k = smelt, salmon. We specify quadratic functions in order to reflect the reality that these relationships are almost certainly nonlinear, but no data are available regarding the precise nature of the nonlinearity. Specifying quadratic functions allows the importance of exports through the Delta and exports through the peripheral canal for fish survival to be much more sensitive to their relative magnitudes, as well as their absolute magnitudes, than would be the case for affine functions. The values of the parameters in these functions were calibrated to match the survival probability estimates presented in the PPIC Report. Because we had a limited number of points for calibration, we were unable to include both linear and quadratic terms.

Event Uncertainty

One of the challenges facing stakeholders seeking to identify a solution is that future events are uncertain regardless of the policy chosen. Our model considers two uncertain events: the recovery of fish populations and a major levee collapse.

Figure 11.3 shows a schematic of these uncertain events and how they contribute to our utility calculations. Although we do not discuss precise utility functions until the next subsection, the figure uses the notation $V(\bullet)$ to refer to the utility generated for a particular interest group by an alternative.

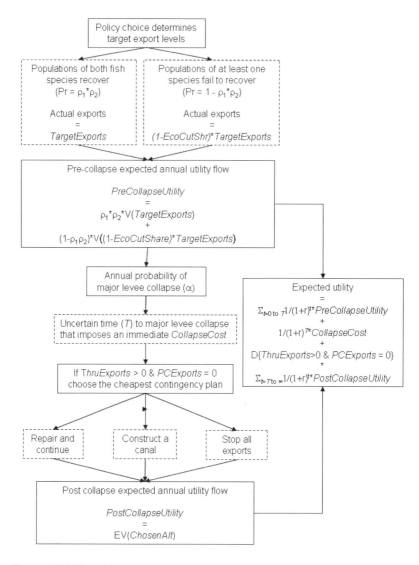

Figure 11.3 Event tree

The selection of a policy vector described corresponds to setting a target value for the level of exports as shown at the top of the figure. As discussed previously, for any export regime, there is some probability that fish populations will recover. If this occurs, the target level of exports can be achieved. However, there is also a probability that at least one species will not recover, triggering ESA-mandated cutbacks.[53]

Following the PPIC, we hypothesize that if fish populations do not recover, exports will be reduced by a constant percentage we call *EcoCutShr*. We therefore have three updated levels of exports:

$$TExC = (1 - EcoCutShr) \times ThruExport,$$
$$PCExC = (1 - EcoCutShr) \times PCExport,$$

and

$$TotalExC = TExC + PCExC.$$

Note that *TotalExC* can also be written as $(1 - EcoCutShr) \times TargetExports$, as we do in Figure 11.3.

We assume that reductions in exports occur if either species fails to show noticeable population improvements. For notational compactness, we create an outcome variable called *Cutbacks*, representing the probability these exports occur. Its value is given by:

$$\text{Cutbacks} = 1 - \rho_{salmon} \times \rho_{smelt}.$$

Following a reduction in exports, fish survival probabilities must be updated to reflect the reduced deliveries. We therefore introduce two new survival outcomes ($\hat{\rho}_{salmon}$ and $\hat{\rho}_{smelt}$) where

$$\hat{\rho}_k = (1 - Cutbacks)^* \; \rho_k \; (ThruExport, PCExport) + Cutbacks^* \; \rho_k \; (TExC, PCExC).$$

The reduction in exports also triggers an updated value for water scarcity costs given by:

$$C = (1 - Cutbacks)^* \; C(TotalExport) + Cutbacks^* \; C(TotalExC)$$

Because of this variability in outcomes, the flow of utility generated by a target export policy is computed using expected utility as shown in the third box of the diagram.

The second uncertain event concerns whether and when a major collapse of the levee system will occur. We follow the PPIC Report in assuming that the construction of a canal insulates the state from this risk. Such a levee failure would impose several major costs on the system. First and foremost, there would be a large immediate cost due to the substantial disruption of the water supply system. We assume that this loss is borne if a canal is not built; the presence of a canal of any size insulates the state against this cost. Moreover, we hypothesize that individual water users would not bear these costs; instead, following a disaster of that magnitude, the state would step in and cover these expenses as occurred when the levees protecting the Jones Tract collapsed.[54]

In the aftermath of a massive failure, the state would face another decision about what recovery strategy to choose. In the dual-conveyance case, we assume that all exports are shifted to the canal postcollapse. In the through-Delta case, we follow the PPIC Report and consider three possible options: build a canal, repair the Delta levees and continue through-Delta pumping, or stop exports. We adopt the PPIC's approach in computing the cost of all three alternatives and choosing the one that has the smallest total cost.[55] We predict that the state would choose to build a peripheral canal in such a scenario, as does the PPIC Report.

Because collapse will occur at some unknown time in the future, we compute precollapse and postcollapse flows of utility. The expected utility is then the discounted flow of precollapse and postcollapse utility plus the discounted immediate *CollapseCost*, with the expectation taken over the time to failure. In the next subsection, we describe the individual stakeholder utility functions.

Stakeholders and Utility Functions

In introducing the outcome variables in the previous subsection, we briefly discussed the interest of various stakeholders. In this section, we develop formal utility functions for each of the five stakeholder groups included in our model.

Our first stakeholder group represents the state's taxpayers. We assume that taxpayers are concerned with reducing the state's total expenditure liability and are risk neutral. This gives us a taxpayer utility function of

$$U_{Tx} = BaseTxBenefit - C_{Tx}$$

where *BaseTxBenefit* is a constant representing the state's base level of benefit from tax expenditures used to support the water sector. We specify *BaseTxBenefit* to equal California's current state budget. We assume that taxpayers are risk-neutral with respect to changes in this expenditure. As a result, the model's predictions are independent of the precise value of this constant.

Our second stakeholder group includes all urban users who depend on the Delta for a portion of their water supply. This group aggregates interests in Southern California with those in the Bay Area.[56] This stakeholder group is concerned with minimizing the cost of meeting its water supply needs. We use the following utility function:

$$U_{Ur} = U_{Ur} (BaseUrBenefit) - C_{Ur}$$

where *BaseUrBenefit* represents an estimate of the benefit to urban users of receiving their current water supply.

Our remaining stakeholders each have constant elasticity of substitution (CES) utility functions[57] with the general form:

$$U_j(x, y) = \left(xWgt_j x^{\omega_j} + \left(1 - xWgt_j\right) y^{\omega_j} \right)^{\gamma_j/\omega_j},$$

where x and y represent outcomes of interest to the stakeholder, $xWgt_j$ describes the stakeholder's willingness to trade one objective for the other, ω_j measures the substitutability between objectives, and γ_j is an exponent between zero and one measuring the stakeholder's level of risk aversion.

Our third stakeholder group represents interests within the Delta, including local residents, farmers, and recreational users. In the context of the policy decisions we model, these users are primarily concerned with the quality of water in the Delta and the amount of levee maintenance that occurs. Although we do not model water quality directly, it is highly correlated with the amount of water flowing into the Delta. Since Delta interests primarily use water upstream within the Delta from where the export pumps are located, the amount of water exported through the Delta has little impact on the quality of their water. Using a general utility function form, Delta interests thus have utility of

$$U_{Dt} = U_{Dt} \left(MaintenanceExpend, DeltaInflow \right).$$

As discussed previously, agricultural groups are concerned about their farming profits and the level of agricultural employment.[58] Using our general form again, the agricultural group's utility is given by

$$U_{Ag} = [(1 - AgEmployWgt)(BaseAgBenfit - C_{Ag})^{\omega_{Ag}} + AgEmployWgt * AgEmply^{\omega_{Ag}}]^{\gamma_{Ag}/\omega_{Ag}}$$

where $BaseAgBenefit$ is an estimate of the farming profit generated with current water export levels.

We adopt a similar structure for the environmental group's utility function. Here the primary concern is fish survival probabilities. As we predict survival probabilities for two different species, our utility function incorporates both species:

$$U_{Ev} = U_{Ev}(\hat{\rho}_{salmon}, \hat{\rho}_{smelt}).$$

Because four of our five groups are risk averse, we calculate expected utility outcomes in our model, using the likelihood of each event as shown in Figure 11.3.

Modeling Caveats

A major challenge to the development of a model such as ours is that there is substantial ambiguity about the appropriate specification of the functions mapping policies to outcomes and outcomes to utilities. We consider two types of ambiguity in our analysis: scientific uncertainty and modeling ambiguity. The mapping from policies to outcomes is characterized by what we call scientific uncertainty. That is, in many cases, science cannot offer precise predictions about how policy choices translate into specific outcomes because scientific experts disagree or are uncertain of the likely impacts. Disagreement about how fish populations will respond to various changes in water export regimes is a particularly notable example. In our analysis, we follow the PPIC Report's approach to scientific uncertainty. That is, for each of the parameters in the model that are subject to scientific uncertainty, we consider a high and a low value and report a range of possible outcomes.

In addition to scientific uncertainty, we must address several kinds of modeling ambiguity. In particular, the utility functions specified in "Stakeholder and Utility Functions" depend on parameters governing stakeholders' degree of risk aversion and their willingness to trade reductions in one objective for improvements in another. We have assigned specific values to these parameters, but our choices are somewhat arbitrary. Moreover, the exact parameters governing the curvature of specific cost functions are unknown. To address these issues, we perform sensitivity testing to determine the robustness of our policy rankings to the specific values of these parameters. Similarly, the specification of functional forms is subject to modeling ambiguity. We have chosen specific functional forms. Our choices are based primarily on their technical properties, such as convexity. We could address this ambiguity by using sensitivity analysis to evaluate the robustness of our policy rankings with respect to the choice of functional forms, as we do for parameters. However, we do not perform this exercise here.

The model presented here also simplifies reality in several important ways. First, it limits attention to a small number of broadly defined stakeholder groups. Second, the model focuses exclusively on water export strategies. As discussed in "Other Decisions," decisions about water infrastructure, upstream diversion changes, and ecosystem restoration will have large impacts on the outcomes of interest to stakeholders. Including these choices requires information not available at the present time.

Results

Using the model presented, we compute expected utility values for each interest group for the four policy options identified in that section: continued through-Delta pumping, construction of a peripheral canal, construction of a dual-conveyance system, and ceasing all exports. Specifically, for each realization of scientific uncertainty (see Table 11.2), we compute each group's expected utility, where expectations are taken over the uncertain events depicted in our event tree (Figure 11.3). Having made these computations, we use an affine transformation to normalize each group's utility function. Under the transformed utility functions, the highest possible expected utility value a group obtains is 1, and the lowest possible utility value is 0. An implication of our normalization procedure is that our transformed utilities convey no information at all about whether the utility difference for a given

Table 11.2   Scientific uncertainty ranges

Parameter name	Low value	High value
CollapseCost ($ billion)	7.8	15.7
RepairCost ($ billion)	0.2	2.5
ConstructionCost ($ billion)	4.75	9.75
TreatCost ($ billion/year)	0.3	1
ϕ_{ag}^{*}	1.58	3.95
ϕ_{ur}^{*}	3.17	6.52
ReductionShr	10 percent	40 percent
Collapse Probability	34 percent	95 percent
CostNX$_{ag}$ ($ billion/year)*	0.49	0.96
CostNX$_{ur}$ ($ billion/year)*	1.10	1.54
MaintainCost ($ billion/year)	1	2
α_{smelt}^{*}	45.19	97.53
α_{salmon}^{*}	77.53	158.63
β_{smelt}^{*}	−0.04	−0.10
β_{salmon}^{*}	−0.10	−0.21
γ_{smelt}^{*}	−1.93	−2.31
γ_{salmon}^{*}	−2.31	−3.86
δ_{smelt}^{*}	−0.78	−1.10
δ_{salmon}^{*}	−1.10	−1.98

Source: 2008 PPIC Report.
*Calibrated.

group between the best possible and worst possible outcome is large or small. On the other hand, our transformed utilities reflect the same risk preferences as the original ones.

Our results are depicted in Figure 11.4. For each interest group, each of the four bars represents the range of possible expected utilities that the group obtains from one of the policies we consider, as scientific uncertainty is varied over the ranges specified in Table 11.2. The top (bottom) of each bar represents the normalized utility associated with the scientific uncertainty realization that is most (least) favorable for that particular group. Note that the degree of scientific uncertainty will be reflected in the length of each bar, while (subject to normalization) the degree of uncertainty over the events listed in Figure 11.3 will be reflected in the placement of the bars in the interval [0, 1]. More concretely, consider the left-most bar in Figure 11.4,

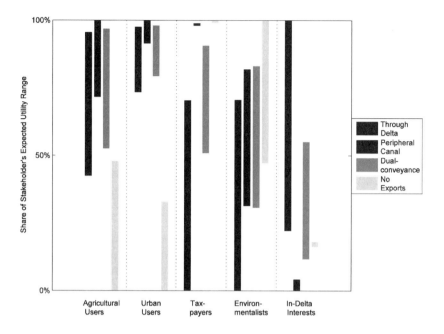

Figure 11.4 Expected utility of policy alternatives by stakeholder

representing agricultural users' utility from the through-Delta policy. A mean-preserving spread of each of the intervals representing scientific uncertainty in Table 11.2 would have the effect of increasing the length of this bar. On the other hand, a mean preserving spread of the uncertainty represented in Figure 11.3 would have the effect of shifting down the entire bar; the more risk averse are the agricultural users, the greater the downward shift.

We now discuss Figure 11.4 in detail. The left-most four bars give the range of utility values for the agricultural stakeholders for each of the four policy alternatives. We see that the agricultural stakeholders prefer the peripheral canal alternative as it generates relatively high expected utility values in all cases. The dual-conveyance alternative is less desirable than the peripheral canal because, depending on parameter values, a wider range of expected utility values are possible, and both the best and worst expected utilities are lower than the corresponding values for the peripheral canal. At its best, the through-Delta alternative performs nearly as well as the canal alternatives for agricultural stakeholders, but at its worst, the lowest expected utility is significantly below the lowest expected utility for the canal alternatives. Moreover, our analysis assumes that the state's taxpayers will bear the costs associated with a disastrous collapse of multiple levees. If the agricultural users were to be liable for some of these expenses, the through-Delta alternative would perform worse. The no-export alternative generates the smallest range of expected utility values but provides low expected utility throughout the range for two reasons: large scarcity costs are imposed by the need to replace water export supplies or fallow land, and reduction in water supplies leads to a decline in agricultural employment.

The next group of four bars reports the urban stakeholder's expected utility ranges. The pattern is quite similar to that of the agricultural group. Stopping exports is clearly the least preferred alternative for this group as well, although urban users are less negatively affected than agricultural users. Urban users pay a premium to replace water supplies but are not affected by a reduction in employment.

The middle group of bars represents the expected utilities of the taxpayer group. It is important to note that in our model the taxpayer group is only concerned with minimizing state expenditures. This group strongly dislikes continuing through-Delta exports because taxpayers bear the financial burden of mitigating the immediate impacts of water supply disruption in the event of major levee collapse. The final bar in this group is only a horizontal line, not a shaded region. This occurs because the no export alternative involves no financial outlay by the taxpayers under any resolution of scientific uncertainty. The costs of reducing exports are borne entirely by the urban and agricultural water users who must replace the lost supplies or adjust their use. The canal alternatives are slightly worse for the taxpayer, because we assume that the state will pay some portion of the costs of constructing a canal.

As we would expect *a priori*, the environmental group strongly prefers ceasing all exports and dislikes continuing through-Delta exports the most. Because environmentalists are modeled as being exclusively concerned with fish survival, this ordering is driven by the varying fish survival probabilities. Our results indicate that the environmental group is essentially indifferent between the two canal alternatives. Although the dual-conveyance has a broader range of expected utility outcomes than the peripheral canal does, its best outcome has a higher value, and its worst outcome has a lower value than the corresponding values for the peripheral canal alternative. This result is dictated by our survival function calibration, which followed the PPIC Report and required the baseline environmental performance of the peripheral canal and dual-conveyance alternatives to be identical.

Our final stakeholder group represents in-Delta interests. This group has a strong preference for continuing at least some through-Delta pumping because this would guarantee that levee maintenance would continue and significant quantities of fresh Sacramento River water would flow into the Delta. The through-Delta alternative is preferred to a dual-conveyance alternative because more maintenance occurs when all exports are routed through the Delta. Stopping exports altogether is preferred to constructing

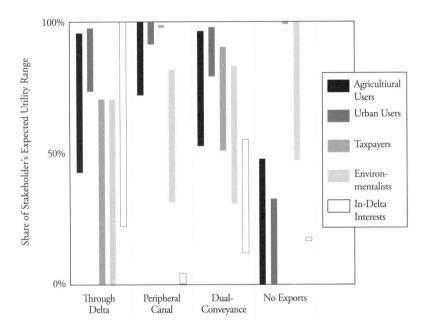

Figure 11.5 Stakeholder expected utility by policy alternative

a peripheral canal. Neither the peripheral canal nor stopping exports results in continued levee maintenance, but stopping exports all together maintains freshwater flows into the Delta.

Figure 11.5 presents the same information as Figure 11.4, reorganized by grouping policy alternatives together and using different-colored shading to indicate each stakeholder group. This grouping facilitates the identification of policy alternatives likely to be acceptable to a broad number of groups. Looking at this figure, we see that stopping all exports and continuing through-Delta exports perform poorly for at least two stakeholders (agricultural, urban, and in-Delta interest for the former, and taxpayers, environmentalists, and perhaps the two export user groups for the latter). The single-conveyance peripheral canal plan performs well for all groups except in-Delta interests. The dual-conveyance alternative emerges as a possible compromise. It performs less well for the agricultural and urban users and the taxpayers, but is still an improvement on either stopping exports or continuing through-Delta pumping. Moreover, it represents a substantial improvement for in-Delta interests.

To assess the robustness of our conclusions to changes in the parameters we had to specify somewhat arbitrarily in the absence of information regarding the appropriate values from the PPIC Report or elsewhere, we varied the values of several key parameters and recomputed utility levels. These experiments indicate that our conclusions are robust to many of these changes. One key parameter is the degree to which levee maintenance expenditures vary with the amount of through-Delta exports. Our baseline results were calculated assuming that maintenance costs are proportional to the level of exports. If, however, this relationship is concave so that most of the maintenance costs are paid even with smaller levels of through-Delta exports, the dual-conveyance alternative performs worse for taxpayers and the water export users. Figures 11.6–11.8 demonstrate how these groups' expected utility varies with changes in Exp_{Maint}, the parameter governing this relationship.

Counterintuitively, increasing stakeholder groups' risk aversion generally increases the expected utility they receive and is especially likely to raise the utility of the worst possible parameter value outcome. This occurs because the sources of risk included in the utility calculations are fish survival and levee failure probabilities. The values in Table 11.2 indicate that the worst values for these probabilities are actually quite certain—a 95 percent probability of levee failure and a 5 percent survival rate for smelt. Increasing stakeholder groups' level of risk aversion thus makes them willing to choose a lower level of average utility in exchange for less variation in utility outcomes. Consequently, the expected utilities from the parameter realizations

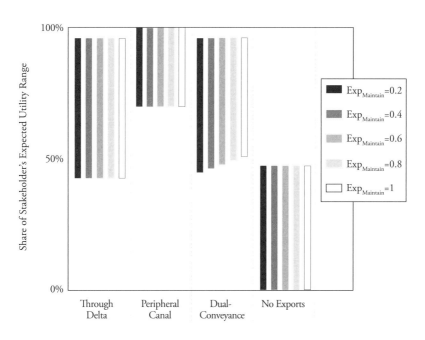

Figure 11.6 Impact of Exp_{Maint} on agricultural stakeholder

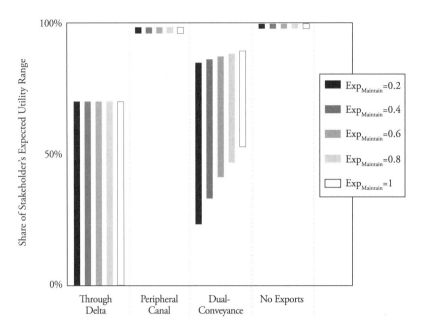

Figure 11.7 Impact of Exp_{Maint} on taxpayer

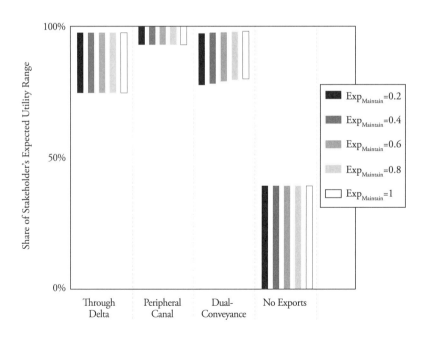

Figure 11.8 Impact of Exp_{Maint} on urban stakeholder

that yield low but predictable utility are closer to those that yield higher, but less predictable utility.

Conclusions

The results presented in Figures 11.4 and 11.5 suggest that among the export strategies available to the state, the dual-conveyance option may be the most politically feasible. At first glance, this may seem to conflict with the PPIC Report's claim that "there seems little reason to prefer a dual facility over a peripheral canal." In reality, however, the results are not contradictory; they simply reflect different modeling approaches.

The PPIC Report explicitly sought to avoid politics and focused on two criteria: maximizing ecosystem performance and minimizing statewide costs. In doing so, the report implicitly weighted the financial gains of each group equally. In contrast, we do not make any comparisons across stakeholders; we simply identify the range of impacts each alternative has for each stakeholder group. The dual-conveyance alternative emerges as a possible compromise because it avoids large losses for any individual group.

Thus far, the political process has tracked our predictions quite well. The *Strategic Plan* selected the dual-conveyance option as its preferred alternative noting that dual-conveyance "recognizes the need to maintain flows through the Delta for water supply and ecosystem health." Our results are consistent with the interpretation that the Blue Ribbon Task Force was sensitive to the political nuances and may have chosen dual-conveyance in part to ensure in-Delta interests that the Delta itself would not be totally abandoned.

Although our findings are consistent with the evolution of the political process to date, the model in its current form excludes some important policy considerations. In future work, we plan to extend the model to incorporate additional policy options and stakeholders, as well as refining the definitions of how the model's components are related. One example of such an extension would be to incorporate the possibility of reduced upstream diversions of Sacramento River water via water trading between upstream users and Delta exporters. In order to do so, an upstream user group would need to be included as a stakeholder, and the relationships between Delta inflows, outflows, and fish populations would need to be refined.

An advantage of the model methodology employed in this chapter is that the incorporation of such extensions is relatively straightforward. The basic structure of the model presented in Figure 11.2 is very flexible. Once the necessary numerical information is obtained, new elements can be added to x, $f(x)$, and $u(y)$ relatively easily. Our approach thus facilitates exploring which extensions or variations have significant impacts on the results.

Notes

1. By contrast, for example, when a government invokes eminent domain to acquire an individual's house, market prices for comparable houses provide a starting point to determine the "appropriate" degree of compensation.

2. Blue Ribbon Task Force, *Delta Vision*; Blue Ribbon Task Force, *Delta Vision Strategic Plan* (October 2008), p. v. http://deltavision.ca.gov/StrategicPlanning Process/StaffDraft/Delta_Vision_Strategic_Plan_standard_resolution. pdf.

3. Blue Ribbon Task Force, *Delta Vision: Our Vision for the California Delta* (2008), http://deltavision.ca.gov/BlueRibbonTaskForce/FinalVision/ Delta_Vision_Final.pdf.

4. Blue Ribbon Task Force, *Delta Vision*; Blue Ribbon Task Force, *Delta Vision Strategic Plan* (October 2008), http://deltavision.ca.gov/StrategicPlanning Process/StaffDraft/Delta_Vision_Strategic_Plan_standard_resolution.pdf; Delta Vision Committee, *Delta Vision Committee Implementation Report* (December 31, 2008), http://www.deltavision.ca.gov/DV_Committee/ Jan2009/08-1231_Delta_Vision_Committee_Implementation_Report. pdf.

5. J. Lund et al., *Comparing Futures for the Sacramento–San Joaquin Delta* (San Francisco, CA: Public Policy Institute of California, 2008), http://www. ppic.org/content/pubs/report/R_708EHR.pdf; J. Lund et al., *Envisioning Futures for the Sacramento–San Joaquin Delta* (San Francisco, CA: Public Policy Institute of California, 2007).

6. H. Cooley, J. Christian-Smith, and P. H. Gleick, *More with Less: Agricultural Water Conservation and Efficiency in California, A Special Focus on the Delta* (Oakland, CA: Pacific Institute, 2008), http://www.pacinst. org/reports/more_with_less_delta/more_with_less.pdf; C. Koehler et al., *Finding the Balance: A Vision for Water Supply and Environmental Reliability in California* (San Francisco, CA: Environmental Defense Fund, 2008), http://www.edf.org/documents/8093_CA_Finding_Balance_2008. pdf.

7. The agencies that signed the original Memorandum of Understanding creating the Bay Delta Conservation Plan process include California Bay Delta Authority, California Department of Water Resources, California Department of Fish and Game, U.S. Bureau of Reclamation, U.S. Fish and Wildlife Service, NOAA Fisheries, Kern Country Water Agency, Metropolitan Water District of Southern California, Zone 7 Water Agency, Santa Clara Valley Water District, San Luis and Delta-Mendota Water Authority, and Westlands Water District.

8. Bay Delta Conservation Plan (BDCP), *The Bay Delta Conservation Plan: Points of Agreement for Continuing into the Planning Process* (November 16, 2007), http://baydeltaconservationplan.com/Libraries/Background_Documents/BDCP-Points_of_Agreement_Final.sflb.ashx; BCDP, *Facts About Conveyance* (August 25, 2008), http://www.water.ca.gov/deltainit/docs/ conveyance_factsheet.pdf; BDCP, *An Overview of the Draft Conservation Strategy for the Bay Delta Conservation Plan* (January 12, 2009), http://baydeltaconservationplan.com/Libraries/Background_Documents/ Overview_of_Conservation_Strategy_1-12-2009.sflb.ashx.

9.   BDCP, *Facts About Conveyance.*

10. Strictly speaking, the Delta is an estuary, not a true river delta, but following popular usage, we refer to the Delta throughout this chapter.

11. Department of Water Resources (DWR), *California Water Plan Update 2005*, http://www.waterplan.water.ca.gov/previous/cwpu2005/index.cfm.

12. M. Brooks, N. Levine, and M. Weiser, "The Delta: An Interactive Map," *Sacramento Bee*, 2008.

13. PPIC Report, 25.

14. In 2006, a legal settlement reached under the threat of litigation and strong pressure from both the judge and elected officials created an obligation to restore San Joaquin River flows to allow the reintroduction of salmon to the river (see Friant Water Users Authority News Release, *Agreement Signals Start to Historic San Joaquin River Restoration* [2006], http://www.fwua.org/sjr/sjr.htm.

15. As discussed later, recent court rulings have reduced water exports to a significantly lower level.

16. BDCP, *Facts About Conveyance.*

17. Ibid.

18. P. Moyle and W. Bennett, "Appendix D: The Future of the Delta Ecosystem and Its Fish," in *Comparing Futures for the Sacramento–San Joaquin Delta* (San Francisco, CA: Public Policy Institute of California, 2008), http://www.ppic.org/content/pubs/other/708EHR_appendixD.pdf.

19. According to one analysis, the average short-term economic impact of these cuts is $500 million annually. Urban users in the South Coast region are expected to be hit especially hard in the short run. Over the long run as urban users are able to adjust to the new cuts, losses fall to approximately $140 million annually. However, if the state were to enter a long drought, losses could be as high as $3.2 billion annually in the short run and nearly $900 million in the long run (see D. Sunding, N. Ajami, S. Hatchet, D. Mitchell and D. Zilberman. *Economic Impacts of the Wanger Interim Order for Delta Smelt.* Berkeley, CA: Berkeley Economic Consulting, 2008, http://www.berkeleyeconomics.com/BEC.FinalReport.8Dec08.pdf).

20. S. E. Ingebritsen, M. E. Ikehara, D. L. Galloway, and D. R. Jones, *Delta Subsidence in California: The Sinking Heart of the State*, USGS Fact Sheet 005-00 (2000).

21. PPIC Report, 38.

22. Ingebritsen, Ikehara, Galloway, and Jones, *Delta Subsidence in California.*

23. D. Bulwa et al., "Deluge in the Delta," *San Francisco Chronicle,* June 4, 2004, A-1.

24. PPIC Report. Economic analysis suggests that repairing the Jones Tract was a sound financial decision. The PPIC Report estimated the total value of assets on the tract at $550 million.

25. South Delta Water Agency public comment by Alex Hildebrand, August 19, 2008. http://deltavision.ca.gov/StrategicPlanningProcess/StaffDraft/Comments/Comment_from_South_Delta_Water_Agency_8-19-08.pdf

26. There is some concern about entrainment of salmon in the new intakes on the Sacramento River. A variety of state-of-the-art fish protection technologies are being considered. Building adequate fish protection into a new system from the beginning is likely to be more effective than trying to reengineer the fish protection system at the South Delta pumping plants, suggesting that the peripheral canal may aid the smelt while the possible negative effects of its intakes on salmon can be mitigated to some extent.

27. BDCP, *Draft Water Operations Conservation Measures* October 31, 2008, 43–44.

28. "Restore the Delta Opposes the Peripheral Canal Because . . . " Restore the Delta, http://restorethedelta.org/?page_id=18.

29. South Delta Water Agency (SDWA), *SDWA Further Comments to the Delta Vision Strategic Plan, Fifth Draft* (October 15, 2008), http://deltavision. ca.gov/StrategicPlanningProcessStaffDraft/Comments/Comment_from_ SDWA_10-15-08.pdf.

30. PPIC Report, xi–xii.

31. Blue Ribbon Task Force, *Strategic Plan*, 101.

32. Bay Institute and Natural Resources Defense Council (NRDC), *Re: 6/18/08 Draft Strategic Plan* (July 2, 2008), http://deltavision.ca.gov/ StrategicPlanningProcess/StaffDraft/Comments/Comment_from_The%20 Bay_Institute_7-2-08.pdf.

33. SDWA, *Further Comments on Fifth Draft*.

34. "Restore the Delta Opposes."

35. Tgianco, Comment on "The Delta Debate: Are You Ready for a Delta Canal?" *Sacramento Bee* forum, 2008.

36. M. Weiser, "Delta Canal Plan Likely to End in Court, Experts Agree," *Sacramento Bee,* January 6, 2009, 4A.

37. SDWA, *Further Comments on Fifth Draft* (emphasis in original).

38. Earthjustice, "Judge Tosses Biological Opinion for Salmon and Steelhead in California," April 16, 2008, http://www.earthjustice.org/news/press/2008/ judge-tosses-biological-opinion-for-salmon-and-steelhead-in-california. html.

39. Delta Vision Committee, *Implementation Report,* 1.

40. Ibid., 1–2.

41. Koehler et al., *Finding the Balance.*

42. SDWA, *Further Comments on Fifth Draft.*

43. *Business Water Caucus Comments on Fourth Draft Strategic Plan* was signed by individuals affiliated with the following groups: California Chamber of Commerce, Kern County Water Agency, Metropolitan Water District of Southern California, San Luis & Delta-Mendota Water Authority, Santa Clara Valley Water District, Southern California Water Committee, Tulare Lake Basin Water Storage District, Water Resources Subcommittee of the California Building Industry Association, and Westlands Water District (see T.W. Birmingham, J. Beck, D. Nelson, J. Kightlinger, G. Zlotnick, T. Hurlbutt, S. LaMar, J. A. Dym and V. Nera. *Business Water Caucus Comments on Fourth Draft Strategic Plan.* September 2, 2008. http:// deltavision.ca.gov/StrategicPlanningProcess/StaffDraft/Comments/ Comment_from_Bus_Water_Caucus_9-2-08.pdf).

44. Birmingham et al., *Business Water Caucus Comments.*

45. M. Weiser, "Nature Conservancy backs Delta canal, with conditions" *Sacramento Bee,* January 7, 2009, A3.

46. Bay Institute and NRDC, *Re: 6/18/08 Draft.*

47. The PPIC Report specifically mentions "the Hayward intertie, the Hetch-Hetchy Aqueduct, Mokelumne Aqueduct, Colorado River Aqueduct, and the proposed New Don Pedro intertie" (see Tanaka, S. K., C. R. Connell, K. Madani, J. R. Lund, E. Hanak, and J. Medellín-Azuara. "Appendix F: The Economic Costs and Adaptations for Alternative Delta Regulations." In *Comparing Futures for the Sacramento–San Joaquin Delta.* San Francisco: Public Policy Institute of California, 2008. http://www.ppic.org/content/pubs/other/708EHR_appendixF.pdf).

48. BDCP, *Third Draft: Habitat Restoration Conservation Measures* October 31, 2008.

49. Sacramento County Farm Bureau, *RE: Preliminary Staff Draft of the Delta Vision Strategic Plan* (July 1, 2008) http://www.sacfarmbureau.org/industry%20issues/BlueRibboncomments.pdf.

50. While a 50–50 decision is an arbitrary choice, altering the allocation of exports between the canal and the through-Delta options is unlikely to affect the qualitative nature of our results. Intuitively, this is the case because the dual-conveyance option has some of the effects of each conveyance method on players' utilities.

51. It is conceivable that increases in the efficiency of conveyance due to the adoption of a peripheral canal may increase total "effective" water exports for a given amount of water diversions. We abstract from this issue here and assume that pre-Wanger exports are the maximum feasible exports.

52. The information provided in the PPIC report's Appendix G provides direct allocation of some costs to these stakeholder groups. For other costs, we estimated the allocation between the two groups. Another consideration is that the costs provided in the modeling results do not reflect payments for water transfers between groups. We generate rough estimates of the size of transfer payments by comparing the willingness to pay of water purchasers and the willingness to sell of water buyers.

53. Strictly speaking, ESA-mandated cutbacks will occur in the future. Following the PPIC Report, we abstract away from the time required to construct a canal and implicitly assume that its impact on fish happens instantaneously.

54. It is quite possible that in the event of a major failure, California and/or the Delta would be declared a disaster area and the federal government would cover some of the costs of collapse. This change would compress the observed utility range for the taxpayers and increase the area of overlap between continuing through-Delta pumping and the dual-conveyance alternative.

55. These computations incorporate the possibility of ESA-mandated export reductions for either the repair-and-continue scenario or the peripheral canal construction scenario.

56. The PPIC Report estimates no impact on urban users located within the Central Valley proper. In the aggregated results, there appear to be small impacts on both San Joaquin Valley and Tulare Basin urban interests. The

impact on Tulare Basin urban interests is not present in the detailed results and was thus not used in our analysis. The detailed results reveal that the impacts identified as San Joaquin Valley urban impacts refer to increased costs borne by two Bay Area entities: the San Francisco Public Utilities Commission and the Santa Clara Valley Water District.

57. A utility function displaying CES requires that a proportional change in the price of two goods results in a proportional change in the quantities of the two goods consumed. The general expression for a CES utility function for two goods x_1 and x_2 is

$$U(x_1, x_2) = \left(p_1 x_1^{\omega} + p_2 x_2^{\omega} \right)^{\gamma/\omega},$$

where p_1 and p_2 are the prices of the two goods, Ω is the constant parameter measuring the substitutability of the two goods for the consumer, and Γ is a parameter between 0 and 1 that represents the consumer's degree of risk aversion.

58. We focus on agricultural employment because it receives substantial attention in the press. The value is computed using a multiplier related to agricultural output. Thus, our results would be qualitatively similar if we instead used agricultural output itself, or a measure of all agriculturally related economic activity or employment.

12

Lessons from Los Angeles: Dealing with Diminishing Predictability in Los Angeles Water Sources

Brian C. Steed

Introduction: The Importance of Predictable Access to Water

Availability of water has been a longstanding concern for the Los Angeles area. Historian H. H. Bancroft notes that, "by the year 1801, the population of Los Angeles had increased to 300. . . . An adequate water supply during the long, dry summers appears to have been one of the major problems."[1] Since the mid-1800s, the Los Angeles, California, area has transformed from a burgeoning agricultural center to one of the largest and most important metropolitan areas in the United States. This economic and population growth occurred despite the fact that the Los Angeles area sits in a semiarid climate zone and receives an average of approximately fifteen inches of rain per year—an amount of precipitation that generates very few local and consistent surface sources of fresh water. This remarkable growth cannot be fully explained without understanding how key individuals in the Los Angeles area took vital steps to increase certainty in water supply.

It is well understood that water is required for economic development and growth.[2] Uncertainty in water availability leads to substantial societal costs including difficulty in planning and reduced investment.[3] In agricultural settings, uncertainty in water availability leads to underproduction. In urban settings, uncertainty leads to stunted economic growth. In this chapter, I focus on how the Los Angeles area has achieved sufficient water predictability to enable growth. I identify two mechanisms used in the Los Angeles area, as must be the case generally in all locations that experience economic and population growth, to garner water stability: the development of infrastructure and the creation and enforcement of water institutions.

Through examining historical and current events surrounding the development and maintenance of infrastructure and water institutions, I conclude that although the infrastructure for increasing water availability remains largely intact, the institutional mechanisms protecting water allocation are increasingly unable to provide predictability in water supply. This is particularly apparent for imported sources of water, which have become unreliable due to the variability in the institutions allocating water. I conclude that the events in Los Angeles provide lessons for future water policy in Los Angeles and throughout the arid western United States.

Before delving into the substance of the analysis, it may be useful to provide some discussion regarding the importance of water resource predictability and the tools used to achieve it. Many researchers have noted the link between water predictability and economic and social development. A recent United Nations report argues "protection against the vulnerabilities associated with uncertainty in water flows is one of the keys to human development."[4] Empirical studies in the developing world have supported these arguments. One recent study, for example, found that variability in water availability decreased economic growth by 38 percent per year and substantially increased poverty rates.[5]

Two important tools have been identified to bolster predictability in water availability. The first is technology. Through technological innovation, infrastructure can be created to augment supply. Examples are more efficient pumps to more effectively access groundwater supplies; the creation of aqueducts, canals, reservoirs, storage tanks, and water delivery systems; and the development of water purification and desalinization techniques.

The second tool identified to bolster predictability in water availability is the creation of institutions—"the prescriptions that humans use to organize all forms of repetitive and structured interactions."[6] Stated differently, institutions are society's "rules of the game."[7] Institutions establish the set of choices available to participants and accordingly establish incentives to act or refrain from acting.

The Los Angeles area increased predictability in water supply through the development of both physical infrastructure and institutions. In terms of infrastructure, the Los Angeles area water supply was augmented through enhancing the physical means to access local groundwater (which percolates from higher elevations into pools under Los Angeles) and the construction of aqueducts to access external sources of water from the Owens Valley, the Colorado River, and the Sacramento–San Joaquin Delta. In terms of institutions, important developments included the creation and enforcement of a water rights system that allowed individuals, businesses, and government agencies to rely on current and future ability to access local groundwater and imported water.

The Water Sources of Los Angeles County

The Los Angeles area receives 40–45 percent of its water from groundwater reserves, depending on the year.[8] The vast majority of the remaining water is imported through the first and second Los Angeles Aqueducts connecting Los Angeles to the Owens Valley, the Colorado River Aqueduct, and the California Aqueduct tapping into the Sacramento–San Joaquin Delta. Each of these sources is discussed in the following sections.

Groundwater Basins

Due to limited surface flows and irregular precipitation, groundwater basins[9] throughout the Los Angeles area have long been vital for meeting local water needs. The process of adjudication established well-understood property rights to groundwater. As a result, long-lasting markets developed for the exchange of groundwater rights. To illustrate the features and functions of clear groundwater rights, I develop examples from four groundwater basins, all occupying western Los Angeles County: the Raymond Basin, the Main San Gabriel Basin, the Central Coast Basin, and the West Coast Basin. Table 12.1 gives the storage capacity of each of these basins in acre-feet (AF),

Table 12.1   Groundwater basin storage capacity and overlying areas

Basin	Storage capacity	Overlying area
Central Coast Basin	13.8 million AF	Artesia, Bellflower, Cerritos, Compton, Downey, Huntington Park, Lakewood, Los Angeles, Long Beach, Montebello, Paramount, Pico Rivera, Norwalk, Santa Fe Springs, Signal Hill, South Gate, Vernon, and Whittier
Main San Gabriel Basin[11]	8.6 million AF	Arcadia, Azusa, Baldwin Park, Bradbury, Covina, Duarte, El Monte, Glendora, Industry, Irwindale, La Puente, Monrovia, Rosemead, San Gabriel, San Marino, South El Monte, South Pasadena, Temple City, Walnut, and West Covina
Raymond Basin	1.37 million AF	Sierra Madre, Arcadia, Pasadena, La Cañada Flintridge, and unincorporated areas of Los Angeles County
West Coast Basin	6.5 million AF	El Segundo, Manhattan Beach, Hermosa Beach, Redondo Beach, Torrance, Inglewood, Hawthorne, Gardena, Lomita, Carson, and Long Beach

as well as presenting the overlying municipalities.[10] Combined, the basins have a total storage capacity exceeding 25 million AF. It is important to note that these figures represent only storage capacity potential and not the actual amount of water which is in each basin. The amount of water withdrawn from each of the basins nearly always results in actual water levels below potential storage capacity. During wet periods, however, the amount of water in each basin significantly increases and may approach storage capacity.[12]

Basin Governance Through Adjudication

Establishing clear and predictable rights within each of the basins was an arduous and time-consuming process. In 1904, the U.S. Geological Survey found over hundred wells operating within the West Coast Basin and in 1908 found 141 wells operating in the Raymond Basin.[13] By 1913, water extraction in the Raymond Basin began to exceed natural replenishment. Overdraft conditions in the West Coast Basin began in 1920. Although extractive pressures were initially somewhat less within the Central Coast and Main San Gabriel Basins, each of these basins eventually entered overdraft conditions by the mid-1950s.[14]

Overdraft within the basins led to extensive problems. Along the coastal plain, overdraft changed groundwater pressure level and flows leading to seawater intrusion into portions of the West Coast and Central Coast Basins. This problem was initially discovered in 1912 in the West Coast Basin when wells in the town of Redondo Beach began drawing saline water. By 1929, the California Department of Water Resources reported that some 45 square miles of subsurface water in the West Coast territory wells were becoming saline.[15] Basins not bordering the sea experienced other problems. Overdraft in these basins caused extensive declines in groundwater levels. Between the 1923 and 1924 water years, groundwater levels in the Main San Gabriel Basin dropped by at least 30 feet. An additional 30-foot decline was observed between 1924 and 1925.[16] Declines in the groundwater table resulted in higher pumping costs, well failures, and surface land subsidence.

In considering options to ameliorate the negative consequences of over-pumping, pumpers sought to establish fixed rights and groundwater extraction limits.[17] In 1937, the city of Pasadena sued the city of Alhambra and other pumpers asserting that it was being harmed by the actions of Alhambra and the other pumpers. Pasadena claimed it had established a right to groundwater in the Raymond Basin predating the other pumpers. In deciding *City of Pasadena v. City of Alhambra*, 75 Cal. App. 2d 91 (1937), the court sought to determine the boundaries and physical limitations of the basin and identify all pumpers in the region. The court asked the California Division of Water Resources, a state regulatory agency, to provide a description of the boundaries and establish a safe yield. The court subsequently brought all known pumpers into the suit. In 1941, the Division of Water Resources reported to the court and all litigants that the Raymond Basin had a yearly overdraft of 8,500 AF above safe yield.

In light of these facts, and the overall uncertainty of what the court would do, the pumpers began serious negotiation with each other.[18] This negotiation led to a stipulated agreement between nearly all of the parties that would grant pumping rights proportional to the actual safe yield of the basin. Pumping rights were determined based on each pumper's historical pumping level, but with a reduction based on the new information regarding basin safe yield. Each of these rights would be transferable among the parties or could be sold to individuals not part of the original adjudication process.[19] Because all parties did not sign off on the stipulation, however, a brief trial was held. After the trial's completion, the judge incorporated all portions of the stipulated agreement on all parties of the suit. The Supreme Court of California eventually endorsed this judgment in 1949 (*City of Pasadena v. City of Alhambra*, 33 Cal. 2d 908, 206 P.2d 17 (1949)).

Through *City of Pasadena v. City of Alhambra*, the Raymond Basin became the first adjudicated basin in California. Each of the other basins was eventually adjudicated in similar manner. In the West Coast Basin, the adjudication process formally began in 1945; a stipulated agreement between the parties was reached in 1955 and was ratified by the court after a brief trial in 1961.[20] The West Coast Basin pumpers, however, did not agree to pump at safe yield. Rather, the physical problem of replenishment was resolved by injecting imported water through injection wells along the coast, essentially increasing underground water pressure to keep the sea at bay. Additionally, the West Coast Basin became part of a special replenishment district along with the Central Basin. Through its incorporating language, the Central and West Coast Basin Water Replenishment District took charge of replenishing the groundwater basins with water captured from natural precipitation and water imported from distant sources.[21]

The Central Basin initially sought to avoid adjudication by importing additional surface water, but this solution was inadequate to stop basin drawdown. To stop declining basin levels, the Central and West Coast Basin Water Replenishment District initiated suit against 750 pumpers in 1962. After reviewing the biophysical information of the basin, pumpers developed a stipulated settlement establishing fixed and tradable "allowed pumping rights." The court eventually agreed to this stipulation after a short trial in 1966. It is noteworthy that similar to the West Coast Basin adjudication, rights were not tied to any notion of safe yield. Rather, it was understood that a physical solution could be achieved by recharging the basins with captured runoff and water imported from external sources.

The Main San Gabriel Basin adjudication formally began in 1968 with a suit naming 190 known pumpers. Like the other cases discussed previously, the pumpers entered into negotiations to establish firm and tradable pumping rights. This effort was ratified after a trial in October 1972, with final judgment being entered in 1973. Like the other cases, the judgment enumerated secure and tradable pumping rights to participating parties. Unlike the other cases discussed, the judgment did not state a fixed number of acre-feet that could be accessed by pumpers per year. Instead, the judgment assigned rights based on a proportion of an operational safe yield. Due to the stochastic nature of precipitation, the groundwater level increases and decreases. Safe yield and the accompanying proportional water rights are also variable based on levels of precipitation, and so every year, the Main San Gabriel Watermaster establishes an operational safe yield based on current water conditions.

Water Markets for Groundwater

Each of the basin adjudication judgments discussed established defined and defensible rights for individual pumpers. These rights gave pumpers the ability to rely on current and future water withdrawals and facilitated temporary or permanent transfers of pumping rights. Accordingly, a robust market for exchange of pumping rights has developed since adjudication, including both the outright sale and the temporary leasing of pumping rights.

Each basin adjudication established a set list of individuals and entities holding pumping rights. In the years immediately following the adjudication, a variety of entities exhibited a great deal of interest in acquiring larger shares of water rights. The West Coast Basin Watermaster recorded seventeen water purchases for 1965–1966. Municipalities (including Dominguez and Torrence), private water companies (e.g., Southern California Water Company), and large private companies (including Mobil and Standard Oil) purchased the largest number of water rights. Those selling the rights primarily consisted of individuals and families with small water holdings.[22] Water purchases in the other basins also generally followed this pattern, where municipalities, water companies, and industrial companies purchased from entities with smaller (and less economically rewarding) endeavors. Once these transfers occurred, the municipalities, water companies, and industries generally retained these rights. These changes were recorded and monitored by watermaster agencies in each of the basins.

This process is evidenced in the consolidation of water rights holders. For Raymond Basin, the judgment in 1945 listed twenty-five holders of pumping rights. By 1990, the number had dropped to seventeen.[23] In 2007, the Raymond Basin Management Board listed sixteen rights holders.[24] The West Coast Basin adjudication found ninety-two holders of rights in 1962. This number had diminished to seventy-three by 1990, and there are sixty-five rights holders today.[25] The Central Basin judgment lists 508 rights holders in 1967, but by 1990, the number had dropped to 174, and rests at 133 today.[26]

Due to this consolidation, outright purchases of rights have become increasingly less common through the years. Between 2001 and 2010 in the

West Coast Basin, for instance, there have been only fourteen purchases of water rights. In the water years 2009–10, 2007–08, and 2001–02, no sales occurred at all.[27] The purchases that did happen ranged in size from as small as 10 AF to as large as nearly 6,200 AF. The majority of these sales involved several hundred AF. Due to its size, the comparative numbers are somewhat higher in Central Coast Basin. Still, over the past ten years, there have only been forty-nine outright sales of rights in the basin. The highest number of purchases occurred in 2008–09 with nineteen purchases, while during 2003–04, there were no recorded sales.[28] The sizes of these sales have been somewhat variable. Similar trends have occurred in the Raymond and Main San Gabriel Basins where outright sales have been somewhat sporadic.[29]

Additionally, the development of a healthy lease market in each of the four basins has reduced the demand for sales. Due to the higher upfront cost of the sale of a water right coupled with the year-to-year variability of water needs of pumpers, water leasing has become an extraordinarily attractive alternative. Although no water sales were recorded during the water year 2007–08 within the Main San Gabriel Basin, the basin watermaster recorded fifty-eight separate yearlong water leases ranging in size from 1.07 AF to 13,571 AF during the same timeframe. These water transfers totaled approximately 45,314 AF.[30] In the year prior (again a year with no recorded water sales), fifty-two separate yearlong water leases were recorded, ranging in size from 1.22 AF to 15,046 AF. The water transfers totaled approximately 48,839 AF.[31]

Similarly, although there were no water right sales in 2008 in the West Coast Basin, there were ten water leases totaling 8,133 AF. In the Central Basin, fifty-seven water leases totaling over 30,000 AF were recorded during the 2007–08 water year. In 2006–07, fifty-eight leases were recorded totaling 22,785 AF of leased water. Throughout the current decade, the number of yearly leases within the Central Basin has varied between forty-seven in 2004–05 and ninety-four in 2000–01. During that period of time, the amount of water leased has not dropped below 17,500 AF leased per year, or approximately 10 percent of total adjudicated rights.[32]

Water Importation

As population in the Los Angeles area increased, it became apparent that local ground and surface water sources would not meet the needs of the growing population at politically acceptable prices. Water managers, therefore, sought to import water from external sources. The city of Los Angeles has twice obtained additional water from the Owens Valley (located over 230 miles to the northeast of Los Angeles) and surrounding areas in the eastern Sierra through the construction of the Los Angeles Aqueduct in 1913 and the second Los Angeles Aqueduct in 1970. Municipalities and other water providers in Los Angeles County also acquired additional water from the Colorado River through the Colorado River Aqueduct in 1941, and the Sacramento–San Joaquin Delta through the California Aqueduct in 1971. Los Angeles obtained water from each of these sources through a variety of sociopolitical and technological mechanisms.

The Los Angeles Aqueduct and the Second Los Angeles Aqueduct

In the early 1900s, it became clear that the city of Los Angeles would soon need more water to sustain its rate of growth. By 1905, the city's population had increased to almost a quarter of a million. At rates of flow received on average from local sources—including water from the Los Angeles River and various wells—and assuming a consumption rate of 150 gallons per citizen per day, water experts assumed the city could support a population of only 300,000. It was clear that the city would soon reach its water capacity.

Seeing this perilous situation, water entrepreneurs began contemplating water importation. The most promising source of external water was the Owens River. Fed by snowmelt from the eastern slope of the Sierra Nevada Mountains, the Owens River ran throughout the year and terminated in Owens Lake. Owens Valley water was especially promising due to geography and ability to appropriate. In terms of geography, the Owens Valley had an altitude about 3,500 feet above sea level. If diverted, simple gravity would produce a water flow from the Owens Valley to Los Angeles without the need of pumping. In terms of appropriation, the Owens Valley was less developed than other water-rich areas, with water rights holders valuing their water rights based on lower-valued agricultural uses. Accordingly, the city of Los Angeles was able to purchase water shares in the Owens Valley for less cost than acquiring water from other sources.[33]

In September 1905, voters in the city of Los Angeles approved a bond measure for the purchase of Owens Valley land which possessed rights to water. In all, 22,670 acres of land were obtained, including 16 miles of land with river frontage with accompanying water rights.[34] In 1907, the voters approved a bond for the construction of the Los Angeles Aqueduct. Construction began soon thereafter and was completed in 1913. The water that began to flow from the Owens Valley quadrupled the amount available to the city of Los Angeles. By 1938, the Owens Valley supplied 70 percent of the city of Los Angeles's water.[35] After World War II, the Los Angeles Aqueduct was extended farther north into the vicinity of Mono Lake. The project tapped four of Mono Lake's tributaries and increased the flow and stability of the aqueduct.[36]

While the Los Angeles Department of Water and Power (DWP) had obtained rights to water in the Mono Basin in the 1940s, officials were concerned that the city could not permanently draw on these rights to their fullest capacity without additional conveyance facilities. City officials were concerned that if the water resources were not fully developed, the California State Water Resources Control Board's Division of Water Rights would cancel Los Angeles' rights due to nonuse and grant these rights to additional parties in the region.[37] To fully develop its water rights, therefore, DWP completed a second aqueduct to the eastern Sierra in 1970.

The second aqueduct begins just south of Owens Lake at the Haiwee Reservoir and parallels the first Los Angeles Aqueduct south to the city of Los Angeles. The second aqueduct essentially doubled the capacity drawn from the eastern Sierra sources. Combined, the first and second Los Angeles Aqueducts supply approximately 430 million gallons of water each day to the city of Los Angeles, representing approximately 35 percent of water consumed by Los Angelinos.[38]

The Colorado River Aqueduct

The water from Owens Valley, however, did not provide a permanent solution for Los Angeles County water needs for two reasons. First, the water primarily served residents of the city of Los Angeles, and county residents outside the city were underserved. Second, sheer population growth, both inside and outside the city, eventually outstripped water availability. Between 1900 and 1930, over two million people entered Los Angeles County.[39] As population increased, significant strains were again placed on all water resources, and fears of water insufficiency grew. This was particularly true for the growing communities which had limited access to surface water.

In the mid-1920s, the city of Pasadena, which depended almost entirely on groundwater pumping, started exploring mechanisms to supplement its ever-shrinking groundwater basin, the Raymond Basin.[40] In searching for potential surface water, Pasadena officials determined that local sources were not available, and they began to explore importing water from the Colorado River. Others in Los Angeles County were similarly interested in obtaining water from the Colorado River—which had recently been divided up via the Colorado River Compact of 1922 between the seven states within the Colorado River system. California was allocated 4.4 million AF of water per year.

In anticipation of even greater water need than could then be accommodated, the city of Los Angeles also sought and was awarded water rights from the Colorado River in 1924, although no delivery mechanism from the river then existed. To pursue these interests, the Metropolitan Water District (MWD) was formed in 1928 with the overall goal of providing water to the area specifically by creating an aqueduct to import Colorado River water. Charter membership in MWD included Pasadena, Los Angeles, and eleven other cities located in Southern California. In September 1931, voters within the district approved a 220-million-dollar bond for the creation of the Colorado River Aqueduct and construction began in 1933.[41]

The Colorado River Aqueduct spans some 242 miles beginning with the Parker Dam located along the California–Arizona border. The first water from the Colorado River arrived in the Los Angeles area in 1941. The aqueduct was built with a capacity of 1.3 million AF of water per year, although the

MWD has never been allocated sufficient water shares from the Colorado River to operate the aqueduct at full capacity.[42] Since its completion, however, the Colorado River Aqueduct has regularly carried a larger amount of water than was allocated under the many agreements governing the Colorado River. Essentially, Upper Basin Colorado River states were not using their full share and California regularly used the surplus. For instance, in the year 2000, California received a total of 5.3 million AF of water. Of that, a large portion flowed through the Colorado River Aqueduct to the metropolitan centers of southern California.[43]

The California Aqueduct

By the mid-1950s, water officials were contemplating matters of water adequacy at the statewide level. Plans were undertaken to capture water from the Sacramento and San Joaquin Rivers that was being lost to the ocean. These plans resulted in the conception of the California Aqueduct, which narrowly gained approval for bonding through a statewide vote in 1960. Although Los Angeles County delivered the largest single bloc of yes votes of any county in the state (over 1.3 million), it also delivered the single largest bloc of no votes (slightly over 1 million) for the project.[44] The disagreement within the Los Angeles area regarding the California Aqueduct can largely be traced to initial resistance by members of the MWD, who wanted assurances that the water flowing south could not be discontinued by interests in Northern California (a worry that turned out to be fully justified as discussed later) and that the project could be self-financed over the long term by water sales.[45]

As part of the State Water Project (SWP), the California Aqueduct begins at the Banks Pumping Facility located within the Sacramento–San Joaquin Delta and travels 444 miles south to serve the San Joaquin Valley and metropolitan areas in Southern California. The Banks Facility is able to pump 10,670 cubic feet per second (CFS) (approximately 0.25 AF per second) from the Delta. At its largest point, the California Aqueduct is able to sustain over 13,000 CFS (approximately 0.30 AF per second) of flow.[46] The project reached completion in 1972–73 as reservoirs in Southern California began receiving Bay Delta water.[47] Thirty agencies eventually contracted to receive water from the SWP—amounting to over 4 million AF of water contracts per year. The largest percentage (2.5 million AF) was obtained by Southern California water agencies. Today, the SWP remains the largest state-built water conveyance system in the United States.[48] (Please see chapter 11 for a discussion of the controversies surrounding Delta water diversions to the South.)

Ability to Provide Predictability in Water Availability

The previous section identified the major sources of water potentially available to Los Angeles County. This section examines whether the institutions governing these sources of water are able to provide predictability of water deliveries to the participants in the water system. Having a water right specified on paper may not sufficiently guarantee water delivery. A right becomes credible when it observably demonstrates to right holders that access to the resource will be guaranteed and maintained over time. If the enforcement of the rights is sporadic or arbitrary, there can be little claim that the rights actually exist. If the rule-in-use is to ignore the specified water right, then it is practically the same as if the right did not exist at all. Here, the inquiry will focus on the acceptance of water rights by resource appropriators and enforcement of water rights by the governing bodies.

Groundwater Resources

Through the adjudication process in the courts, groundwater resource users came to understand their rights and obligations. Each of the adjudications fixed a quantifiable amount of water that could be withdrawn from the aquifer without penalty. For Raymond, West Coast, and Central Coast Basins, this right is a fixed amount that resource users can rely on. In the case of the Main San Gabriel, the number is somewhat more variable due to the variability of the operational safe yield established by the Main San Gabriel Water Management Board. Regardless, each pumper in the Main San Gabriel understands the percentage of right they have to the amount of water that can be safely withdrawn from the basin.

As described previously, individual pumpers and associations of pumpers negotiated settlements in each of the basins that were eventually adopted as judgments establishing water rights. The agreements reached have remained largely intact, and state and federal governments have deferred to the established rights. The only significant exception is in the area of water quality. Where volatile organic compounds, perchlorate, nitrates, and other contaminants have contaminated areas, the federal government through the Environmental Protection Agency has taken a role in mandating cleanups through the Superfund statutory process. The state has also acquired some role through the setting of acceptable contamination levels by the California State Department of Public Health.

Otherwise, the rights can be altered only by amending the adjudicated judgments, which occurred historically at the request of nearly all of the pumpers. After prolonged drought in the Los Angeles area in the early 1990s, for instance, pumpers in the West Coast Basin requested that the judgment be readjudicated to allow for a one-year carryover extension enabling pumpers to take additional water to ameliorate the effects of the reduced amount of surface water available during drought years.[49] This amount would then be subtracted from the water available to the pumpers during the year immediately following the over-extraction.[50] While this alteration of the original adjudication may not provide a long-term solution for meeting all water needs during extended drought, it does provide some ability to more effectively draw on groundwater during times of water shortages.

Because these rights are secure, a market for water rights and leases has developed. This market has largely continued through the present, with rights holders selling or leasing shares within the market. The self-managed rights system has also allowed some security against threatening policy directions taken by external governing agencies. For example, although the initial adjudication of the Central and West Coast Basins allocated pumping rights, it did not clearly establish who had rights to put water in the basin for storage. Hence, while appropriation rights were clear, the right to store water in the basin was somewhat uncertain. Conflict arose as the cities of Long Beach, Downey, Lakewood, Signal Hill, and nine other pumpers asserted that they and the other adjudicated right holders had the exclusive right to manage the storage space within the basin. The Water Replenishment District, which controls groundwater replenishment activities within the basin, disagreed and asserted that it had the exclusive right to control groundwater storage as part of replenishment activities. The conflict went before the California Superior Court and the California Court of Appeals, both of which decided that according to the statutory purpose of the Replenishment District, this entity would be in charge of all storage space.

The majority of pumpers was generally dissatisfied with this result because their individual right to store water in years of abundance and draw on stored water in years of scarcity did not seem to be recognized by the court. Over the last several years, however, the dissatisfied pumpers and associations of pumpers have worked together with the Water Replenishment District to amend the judgments of each basin to clarify storage rules allowing for each pumper a percentage of storage space based on pumping rights held and supervised by a new watermaster service. Through a mediation process, the pumpers and replenishment district are working to reach sufficient consensus to present a unified plan before the court.

Enforcement of pumpers' rights has occurred through the watermasters in each of the four basins who have the responsibility to monitor pumping activities. The findings of these monitoring activities are then published in a yearly report detailing individual pumping amounts of each of the pumpers operating in the basin. Watermasters are also charged with alerting the court and other pumpers of violations of the adjudicated rights. If a pumper takes more than his allocated right, court action may be taken, although violations have been uncommon since the adjudication process. The West Coast Basin and the Central Basin have traditionally contracted with the California State Department of Water Resources to provide the watermaster service.[51] Raymond and Main San Gabriel, on the other hand, have each hired their own watermaster services.

The Owens Valley

Rights to imported water are less clear than rights to groundwater. Intervention by individuals and groups who hold no formal rights to water often obfuscates established historical rights. (This issue is more fully discussed by Bretsen and Hill in chapter 6.) In the case of the Owens Valley water, despite acquiring substantial water rights to the upper Owens Valley and Mono Lake, a series of court rulings have greatly diminished the amount of water actually flowing through the Los Angeles Aqueducts. Notable reductions in the amount of water accessible to Los Angeles have occurred as a result of lawsuits under the California Environmental Quality Act (CEQA), the public trust doctrine, and other environmental claims.

As noted, the city of Los Angeles obtained rights to groundwater as well as surface water in the Owens Valley and Mono Basin in the first half of the Twentieth Century. Despite these rights, various lawsuits have capped pumping at an amount much lower than the rights specified on paper. Environmental groups, for instance, have successfully used complaints under CEQA to delay pumping and water deliveries regardless of the rights held by the parties. One common argument has alleged that the Environmental Impact Review (a step required by the CEQA) performed by the city of Los Angeles prior to undertaking pumping activities was legally inadequate. In one such instance, the city of Los Angeles was forced to delay proposed pumping until a legal settlement mandated that Los Angeles pumping in the Owens Valley be coordinated with Inyo County officials.[52]

Other actions by external governments have equally disregarded established rights. In 1983, the California Supreme Court held 6–1 that historical rights to the waters flowing into the Mono Basin held by the city of Los Angeles did "not preclude a reconsideration and reallocation which also takes into account the impact of water diversion on the Mono Lake environment" (*National Audubon Soc'y v. Superior Court*, 33 Cal. 3d 319 (1983)). In reaching this conclusion, the court relied on the public trust doctrine, asserting that the public had a right to environmental outcomes which trump the city's right to water. (See chapter 7 by James Huffman, which deals with the public trust doctrine.) *National Audubon Soc'y v. Superior Court* established precedent that has resulted in numerous cases challenging existing water appropriations under the theory that such appropriations violate the public trust.

In *Dahlgren v. Los Angeles* (Mono Co. Superior Court No. 8902, 1985), the Mono County Superior Court found that the public trust doctrine along with a 1937 provision of the California Fish and Game Code prohibiting the dewatering of streams below dams required a flow of at least nineteen CFS in Rush Creek (located in the Mono Basin). Dahlgren, an avid fly-fisherman, sued to preserve trout habitat in Rush Creek after noting that brown trout had reestablished themselves there after being washed over the spillway of the Grant Lake Reservoir during a particularly high water year.[53]

In 1987, the Mono County Superior Court used the public trust doctrine to order increased flows in Vining Creek (*Mono Lake Committee v. Los Angeles* (Mono County Superior Court No. 8608, 1987)). Similarly, a 1994 lawsuit filed by environmental groups used the public trust doctrine to force the State Water Resources Control Board to change diversion rights held by the city of Los Angeles to include a required water level at Mono Lake of 6,392 feet above sea level.[54] This level is projected to be reached sometime around 2015. Even after the desired lake level is met, the new regulation mandates that Los Angeles be allowed to appropriate water at only one-third of its historical average from the Mono Lake Basin.[55]

In 1997, the city of Los Angeles settled with the Concerned Citizens of Owens Valley and the Great Basin Unified Air Pollution Control District[56] to mitigate dust blowing off Owens Lake—the original termination point for the Owens River. This settlement was reached after many years of litigation. The settlement mandated that Los Angeles divert 13 percent of its Owens Valley water supply toward dust mitigation. Since the agreement, the city of Los Angeles has spread 40,000 AF of water per year on the Owens Lake lakebed.[57]

Despite historic drought conditions in Los Angeles during 2007, the Los Angeles DWP was forced to permanently divert 40 CFS of water (approximately an additional 5 percent reduction) from the Los Angeles Aqueduct to restore the Lower Owens River to meet obligations under *Sierra Club and Owens Valley Committee v. City of Los Angeles* (Inyo County Superior Court Case No.: S1CVCV01-29768).[58] This case, pending in Inyo County Superior Court since 2001, sought to enforce a 1977 memorandum of understanding reached between the city of Los Angeles and a variety of interested parties seeking to mitigate the effects of water diversions from Owens Valley. Even though the restoration of the Lower Owens was part of longstanding obligations, the 5-percent reduction in water available to the city of Los Angeles was especially costly given the previous reductions in the amount of water flowing through the Los Angeles Aqueduct.[59]

These environmental and legal challenges have greatly weakened the rights to deliver water to Los Angeles. To satisfy the environmental concerns and habitat restoration projects, the water flowing from the Owens Valley has diminished by between 30 and 40 percent from historic levels and has made Los Angeles increasingly dependant on water from the Colorado River and the Sacramento–San Joaquin Delta.[60]

The Colorado River

Disagreements over the rights to the Colorado River have resulted in similar uncertainty to established rights to water. Three conflicts over water affect Los Angeles County's rights to the Colorado River—international conflicts, disagreements between the states drawing from the Colorado, and conflict within California between the various holders of water rights.

International conflicts along the Colorado have arisen between the United States (the river's main country of origin) and Mexico (where the river flows ultimately into the Gulf of California and the Pacific Ocean). U.S. leaders entered into an agreement with Mexico in 1944 granting 1.5 million AF of water to Mexico per year. While previous disputes have appeared due to the salinity content of the Colorado when it reaches Mexico,[61] conflict is currently brewing over maintaining the Colorado River Delta and its historic ecosystem functions. While the Colorado Delta was once rich in biodiversity, the amount of water flowing pursuant to the 1944 agreement has been insufficient to maintain ecological conditions once present, and some have advocated increasing the flow out of the United States.[62] Where the additional water will come from is an open question.

Conflicts between U.S. states sharing the Colorado River have also been longstanding and bitter. The 1922 Colorado River Compact allocated 7.5 million AF of water both to upper Colorado River States (Colorado, New Mexico, Utah, and Wyoming) and 7.5 million AF to the lower Colorado River States (Arizona, California, and Nevada).[63] In 1963, the U.S. Supreme Court found in *Arizona v. California*, 373 U.S. 546 (1963), that Congress had allocated substantially more rights from the Colorado to the states of Arizona and Nevada—and away from California—than were established in the original 1922 Colorado River Compact.

Despite the *Arizona v. California* ruling, which held California's allocation at 4.4 million AF per year, the state frequently took about 800,000 AF more than its share from the surplus water—much of which was captured by the MWD to supply water to metropolitan areas in Southern California. The practice of using surplus water became something of a de facto right and continued for decades. However, in 2002, the U.S. Department of Interior announced that it would impose its "nondiscretionary obligation" to hold California's right to the Colorado at 4.4 million AF, cutting off access to surplus water. Of this, approximately 550,000 AF (about one-fourth of California's allotment) would be allocated to the MWD.[64] The remaining water was divided between three irrigation districts holding priority rights: the Palo Verde Irrigation District, the Imperial Irrigation District, and the Coachella Valley Water District.[65]

Additional fights over the Colorado River are virtually guaranteed. Water officials in Nevada have asserted in recent years that they may be forced to renegotiate the Colorado River Compact in order to get a larger share of the water to meet the needs of their ever-growing population. It is unclear at this time who would receive less water than apportioned in the original agreement. Making matters worse, recent evidence illustrates that the Colorado River Compact was decided in a period of high water. In 1922, when the Compact was made, predicted annual flows of the Colorado were assumed to be 16.4 million AF. By 1960, that number was reduced to 13.5 million AF based on newer stream flow studies.[66] More recent studies using tree-ring widths as a proxy for high and low water years over the last 500 years have determined that sustained droughts have been frequent along the Colorado and that the Compact was agreed to during an unusually wet period.[67] Accordingly, policymakers will likely need to revisit allocation amounts to bring them into line with actual biophysical conditions, especially during times of prolonged drought.

Within California, competing uses for Colorado River water have added additional uncertainty to the rights in Colorado River water. As noted, only about one-fourth of California rights to the Colorado River are held by MWD. The other three-fourths are held by irrigation districts. Without access to surplus water from the Colorado River, MWD has sought to purchase water from the irrigation districts. Prolonged litigation brought by the irrigation districts, however, has hampered water transfers.

Additional complications involve environmental concerns. For instance, recent controversy has surrounded the future of the Salton Sea—an artificial lake in the Imperial Valley originally created in 1905 by a breach in irrigation levees in the Imperial Valley which resulted in water flooding salt flats on the bed of a then-dry prehistoric sea. Currently fed by water return flows from irrigation in the Imperial and Coachella valleys, the Salton Sea is California's largest inland lake and is below sea level. Advocates for the Salton Sea assert that because it has become important habitat for migratory waterfowl and other species, additional water deliveries must be maintained to enhance the lake's environmental benefits.[68]

The effect of these challenges has resulted in substantial decreases in water deliveries to Southern California from the Colorado River over time. By 2015, MWD's share of the Colorado River is expected to be .55 million AF per year. This represents a steep decline from historical amounts of 1.2 million AF per year.[69]

The Sacramento–San Joaquin Delta

The California Aqueduct running south from the Sacramento–San Joaquin Delta has faced similar uncertainty regarding rights. (For a discussion of this uncertainty, see chapter 11.) Uncertainty over the Delta has most recently come to light in suits over endangered and threatened fish species located there. In 2007, a state court judge acted to protect the delta smelt, a two- to three-inch fish found only within the Sacramento–San Joaquin Delta. Under the auspices of the California Endangered Species Act (a California statute distinct from the federal Endangered Species Act), in March 2007, Alameda Superior Court Judge Frank Roesch ordered that the pumps feeding the California Aqueduct be shut down within sixty days of his ruling, unless the California Department of Water Resources obtained an incidental take permit for the fish (then listed as threatened under California law).[70] After failing to obtain the necessary permit, the pumps were shut down entirely for twelve days and operated for only four hours/day for an additional week in June 2007. After finding that the majority of fish migrated away from the pump intakes, the pumps were allowed to restart. This was not, however, the end of the controversy.

In late 2007, U.S. District Judge Oliver Wanger from California's Eastern District found that California had violated its obligations under the U.S. Endangered Species Act (ESA) in regards to the delta smelt. Judge Wanger ordered a 25–30 percent reduction of water pumped out of the Delta. This cut represented a loss of 730,000 AF to those who relied on water from the SWP.[71] Judge Wanger's ruling was seemingly made permanent in December 2008, when the U.S. Fish and Wildlife Service issued a Biological Opinion under the authority of the ESA that the pumping reduction remain in effect as a necessary condition for the fish species' recovery.[72] The opinion further mandated that the pumps providing water to the California Aqueduct be shut down during certain periods of the year when the delta smelt were spawning. Finally, in dry years, water exports will be reduced as much as 50 percent of pre-2007 levels to provide sufficient flow to maintain the smelt's habitat.[73]

The status of this plan spelled out under the biological opinion is currently uncertain. In May 2009, Judge Wanger enjoined the implementation of the biological opinion on grounds that it violated the U.S. National Environmental Protection Act (NEPA). Specifically, Judge Wanger found that the U.S. Fish and Wildlife Service failed to perform the necessary environmental assessment and environmental impact review of financial impacts that shutting down the pumps would have imposed on farmers who depend on imported irrigation water. NEPA compliance will likely take time and delay reductions in upcoming years.[74]

The delta smelt is just the beginning of a string of potential changes affecting the ability of Southern California to draw water from the Sacramento–San Joaquin Delta. In July 2008, Judge Wanger ruled on a separate suit that water diversions harmed, threatened, and endangered winter-run Chinook salmon, spring-run Chinook salmon, and steelhead trout. The biological opinion regarding the salmon and trout species released in early 2009 mandates an additional 8 percent cut in water exported from the Sacramento–San Joaquin Delta.

In 2009, the California Department of Fish and Game listed a separate species of smelt, the longfin smelt, as a threatened species under the California Endangered Species Act, despite the fact that the U.S. National Marine Fisheries Service decided earlier in 2009 not to list the fish as threatened under the U.S. Endangered Species Act.[75] No new action has been taken to reduce flows based on the longfin, but past experience with endangered and threatened fish suggests that future reductions will likely be pursued by interested parties. Additional suits under the ESA will almost certainly follow for the protection of the green sturgeon, a fish that inhabits the Sacramento–San Joaquin Delta in small numbers. The species was listed as threatened under the U.S. Endangered Species Act in 2006. In May 2009, the U.S. National Marine Fisheries Service proposed protection under Rule 4(d) of the U.S. Endangered Species Act ensuring the species protection, including protection against habitat loss.[76]

Finally, a separate suit filed in late 2008 by the California Water Impact Network (C-WIN) and the California Sports Fishing Alliance threatens to reduce pumping activities through application of the public trust doctrine. The petitioners allege that in addition to harming habitat, water diversions and the pumps themselves harm other recreational and aesthetic attributes which should be held in trust for the public.[77] C-WIN asserts that the suit was inspired by use of the public trust doctrine in the Mono Basin to limit water diversions. In describing its goals in filing the suit, C-WIN states that it wants to "spread enforcement of the public trust doctrine throughout California" and prohibit "waste and unreasonable use of water, starting with protecting fisheries and aquatic ecosystems now directly injured by excessive water diversions of the California State Water Project."[78] Although there has not been a ruling in this case to date, the use of the public trust doctrine in the Sacramento–San Joaquin Delta has opened a new line of attack on historical water rights in the area.

The upshot of this plethora of legal and environmental challenges has been diminished flows through the California Aqueduct. For the past ten years, the California Department of Water Resources reports that, on average, only 68 percent of water promised from the SWP has actually flowed. In 2009, that number had diminished to only 40 percent of water flowing from the SWP and projected deliveries for the 2009–10 water year are the lowest in the history of the project.[79]

Conclusion and Implications: Lessons from the Los Angeles Area

The foregoing analysis demonstrates that the complex institutions governing water allocations from the Owens Valley, the Colorado River, and the Sacramento–San Joaquin Delta have been inconsistently applied and enforced over time. Legal and political challenges by private parties, by interest groups, and from both national and state governmental authorities have undermined longstanding institutions allocating water to individuals and entities within the Los Angeles area. Inconsistency in the application and enforcement of water allocation institutions has prevented meaningful predictability in the degree to which residents of the Los Angeles region can rely on imported sources of water.

This variability in institutions allocating imported water has led to a substantial disconnect between demand and supply. Through the past five years, the Los Angeles area has experienced severe drought. The 2006–07 water year yielded the lowest ever recorded rainfall for portions of Los Angeles County.[80] The previous year had also been drier than average. Under these drought conditions, drawing on rights to imported sources of water would seemingly become more vital to meeting local water demands. Notwithstanding these conditions, water allocated from the imported sources has actually been reduced. These reductions have generally been made not because of drought conditions in the headwaters of the Owens Valley, the Sacramento–San Joaquin Delta, and the Colorado River, but rather have been made in response to political and legal challenges.

Lessons from Los Angeles

There are several lessons to be learned from the Los Angeles experience. These include (1) water from imported sources may involve temporal and spatial trade-offs, (2) more emphasis needs to be placed on understanding and strengthening water rights, and (3) diversification of an area's local water portfolio is important. Each of these will be discussed in the following sections.

Lesson 1: Spatial and Temporal Trade-offs in Imported Water

Importing water from distant sources almost always involves spatial and temporal trade-offs. In spatial terms, by drawing water from the Colorado River, Northern California, and the eastern Sierra, the people of Los Angeles County have become somewhat dependent on the biophysical and social conditions of the areas-of-origin. Los Angeles has essentially become linked to far-distant areas. Droughts in places as far away as Wyoming and Colorado potentially impact water availability in Los Angeles. Moreover, by increasing the scale of their water delivery system, the people of Los Angeles have set up potential conflicts with a much larger set of players with a diverse set of interests. The population of the San Francisco Bay regions has different plans for the Sacramento–San Joaquin Delta than those living in metropolitan Southern California.

In temporal terms, many of the areas where the water is drawn from have significantly changed overtime. There is more demand on the resources from local populations along the Colorado River and the Sacramento–San Joaquin regions. More importantly, general preferences regarding the use of water have changed over time. Although diversion and extraction were historically acceptable, many now view these actions as normatively wrong. This is particularly apparent in the seemingly endless environmental legislation and litigation impacting the ability to access the resources. Simply put, people do not only want water flowing from their taps—many also want a flourishing ecosystem in the area where the water originates.

Lesson 2: More Emphasis on the Importance of Defending Water Rights

In recognizing the trade-offs inherent in any water importation system, sound policy requires strengthened water rights to provide credibility in the commitments offered to participants relying on the imported water. Unfortunately, strengthening water rights has not generally been the current trend. Indeed, the problem of weakening property rights to water is pervasive across the state of California, as well as the entire United States.

Recent developments in California, however, may indicate a change in direction toward increased recognition of property rights to water. In late 2008, the Federal Court of Appeals decided *Casitas Municipal Water District v. United States*, 543 F.3d 1276 (Fed. Cir. 2008), holding that water diverted under the U.S. Endangered Species Act to provide flows for the steelhead trout constituted a takings under the Fifth Amendment of the U.S. Constitution. Specifically, the court found that Casitas was granted "the perpetual right to use all water that becomes available through the construction and operation" of the Ventura River Project through a contract with the U.S. Government (2007 5153 6). After the listing of the steelhead trout as endangered, the government required Casitas to divert water for the construction of a fish ladder. The court reasoned that because the water was permanently diverted away from Casitas, the U.S. Government's actions could be classified as a physical takings. While an appeal will certainly follow, the court's recognition of the loss of flows as a loss of property right indicates a substantial departure from previous jurisprudence.[81]

Lesson 3: The Importance of Portfolio Diversification

Although institutional reform leading to more enforcement of established rights would alleviate the water supply problem somewhat, such sweeping institutional changes are highly unlikely in the current political climate. Accordingly, the diversification of local water portfolios has become exceedingly important. Water portfolio diversification would produce two benefits. First, portfolio diversification would reduce risk by providing more sources of water from which the Los Angeles area could draw. In the event that one source became unavailable, there would be other sources to draw on. Second, portfolio diversification would likely increase the amount of water available to the Los Angeles area. To obtain these two benefits, four sources of water would have to be developed. These include the maximization of local water sources, increased conservation efforts, further development of water recycling, and desalinization.

MAXIMIZING LOCAL SOURCES

Maximizing local water sources will involve further reliance on groundwater basins which may prove to be problematic. Although local sources involve more ability by pumpers to govern the use and trading of the resource,

340

groundwater is limited and the rights to access groundwater do not allow for extended overpumping. Moreover, the Main San Gabriel, West Coast, and Central Coast Basins have historically relied to some degree on imported water to recharge the groundwater basins. In wet periods, spreading grounds are used to capture run-off flowing through the channels of the Main San Gabriel River and Rio Hondo. During other periods, imported water has been purchased from the MWD and spread to replenish the groundwater basins and injected along the coast to prevent further seawater intrusions. Due to reductions in imported water, there has been less water to spread. Indeed, MWD predicts that replenishment water will only be available during three out of ten years.

Based on these conditions, it is possible that the basin adjudications will have to be amended to bring pumping in line with biophysical conditions during times of extreme drought. While on its face, the likelihood of amending the judgment to reduce pumping does not appear high, it is important to remember that this is exactly what happened during the time of the original adjudications. There is no reason to believe that in the face of long-term necessity, the judgments would not be reevaluated to preserve the important water resource for all users.

It is very important to reemphasize here the role of water markets to stretch local groundwater supplies and allocate water to higher-valued uses. Because the adjudication of groundwater basins that became accepted by all interested parties, clear property rights were established and water markets developed. Markets developed because it became clear what the sellers had to offer and the buyers could determine with almost certainty what they were getting in such a market transaction. It is difficult to envision how such markets could develop for imported water given all of the institutional complexity that spreads across so many political and economic jurisdictions. Further empirical work is needed to determine how much economic value has been created by these water markets in the Los Angeles area, but it would appear to be very significant.

CONSERVATION

Water portfolio diversification will also inevitably involve further conservation efforts. Conservation through technologies such as low-flow toilets, washing machines, and other appliances and devices that reduce water use has been effective in diminishing water demand. Conservation has also been obtained through regulations controlling the use of water. Regulations have been set, for instance, to control the duration and frequency of lawn watering and not using potable water to wash driveways. Additional gains in conservation could be achieved through revisions of water pricing. Although not politically popular, many water delivery agencies have begun to experiment with price tier arrangements to charge more to those who use the most water.

(See chapter 9 for a discussion of the power of price conservation.)

RECYCLED WATER

Recycled water provides a third opportunity for enhancing local water portfolios. Recycled water generally refers to sewer water, which has undergone treatment for reuse in the community. The State of California currently prohibits the use of recycled water for potable purposes. The Sanitation Districts of Los Angeles County operate a series of treatment facilities throughout the Los Angles area. Water from these treatment facilities is distributed through a separate plumbing system utilizing "purple" pipes to distinguish it from potable water.

Approximately 40 percent of the water spread by the Water Replenishment District in the Montebello Forebay to recharge the Central Coast and West Coast Basins is recycled water.[82] It is likely that recycled water will become even more important for groundwater recharge in the future. The Water Replenishment District and the West Coast Basin Municipal Water District, for instance, recently teamed up to inject 100 percent recycled water, which has been treated to potable standards, in the injection barrier wells protecting the West Coast and Central Coast Basins against saltwater intrusion. Finally, the Main San Gabriel Municipal Water District is currently developing an extensive plant to recycle wastewater to meet water needs and replenish the Main San Gabriel Basin.

DESALINIZATION

Water desalinization of sea and brackish water represents the final component of local portfolio diversification. While the cost of desalinization has historically made the practice prohibitive for most uses and in most places, the current uncertainty in the water situation of Los Angeles has made the option appear increasingly attractive. Several desalinization operations are ongoing for brackish groundwater which infiltrated the West Coast and Central Coast Groundwater Basins prior to adjudications. The Brewer Desalter converts 5 million gallons per day of brackish groundwater into water available to consumers of the California Water Service Company.[83] The Goldsworthy Desalter treats 2.75 million gallons of brackish groundwater per day.[84]

Plants for desalinizing water taken from the ocean are currently in planning phases or are under construction in the Los Angeles area. Cities and water agencies in Orange County and San Diego County are performing environmental reviews for constructing desalinization plants to serve the populations south of Los Angeles County. The cities of Long Beach and Los Angeles, as well as the West Basin Municipal Water District, have announced plans for constructing water desalinization plants within Los Angeles County. Although it is unclear how long this construction will take, it is likely that water deliveries from the sea are a not-too-distant reality for the people of

Los Angeles County. On the upside, these processes will provide a larger degree of water security for the region. On the downside, desalinized water is generally far more expensive than other sources of water, although it is difficult to predict how much cost might be reduced if desalinization is performed on a larger scale.

Learning the Lessons of Los Angeles

There unfortunately appears to be no simple way out of the current water conundrum for the people of Los Angeles County and surrounding areas. Reducing reliance on imported water will not be easily accomplished, and yet it is almost certain that disputes over imported water will continue to frustrate efforts at generating water stability for the region in the near future. Water portfolio diversification plans, with the exception of conservation, will take substantial time to implement.

Areas around the nation are currently considering extensive imported water projects. Perhaps most visible are the efforts of Las Vegas, Nevada, to continue drawing from the Colorado River and to import water from groundwater basins located over 200 miles north of the city. In considering these actions, it may be wise to consider the ability to provide water predictability over long time horizons. Water managers must be aware that in the absence of substantial institutional protections, these external sources may not be as reliable as now thought. As the Los Angeles case illustrates, establishing such predictability in imported sources may not prove easy.

Notes

1. Hubert Howe Bancroft, *The History of California,* vol. 2 (San Francisco, 1888). Here, Bancroft is referring to the city of Los Angeles, yet the same water scarcity issues are applicable to the greater Los Angeles area.
2. R. Maria Saleth and Ariel Dinar, *The Institutional Economics of Water* (Northampton, MA: Edward Elgar and the World Bank, 2004).
3. Barton H. Thomspon Jr., "Uncertainty and Markets in Water Resources," *McGeorge L. Rev.* 36 (2005): 117.
4. United Nations (UN), *Human Development Report 2006, Beyond Scarcity: Power, Poverty, and the Global Water Crisis* (New York: Palgrave Macmillan, 2006), 133.
5. Claudia Sadoff, *Can Water Undermine Growth? Evidence from Ethiopia*, World Bank Agricultural and Rural Development Notes 18 (September 2006), http://siteresources.worldbank.org/INTARD/Resources/Note18_Ethiopia_web.pdf.
6. Elinor Ostrom, *Understanding Institutional Diversity* (Princeton, NJ: Princeton University Press, 2005), 3.
7. Douglass North, *Institutions, Institutional Change And Economic Performance* (New York, NY: Cambridge University Press 1990), 3.
8. Dorothy Green, *Managing Water: Avoiding Crisis in California* (Berkeley, CA: University of California Press, 2007).

9. A groundwater basin is defined as "an area underlain by permeable materials capable of furnishing a significant supply of groundwater to wells or storing a significant amount of water" (see California Department of Water Resources, *California's Groundwater, Bulletin 118—Update 2003*. Last modified December 21, 2010. http://www.water.ca.gov/groundwater/bulletin118/bulletin118update2003.cfm.1). Depending on the subsurface geology, groundwater basins may be distinct or connected with surface water basins, such as rivers or lakes.

10. As may be noted, the geographic boundaries of municipalities do not conform to the geologic boundaries of the groundwater basins. For instance, Long Beach overlies portions of both the Central Coast and West Coast Basins.

11. This includes both Main San Gabriel Basin and Puente Subbasin. Despite being considered a subbasin of the Main San Gabriel, the Puente is a separately adjudicated basin. However, the two basins are frequently considered as being joined, including within the annual report of the Main San Gabriel Basin Watermaster.

12. The basins rarely fill to near capacity due to the amount of water pumped out yearly from the basins. This has left room within each of the basins for storage of water over time. This natural storage space has become important to area basin managers who are considering leasing storage space to a variety of interested parties. Due to the storage of imported surface water and banked groundwater, it is likely that the basins will be maintained at near capacity in the future.

13. William Blomquist, *The Performance of Institutions for Groundwater Management, Vol. 1: Raymond Basin* (Bloomington, IN: Indiana University, Workshop in Political Theory and Policy Analysis, 1987); Blomquist, *The Performance of Institutions for Groundwater Management, Vol. 2: West Basin* (Bloomington, IN: Indiana University, Workshop in Political Theory and Policy Analysis, 1988).

14. Institutional factors fueled overpumping. Under California law, overlying owners were deemed to hold the right to pump and were granted seniority based on first in time, first in right. In *Katz v. Walkinshaw*, 141 Cal. 116 (1903), the California Supreme Court modified these rights to include a provision that in times of water scarcity a court could be called in to adjudicate the rights to pump. In such cases, each landowner could be deemed to have "correlative rights," where adjacent pumpers would be found to be coequal owners of the water and would each proportionally share in water rights reductions. California water law further recognized prescriptive rights. If there were no "surplus" water in the basin, then pumpers who began pumping activities could obtain a prescriptive pumping right. Common property law asserts that a prescriptive right may be acquired by a nonproperty owner after "open, adverse, non-permissive use" of another's property for a specified period of time (see J. Gordon Hylton, David L. Callies, Daniel R. Namdelker, and Paula A. Franzese, *Property Law and the Public Interest* Charlottesville, VA: Lexis Law Publishing, 1998: 82–83). A prescriptive right is generally held to be a use right and is often described as an easement. In California, the specified time for prescription of a water right is five years (see William Blomquist, *Dividing the Waters*

(San Francisco, CA: ICS Press, 1992). Prescriptive rights are similar to squatter's rights on real estate acquired through adverse possession. Right to the water of another was acquired after five years of continuous adverse use. Making prescriptive rights particularly problematic was the fact that pumpers could not know when their rights were being prescribed. This generated substantial uncertainty regarding the rights of overlying owners. Under these conditions, lawyers advised their clients to put as much water to beneficial use as possible so as to firmly establish their date of priority and their place at the table in the event of court action (see Elinor Ostrom, "Public Entrepreneurship: A Case Study in Ground Water Basin Management" (PhD dissertation, University of California, Los Angeles, 1965)).

15. (California DPW, 1930, 73). California Department of Public Works, Division of Water Resources *South Coastal Basin* Bulletin No. 32 (Sacramento, CA: Government Printing Office, 1930, 73). While not as extensive as that found in the West Coast Basin, sea water intrusion was reported in the Central Basin in the area around Alamitos Gap near Long Beach by 1949 (see Blomquist, *Dividing the Waters*).

16. (California DPW, 1925) California Department of Public Works, Division of Engineering and Irrigation, *Supplemental Report on the Water Resources of California.* Bulletin No. 9. (Sacramento, CA: State Printing Office, 1925).

17. In addition to limiting pumping, actors sought new sources of imported water as will be discussed below.

18. Collaboration between resource users to create governance institutions and manage local resources has been identified as an effective mechanism of resource management (see, Elinor Ostrom, *Governing the Commons* (New York: Cambridge University Press, 1990); Jean-Marie Baland, and Jean-Philippe Platteau. *Halting Degradation of Natural Resources: Is There a Role for Rural Communities?* (Oxford: Clarendon Press, 1996); T. Dietz, E. Ostrom, and P. Stern. "The Struggle to Govern the Commons." *Science* 302, no. 5652 (2003): 1907–12). Elinor Ostrom was recently awarded the Nobel Prize in Economic Sciences for her work in identifying how and under what circumstances resource users will act collectively to govern shared resources. In Chapter 4 of *Governing the Commons*, Ostrom identifies the collaboration of groundwater users to solve problems of overuse in the Los Angeles area as an example of successful collective resource management.

19. Within-basin transfers of rights were contemplated through the adjudication process. It appears less attention was paid to transfers outside of the basin. While out-of-basin transfers appear possible, they have not regularly occurred. Rather, entities within the basin have purchased and leased rights and have not exported water out of the basins. This pattern has generally held for each of the basins in this study. The majority of rights transfers *has* been within basin. The few out-of-basin transfers noted have been by entities that have service areas both inside and outside of the basin. The Southern California Water Company, for instance, transferred part of its pumping share from the West Coast Basin to supply water to its service area lying to the west of Palos Verde Hills (see California Department of Water Resources 2007).

California Department of Water Resources, *Annual Report of Watermaster Service in the West Coast Basin, Los Angeles County July 1, 2006–*

June 30, 2007 (Glendale, CA: Department of Water Resources Southern District, 2007), http://www.water.ca.gov/watermaster/sd_documents/west_basin_2007/westcoastbasinreport2007.pdf.

California Department of Water Resources, *Annual Report of Watermaster Service in the West Coast Basin, Los Angeles County July 1, 1996–June 30, 1997* (Glendale, CA: Department of Water Resources Southern District, 1997).

California Department of Water Resources, *Annual Report of Watermaster Service in the West Coast Basin, Los Angeles County July 1, 2008–June 30, 2009* (Glendale, CA: Department of Water Resources Southern District, 2009), http://www.water.ca.gov/watermaster/sd_documents/west_basin_2009/westcoastbasinwatermasterreport2009.pdf.

20. See Carl Fossette and Ruth Fossette, *The Story of Water Development in Los Angeles County* (Downey, CA: Central Basin Municipal Water District, 1986). Final settlement of the West Coast Basin actually required a second suit listing over one hundred small pumpers not named in the original suit, and a settlement agreement was reached in 1966 (see Blomquist, *Dividing the Waters*).

21. Ostrom, "Public Entrepreneurship"; Fossette and Fossette, *Story of Water*. The imported water was purchased through municipal water districts such as the Central Basin Municipal Water District and the West Basin Municipal Water District.

22. California Department of Water Resources, *Annual Report of Watermaster Service in the West Coast Basin, Los Angeles County 1965–1966* (Los Angeles, CA: Department of Water Resources Southern District, 1966)

23. Blomquist, *Dividing the Waters.*

24. Raymond Basin Management Board 2007. Raymond Basin Management Board *Watermaster Service in the Raymond Basin 2006–2007* (Asuza, CA, 2007).

25. California Department of Water Resources, *Annual Report of Watermaster Service in the West Coast Basin, Los Angeles County July 1, 2008–June 30, 2009* (Glendale, CA: Department of Water Resources Southern District, 2009), http://www.water.ca.gov/watermaster/sd_documents/west_basin_2009/westcoastbasinwatermasterreport2009.pdf.

26. Blomquist, *Dividing the Waters*; California Department of Water Resources, *Annual Report of Watermaster Services in the Central Basin, Los Angeles County July 1, 2009–June 30, 2010* (Glendale, CA: Department of Water Resources Southern District, 2010), http://www.water.ca.gov/watermaster/sd_documents/central_basin_2010/centralbasinwatermasterreport2010.pdf.

27. This information was obtained from the Annual Reports of the Watermaster Services for the West Coast Basin produced by the California Department of Water Resources, Southern Division between 2001 and 2010. These reports can be accessed online at: http://www.water.ca.gov/watermaster/sd_reports/westcoastbasin.cfm.

28. This information was obtained from the Annual Reports of the Watermaster Services for the Central Basin produced by the California Department of Water Resources, Southern Division between 2001 and 2010. These reports can be accessed online at: http://www.water.ca.gov/watermaster/sd_reports/centralbasin.cfm.

29. A more complete explanation for the reduction of transfers likely involves the functioning of an efficient water market. When the original adjudication occurred, the values of water were highly disparate among the recipients of rights. The market facilitated the movement of water from lower to higher values until these differences in values were reduced. During the adjudication process, an attempt was made to do what was fair and give rights to those who had historically used the water. Then after adjudication and the firming up of rights, disparities in values became relevant and transfers to higher-valued uses were quickly made, but have diminished through time.

30. Main San Gabriel Watermaster, *Annual Report of the Main San Gabriel Watermaster 2007–2008* (Azusa, CA, 2008).

31. Main San Gabriel Watermaster, *Annual Report of the Main San Gabriel Watermaster 2006–2007* (Azusa, CA, 2007).

32. It should be noted that leases and purchases are not perfect substitutes. Leases are more flexible. Demand by resource users is somewhat stochastic based on variable amounts of surface water available and the prices of that water. Lessees are not committing to a permanent arrangement and are thereby able to game the system, believing that groundwater will be more available and/or less expensive than surface water. But leasing is also much more risky because lessees may not be able to augment supplies with certainty in a lease market where all parties are subject to similar supply variation such as drought. It appears from the data that flexibility has been quite important relative to problems with uncertainty.

33. Gary D. Libecap, *Rescuing Water Markets: Lessons from Owens Valley* (Bozeman, MT: PERC Policy Series, 2005); Libecap, *Owens Valley Revisited* (Stanford, CA: Stanford University Press, 2007).

34. The manner in which this property was obtained has been the source of a fair amount of historical controversy. Residents of Owens Valley have long complained that the city took advantage of them in purchasing the water rights. The facts of the purchase suggest that there may indeed have been some degree of subterfuge involved. The individual operating on behalf of the city, Fred Eaton, represented that the purchases were occurring to establish a cattle operation in the area and did not fully disclose his involvement with city of Los Angeles (see Vincent Ostrom, *Water and Politics* (Newbury Park, CA: Haynes Foundation, 1953)). Others have alleged that the city official pretended to be an official from the U.S. Bureau of Reclamation, although the evidence of this claim appears tenuous (see Abraham Hoffman, "Did He or Didn't He? Fred Eaton's Role in the Owen's Valley—Los Angeles Water Controversy," in *Water in the West*, ed. J.B. Smallwood, Jr. (Manhattan, KS: Sunflower University Press, 1983, 30–38). Work by economists has asserted that the water purchase represented a fair market transaction (see Libecap, *Rescuing Water Markets* and *Owens Valley Revisited*). Regardless of these debates, the fact remains that the water transfer has been long lamented as a source of regional hardship. Over the years, some local parties were so strongly against the transfer that they dynamited the Los Angeles Aqueduct (see Norris Hundley Jr., *The Great Thirst* (Los Angeles, CA: University of California Press, 2001)). More recently, the water transfer has been denounced by academics, en-

vironmentalists, and conservationists who were never privy to the original negotiations and whose opposition to the transfer may have more to do with their personal worldview than with the equity of the actions (see, e.g., Mark Reisner, *Cadillac Desert: The American West and Its Disappearing Water,* rev. ed. (New York, NY: Penguin Books, 1993)).

35. Libecap, *Owens Valley Revisited.*
36. *A Second Aqueduct,* Los Angeles Department of Water and Power (DWP), accessed June 2, 2011, http://wsoweb.ladwp.com/Aqueduct/historyoflaa/secondaqueduct.htm.
37. Hundley, *Great Thirst.*
38. *The Story of the Los Angeles Aqueduct,* Los Angeles DWP, accessed June 2, 2011, http://wsoweb.ladwp.com/Aqueduct/historyoflaa/index.htm.
39. United States Census, *California Population of Counties by Decennial Census: 1900 to 1990,* 3/27/1995, accessed July 8, 2011, http://www.census.gov/population/cencounts/ca190090.txt.
40. Blomquist, *Dividing the Waters.*
41. Steven P. Erie, *Beyond Chinatown: The Metropolitan Water District, Growth, and the Environment in Southern California* (Stanford, CA: Stanford University Press, 2006). Member agencies of the MWD presently include fourteen cities, twelve municipal water districts, and one county. The MWD currently supplies approximately 60 percent of municipal water from Ventura County to the Mexican border with water from the Colorado River and Northern California (see David Carle, *Introduction to Water in California* (Berkeley, CA: University of California Press, 2004)).
42. Erie, *Beyond Chinatown.*
43. Carle, *Introduction to Water.*
44. Hundley, *Great Thirst.*
45. *State Water Project—History,* California Department of Water Resources (DWR), last modified October 28, 2008, http://www.water.ca.gov/swp/history.cfm.
46. CA DWR, *State Water Project—History.*
47. Erie, *Beyond Chinatown.*
48. *DWR Releases Initial 2010 State Water Project Allocation,* CA DWR, December 1, 2009, http://www.c-win.org/news/dwr-releases-initial-2010-state-water-project-allocation.html.
49. The amended judgment stipulated that parties could pump an additional 2 AF or an additional 20 percent of the adjudicated right (whichever was greater) per year.
50. West Basin Watermaster, *Watermaster Service in the West Coast Basin, Los Angeles County July 1, 1996–June 30, 1997* (Glendale, CA: Department of Water Resources Southern District, 1997).
51. This arrangement is slated to change under the readjudicated judgment dealing with storage rights. Under the new arrangement, the watermaster service will be undertaken by the Water Replenishment District.
52. Inyo County Water Department, *The City of Los Angeles and the Owens Valley: Chronology of Key Events* (January 2008), http://www.inyowater.org/Water_Resources/Chronology_1900_2008.pdf.
53. Judith A. Layzer, *Natural Experiments: Ecosystem Based Management and the Environment* (Cambridge, MA: MIT Press, 2008).

54. Libecap, *Owens Valley Revisited.*
55. Green, *Managing Water.* Other suits regarding the Owens Valley operations have relied on CEQA.
56. The Great Basin Unified Air Pollution Control District is a California governmental agency that monitors and enforces air pollution in Mono, Alpine, and Inyo counties.
57. Erie, *Beyond Chinatown.*
58. Randall C. Archibald, "A Long Dry California River Gets, and Gives, New Life," *New York Times*, January 12, 2008, http://www.nytimes.com/2008/01/12/us/12water.html?ref=science. Much of the water flowing in the Lower Owens River is recaptured by the city of Los Angeles before it enters Owens Lake. During the course of its flow through the Lower Owens River, a significant amount of water percolates into local groundwater or evaporates. The city of Los Angeles also uses a great deal of water which it recaptures in dust abatement activities in the Owens Valley pursuant to other legal obligations (see Archibald, "Long Dry California River"). For these dust abatement activities, water is sprinkled over large areas to reduce particulate matter blowing from the dry lakebed. Accordingly, very little of the water released to increase the flow of the Lower Owens is actually returned into the Los Angeles Aqueduct.
59. Liebcap (*Owens Valley Revisited*) and Kahrl (*Water and Power*; see References) each provide an excellent history of the cutbacks in water appropriated to the city of Los Angeles from the Owens Valley and surrounding areas of the Eastern Sierra.
60. Green, *Managing Water.*
61. See, e.g., B. Delworth Gardner and Clyde E. Stewart, "Agriculture and Salinity Control in the Colorado River Basin," *Natural Resources Journal* 15, no. 1 (January 1975): 63–81.
62. Joe Gelt, "Sharing Colorado River Water: History, Public Policy and the Colorado River Compact," *Arroyo* 10, no. 1 (August 1997), http://ag.arizona.edu/AZWATER/arroyo/101comm.html.
63. The dividing point between the upper and lower Colorado River is Lee's Ferry, Arizona. The location of this dividing point means that small parts of Arizona actually fall in the Upper Basin, and small parts of Utah and New Mexico actually fall in the area classified as Lower Basin.
64. Erie, *Beyond Chinatown.* In addition to the 550,000 AF, MWD was promised a high priority to using any additional water not used by other users in California. To qualify for this additional water, MWD would have to demonstrate conservation activities and other collaborative projects with the Imperial Irrigation District. Despite these promises, to date little additional water from the Colorado has materialized for the use by the Metropolitan Water District (see *California's Colorado River Allocation*, Metropolitan Water District, last modified March 18, 2009, http://www.mwdh2o.com/mwdh2o/pages/yourwater/supply/colorado/colorado04.html).
65. Carle, *Introduction to Water.*
66. Erie, *Beyond Chinatown.*
67. Connie Woodhouse, Steven T. Gray, and David M. Meko, "Updated Streamflow Reconstructions for the Upper Colorado River Basin," *Water Resource Research* 42 (2006), doi:10.1029/2005WR004455.

68. Erie, *Beyond Chinatown.*
69. Green, *Managing Water.*
70. An "incidental take permit" is a permit allowing the continuance of ongoing business operations despite the presence of a threatened or endangered species. Normally, under both the California Endangered Species Act and United States Endangered Species Act, "taking" an endangered or threatened species is expressly forbidden. Taking includes killing or harming of an endangered or threatened species. Harming includes engaging in any activity that damages species' habitat. These prohibitions apply to intentional takings and unintentional takings. Incidental take permits allow for the occasional, unintentional takings of small numbers of a protected species if the permit holder makes efforts to ameliorate habitat loss and/or implements a plan to minimize the unintentional taking of the species.
71. Peter Fimrite, "U.S. Issues Rules to Protect Delta Smelt," *San Francisco Chronicle*, December 16, 2008, http://www.sfgate.com/cgi-bin/article. cgi?f=/c/a/2008/12/16/MNDD14OIOF.DTL.
72. U.S. Fish and Wildlife Service (USFWS), *Formal Endangered Species Act Consultation on the Proposed Coordinated Operations of the Central Valley Project (CVP) and State Water Project (SWP)*, Reference Number: 81420–2008-F-1481–5 (2008), http://www.fws.gov/sacramento/es/ documents/SWP-CVP_OPs_BO_12-15_final_OCR.pdf.
73. Fimrite, "U.S. Issues Rules."
74. Jacqueline McDonald, "Fish and Wildlife Service Required to Justify Pumping Restrictions in the Delta," *Environmental Law and Policy Alerts* (Sacramento, CA: Somach Simmons & Dunn, 2009), http://www.somachlaw. com/alerts.php?id=29.
75. California Fish and Game Commission, *Notice of Findings: Longfin Smelt*, 2009, http://www.fgc.ca.gov/regulations/new/2009/lsntcfindings ISWARRNTED.pdf.
76. USFWS, Endangered and Threatened Wildlife and Plants: Proposed Rulemaking to Establish Take Prohibitions for the Threatened Southern Distinct Population Segment of North American Green Sturgeon, 74 Fed. Reg. 23822 (proposed May 21, 2009) (to be codified at 50 C.F.R. pt. 223).
77. Mike Taugher, "Activists Sue to Shut Down Delta Pumps," *Oakland Tribune*, December 1, 2008.
78. California Water Impact Network (C-WIN), *Water Politics and Social Justice*, 2009, http://www.c-win.org/paperwater.html.
79. CA DWR, *DWR Releases.*
80. Main San Gabriel Watermaster 2007. Main San Gabriel Watermaster, *Annual Report of the Main San Gabriel Watermaster 2006–2007* (Azusa, CA, 2007).
81. The degree to which the acknowledgement that diverting flows amounts to a physical takings will impact governmental respect for current water allocations is unclear. The ruling does not assert that governments cannot divert flows for different purposes. But, if the ruling stands, it will at the very least increase the cost to governmental agencies seeking to divert flows away from established rights holders toward other uses.
82. Theodore Johnson, "Groundwater Replenishment at the Montebello Forebay

Spreading Grounds," *WRD Technical Bulletin* 14 (Winter 2008), http://www.wrd.org/engineering/groundwater-replenishment-spreading-grounds.php.

83. "Groundwater Recovery: Brackish Groundwater," West Basin Municipal Water District, http://www.westbasin.org/water-reliability-2020/groundwater/groundwater-recovery.

84. "Robert W. Goldworthy Desalter," Water Replenishment District of Southern California, http://www.wrd.org/engineering/groundwater-los-angeles.php?url_proj=robert-goldsworthy-desalter.

13

Dams, Water Rights, and Market Transfers in California

Richard W. Wahl

Introduction: Who Owns Water, and Can Owners Sell Their Supplies?

If you lived in or near the small town of San Jose Chacaya, several miles up a winding road from Lake Atitlan in Guatemala before 1965, you got your water by walking to the town fountain where you filled up your earthen or metal pots. You then carried them home as best you could, possibly—as has been the custom of the world over for centuries—on your head. Given that you filled and carried the pots, one could say that you "owned" the water in your pots, but not the water while it remained in the community well.

So it is today that most of us rely on water conducted through pipes extending not just into a central city well or tap, but into our individual homes— water, we can use at our discretion; for drinking, cooking, and washing inside and for watering grass and plants outside. Do we own such water? Maybe, in the sense that we pay for it and that no one else can take water from our pipes without our permission. But, if you live in Denver, Colorado, you as an individual customer cannot sell your domestic supply to the nearby growing suburbs of Aurora or Arvada. Even if you owned that water and could sell it, how far "upstream" in the supply system would you own the right? How about up in the mountains at water's natural source or in Denver's storage facilities on the South Platte such as Cheeseman Reservoir? The answer, in most cases, is that you don't "own" the water—you have no underlying water right recognized under state law; rather, your city, county, or water district holds the rights for the water it treats and delivers to individual water taps and contracts with you for delivery of its product. But water districts, whether municipally owned or owned by irrigation or other public districts, can and do buy, exchange, and occasionally sell water rights as part of their business in order to supply their customers.

Some districts own the rights to their water supply, but others receive water under contract from still larger districts or from state or federal projects— with these latter entities owning the water rights. Another variation is the "mutual water company" in which customers own shares of the district's water rights: individuals within the company might have the right to sell their shares under conditions set by the district. This routinely occurs, for example, in the Northern Colorado Water Conservancy District, whose market transactions have been studied by economists for a long time.[1]

This brief narrative highlights some of the differences in water ownership that have evolved in the arid West of the United States—an evolution that is multifaceted. A historian might ask: How did this maze of interlocking institutional arrangements arise? A lawyer you consulted about selling or transferring your water rights might know this history and would certainly be able to inform you about the different types of water rights and governing institutions in your state, the type of ownership or contractual rights in your water utility or district, and the rules that followed from this status regarding any possible sale or transfer of such rights. An economist could probably tell you whether these historical institutions, the water rights, and the rules for transfer provide accurate prices—either in the water rates of the supplying district or through possible sale to a higher-value use nearby or even elsewhere in your state or region. An economist might also ask whether the transactions costs of transferring water, be it at the district level or the administration of transfers by the state, impose unnecessary or artificially high barriers in terms of fees, the time required for review and approval, or other aspects of the process. If market signals (prices) are not "accurate" to the final users of water, and if transactions costs are artificially high, then it is not possible for water resources and existing facilities to be used efficiently. (Chapter 9 by Gardner in this volume focuses on this issue.)

As regions grow, the economic demands for water are bound to increase and change. It is not uncommon that as population grows, urban water districts can offer a higher price than agricultural users for "raw," untreated water. These urban districts may be able to make offers directly to agricultural users who own the water rights, probably because the latter have rights with earlier priority dates under the appropriative system of ownership. Similar transactions might occur where individual farmers own shares in a mutual water company if company rules allow. Otherwise, transfers may be initiated by water district management serving as an intermediary in those cases where individual farmers do not directly have title to their own water rights, but the district does.

Districts might also consider raising water prices to engender conservation, but more common would be for their boards of directors to pursue the option of upgrading district facilities to conserve water and then selling some or all of the saved resource and using the proceeds to finance the upgrades. Alternatively, the district might offer positive incentives to growers to husband their water supplies more carefully, or the district might develop rules to evaluate sales proposed by its members of water they currently receive under contract with the district. District-level conservation measures might include updating the district's own water storage facilities or employing underground storage in aquifers, replacing earthen ditches with those that are concrete-lined or with pipes. Some individual growers might lower conveyance losses within their farming operations by similar measures or by employing water delivery scheduling systems that use data on soil moisture, crop needs, and other conditions. All of these practices will effectively stretch existing supplies of water to meet increasing demands.

In this respect, it is worth noting that in the more arid western states in which irrigation is in widespread use (Arizona, California, Colorado, New Mexico, Idaho, Utah, and Wyoming), the consumptive water use in agriculture ranges from 85 percent to 96 percent of the total.[2] In California, the percentage is 91 percent. Hence, by conserving just 10 percent of the water used in agriculture (or 9 percent of the total), all other consumptive uses can double.

The California Case

Both in terms of water management and water rights law, California is a special case in the western United States. Due in part to the state's geography extending 600 miles from north to south, topographical and climatic factors vary widely. Rainfall is relatively more plentiful in California's northern forests compared to the southern portions of the state, which are desert extending down to the border with Mexico. In fact, "in an average year, some areas receive as little as two inches of precipitation while others receive 100 inches or more."[3]

Settlement by Europeans began at the drier extremity, moving north from Mexico. At the behest of King Charles III of Spain, a string of some twenty Catholic missions was founded near the coast to facilitate trading and to colonize the area for Spain. San Diego was the first, established in 1769, and over the next fifty-four years, the Camino Real had been extended over 600 miles north to the San Francisco area. Many of these missions are now familiar names as California communities—Santa Barbara, Santa Cruz, Santa Clara, San Jose, and San Rafael. As the communities around these missions grew, fishing and agriculture sent inhabitants upstream, past the state's coastal range and into the expansive and relatively flat and arid Central Valley, where the valley floor length extends some 400 miles from north to south and averages 45 miles in width.[4]

Traveling upstream from the San Francisco Bay, one enters the San Pablo Bay, the Carquinez Straits, and the Suisun Bay. From there one passes into a large Delta fed by two of the state's principal freshwater rivers, the Sacramento and the San Joaquin. The Sacramento River extends far northward within the Central Valley, past current-day Redding. Also within the northern half of the Central Valley flow the Feather and American rivers as major tributaries originating in the Sierra Nevada Mountains that extend nearly to state's eastern boundary. Similarly, the San Joaquin River drains the Central Valley south of the Sacramento–San Joaquin Delta with its own tributaries, the Kings River far to the south and moving north to the Fresno, Merced, Tuolumne, and Stanislaus rivers, all draining snowmelt and rain from the southern and middle portions of the Sierras.

Urban communities and agricultural development first clung to these watercourses, and they adopted the English common-law custom of riparian (or streamside) water rights.[5] Riparian rights are "appurtenant" to or attached to those land parcels immediately adjacent to rivers and streams. These rights had certain advantages for those fortunate enough to be streamside landowners—the rights were perpetual, there was no definite measure or limit to the amount of water that could be used on the land, and the rights, or any part of them, could not be lost because of nonuse. One disadvantage was that a riparian water right could not be transferred to another location or away from the stream—the water had to be used on the same streamside tract of land, although that parcel could be subdivided.[6] This limitation was hardly conducive to the irrigation of lands far removed from the water source.

A different tradition of water rights, however, was adopted when gold was discovered in California and the mining boom was on—the prior-appropriation system. Like mining claims, water belonged to the first to claim it and to demonstrate use. And this first-in-time, first-in-right aspect of the water right had another feature: in times of low river flow, the most recent rights holders were cut off first, giving more security of use to the most senior (earliest) claimants. By contrast, in times of low flow, holders of riparian rights shared the available water. As placer deposits played out in the stream gravels, mining claims were filed farther and farther off the main rivers, and water was conducted to them via canals or pipes so the miners could employ hydraulic mining—forcing soil lose by using water under pressure and sorting out the gold ore in sluice boxes. Hence, appropriative rights differed from riparian rights in two important ways—the water did not necessarily have to be used on a streamside land parcel, and they were not attached in perpetuity to a particular land parcel at all. An appropriative water right, once claimed and put to use, could subsequently be transferred to another land parcel or subsequently be sold in whole or in part for use elsewhere, either for the same or for a different use (say agriculture instead of mining). An appropriative right, therefore, treats water more like a commodity: The resource can be marketed and therefore adapted to changing water needs with different purposes and locations of use. The use of the water, however, had to be continuous from year to year and could, unlike a riparian right, eventually be challenged and lost through nonuse.

Although this dual system of water rights—riparian and appropriative—has undergone some transformations, it remains in California to this day, setting the state apart from other western states which now rely almost exclusively on appropriative water rights. Some regard riparian rights as an anachronism and as out of touch with the need to transfer water to new uses. Not only is this argument made now, but it has been made throughout California's history in its courtrooms and in the legislature. Therefore, it is natural to ask if the substantial holdings of riparian rights in the state today, mostly in the lower Sacramento River area and in the Sacramento–San Joaquin Delta, are not an important deterrent to the most efficient use of the water resources of the state, especially in this time of increasing competition for water, both among human uses (such as agriculture, municipal and industrial, and recreation) and for preserving aquatic habitats and protecting the migration of anadromous fish through the Delta. (This question is discussed later in the chapter.)

California water management is unusual in other ways as well. By the 1920s, the state's visionaries were planning water diversions on a much grander scale. By this time, the diversion of the Sacramento and Feather Rivers to irrigate lands throughout the most suitable lands in the northern Central Valley had become extensive. Similarly, the diversion of water to lands in the southern half of the Central Valley, particularly on the valley's east side, was well established—principally by diversions from the San Joaquin River tributaries flowing out of the Sierras. But the more expansive vision was to transport water from the water-rich areas of northern California to areas south of the Sacramento–San Joaquin Delta, particularly to the vast expanses of arable land on the west side of the southern Central Valley. Water was also planned for delivery to the growing towns and cities amidst the farmlands in the southern half of the Central Valley and still farther south over the Tehachapi range to the large and growing population centers surrounding Los Angeles. In the southernmost parts of the state, urban and agricultural water purveyors had already constructed conveyance facilities to use water from the Colorado River, which flowed along the state's eastern boundary. But northern California was another promising water source and one without the interstate and upstream competition on the Colorado River.[7] (See chapter 12 for further discussion of the Colorado River and other diversions to the Los Angeles area.)

At an early stage, the plans for using northern California's water were not specific as to how the water would be transported—around the Delta, over it, or through it. Such transport would be not only an engineering challenge, but also an ecological one. The north-to-south transport had the potential to interfere with the slow east-to-west flows in the lower, almost level reaches of the Delta—through its large and extensive network of both natural and man-made channels to reach the Suisun Bay and eventually the San Francisco Bay. Indeed, today the Delta remains the Gordian knot of California water management. In its tangle of water channels, the freshwater flows of the Sacramento and San Joaquin mix with saline waters of the estuaries below, resulting in an extensive zone of high biological productivity and diversity. In any year of low rainfall, or with increased diversions of water from the rivers emptying into the Delta, higher salinity levels can intrude farther upstream, affecting not only biological processes, but also those residents on islands in the Delta who pump water from its channels for agricultural and domestic use. These lands are extensive, totaling about 740,000 acres.[8] And because the facilities that were ultimately built to convey Sacramento River water south *through* the Delta channels utilized large pumping plants near its southern margins, the suction from increased pumping rates affected the velocity of flow and even, at times, the direction of flow through some of the Delta channels. Therefore, how to balance increased demand for diversions elsewhere against the fishery and other ecological values of the Delta became an inherent and ongoing challenge. (See chapter 11 for an excellent discussion of possible resolutions to the problems of the Delta.)

These effects on the natural flows in the Central Valley rivers and the Delta channels are the result of not just one, but two large-scale water development projects, each pumping water from the southern Delta into its own system of canals for conducting water farther south—the federal Central Valley Project (CVP), commenced after 1937 authorizing legislation, and a somewhat parallel state project, the State Water Project (SWP), initiated after voters approved bonds for its construction in 1960. These dual projects make the state unique in yet another way. In fact, the SWP taken by itself is noteworthy: Davis observes that "as a rule, state agencies do not engage in the production and marketing of water services. The major exception is in California where there is a large-scale water development program."[9]

The upshot of both federal and state projects means that large portions of the state's rivers and farmland are managed under different legislative mandates and regulations. The various points of divergence and convergence of these two public projects—whether in terms of their physical facilities, water rights, water contracts, or applicable state and federal law and regulation—produce considerable tensions, as well as some interesting contrasts.

Perhaps the principal focus of this entire volume is how market forces have arisen to reallocate water in the face of changing demands. This issue is of paramount interest in the case of California, where water problems are so critical to the economy of the state. The variety of physical and institutional conditions described previously is at the core of the development of trades or exchanges of water in California. These exchanges include the transfer of full ownership of appropriative rights; trades of water deliveries received under contract with the CVP, the SWP, or a water district; and market-like innovations involving riparian uses, despite such rights remaining associated with their original riparian lands. The concluding section of this chapter includes some recommendations for change in administering riparian water rights, based in part on general recommendations extending as far back as the 1973 National Water Commission reports, produced more than thirty-five years ago.

Some History of the Rise of Market Transfers of Water in the West in General

The increased use of market transfers of water as a way of promoting efficient use of this resource in the western United States was one of those ideas that although it had been around for some time and been discussed in "academic" circles to some extent had not widely entered the consciousness of water managers before the 1980s. In the late 1960s, Gardner and Fullerton had shown how actual market trades of water among irrigation companies in central Utah had approximately doubled the value of water.[10] The most important reason was that only two of four irrigation companies had ownership of water storage facilities, and the market effectively made these facilities available to all four, thus giving all access to highly valued late-season water.

By the mid-1980s, however, discussions of markets appeared to have sprung nearly full-blown from almost every corner and discipline—economic, legal, and institutional. This was due to several factors—the increased competition for water generally in the western United States, the fact that the most promising locations for new storage had been utilized, increasing publication of the negative impacts of large storage structures on everything from normal migration of anadromous fish to reduced habitat in wetlands, and, especially in the case of federally supplied irrigation water, tighter federal budgets and greater scrutiny of federal subsidies. Within a few years, several of the more abstract treatments of the subject were translated into descriptions of the details of a variety of past market or market-like transactions, detailed examinations of state law with regard to water transfers, and a detailed review of federal policies and law.[11] Not surprisingly, there was considerable overlap in the conducting and findings of these studies—indeed, economists and lawyers collaborated to work on common problems and federal and state workers joined efforts to solve water problems. In turn, researchers and agency staff were given more time and resources to research more fully the specifics of how existing federal and state law and policy would affect water transfers and to make recommendations for change. Indeed, some periodicals arose that were devoted almost exclusively to the subjects of water markets and water transfers.

Although this chapter makes no attempt to exhaustively review this explosion of publications before, during, and after this period, it does discuss some key building blocks. Before the 1980s, if you were a graduate student in water resources—say engineering or applied economics—it would be unlikely that market trades would have been prominent in your courses or perhaps even mentioned in your textbooks. Scholars in institutions of higher learning were applying the techniques of scientific management in great detail to the subject of water resources, mostly in the elaboration of benefit-cost analysis and the application of systems-analysis techniques, particularly where multiple reservoir systems were involved. As one example, the *Economics of Water Resources Planning*, by L. Douglas James and Robert R. Lee (1970), discusses several benefit categories of multipurpose water projects, such as water supply, hydropower, flood control, recreation, and fish and wildlife enhancement, as well as intangible values, incremental cost, planning horizons, present worth of costs and benefits, price elasticity of demand for water, and charging for project outputs. Chapter Seven in that book on "Institutional Framework," however, does not even mention market transfers of water. Although it contains detailed definitions of riparian and appropriative water rights, for the most part these are treated as "constraints," not as background for discussing the buying and selling of water rights and certainly not as instruments of policy that can be modified or fine-tuned to lower the transactions costs of market transfers of water. Rather, the forefront in the discipline of economics applied to water resources was scrutiny of whether a benefit-cost study treated both costs and benefits correctly, whether all alternative plans for a project had been given a careful and thoughtful treatment, and whether the externalities associated with the alternatives had been considered. This is not to say that the subject of water markets and the adaptability of water law to facilitate markets had not received any academic or scholarly attention (as discussed more fully later), but merely that these topics had not entered the mainstream of graduate school training or the parlance of water district managers.

One of the first entities to give full treatment to water market transfers and to achieve wide recognition were the conservative think tanks and university centers, as represented by Anderson from the Political Economy Research Center and Montana State University with the clever title *Water Crisis: Ending the Policy Drought*, followed by *Water Rights*, both dealing with water markets.[12] Also in 1983, Gardner laid out the theoretical rationale for market transfers of water, discussed some examples of operating markets for water, and listed some of the legal and institutional impediments to market formation that were still prevalent in the West.[13] Shortly thereafter, in 1985, "Voluntary Transfers of Water in the West" was published as a chapter in the U.S. Geological Survey's *National Water Summary*.[14] The writing and publication of that chapter was undertaken at the impetus of Dr. Herbert Fullerton, a Utah State University economist working at the time on the staff of Assistant Secretary for Land and Water Resources, Garrey Carruthers, a political appointee (and PhD economist) in the Department of the Interior, and Dr. Robert K. Davis, Director of the Economics Staff of the Office of Policy Analysis at Interior, who also had a long history of scholarship in water resources.[15] The principal insight of this work was that a careful treatment of a limited number of past water transfers and market-like trades might lay the groundwork for more acceptance of this "new" management option. Not surprisingly, this attention to the topic occurred during Ronald Reagan's first administration, which was more supportive of market principles than previous administrations. Concurrently, as noted later, the Environmental Defense Fund, an environmental and conservation organization, had also begun to champion the application of market principles to solving environmental problems at lower cost.

Resources for the Future (RFF), a think-tank that played a pioneering role in resource economics, was also a pioneer in water markets. Kenneth Frederick, for example, produced an edited volume titled *Scarce Water and Institutional Change* in 1986. Authors of two chapters in this volume, Wahl and Shabman, contributed case studies in which Frederick highlighted the need for effective water markets and more secure water rights (concerns that remain today).

Water attorneys who happened to be in the right place and close to one facet or another of policymaking for water resources had the same insights. Under the auspices of the Western Governor's Association (WGA), attorney Bruce Driver spearheaded a report issued in 1986, *Western Water: Tuning the System,* which was submitted to the WGA by a Water Efficiency Task Force.[16] The report focused on water efficiency, especially through conservation, salvage, and transfers. This was followed by a second report, published in 1987, *Water Efficiency: Opportunities for Action,*[17] also managed by Driver, but with even more direct involvement of the governors, their representatives, and a wider circle of major participants in western water use and development. This report garnered considerable attention as it was transmitted to the governors from WGA's Water Efficiency Working Group, which included not only three governor's representatives, but also three members of the Western States Water Council and three high-ranking officials in the U.S. Department of the Interior. Like many government reports, and in this case by design, the report did not list the names of the some of the staff authors of its various sections or even the staff manager, Bruce Driver.

A graduate of the University of Colorado School of Law, Stephen J. Shupe, understood how important market transfers of water might be in the West and seized the opportunity to organize some two-day conferences under the auspices of the University of Denver School of Law: "Water Marketing 1987: Profits, Problems, and Policies in the Western States" and "Water Marketing 1988: The Move to Innovation." A wide variety of scholars as well as practitioners, such as water district managers and staff, were invited to these conferences.[18]

The WGA reports mentioned previously led to almost immediate results, at least by bureaucratic speed limits. On December 16, 1988, the Department of the Interior issued a two-page set of "Principles Governing Voluntary Water Transactions That Involve or Affect Facilities Owned or Operated by the Department of the Interior."[19] The one-page preamble makes clear that the principles were issued in direct response to a July 1987 resolution of the WGA (which in turn grew out of the WGA report mentioned previously). The preamble references several types of transactions that had become increasingly common in the western states, such as "direct sale of water rights; lease of water rights; dry-year options on water rights; sale of lands associated with water rights; and conservation investments with subsequent assignment of conserved water." The stance taken in the "Principles" is that the federal government would utilize existing state and federal water law to govern such transactions (avoiding thereby the red flag of new legislation) and would facilitate transfers involving federal facilities, water rights, or contracts, but would not generally initiate or propose a water transfer "except when it is part of an Indian water rights settlement, a solution to a water rights controversy, or when it may provide a dependable water supply the provision of which would otherwise involve the expenditure of Federal funds." Note that this statement if taken seriously fills in the gap, discussed later, between the 1973 National Water Commission recommendations and the federal government's procedures for benefit-cost analysis as part of water project planning.[20] The "Principles Governing Voluntary Water Transactions" were supplemented by a somewhat more detailed, seven-page "Criteria and Guidance," issued at the same time.[21] These documents can be set in the larger context of efforts within the Interior Department to reorient parts of the traditional Bureau of Reclamation mission, as explained in a twenty-page report (*Assessment '87… A New Direction for the Bureau of Reclamation*) issued in the fall of 1987 by assistant secretary for Water and Science, James Zigler.[22]

The Natural Resources Law Center at the University of Colorado produced a number of research reports related to water transfers during this same period.[23] The center benefited from the able leadership of Lawrence MacDonnell who had a background in both law and economics and who had interaction with other law professors with an interest in natural resources and public policy, such as David H. Getches and Charles Wilkinson. MacDonnell also invited other scholars and practitioners to the center's annual June water conferences that were part of its continuing legal education program (and which attracted participants from throughout the west with a wide variety of backgrounds). The center also had close proximity to the offices of the WGA in Denver and its Scholar in Residence, Bruce Driver.

At the federal level, the use of markets and market incentives to assist in addressing environmental problems got a tremendous endorsement and forward momentum with the publication and distribution of *Project 88— Harnessing Market Forces for the Environment: Initiatives for the New President*, a public policy study sponsored by Sen. Timothy E. Wirth, (D-Colorado) and Sen. John Heinz (R-Pennsylvania).[24] The chapter on federal water policy noted that "federal water development policy originated in the last century to serve the goal of westward expansion and frontier development,"[25] but that the Bureau of Reclamation and the U.S. Army Corps of Engineers were beginning "a transition to new missions, responsibilities, and outlooks," and offered that "water markets can facilitate the provision of adequate supplies at the least overall cost."[26] Recommendation 20 is to "remove barriers to water markets," so as to create "economic incentives for water conservation," and notes that "when farmers have a financial stake in conserving water, when urban needs are met without shrinking agriculture, and without building new dams and reservoirs, environmental protection gains."[27] This report was reinforced by *Project 88—Round II* prepared under this same sponsorship. Among other more specific recommendations, this *Project 88* called for the U.S. Department of the Interior to issue a "generic policy statement affirming the transferability of contractual rights to reclamation water supplies,"[28] which the Bureau of Reclamation was already in the process of doing.

The Office of Policy Analysis at Interior granted Richard Wahl part of one year's leave from the department to locate at RFF, a think tank in Washington, DC, so that he might synthesize some of his work on various interrelated water issues. He first produced a Working Paper, "Promoting Increased Efficiency of Federal Water Use Through Voluntary Water Transfers."[29] This was followed by publication in 1989 of *Markets for Federal Water: Subsidies, Property Rights, and the Bureau of Reclamation*, with separate chapters treating the early history of the Bureau of Reclamation, water subsidies for irrigation, construction costs on federal projects, acreage limitations, and laws and agency practices which related to the transferability of water. The second part of Wahl's book deals with the potential applicability of market principles to various water projects and issues facing the department—water pricing within the large CVP in California, salinity in the Colorado Basin, and water efficiency within the Central Arizona Project, a chapter largely drafted by Robert Johnson, an economist who later became a regional director and a commissioner of the Bureau of Reclamation. The principal thesis of this book was that not only could water transfers be applied to the underlying water rights for reclamation projects, usually held by water districts or state or federal agencies, but also to the contractual rights of individual districts within large projects (or even individual irrigators).

But this flurry of activity in the 1980s was not the first time that legal and economic scholars had delved substantially into the subject of market transfers of water. Even though he did not write directly on the subject, as in so many areas of natural resources economics, Allen Kneese of RFF had been there first. Kneese is thanked in the acknowledgment section of the Hartman and Seastone book, published by RFF in 1970, as were John Krutilla, Irving Fox, and Charles Howe, and this introductory material notes that "the original conception of the[ir] study was developed within the staff of RFF and crystallized in correspondence with the authors."[30] Some of the structure of studies done in the 1980s followed this 1970 RFF book, even though some of those authors may not have read the RFF book nor referenced it. The Hartman and Seastone book, in addition to a general discussion of the benefits of transfers and the water laws that affect transfers, provides some substantial details on past or then-existing locations in which transfers were common, including the Northern Colorado Water Conservancy District, the Southeastern Water Conservancy District in Colorado, and the North Poudre Irrigation Company, a mutual ditch company in Colorado.

Shortly after Hartman and Seastone's book was published, the National Water Commission stated its conclusions regarding water transfers in no uncertain terms: "Allowing the transfer of water rights offers promise of promoting more efficient use of water, particularly in the West," and "immutably fixing allocations of water in a rapidly changing world is almost guaranteed to make those allocations inconsistent with future needs."[31]

The commission went on to present a conclusion directly related to the construction of new reservoirs: "Each proposal for a new water supply project should contain, among other information, a report on the possibility of transfer of water rights as an alternative to construction of the new project."[32]

Still, the *Principles and Guidelines*, the federal government's own manual for evaluating new projects, fails to require a water purchase option or other market variants in its list of alternative to be evaluated.[33] This is more than a little strange in light of the fact that the staff work on this manual was done by an interagency team which included three PhD economists—G. Edward Dickey of the Office of the Assistant Secretary of the Army for Civil Works and Richard Wahl of the Economics Staff in the Office of Policy Analysis from Interior, assisted by Robert K. Davis in Interior's Office of Policy Analysis. One might logically have expected to find the trading of water rights mentioned in one of several places in the *Principles and Guidelines*: the alternative plans (alternatives to the proposed project, Section 1.3.5) or perhaps in costing an alternative (the cost of purchase of water rights or contractual deliveries). But inexplicably Section 1.3.5 contains only a general admonition to be sure that "all reasonable alternatives are evaluated," and the cost section deals exclusively with costing the materials and resources used by the project.[34] In these omissions, the *Principles and Guidelines*, not surprisingly, followed the general content of the graduate level water resources textbooks and training of the time, discussed previously.

The Rise of Market Transfers of Water—California

The rise of market transfers of water in California is perhaps best understood as the struggle between (1) traditional water interests who understandably wanted to protect the water rights that they had established many decades earlier and which they viewed as essential to their commercial success, and (2) innovators in the state who viewed water allocation as extremely inefficient and which could be markedly improved by market transfers from lower-valued to higher-valued uses. The latter group included academic economists who were making the case for water markets in the early 1980s.[35] Also prominent was the Environmental Defense Fund (EDF) which was later to champion market principles for environmental purposes at the national level in *Project 88* and *Project 88 Round II*, members of the California Assembly who represented urban interests and saw the need for additional water, and a few senior staff advisors working either for government agencies, such as the California Department of Water Resources (DWR), or for major water purveyors, such as the Metropolitan Water District of Southern California. But aside from the case made for markets by economists on grounds of economic efficiency, most of the pressure for stretching water supplies came not from market transfers but from conservation resulting from government regulation and the actions of two of the largest water districts in the state.

In 1980, the Imperial Irrigation District (IID) located at the border with Mexico in Southern California, and which has a large entitlement to import water from the Colorado River via the All-America Canal, was formally accused of water waste and unreasonable use by one of its own members (Elmore).[36] This led the state DWR in 1981 to publish a report of findings detailing what conservation measures could be undertaken to prevent waste along with an estimate of the quantities of water savings and cost per acre-foot (AF) for each measure. In 1983, the U.S. Bureau of Reclamation published a report with similar findings. Then, in 1994, the State Water Resources Control Board rendered its decision on Elmore's complaint, finding IID's use of water under the law "unreasonable," but not "wasteful." The board required the district to prepare a conservation plan that would include repairing defective tailwater recovery structures and constructing regulatory reservoirs for water deliveries in the district. All this activity set the stage for the Metropolitan Water District of Southern California to offer to fund the cost of some of the conservation investments in exchange for receiving the conserved water. As indicated previously, economists within the Environmental Defense Fund also began writing about such trading possibilities.[37]

Traditionally, water interests had viewed, probably correctly, the appropriative doctrine of water rights as fundamentally "use it or lose it."[38] One of the foundations of prior-appropriation law is that if the right holder failed to put the water to beneficial use over a number of years, the right would be subject to challenge, and the water could be forfeited and made available for reappropriation. Also, the traditional wisdom was that if the water were conserved in order to sell the conserved fraction, the right could be forfeited since clearly the saved amount was no longer being put to beneficial use by the right holder. In short, the act of sale itself demonstrated that some portion of the original right provided more water than the original water user needed. However, people who thought carefully about western water institutions realized that these interpretations of western water law left no incentive for conservation and that these views were running head on into an era of increased population; increasing demand for water for municipal, agricultural, and environmental purposes; and more limited opportunities for the traditional solution of constructing new storage and delivery facilities.

Two California assemblymen, Katz and Bates, set out to remedy these problems by proposing an amendment to the California Water Code. The legislature followed by addressing water user concerns through several additional changes in the state's water law that were to be made over a number of years. As a result of these efforts, the California water code now has several provisions related to both long-term water transfers and temporary transfers, the latter defined as being of duration of one year or less. These provisions are discussed in the following paragraphs, along with their dates of passage.

The California Water Code clearly states that for all appropriative water rights, users may seek a (permanent) change in the point of diversion, place of use, or purpose of use.[39] The code allows an entire water right to be sold for use elsewhere or for a different purpose and also, in the case of a conservation practice, the sale of only the conserved portion. The quantity transferable is based on consumptive use, and any change in the three parameters listed above must not injure other water users (as is standard throughout the West). A separate and somewhat repetitive portion of the code, sections 1735 and 1737, enacted in 1991, provides for "long-term transfers," (those for any period longer than one year) with additional provisions: the State Department of Fish and Game is allowed to review the transfer and participate in the required public hearing before the State Water Resources Control Board. The board must find, among other things, that the transfer "would not unreasonably affect fish, wildlife, or other instream beneficial uses of the water." At the end of the transfer period, the water reverts to its original purpose and place of use. Similar provisions apply to "temporary transfers,"[40] which have a duration of not more than one year and have the additional condition that the transfer "would not unreasonably affect fish, wildlife, or other instream beneficial uses." Temporary transfers (such as during a drought) can be implemented under an expedited procedure.

But as alluded to earlier in this chapter, because of the large water projects constructed by government agencies, the CVP and SWP, and because of large irrigation districts that supply water, many individual users in California do not themselves own a water right but have a right to use water under a contract with a supply agency. The question is: Do those with contracts for water have the right to transfer it? In *Markets for Federal Water*, Wahl posited that there was no apparent prohibition in federal law against such transfers on reclamation projects and, in fact, such transfers would be advantageous. An even more extensive answer to the transfer question is given in a study that focused not only on California state law, but on how that law interacts with federal law in relation to water transfers.[41] This study concludes that (1) transfers among CVP users within the same service area (within a single season, but from one location to another) were commonplace and found examples of transfers between districts, (2) Section 8 of the 1902 Reclamation Act basically places water on federal projects under state law, and (3) in California, water law was moving to facilitate transfers and addressed this topic directly. In a series of 1992 amendments, Section 1745 (Water Supplier Contracts), subsections 1745.02–1745.10, the legislature provides that the supplier (district) can enter into a contract with its members to "reduce or eliminate for a specified period of time their use of water" and that the supplier "may contract with a state drought water bank or with any other state or local water supplier or user inside or *outside* [emphasis added] the service area" of the water supplier for the transferred water so long as other district members are not injured. For a district to be able to contract with entities outside its own service area was, to be sure, a giant step toward freer transfers. These subsections go on to specify that reductions in use may be due to conservation, use of an alternate water supply, and land fallowing; that the water to be transferred does *not* have to be surplus to the needs of other water users in the district's service area; that "no transfer of water pursuant to this article or any other provision of law shall cause a forfeiture, diminution, or impairment of any water rights;" and that "a transfer [that is consistent with these provisions of California water law] is deemed to be beneficial use by the transferor." Section 1745.09 makes clear, moreover, that these measures do not alter the underlying water rights of the district: they do not, for example, reduce the water rights of the district and confer them to the transferring party.

One additional item addressed by amendments to the water code relates to the central role played by the CVP and the SWP canals in delivering water to many areas of the state. Must those projects make available any surplus capacity in their conveyance facilities for proposed water transfers? This question is answered in the affirmative by sections 1810–1812 (enacted in 1986) providing that (1) the transferring party pay reasonable costs for use of the facilities, (2) there is no adverse impact on the use of the facility by other entities with rights to it, and (3) there are no adverse impacts on water quality of other users of the facility.

In summary, little by little, the attention that had been devoted to the potential beneficial effects of water transfers in California gained wider circulation for and acceptance of the concept. As elsewhere in the West, the acceptance of water transfers was pushed forward by a number of water conferences held in the state.

Drought as a Catalyst for Change

It is a useful maxim for economists and others involved in policy analysis to remember that crises can be catalysts for change—and drought is often such a crisis.[42] Hence, in California, a period of major drought in the late 1980s and 1990s served the purpose of focusing attention on market transfers of water to ameliorate water shortages. A drought water bank was established under which state agencies were organized to process a large number of transfers within a short period of time. This program is examined in detail in a California DWR report and cogently summarized by the manager of the drought water bank, Steve Macaulay.

> Although California has successfully weathered 6 years of drought (beginning in 1987), it has not been without sacrifice to all segments of the water community. Many urban areas have imposed mandatory water rationing programs, and water rates have gone up by more than 40 percent throughout much of the state, State Water Project agricultural deliveries dropped to an unprecedented *zero* in 1991 and many federal Central Valley Project users were limited to a 25-percent supply in 1991 and 1992. The environment has suffered, particularly California's anadromous fisheries. Waterfowl habitat has also been greatly diminished by low rainfall and reduced water supplies.
>
> Water transfers have come into their own during this drought. A number of successful [individually negotiated] transfers came about in the early part of the drought, although individual transactions took several months to coordinate. [In order to respond more quickly and on a larger scale,] Governor Wilson formed the 1991 Drought Water Bank as a new institution to respond to the water supply crisis. Through the cooperation of about 350 sellers and 20 buyers, the Water Bank was able to meet eventual critical demands of 400,000 acre-feet while carrying another 265,000 acre-feet for the State Water Project into the next year. The Drought Water Bank continued in 1992 and successfully met the full critical water demands of more than 150,000 acre-feet.[43]

Table 13.1 shows summary statistics for the trades consummated under the water bank by source, the Delta "carriage water" requirements, and the destinations of the water from the bank. In 1991, land fallowing was the most productive water source, whereas in 1992, there was no land fallowing and most of the water was acquired from groundwater substitution (under which growers utilized more of the groundwater to which they had access, while selling more of their surface water supplies). The third source was direct purchase of stored water. "Carriage water" is subtracted from the total of those sources—the extra amount of outflow through the Delta which transferees were required to provide. This "water tax" was intended to limit adverse impacts on water quality in the Delta and to prevent any reverse stream flow in the Delta (carriage water amounts are set by state administrative processes independent of the water bank). The final section of the table shows that

Table 13.1 Trades of the 1991 and 1992 drought water banks

	1991 Quantities (1,000s AF)	1992 Quantities (1,000s AF)
Water source		
Land fallowing	420	0
Ground water substitution	258	150
Surface water purchased	142	35
Total water purchased	820	185
Extra water required at Delta	−165	−31
Net water available	655	154
Water destinations		
Urban	307	39
Agricultural	83	95
Wildlife	0	20
Carryover storage	265	0
Total of destinations	655	154

Source: California Department of Water Resources (DWR), *State Drought Water Bank*, 1993, Table 1–1, p. 7.

urban entities accounted for the largest share of purchases in 1991, but not in 1992, when agricultural purchases predominated.

The Central Valley Project Improvement Act

In California, various interests advocating pricing reform, greater utilization of markets, and more water for environmental purposes were successful in getting such measures forged into law within the fiery furnace of federal legislation. The Central Valley Project Improvement Act (CVPIA) was the culmination of these efforts. The intensity of the debate and the focus on details in the wording of the act's numerous interlocking provisions are reflected in the fact that workers in the Interior Department could not get a final copy of the bill *for many days after the bill was voted on and passed* because Congressional staff were still reconciling the various amendments and working out other details. Whatever the pangs of its birth, this legislation, along with the administration of the Endangered Species Act (ESA), is likely to be a central feature of water management in California for decades to come, especially for those districts and state agencies that must deal with water uses within the Delta, such as (1) agriculture on the Delta islands, (2) the suitability of the Delta's aquatic habitat for certain water species, as well as fish migration through the Delta, or (3) water transported south of the

Delta.[44] (Chapter 11 contains a discussion of political and economic issues relating to the Delta.)

The stated purposes of the CVPIA (Section 3402) pertain mostly to protecting fish and wildlife and their associated habitats. The CVPIA amends the 1937 authorizing legislation of the CVP to include fish and wildlife "mitigation, protection, and restoration." The act, however, also addresses water use more generally and has as one purpose to increase water-related benefits of the project to the state "through the expanded use of voluntary water transfers and improved water conservation." To this end, Section 3406 specifies that any individual or district that receives water under a CVP contract is "authorized to transfer all or a portion of the water subject to such contract to any other California water user or state or federal agency, Indian tribe, or nonprofit organization," thereby settling any remaining doubt about the legal foundations under federal law to transfer CVP project water not only to other CVP contractors but to users outside the CVP. If water is transferred outside the CVP for irrigation, however, the costs to be paid to the federal government are set at the greater of the CVP cost-of-service rate (which could be higher than the existing contract rate) or the Reclamation Reform Act's "full cost" rate.[45] Paralleling another provision of state law, Section 3406 (a)(1)(E) of the CVPIA states that transfers of CVP water "shall be deemed a beneficial use of water by the transferor for the purposes of section 8 of the Act of June 17, 1902," the original legislation for the federal Reclamation program, which requires that water be put to beneficial use. And somewhat similar to the provisions of current California law protecting fish and wildlife from adverse affects of water transfers, subsections 3405(a)(1) subsections (H) and (L) limit the adverse effects of transfers on fish and wildlife uses supplied by CVP contract.

The CVPIA contains about twenty-five pages and is a set of densely packed and interwoven provisions, including (1) a reallocation of 800,000 AF of project water to fish and wildlife purposes; (2) surcharges on water rates, which can be used for, among other things, provision of water for fish and wildlife purposes; and (3) planning for an increase in project water yield for the future. This increase in yield is to be a search for a "least-cost plan" and is to include, among other options, "transfers, purchase of water, purchase and idling of agricultural land; and direct purchase of water rights" (Section 3408(g)), thereby requiring a more complete examination of options than provided for in the federal *Principles and Guidelines* for benefit-cost analysis of federal water projects[46] and that would be consistent with the Water Transfer Principles and Guidelines of the Interior Department adopted in 1988.

CALFED

The acronym is witness to the obvious—federal-state cooperation is necessary to solve Delta water-quality problems, given that both federal and state projects transport large quantities of water through the Delta from the Sacramento–San Joaquin Rivers to major pumping plants on the south margins of the Delta. Both federal legislation (such as the ESA and the CVPIA) and state legislation and regulation affect water in the Delta, and both federal and state contractual rights to water are involved in Delta transport as well as major holdings of riparian rights within the Delta itself. The CALFED Bay-Delta Program was initiated in 1995 by Governor Pete Wilson and the Clinton Administration. The program draws largely from existing staff of the agencies involved in federal and state water management and the protection of fish and wildlife, with the staff managed by a CALFED program director and with a steering committee of agency managers with decision-making capability. The committee meets frequently to consider findings and to guide future work of the staff. CALFED identified its scope not just as the formal Delta, but the entire drainage area of the Central Valley. Among the six groupings of CALFED studies in 1999 were water use efficiency and water transfers.[47]

Progress Toward Recognizing Water Markets

To show how far things have come since the days when one feared that even mentioning "water markets" or "water transfers" in California might threaten the viability of water district managers and other water interests, a Google search of "California DWR water transfers" now produces the top entry "Water Transfer Office," with a lead sentence "The U.S. Bureau of Reclamation, the Department of Water Resources and the State Water Resources Control Board are implementing the CALFED Water Transfer Program." The same page points to five "papers" on water transfers. Most are outlines of rules and procedures utilized by the agencies that manage transfers within the state, such as the offices within the Department of Water Resources that deal with transfers and including the quasi-judicial arm managing water rights, the State Water Resources Control Board. One paper describes past transfers in the state. A click beyond this initial page yields the agency application forms for transfers, as well as the name, address, and phone number for the Water Transfer Coordinator. Hence, initiating water transfers is just a phone call or a few computer clicks away: in California, water transfers have entered the mainstream.

Permits for Riparian Rights

California has a wide range of water resources, water storage, transfer facilities, and water-related ecological resources. Water from streams in the Sierra Nevada Mountains has been stored in mountain reservoirs and conducted both to farmland in the Central Valley below and, in some cases, transported over long distances to the population centers of San Francisco and Los Angeles. (See chapter 12 in this book for a discussion of these issues.) The state has substantial fisheries and estuaries that depend on flows of fresh water. The most prominent is the Delta which has been discussed previously. This estuary has suffered as diversions of fresh water have increased—north of the Delta, south of the Delta, and through the Delta.

Complicating matters, different water users within the state have adopted different traditions of water law—riparian rights that stay fixed to the land next to a stream and appropriative rights that allow water to be transported far from original sources. This complex legal framework, coupled with increased demands and major facilities to transport water, has presented and will continue to present challenges unique to this state. In fact, as one might expect, the state's history is replete with conflicts over these two formulations of water law (riparian and appropriative) as well as between state law and federal law and regulation—the advocates of each trying to secure their rights to more water and to receiving water at the lowest cost. Even though the history of California water is filled with numerous legal challenges, the state supreme court has upheld riparian rights as primary. From time to time, legislators have reshaped both riparian and appropriative rights to some degree. And in the area of voluntary water transfers and water marketing, the legislature passed a number of bills to protect existing water rights holders who desired to transfer water or to conserve water and transfer the amount conserved. Federal legislation specific to California, such as the CVPIA discussed above, has facilitated transfers, including purchases for fish and wildlife.

Yet, for all this innovation, there is one area that begs for change. The National Water Commission suggested reform of riparian rights (aimed nationally and not specific to any one state) more than thirty-five years ago: "The present riparian law applied in most Midwestern and Eastern States provides an inadequate foundation on which to plan, construct, and operate water resources projects."[48] The commission's summary report goes on to recommend that riparian rights be converted into a permit system, under which permits would be akin to appropriative rights.[49]

The words of the commission's background reports dealing with water transfers and riparian rights are also strong and unambiguous. The summary section of *Legal Study Number 2, Riparian Water Law: A Functional Analysis* states that "the riparian system stands *indicted* [emphasis added] on several counts"[50] and reiterates a conclusion of *Legal Study Number 1* that typically a riparian system of state law "gives water users no legal certainty as to future supply (and) it also seems ill-adapted to transfers since there are no definite property rights to be sold."[51]

In California, riparian rights have undergone some transformations as the state has developed. For one, water under such rights must now be put to "beneficial use"—always a requirement under the prior-appropriation doctrine. Second, with the advent of the CVP and the SWP, many early water rights, both appropriative and riparian, were exchanged in some form for deliveries of defined quantities of project water. The process of determining precisely what quantities of water could reasonably be used under early rights was difficult and time-consuming.

With respect to market transfers of riparian rights, California has made one significant innovation: payment to riparian holders to forgo their use of water in order to enhance instream flows is allowed. This is particularly important in increasing flows through the Delta. But many of the several eastern states, where the riparian doctrine was the sole basis for water rights, have moved even farther in this direction than has California (see chapter 2). As water conflicts have become more intense, most of these states have shifted to a permit system that has more in common with prior appropriation than with traditional riparian systems. The most important difference is that water shortages are typically handled through a type of forced sharing rather than priorities established in prior appropriation.

From the standpoint of administration, California should be able to implement a system of permits for riparian rights. Many records are available that could facilitate such a conversion. For example, the DWR regularly overflies state agricultural lands to record acreages irrigated and keeps records on the types of crops grown by acreage. Existing data on consumptive water use by various crops could then be used to estimate water used on riparian land parcels. These estimates could be checked against water records where such records are available and reconciled with estimates of diversions and return flows.

Clearly, many technical details would have to be worked out. But a permit system would be a major step forward toward more general transfers of riparian rights to the benefit of both sellers and buyers and more effective use of water in the state. In summary, given California's increasing experience with evaluating and processing transfers of appropriative water rights, state and federal agencies should be well-equipped to deal with the quantification of riparian rights and the evaluation of voluntary transfer proposals involving such rights.

Conclusions

Two approaches are basic to thinking about existing water problems and those that may emerge in the future. The first is to study the existing and proposed physical structures necessary to store and convey water, and there are many options. These studies require engineering, hydrological, and planning analyses. The physical structures must be juxtaposed to future demands for water, projections of which may or may not prove to be accurate. Economics and benefit-cost analysis clearly have a major role to play in evaluating the options presented in such studies. With such an interconnected system as California has in place (privately developed and local water sources set along side two enormous public projects, the CVP and SWP) in addition to its highly complex economy, the state faces an enormous water infrastructure problem.

Especially vexing are the problems tied to the hydrology and environment of the Delta. Complex physical flow models, systems analyses, and economic models with regional demands and transportation costs built in will have an essential role to play. Fortunately, all have been employed extensively already.

A second approach, not exclusive of the first, is to evaluate if the existing water institutions align the incentives necessary to produce efficient outcomes. Does the price of water to final users accurately reflect its value in other uses, including instream flows? If not, the growers and districts that supply and apply water cannot be efficient in the sense that economic output is maximized. Unless prices represent the opportunity costs in the use of water, the decision to use or to market water supplies cannot hope to produce an efficient allocation between the two. In addition, market forces must be allowed to express themselves so that the price (or opportunity cost) can change as demand changes. Economists argue that if you can get the incentives correct, then the choices about the best future options will be economically efficient. And if governments can structure markets well, voluntary transactions will prove to be efficient in meeting future demand through trading of existing supplies. Market transactions can also provide accurate price signals for the value of water from new facilities—a price that might well vary from one location to another, particularly in a state as large as California where water transportation costs are not trivial and where a system of charges by both the SWP and CVP already heavily influence transportation rates for water.

If projections of future demand by government agencies are not accurate, then prices set in the marketplace can signal needed corrections. Unless incentives are correctly aligned, the value of water provided by additional structures cannot be accurately evaluated and water will not be efficiently produced and used.

The above discussion is not meant to imply that no more large dams should be built in California (see the discussion in chapter 1). For example, one type of project that repeatedly surfaces in studies of how best to meet California future water demands, including meeting environmental constraints, such as those stemming from the ESA, is the addition of another large storage facility south of the Delta, similar in function to the existing San Luis Reservoir. Such a facility would allow more water to be moved through the Delta when it is least detrimental to fish populations and then stored until the time when it is most needed by districts farther south. The discussion here is meant, however, to caution that other alternatives, including market incentives and buying water for environmental purposes, need to be carefully examined first.

Before new large physical structures are built, instituting broader water markets would demonstrate how much additional water might be obtainable through more efficient use, both in cities and agricultural areas. And if structured correctly, water markets could demonstrate how governments and other organizations can continue to obtain water for wild-life refuges and other environmental purposes. These markets will further signal how and when individual farming operations or irrigation districts can profitably sell part of their water as they voluntarily seek out and implement the most efficient and cost-effective water conservation measures.

Notes

1. L. M. Hartman and Don Seastone, *Water Transfers: Economic Efficiency and Alternative Institutions* (Baltimore, MD: Johns Hopkins Press, 1970), chap. V. Hartman and Seastone describe transactions in other districts as well.
2. Lawrence J. MacDonnell, *The Water Transfer Process as a Management Option for Meeting Changing Water Demands* (Boulder, CO: University of Colorado School of Law, 1990), Table 7, compiled from USGS data.
3. California Department of Water Resources (DWR), *Bulletin 132-96: Management of the California State Water Project* (Sacramento, CA: DWR, 1997), xix.
4. CA DWR, *State Drought Water Bank* (Sacramento, CA: DWR, 1993), 16.
5. William L. Kahrl, ed., *The California Water Atlas* (Sacramento, CA: California Assembly Office of Planning and Research and CA DWR, 1978), 47 and 49.
6. For an accessible and more detailed description of riparian water rights, appropriative rights, and water law in general, see David H. Getches, *Water Law in a Nutshell* (St. Paul, MN: West Publishing, 1984).
7. Richard W. Wahl and Robert K. Davis, "Satisfying Southern California's Thirst for Water: Efficient Alternatives," in *Scarce Water and Institutional Change*, ed. Kenneth D. Frederick, (Washington, DC: Resources for the Future, 1986).
8. CA DWR, *Bulletin 132-96*, xxi.
9. Robert K. Davis, *The Range of Choice in Water Management* (Baltimore, MD: Johns Hopkins Press, 1968), 8.
10. B. Delworth Gardner and Herbert H. Fullerton, "Transfer Restrictions and Misallocation of Irrigation Water," *American Journal of Agricultural Economics* 50, no. 3 (August 1969): 556–71.
11. In the 1950s, the land-grant universities of the western region established a committee called the Western Agricultural Economics Resources Council Committee on Economics of Water Resource Development. This committee spearheaded investigations of water transfers and related matters. The committee held annual meetings and published proceedings for over twenty years.
12. Terry L. Anderson, *Water Crisis: Ending the Policy Drought* (Washington, DC: Cato Institute, 1983); Terry L. Anderson, ed., *Water Rights: Scarce Resource Allocation, Bureaucracy, and the Environment* (Cambridge, MA: Ballinger Publishing, 1983).
13. B. Delworth Gardner, "Market Versus Political Allocations of Natural Resources in the 1980's," *Western Journal of Agricultural Economics* 8, no. 2 (December 1983): 215–29.

14. Richard W. Wahl and Frank H. Osterhoudt, "Voluntary Transfers of Water in the West," in *National Water Summary*, U.S. Geological Survey Water Supply Paper 2300 (Washington, DC: U.S. Government Printing Office, 1985).

15. Another economist with promarket credentials, Professor Richard L. Stroup from Montana State University, served as director of the Office of Policy Analysis during this same general time period.

16. Western Governors' Association (WGA), *Western Water: Tuning the System* (Denver, CO: WGA, 1986).

17. WGA, *Water Efficiency: Opportunities for Action System* (Denver, CO: WGA, 1987).

18. Steven J. Shupe, ed., *Water Marketing 1987: Profits, Problems, and Policies in the Western United States* (Denver, CO: University of Denver College of Law, 1987); Steven J. Shupe, ed., *Water Marketing 1988: The Move to Innovation* (Denver, CO: University of Denver College of Law, 1988). One is hard-pressed to find the conference proceedings, even in most university libraries in the West, which is unfortunate given how central they were in gaining wider acceptance of markets by water users.

19. Reproduced in Robert E. Beck, ed., *Waters and Water Rights* (Charlottsville, VA: Michie, 1991), 426–27.

20. U.S. Water Resources Council, *Economic and Environmental Principles and Guidelines for Water and Related Land Resources Implementation Studies* (Washington, DC: U.S. Government Printing Office, 1983).

21. Also reproduced in Beck, *Waters*, 419–25.

22. U.S. Department of the Interior, Bureau of Reclamation (U.S. DOI/BR), *Assessment '87 . . . A New Direction for the Bureau of Reclamation* (Washington, DC: U.S. DOI/BR, 1987).

23. Bonnie G. Colby et al., *Transferring Water Rights in the Western States—A Comparison of Policies and Procedures* (Boulder, CO: Natural Resources Law Center, University of Colorado School of Law, 1989); MacDonnell, *Water Transfer Process*; Lawrence J. MacDonnell, Richard W. Wahl, and Bruce C. Driver, *Facilitating Voluntary Transfers of Bureau of Reclamation–Supplied Water* (Boulder, CO: University of Colorado School of Law, 1991).

24. Eight years earlier a June 13, 1980, memorandum from President Carter heralded an initiative on increasing the efficiency of government services, which included several economic-based incentives, such as marketable rights.

25. WGA, *Project 88—Harnessing Market Forces for the Environment: Initiatives for the New President* (Washington, DC: WGA, 1988), 47, http://www.heinz.org/UserFiles/Library/Project88.PDF.47.

26. WGA, *Project 88*, 48.

27. Ibid., 43.

28. WGA, *Project 88—Round II: Incentives for Action: Designing Market-Based Environmental Strategies*, 171, http://www.hks.harvard.edu/fs/rstavins/Monographs_&_Reports/Project_88-2.pdf.

29. Richard W. Wahl, *Promoting Increased Efficiency of Federal Water Use Through Voluntary Water Transfers*, National Center for Food and Agricultural Policy Discussion Paper Series No. FAP87-02 (Washington, DC: Resources for the Future, 1987).

30. Hartman and Seastone, *Water Transfers*, vii.

31. U.S. National Water Commission, *Summary, Conclusions, and Recommendations* (Washington, DC: U.S. DOI, 1973), 59.

32. U.S. National Water Commission, *Summary*, 60.

33. U.S. Water Resources Council, *Economic and Environmental Principles*.

34. Interestingly, the *P&G* did open the door to evaluating agricultural benefits not by the traditional method of farm budgets, but by using the market value of similar agricultural land (Section 2.3.5(i)).

35. B. Delworth Gardner, "The Untried Market Approach to Water Allocation," in *New Courses for the Colorado River*, eds. Gary D. Weatherford and F. Lee Brown (Albuquerque, NM: University of New Mexico Press, 1983), 155–76; B. Delworth Gardner, "Market Versus Political Allocations of Natural Resources in the 1980's," *Western Journal of Agricultural Economics* 8, no. 2 (December 1983): 215–29.

36. This paragraph summarizes material from Wahl and Davis "Southern California's Thirst," 118–24.

37. Robert N. Stavins and Zach Willey, "Trading Conservation Investments for Water," in *Regional and State Water Resources Planning and Management*, ed. R. J. Charbeneau (Bethesda, MD: American Water Resources Association, 1983), 223–30.

38. Wahl and Davis, "Southern California's Thirst," 128–32; Brian L. Gray, Bruce C. Driver, and Richard W. Wahl, *The Transferability of Water Provided by the State Water Project and the Central Valley Project: A Report to the San Joaquin Valley Drainage Program* (1990) 110–125.

39. California Water Code §§1701–1705, enacted in 1988.

40. California Water Code §§1725–1732.

41. Gray, Driver, and Wahl, *Transferability of Water*.

42. In "Ten Commandments for Policy Economists," political scientist Christopher K. Leman and economist Robert H. Nelson, word their commandment 8 as follows: "Profit from Action-Forcing Events: There is an inertia in bureaucratic behavior that ordinarily tends to prevent significant change. Initiatives usually occur in response to a crisis activated by an external event—a court case, a revenue shortfall, a change in leaders, a media issue, a social movement, and so on. The policy economist must be on the lookout for these action-forcing events and be ready to use them" (*Journal of Policy Analysis and Management* 1, no. 1 (Fall 1981): 190, doi:10.2307/3324112).

43. CA DWR, *State Drought*.

44. Delta problems did not begin with the ESA. A period of below-average rainfall beginning in 1917 resulted in saltwater intrusion into the Delta severe enough to prevent the cities of Antioch and Pittsburgh from utilizing water from the Suisun Bay for drinking water (see Mary Montgomery and Marion Clawson. *History of Legislation and Policy Formation of the Central Valley Project*, (Berkeley, CA: U.S. Department of Agriculture, Bureau of Agricultural Economics Research, 1946).

45. For details on these definitions, see Richard W. Wahl, *Markets for Federal Water: Subsidies, Property Rights, and the Bureau of Reclamation* (Washington, DC: Resources for the Future, 1989), 53–56; and U.S. DOI/BR, *Irrigation Water Rates* (Sacramento, CA: Mid-Pacific Region, 1987)

especially Schedule A-1, "Schedule of CVP Irrigation Contract, O&M, Cost of Service, and Full Cost Rates per Acre-Foot by Contractor."

46.   U.S. Water Resources Council, *Economic and Environmental Principles.*

47.   CALFED, *CALFED Bay-Delta Program: Working Together for a Solution* (Sacramento, CA: DWR, 1999), 12–15.

48.   U.S. National Water Commission, *Summary*, 60.

49.   Ibid.

50.   Clifford Davis, *Riparian Water Law: A Functional Analysis*, Legal Study Number 2, prepared for the National Water Commission (Springfield, VA: National Technical Information Service, 1971), S-1.

51.   Ibid., 39.

About the Authors

The Editors

B. Delworth Gardner, Research Fellow at the Independent Institute, is Professor Emeritus of Economics at Brigham Young University and Professor Emeritus of Agricultural Economics at the University of California-Davis. He received B.S. and M.S. degrees in Agricultural Economics from the University of Wyoming and a PhD in Economics from the University of Chicago. He has held professorial appointments at Colorado State University, Utah State University, University of California-Davis, and Brigham Young University.

Gardner was director of the Giannini Foundation of Agricultural Economics at the University of California from 1976–1984 and was visiting professor, University of California—Berkeley in 1965. He was also visiting scholar at Resources for the Future, Washington, DC in 1966–67, and the Julian Simon Fellow at the Property and Environment Research Center, Bozeman, Montana, in 2002. He is a Fellow of the American Association of Agricultural Economics and served as president of the Western Agricultural Economics Association. He has taught courses and done research abroad in Bolivia, Ecuador, Egypt, India, Iran, and China. He is the author of two books (*Plowing Ground in Washington* and *Regional Growth and Water Resource Development* [coauthored with W. Cris Lewis, Jay C. Anderson, and Herbert H. Fullerton) along with some two hundred professional papers and journal articles in agricultural and resource economics.

Randy T. Simmons, Senior Fellow at the Independent Institute, is Professor of Political Economy in the Department of Economics and Finance at Utah State University where he teaches about politics, law, and economics. He is also a Senior Fellow at the Property and Environment Research Center (PERC) in Bozeman, Montana. He emphasizes the importance of economic reasoning to better understand public policy. The real challenge of the social process, as he sees it, is to design institutions that have outcomes that closely represent the wishes of individuals. His books include the public choice primer *Beyond Politics: The Roots of Government Failure*, *Critical Thinking about Endangered Species* and *Wilderness and Political Ecology*.

The Contributors

Bruce Aylward is a director at Ecosystem Economics LLC, where he provides strategic advice and capacity-building on water rights acquisition for ecosystem purposes to foundation, nonprofit, and agency initiatives in the western United States. From 2002–2007, Bruce led water market and water bank development efforts at the Deschutes River Conservancy in Oregon. During that time, he also served as convening lead author on Freshwater Services for the policy track of the Millennium Ecosystem Assessment and wrote the economics chapter for *FLOWS*, a World Conservation Union (IUCN) guide to environmental flows. Bruce has a bachelor's degree from Stanford and master's and doctorate from Tufts University. He is an adjunct faculty member for Oregon State University's Water Resources Graduate Program and teaches natural resource economics at the OSU Cascades campus in Bend, Oregon.

Todd K. BenDor is an assistant professor of City and Regional Planning at the University of North Carolina at Chapel Hill. Dr. BenDor is an environmental planner with a background in systems modeling and policy analysis. His research and teaching focus on understanding the impacts of urban development and expansion on urban infrastructure, ecological and environmental resources, and environmental-related conflicts. In 2009, he was a GlaxoSmithKline Faculty Fellow at North Carolina State University's Institute for Emerging Issues. He holds a BS from the Worcester Polytechnic Institute, an MS from Washington State University, and a PhD from the University of Illinois at Urbana-Champaign.

Stephen N. Bretsen is the William Volkman Associate Professor of Business and Law at Wheaton College (Illinois). Bretsen received his BA from the College of William & Mary and his JD from the University of Colorado Law School. His journal articles have addressed water rights in the American West.

Martin W. Doyle is a professor of River Science and Policy in the Nicholas School of the Environment at Duke University. He is an environmental hydrologist and geomorphologist, with training in river engineering and earth science. Professor Doyle received his master of Environmental Engineering at the University of Mississippi and his PhD in Geomorphology at Purdue. His research is at the interface of physical science, economics, and policy of environmental management and restoration. He focuses on the use of market mechanisms for environmental restoration and the future of river infrastructure, such as water supply dams and levees, under changing climate and increasing population.

Dr. Doyle has received a Guggenheim Fellowship, a National Science Foundation Early Career Award, a Julian Simon Fellowship, and the Dimitrius M. Chorafas Prize (Switzerland). For his work in bridging environmental science and policy, in 2009, he was named the inaugural Frederick J. Clarke Scholar by the US Army Corps of Engineers. In 2008, Dr. Doyle was named an Aldo Leopold Leadership Fellow by Stanford University, and he received a GlaxoSmithKline Faculty Fellowship for Public Policy from the Institute for Emerging Issues.

Rachael E. Goodhue is professor, Department of Agricultural and Resource Economics, University of California-Davis, and a member of the Giannini Foundation of Agricultural Economics. Her research interests include agricultural and agri-environmental policy, agricultural marketing and contracting, pesticide use and regulation, and property rights and natural resource management. Goodhue earned a BA in Economics from Swarthmore College and a MS and PhD in Agricultural and Resource Economics from the University of California-Berkeley.

Goodhue is a member of Gamma Sigma Delta and Phi Beta Kappa. Awards include Most Downloaded Article, *ARE Update*, Giannini Foundation of Agricultural Economics; Associated Students of the University of California Davis Excellence in Education Award; Verona d'Oenometric Award for the Outstanding Conference Paper; and Best Paper by a Younger Scholar Published in *Review of Industrial Organization*.

Ray Hartwell is a director at Ecosystem Economics LLC, a consulting firm that supports the design and implementation of market-based approaches to environmental management challenges. Ray brings substantial expertise in water rights transactions, conservation finance, ecosystem services markets, and econometric analysis. He also has experience in energy efficiency planning and implementation.

Prior to joining Ecosystem Economics, Ray worked at the Deschutes River Conservancy, Environmental Defense Fund, and Cornerstone Research. In addition, he taught courses in statistics at New York University. Ray holds a BA *summa cum laude* from Williams College and a master's from New York University.

Peter J. Hill is professor Emeritus of Economics at Wheaton College (Illinois) and a Senior Fellow at PERC (Property and Environment Research Center). Hill received his BS from Montana State University and his PhD from the University of Chicago.

Professor Hill has edited several books on environment and resource issues and has coauthored, with Terry Anderson, *The Birth of a Transfer Society* and *The Not So Wild, Wild West: Property Rights on the Frontier*. His journal articles have dealt with the evolution of property rights and the history of water rights in the United States.

Benjamin F. Hobbs earned a PhD (Environmental Systems Engineering) in 1983 from Cornell University. He holds Theodore M. and Kay W. Schad Chair of Environmental Management at the Johns Hopkins University, where he has been in the Department of Geography & Environmental Engineering since 1995. He also holds a joint appointment in the Department of Applied Mathematics & Statistics, and directs the JHU Environment, Energy,

Sustainability & Health Institute. Previously, he was at Brookhaven and Oak Ridge National Laboratories and a member of the Systems Engineering and Civil Engineering faculty at Case Western Reserve University. His research and teaching concerns the application of systems analysis and economics to electric utility regulation, planning, and operations, as well as environmental and water resources systems. Dr. Hobbs has had visiting appointments at the Helsinki University of Technology, University of Washington, Netherlands Energy Research Center, and Cambridge University. He chairs the Market Surveillance Committee of the California Independent System Operator and is a member of the Public Interest Committee of the Gas Technology Institute. Dr. Hobbs is a Fellow of the IEEE and INFORMS.

James L. Huffman is dean emeritus of Lewis & Clark Law School. He holds a BS degree from Montana State University, an MA from the Fletcher School of Law and Diplomacy at Tufts University, and a JD from the University of Chicago Law School. He has taught at Lewis & Clark since 1973 and has had visiting appointments at the University of Oregon, Auckland University (New Zealand), Francisco Marroquin University (Guatemala), and the University of Athens (Greece).

Professor Huffman has been a Bradley Fellow of the Heritage Foundation, and he serves on the boards of the Rocky Mountain Mineral Law Foundation, the Western Resources Legal Center, and the Classroom Law Project. He serves on the Executive Committee of the Environment and Property Rights Practice Group of the Federalist Society and is a member of the Hoover Institution Task Force on Property Rights, Freedom and Prosperity. He was the Republican nominee for United States Senator from Oregon in 2010. Professor Huffman has written over 150 academic articles and chapters as well as dozens of opinion pieces for *The Wall Street Journal*, *The Los Angeles Times*, *The Oregonian*, *The Washington Times,* and several other newspapers.

Joseph F. Koonce received his BA degree from Dartmouth College and MS and PhD degrees from the University of Wisconsin, Madison, in Zoology. He is currently professor at Case Western Reserve University with a secondary appointment as professor in the Department of Electrical Engineering and Computer and Science. He joined the faculty of the Department of Biology at Case Western Reserve University in 1973 and served as Chair of the Department of Biology from 2000 to 2009. Dr. Koonce has broad research interests in aquatic systems ecology. He has served on a number of boards and advisory committees for the Great Lakes Fishery Commission, the International Joint Commission, National Research Council, and the U.S. Environmental Protection Agency. He served as the Ecosystem Partnership Coordinator for the Great Lakes Fishery Commission (1992–1993) and as U.S. cochair of the Habitat Advisory Board of the Great Lakes Fishery Commission (1997–1999). Dr. Koonce is the leader of the Lake

Erie Ecological Modeling Project, and he is a member of the International Association of Great Lakes Research and the American Fisheries Society.

Jeffrey M. Peterson is an associate professor in the Department of Agricultural Economics at Kansas State University. He also has held a visiting faculty appointment in the Department of Agricultural and Resource Economics at Oregon State University. He earned a BS degree from the University of Wisconsin-River Falls and MS and PhD degrees from Cornell University.

Peterson conducts research and teaching in the field of environmental and resource economics. His research focuses on environmental policy analysis, emphasizing the roles that hidden information and uncertainty play in individual policy responses. Many of the applications of his research have been at interface between agriculture and the environment. Major research topics have included groundwater extraction, payment for environmental service contracts, and agricultural land use responses to climate change.

Susan Stratton Sayre is an assistant professor in the Economics Department at Smith College and is affiliated with the college's Environmental Science and Policy Program. She earned a BA in Economics and Religion from Swarthmore College and MS and PhD degrees in Agricultural and Resource Economics from the University of California, Berkeley. Her research addresses how political and economic forces influence the development of environmental and resource policy, with a particular focus on water policy. She is especially interested in groundwater policy. Recent projects look at water policy in both water-scarce areas, including California and Spain, and relatively water-rich areas like the Northeastern United States.

Brandon Scarborough is a Research Fellow at the Property and Environment Research Center (PERC) and an independent environmental economics consultant in Bozeman, Montana. He specializes in water markets for economic as well as environmental applications and the associated institutional structures that promote or inhibit trading. Other interests include payments for ecosystem services, alternative energy policies, climate change, and the efficacy of using forests to sequester carbon as part of a national or international abatement strategy. He holds BS degrees in Business and Environmental Biology and a MS in Applied Economics from Montana State University.

Leonard Shabman is a Resident Scholar at Resources for the Future. Until 2002, he was on the faculty in the Department of Agricultural and Applied Economics at Virginia Tech, where he is now an emeritus professor. He has served as a staff economist at the United States Water Resources Council, scientific advisor to the assistant secretary of Army, Civil Works, and as a member of the National Academy of Sciences, National Research Council, Water Science and Technology Board. He has been appointed to and chaired several academies committees and has been recognized as an associate of the National Academies. Dr. Shabman has published papers on subjects ranging from natural hazard management to wetlands and water quality management and public investment analysis methods; he has provided consultation to governmental and nongovernmental organizations on these same topics.

Leo K. Simon is an adjunct professor in the Department of Agricultural and Resource Economics, University of California-Berkeley. He holds a BA degree and a Concert Diploma of Music from the University of Melbourne, Australia. He obtained MS degrees in International Relations and in Economics from the London School of Economics, and a PhD in Economics from Princeton University. Simon's research interests range from theoretical game theory to simulation modeling to applied political economy. His recent work in political economy applies a game-theoretic model of multiissue, multiplayer negotiations developed in collaboration with Gordon Rausser. With Rausser and others, he recently completed a study of water resource allocation across subbasins of the Adour Basin of Southern France. One current application studies the current negotiations over the Water Transfer Agreement between IID and SDCWA in Southern California. Another compares the political economics of agri-environmental policy formation in Europe and the United States, and the role played by the WTO in these two regions.

Craig M. Smith is an assistant professor of Agricultural Business at Fort Hays State University. He has been at FHSU since August 2011. He teaches courses in agricultural marketing, precision agricultural technologies, advanced farm management, and quantitative methods of analysis for decision-making. Craig grew up in rural south-central Kansas, near Yoder and spent much of his time working in farming and construction. He holds a BS in Agricultural Technology Management, an MS in Agricultural Economics, and a PhD in Agricultural Economics—all from Kansas State University. Previously, Craig has worked as a natural resource engineering specialist in northwest Missouri for MU Extension and as an extension watershed economist for Kansas State. Much of his research is related to analyzing water resource issues (both quality and quantity) from an economic perspective. Additionally, Craig is involved with several precision agricultural and farm machinery economic analysis projects.

Brian C. Steed is an Instructor and Researcher in the Political Science Department at Utah State University. He earned BA and MA degrees from Utah State, a JD from SJ Quinney College of Law, University of Utah, and a PhD from Indiana University-Bloomington. His research concentrates on public and environmental policy, and he has published articles in a variety of journals including *Ecological Economics, Southern Economic Journal, Harvard Latino Law Review*, and *Journal of Land Use and Environmental Law*. Steed is also a member of the American Bar Association and the Utah State Bar Association.

Kurt Stephenson is a professor in the Department of Agricultural and Applied Economics at Virginia Tech. Stephenson's research interests include market-based environmental policies, water resource economics and policy, and the role of economic analysis in public policy. He has served on numerous water quality policy and regulatory advisory boards. Dr. Stephenson received his BS in Economics from Radford University, his MS degree in Agricultural Economics from Virginia Tech, and his PhD in Economics from the University of Nebraska-Lincoln.

For 13 years, **Richard W. Wahl** was a senior-level economist in the Office of Polity Analysis in the U.S. Department of the Interior. After moving to Boulder, Colorado, he was an economist in the Environment and Behavior Program at the Institute for Behavioral Sciences at the University of Colorado in Boulder and a consultant on natural resource issues. Wahl holds a BS degree from the University of Colorado, an MA from Harvard, and a PhD from Johns Hopkins University. He continues his consulting work and maintains a strong interest in water policy. He is the author of *Markets for Federal Water: Subsidies, Property Rights, and the Bureau of Reclamation*, published by Resources for the Future.

Pearl Q. Zheng, PhD, PEng. is an engineer and a scientist, specializing in water resources management. She holds a BEng. in Environmental Engineering and BA in English from Tianjin University in China; an MEng. in Environmental Engineering from McMaster University in Canada; and an MA in Applied Mathematics and Statistics and a PhD in System Analysis and Economics for Public Decision Making from the Johns Hopkins University. She is a registered professional engineer and currently a senior analyst at Abt Associates Inc., conducting interdisciplinary research and providing engineering services for effective environmental policy-making and planning. Dr. Zheng has extensive statistical, hydrological, and Geographic Information System modeling skills. She has also supervised emission control projects in Canada and designed wastewater treatment facilities in China.

Index

Compensatory Mitigation Rule (2008), 21, 24–25, 32
competition in auctions, 112, 113, 138, 139n23
compliance, cooperative enforcement of, 218
Conatser v. Johnson, 198–99, 201
Conservancy Act, New Mexico, 165–66
conservation
  biodiversity and dam removal, 250
  Biodiversity Benefits Index, 116
  biodiversity contracts, 116–17
  and CVPIA, 370
  and direct user charges vs. property tax revenue, 226
  district-level, 354–55
  ecological quality and compensatory mitigation, 34–35
  elasticity of demand and water conservation, 232–35, 246n14
  establishing value of instream water, 122, 141n44
  fish ladder requirement at Casitas water project, 184–86, 202, 206nn5–6, 340
  fish riparian habitat dam decommissioning model, 259–61
  and fish species in the Delta, 287–88, 303–5, 319n53
  habitat conservation banks, 18–19, 23–24, 25
  incentive for, 366
  legislation, 78–80
  in Los Angeles, 341
  overview, 6
  Sacramento–San Joaquin Delta stakeholders, 281–82, 295–97, 303, 309–10, 311
  and taxes vs. pricing, 10–11, 243
  See also habitat restoration; *entries beginning with* "ecosystem"; *entries beginning with* "instream"
contracts
  Bureau of Reclamation alleged breach of contract, 155
  for carbon credits, 68–69
  IID and MWD, 161–62
  procurement auction, 69
  right to transfer question, 366–67
  stakeholder sensitivity to violations of, 51

USBR and public water districts, 237–40, 244
  in WQT programs, 55
conveyance losses, 355
corporate governance of mutual irrigation companies, 146–47
Corps. *See* U.S. Army Corps of Engineers; U.S. Army Corps of Engineers (Corps)
cost differences for WQT, 44, 47, 48–49, 57, 63
cost effectiveness in markets, 213–14
cost model for dam decommissioning, 262–63
credit stacking, 36–37
credits
  carbon credits, 68–69
  nitrogen or phosphorus credits, 22–23, 37
  nonpoint credit sales to NPSs, 220–22
  public relations and pollution credit purchases, 49
  USACE and EEP-generated mitigation credits, 26–27, 28
  waste assimilation credits, 221
  See also allowances; mitigation credits; offsets
crisis in Sacramento–San Joaquin Delta, California, 282–83, 286–89, 317n14
Crooked River, Oregon, 124, 141n45
cross-sectional analyses, 233–34
Crutchfield, S., 53
cubic feet per second (CFS), 75, 98n2
cultural barriers to instream flow markets, 96–97
cultural ecosystem services, 18
Cummings, R., 111
CVP (Central Valley Project), 286, 358, 366–67, 372–73
CVPIA (Central Valley Project Improvement Act), 369–71, 377n44
CWA. *See* Clean Water Act

D
Dahlgren v. Los Angeles, 333
dams
  decommissioning (*See below*)
  high hazard potential classification, 248, 249, 265, 274n3
  overview, 248–49
  and river ecosystems, 249–50

incidental take permits, 336–37,
  350n70
income equalization, 242–43
industry
  EPA industry classes, 210–11
  and private ownership of instream
    rights, 89–90, 98
  and water-based transportation,
    190
  WQT trading priorities, 50, 51
  See also point source (PS) pollution
    and polluters; wastewater
    treatment plants
inelastic demand, price, 236
information levels
  and auctions, 111, 112–13, 116,
    136–37, 139nn19–20, 140n27
  revealing previous year's reserve
    price, 124
  and WQT, 54–56, 60–61, 64–66
infrastructure
  Bureau of Reclamation and MRGCD
    infrastructure, 166–67
  capital costs, 108
  failures (*See below*)
  for irrigation, 146
  in Los Angeles area, 322
  at Sacramento–San Joaquin Delta,
    282, 286, 290, 297, 302
  science-based recommendations for,
    373
  for water transport, 168–69
  See also entries beginning with
    "dams"
infrastructure failures
  dams, 250–51
  levee failures in the Delta, 288–89,
    291–92, 303–4, 305–6, 319n54
innovation. *See* technological
  innovation
institutional entrepreneurs, 3. *See also*
  private entities
instream flows
  cubic feet per second, 75, 98n2
  market activity for, 83–88, 101n35,
    102n43, 102nn38–39
  market transactions related to, 8–9,
    75–76, 80–83
  markets (*See below*)
  overview, 2, 6
  and private property rights, 9–10
  protecting, 77–83

state laws on, 77, 78–80, 100n10,
    100n15, 100n21, 101n31
  status quo flows, 78–80, 100n15,
    100n21
  water quality and nitrogen allot-
    ments, 31
  See also Sacramento–San Joaquin
    Delta, California
instream flow markets
  acre-foot of water measure, 83,
    101n37
  administrative barriers, 95–96,
    105n76
  AF/year prices, 84, 86, 87–88
  cultural barriers, 96–97
  enforcement, 93–95
  establishing value of instream water,
    122, 141n44
  instream flow prices, 84, 86, 87–88
  legal barriers, 88–91, 102nn45–46,
    103nn50–51
  overview, 97–98
  participants, 83–84, 85, 122
  rights poorly defined, 91–93, 98,
    105n84
  See also Ochoco Irrigation District
    stream flow restoration
intangible costs of WQT, 49–51
Interagency Review Team (IRT), 20
Interior Department involvement in
  water transfer, 161–62
irrigation districts
  and Bureau of Reclamation, 152–55,
    175n43
  Edwards Aquifer auctions, Texas,
    115–16
  exclusion rights via, 146–52
  and heterogeneity of rights, 113
  Imperial Irrigation District, 160–62,
    365
  irrigation reduction auctions,
    114–15
  Middle Rio Grande Conservancy
    District, 164–67, 178n91, 179n102
  overview, 148–52, 173
  and trade between districts, 108
irrigation works, Native American, 3
IRT (Interagency Review Team), 20
"isolated conveyance" (peripheral canal)
  for Sacramento–San Joaquin Delta,
    California, 291, 292–93, 294, 312–15,
    319n51

J
James, L. Douglas, 360
J.J.N.P. Co. v. Utah, 198–99
John Day River, Oregon, 75
Johnson, Conatser v., 198–99
Johnson, Robert, 363
jus privatum legal interest in coastal
lands, 189
jus publicum legal interest in coastal
lands, 189, 190
jus regium legal interest in coastal
lands, 189
Just v. Marinette County, 196, 199–200
Justinian, emperor of Rome, 186–87

K
Kansas WQT market study, 50
Katz, Richard, 366
Kearney, J. D., 194
Kent, James, 190
Kirkpatrick, Andrew, 191
Klamath Hydroelectric Settlement
Agreement, 11
Klemperer, P., 110, 112
Kneese, Allen, 363
Koonce, Joseph F., 11, 247–79, 382

L
Lake Erie Dam Database, 269
Lake Erie Ecological Model (LEEM)
ecological model, 261
habitat–ecosystem linkage, 261
multidam decommissioning case
study, 258, 269–72
overview, 255–56
restoration, 258–59
riparian habitat models, 260–61
single dam decommissioning case
study, 257–58, 264–69
walleye restoration and lamprey
control, 259–61, 263, 267–68,
271–72
lamprey in Great Lakes, 259–61, 263
Lamprey v. State of Minnesota, 197, 200
Laury, S., 111, 115
lawsuits. *See* claims/challenges/lawsuits
leases. *See* water leases
Lee, Robert R., 360
LEEM. *See* Lake Erie Ecological Model
legal barriers to instream flow water markets, 88–91, 102*nn*45–46,
103*nn*50–51

Leman, Christopher K., 377*n*42
Letson, D., 53
levee failure in Sacramento–San
Joaquin Delta, California, 288–89,
291–92, 303–4, 305–6, 319*n*54
life expectancy of dams, 250
limit of treatment technology (LOT),
210–11, 212
Los Angeles, California
Dahlgren v. Los Angeles, 333
desalinization plants, 342–43
groundwater basin governance
through adjudication, 323–26,
331–32, 341, 347*n*29
lessons from, 339–43
and Mono Lake, 99*n*8, 196–97, 200,
328–29, 333–34
overview, 338–39
and Owens Valley, 103*n*53, 328,
333–34, 347*n*34, 349*n*56
portfolio diversification, 340–43
*Sierra Club and Owens Valley
Committee v. City of Los Angeles,*
334
See also water supply predictability in
Los Angeles
Los Angeles area water sources
California Aqueduct, 330
Colorado River aqueduct, 329–30,
348*n*41
groundwater basin governance,
324–26, 344*n*14, 345*nn*18–19,
346*n*20
and groundwater basins, 323–24,
344*nn*9–12 (*See also* groundwater
basins in California)
and groundwater markets, 326–27,
331, 346*n*28, 347*n*29, 347*n*32
Los Angeles aqueducts, 328–29,
347*n*34
water importation, 327–30, 333–34,
339, 347*n*34
Los Angeles Basin, 13
Los Angeles Department of Water and
Power (DWP), 328–29, 334
LOT (limit of treatment technology),
210–11, 212

M
MA (multicriteria analysis), 247–48,
254–55, 257–58, 261
Macaulay, Steve, 368

Nature Conservancy, The (TNC),
296–97
navigable waters, 186–87, 189, 190, 191,
193–94, 196–98, 207n24
negotiations
bilateral, vs. central exchange, 51, 54,
55, 56
costs of, 93, 215
IID and MWD, 161–62
for Los Angeles basin water, 325,
345n18
negotiated individual transactions,
102n43, 107, 368
for Owens Valley water, 347n34
for price, 59, 87–88
for pumping rights in Sacramento–
San Joaquin Delta, 325–26, 331
in quantitative decision analysis, 254,
270–71
Santa Fe and Sierra Waterworks,
168–72
and value of resource, 113, 131
Nelson, Robert H., 377n42
Nentjes, A., 54–55
NEPA (National Environmental Protection Act), 337
Neptune City v. Avon-By-The-Sea, 198,
201
Netusil, N., 52–53, 55–56, 64
Neuse River Basin, North Carolina,
30–31, 219, 220
Neuse River Compliance Association
(NRCA), 30, 31
Nevada
instream flow rights and private
entities, 89–90, 98
instream water laws and market
transfers, 82
new appropriations for instream
flows, 79
New Jersey
oyster bed ownership question,
191–93
on right of public access, 198, 201
New Mexico
Conservancy Act, 165–66
Estancia Basin, 167–72
instream flow laws, 100n10
instream flow rights and private
entities, 89–90, 98
instream water laws and market
transfers, 82, 102n46

MRGCD, 164–67
population growth, 163, 177nn78–79
public interest protection, 158–59
rainfall and water usage, 163,
178nn82–83
San Juan–Chama Project, 163
water code, 165, 170
New Mexico Office of State Engineer
(NMOSE), 163, 168–70, 172
New York
Appleby v. City of New York, 194
Fort Edwards Dam, 251
NID (National Inventory of Dams), 11,
248, 274n3
NID database, 248, 249, 250, 274n3
nitrogen (N), 31, 69n5
nitrogen (N) credits, 22–23, 37
nitrogen (N) retention, 18
no-injury rule, 89–90, 92–93, 103nn
50–51, 105n76, 108, 156–57
no net loss goal for streams and wetlands, 19, 28–29, 35, 38
nonpoint credit sales to NPSs, 220–22
nonpoint loading, reducing variability
of, 53
nonpoint source (NPS) pollution and
polluters
BMPs for pollution reduction,
22–23, 44
BMPs paid for by PSs, 212–13,
223n9, 224n19
as credit resale program sellers,
221–22
EPA on, 8
mandatory mass load limits on,
219–20
nonpoint credit sales to, 220–22
overview, 210
reclassifying as PS, 223n6
regulatory leniency toward, 43–44,
210
TMDL requirements, 22
unit cost function, 46
and water quality trading, 211–13
See also best management practices;
point source–nonpoint source
markets
North Carolina
DENR, 26–27, 30–31
DOT, 26–27
Ecosystem Enhancement Program,
26–30, 33–34

Independent Studies in Political Economy

LIBERTY FOR WOMEN | *Ed. by Wendy McElroy*

MAKING POOR NATIONS RICH | *Ed. by Benjamin Powell*

MARKET FAILURE OR SUCCESS | *Ed. by Tyler Cowen & Eric Crampton*

MONEY AND THE NATION STATE | *Ed. by Kevin Dowd & Richard H. Timberlake, Jr.*

NEITHER LIBERTY NOR SAFETY | *Robert Higgs*

THE NEW HOLY WARS | *Robert H. Nelson*

NO WAR FOR OIL | *Ivan Eland*

OPPOSING THE CRUSADER STATE | *Ed. by Robert Higgs & Carl P. Close*

OUT OF WORK | *Richard K. Vedder & Lowell E. Gallaway*

PARTITIONING FOR PEACE | *Ivan Eland*

PLOWSHARES AND PORK BARRELS | *E. C. Pasour, Jr. & Randal R. Rucker*

A POVERTY OF REASON | *Wilfred Beckerman*

PRIVATE RIGHTS & PUBLIC ILLUSIONS | *Tibor R. Machan*

PROPERTY RIGHTS | *Ed. by Bruce L. Benson*

THE PURSUIT OF JUSTICE | *Ed. by Edward J. López*

RACE & LIBERTY IN AMERICA | *Ed. by Jonathan Bean*

RECARVING RUSHMORE | *Ivan Eland*

RECLAIMING THE AMERICAN REVOLUTION | *William J. Watkins, Jr.*

REGULATION AND THE REAGAN ERA | *Ed. by Roger E. Meiners & Bruce Yandle*

RESTORING FREE SPEECH AND LIBERTY ON CAMPUS | *Donald A. Downs*

RESURGENCE OF THE WARFARE STATE | *Robert Higgs*

RE-THINKING GREEN | *Ed. by Robert Higgs & Carl P. Close*

SCHOOL CHOICES | *John D. Merrifield*

SECURING CIVIL RIGHTS | *Stephen P. Halbrook*

STRANGE BREW | *Douglas Glen Whitman*

STREET SMART | *Ed. by Gabriel Roth*

TAXING CHOICE | *Ed. by William F. Shughart, II*

TAXING ENERGY | *Robert T. Deacon, Stephen DeCanio, H. E. Frech, III & M. Bruce Johnson*

THAT EVERY MAN BE ARMED | *Stephen P. Halbrook*

TO SERVE AND PROTECT | *Bruce L. Benson*

TWILIGHT WAR | *Mike Moore*

VIETNAM RISING | *William Ratliff*

THE VOLUNTARY CITY | *Ed. by David T. Beito, Peter Gordon, & Alexander Tabarrok*

WINNERS, LOSERS & MICROSOFT | *Stan J. Liebowitz & Stephen E. Margolis*

WRITING OFF IDEAS | *Randall G. Holcombe*